ISSUES IN CARIBBEAN INTERNATIONAL RELATIONS

Edited by

Basil A. Ince
Anthony T. Bryan
Herb Addo
Ramesh Ramsaran

Institute of International Relations
University of the West Indies
St. Augustine, Trinidad and Tobago

UNIVERSITY
PRESS OF
AMERICA

LANHAM • NEW YORK • LONDON

University Press of America,™ Inc.

4720 Boston Way
Lanham, MD 20706

3 Henrietta Street
London WC2E 8LU England

Library of Congress Cataloging in Publication Data
Main entry under title:

Issues in Caribbean international relations.

Based on papers from a conference on Contemporary
trends and issues in Caribbean international affairs held by the
Institute of International Relations of the University of the West
Indies, St. Augustine, at the Hilton Hotel, Port-of-Spain, Trini-
dad, May 23–27, 1977.
Includes indexes.
1. Caribbean Area–Foreign relations–Congresses. 2.
Caribbean Area–Economic integration–Congresses. I. Ince,
Basil A. II. University of the West Indies (Saint Augustine,
Trinidad and Tobago). Institute of International Relations.
JX1524.I85   1983   327'.09729   82–21733
ISBN 0–8191–2913–5
ISBN 0–8191–2914–3 (pbk.)

Co-published by arrangement with the Institute of International Relations University of the West Indies St. Augustine, Trinidad and Tobago

Issues in Caribbean International Relations

Edited by
Basil A. Ince
Anthony T. Bryan
Herb Addo
Ramesh Ramsaran

Preface

In May 1977, the tenth anniversary of the establishment of the Institute of International Relations, the Institute convened a conference on *Contemporary Trends and Issues in Caribbean International Affairs* at the Hilton Hotel, Port-of-Spain, Trinidad. The conference was held from May 23 to 27 and was attended by more than sixty Caribbean and International scholars. Some twenty-eight papers were presented from which this volume, *Issues in Caribbean International Relations*, has emerged.

The volume has been divided into four parts, representing areas of importance to the developing countries of the Caribbean: *Small Size and Foreign Policy; Regional Integration; Negotiation;* and *Decision-Making*. Although several years have elapsed since the preliminary versions of these papers were written, several have been revised and the Editorial Committee of the Institute believes that their quality, as well as the growing scholarly interest in Caribbean Affairs, warrant the publication of this volume.

The conference was a success because of the high level of participation of the conferees and because of the co-operative effort of the Institute's staff. This volume serves first of all as a tribute to the energy and foresight of Professor Leslie F. Manigat, former Director of the Institute, whose brainchild the conference was and who worked indefatigably in its organization. Mrs. Norma Ferreira and members of the Conference Secretariat, Misses Cynthia Baptiste, Jeanne Callender, Anne Pereira and Mrs. Dianne Cedeno; Yola Alleyne and the Library staff; Joan Darcheville and members of the Documentation Centre; Mirlande Manigat, Donna Carter, Henry Gill, Peter Gonzales and David Ramjattan spent long hours working to ensure its success.

i

Special thanks must go to the Ford Foundation, without whose generous financial assistance the conference would not have been possible. Mrs. Margaret Blenman-Harris, whose editorial skills shaped the final manuscript, deserves special mention. The editors, however, accept responsibility for any shortcomings in this volume.

Basil A. Ince
Anthony Bryan
Herb Addo
Ramesh Ramsaran

June 1981.

List of Contributors

Herb Addo, Senior Research Fellow, Institute of International Relations, University of the West Indies, St. Augustine, Trinidad, W.I.

Robert Anderson, Professor of Political Science, University of Puerto Rico, Rio Piedras, Puerto Rico.

Havelock Brewster, Senior Economist, United Nations Conference on Trade and Development (UNCTAD), Geneva, Switzerland.

Anthony T. Bryan, Senior Lecturer, in Latin American Studies, Institute of International Relations, University of the West Indies, St. Augustine, Trinidad, W.I.

Winston Extavour, Foreign Service Officer, Ministry of External Affairs, Trinidad, W.I.

Trevor Farrell, Senior Lecturer, Department of Economics, University of the West Indies, St. Augustine, Trinidad, W.I.

George Goodwin, Eastern Caribbean Common Market Secretariat, St. John's, Antigua.

Basil A. Ince, Acting Director, Institute of International Relations, University of the West Indies, St. Augustine, Trinidad, W.I.

Morton Kaplan, Professor of International Relations, Committee on International Relations, University of Chicago, U.S.A.

Yolande Lake, Eastern Caribbean Common Market Secretariat, St. John's, Antigua.

Jacques Levesque, Director, Centre Interuniversitaire d'Etudes Européennes, Université du Québec à Montréal, Canada.

Vaughan E. Lewis, Director, Institute of Social and Economic Research, University of the West Indies, Mona, Jamaica.

Anthony P. Maingot, Professor of Sociology, Florida International University, Miami, Florida, U.S.A.

Ramesh Ramsaran, Research Fellow, Institute of International Relations, University of the West Indies, St. Augustine, Trinidad, W.I.

James Rosenau, Professor and Director, Institute of Transnational Studies, University of Southern California, U.S.A.

iii

Part I:

Small Size and Foreign Policy

The Adaptation of Small States*

*James N. Rosenau***
University of Southern California

There is no shortage of research on the external behavior of small states. A recent survey identified fifty-five major investigations in which generalized observations are made about the problems and dynamics whereby small states ward off, procure from, and otherwise cope with their external environments.[1] If case studies of the circumstances of specific small states at particular moments in history had been included in the survey, presumably the history would be considerably larger. More specifically, assuming that by some conservative definition one hundred small states could be identified as political entities in the last two centuries—a not unreasonable assumption—and if it is presumed that each of these has been the focus of some one hundred case analyses—again a not unreasonable presumption—then the literature on the subject can be estimated to exceed ten thousand entries.

So compelling have been the problems of small states that it is even possible to discern historical periods in the study of them. As long ago as the 18th century, many observers were preoccupied with the idea of the small state, seeing it as an attractive alternative to the dangers of centralized and autocratic large states. In the 19th century, on the other hand, observers tended to take a contrary position, perceiving in the small state an obstacle to the unification of similar cultural entities that could give meaning to a vigorous nationalism. Still later, during World War I, the interwar years, World War II, and the Cold War, analyses focused on small states as, respectively, instruments of belligerent powers, occupants of key roles in international organizations, precipitants of major international conflicts, and arenas of competition among superpowers.[2]

*In writing this paper I have had invaluable help from Niels Amstrup, Thomas Johnson, and Edwin P. McClain. I am also grateful for the support provided by the Institute for Transnational Studies of the University of Southern California.
**This paper has appeared in James Rosenau's, *The Study of Political Adpatation*, by F. Pinter, and appears here with the kind permission of the publisher.

Prior work on small states is marked by still another unique characteristic. Unlike most research on foreign policy phenomena, small state analyses tend to be pervaded by a "genuine puzzle." Elsewhere I have suggested that research in the field has lagged in recent years because of a lack of important and challenging questions that motivate investigators to press forward in such a way that their work cumulates, ever expanding the base on which knowledge about the dynamics of foreign policy is founded. Not all questions are so important and challenging as to sustain the curiosity of successive generations of observers. Only certain kinds are likely to provide cumulative research; namely, those questions that concentrate on (1) important outcomes that can be (2) clearly specified and that occur with (3) sufficient regularity to be deemed worthy of explanation. Such questions I call "genuine puzzles," since the importance and regularity of the outcomes evoke and maintain the curiosity of investigators while the specificity of the outcomes disciplines their curiosity and prevents them from pursuing unrelated lines of inquiry.[3] While most foreign policy research focuses on important issues, it tends not to be cumulative because it lacks a concern with either recurring or specified outcomes. Even those investigations which probe recurrent phenomena, for example, normally fail to be specific about the outcomes involved. Instead such inquiries tend to focus on the question of why states do what they do when they engage in external behavior, a query that allows each researcher to probe whatever is of interest at the moment and thus results in a multitude of diverse and even contradictory studies.

Through much of its history, on the other hand, small states analysis has concentrated on a genuine puzzle, what one observer calls the "small state paradox."[4] The paradox can be posed succinctly in the form of a question: "Why do small states survive?" This would appear to be a genuine puzzle because it specifies a recurrring outcome (survival) and challenges comprehension because it can be readily argued that in the long sweep of time small states are likely to be conquered or otherwise absorbed by larger ones. Inasmuch as recent centuries do not uphold such reasoning, with innumerable small states having managed to persist intact, small state analysis has enjoyed a long history through the provocation of what would appear to be a genuinely puzzling outcome.

Yet, notwithstanding the voluminous literature on small states, the existence of discernible and logical periods of history in the study of them, and the persistence of genuine puzzlement about their survival, the dynamics of small state behavior in the international system remain obscure, eluding the grasp of present-day scholars as well as those of prior generations. No less than six different definitions of and approaches to small states have been identified,[5] and more than a few of these are contradictory at best and mutually exclusive at worst. As one observer puts it, all the many inquiries into the international circumstances surrounding small states are marked by "an astonishing lack of cumulation." Indeed, in spite of all the recent attention scholars have paid to small states, "the confusion seems greater today than, say, ten years ago," amounting to what has been characterized as "the malaise of small state analysis."[6]

CONCEPTUAL DIFFICULTIES

It is not difficult to identify some of the reasons for the malaise. Size, be it small, large, or anything in between, is an elusive variable. Its boundaries are defined not by objective circumstances, but by the concerns of observers. Small states are not inherently small. They are small only in relation to other states that are conceived not to be small. And, even as such, their smallness acquires meaning only in the context of a variety of other variables that may be operative. Underdeveloped mini-states may be viewed as small, but so may industrialized states adjacent to superpowers. Offshore island states may be treated as small if water separates them from the African continent, but not if they are like England or Japan located off the coasts of Europe or Asia. The relational context in which smallness is assessed thus fosters a tendency to equate smallness with weakness, a tendency that surely can be viewed as a source of malaise when it is recalled that such states as England and Japan have dominated whole eras of history, not to mention "large" neighbors on the mainland.

Stated differently, there are all kinds of small states and this great variety is likely to hinder conceptual clarity and empirical cumulation. Or, even worse, the variety can tempt analysts to achieve clarity through precise operational definitions that confine smallness to a single dimension (e.g., population size or proximity to a superpower), a solution that reduces confusion but at the same time excludes so many cases as to also reduce the puzzlement that sustains inquiry. Perhaps still worse, the elusiveness of the size variable can lead researchers to define smallness in terms of several additive dimensions (e.g., population plus underdevelopment plus geographic location in the Caribbean), a solution that insures clarity but so narrowly defines the scope of inquiry as to virtually prohibit the cumulation of generalized knowledge.

Much of the disarray in small state analysis also arises out of a concern with the special problems of specific small states. It is understandable and appropriate that scholars in Caribbean countries are inclined to focus on the particular dilemmas of states in that region; but while this applied-research orientation may provide insights that facilitate the movement of Caribbean states toward the realization of their policy goals, it does not necessarily contribute to the expansion of a generalized knowledge base pertaining to small states. For this kind of cumulation to occur, studies of particular states or regions must be undertaken in the context of concepts and theories that are widely shared and thereby yield empirical findings which are comparable across states and regions. Until such a theoretical perspective is developed and widely accepted, the great variety of small states is likely to continue to foster a multitude of unrelated and noncumulative inquiries.

Another major reason for the malaise that marks small state analysis can be traced to the problem of distinguishing between the objective circumstances of world politics and subjective assessments of them. Difficult to preserve at best, this distinction is especially challenging when applied to small states. However smallness may be defined, there are certain realities that can severely constrain their freedom of action and that can therefore delude analysts into treating the constraints as determinants of behavior. Small states cannot put millions of men into uniform, sustain extensive scientific establishments, maintain elaborate foreign offices and (in many instances) separate diplomatic representation in all the world's capitols, or otherwise draw upon the vast panoply of resources through which foreign policy decisions are most readily implemented. However, while such objective circumstances may thus encourage small states to scale down their aspirations, to eschew consideration of certain policy alternatives, to avoid offense to trading partners, or otherwise to become responsive to demands from abroad and dependent on those who make them, the external realities with which they must contend do not dictate their foreign policy decisions. The realities can be discounted, misperceived, reinterpreted, or otherwise ignored. The results of doing so may be disastrous, but such outcomes are always possible precisely because the external behavior of small states, like that of large states, springs from the perceptions, evaluations, and choices of identifiable individuals and not from the circumstances of the outside world.

Indeed, recent history provides ample evidence of how subjective redefinition by policy makers can alter the circumstances that were long viewed as objective constraints which small states had to accept. The newly acquired political clout of the oil-rich small states of the Arab world are a case in point. While mounting energy consumption in the industrial world was altering the objective circumstances pertaining to the need for Middle Eastern oil reserves, it was not until identifiable leaders of the small states of that region redefined their relationship to what had been the constraints in their external environments that their "smallness" became, in effect, "largeness" in world politics. And who would have thought only a few years ago that objective circumstances were so fragile, so subject to reinterpretation, as to permit Cuba—that "small" island but ninety miles off the coast of a superpower—to send troops to Africa and substantially affect the course of events in that distant continent?

But, it might be argued, the presence of a genuine puzzle relevant to small states should have served to offset these conceptual difficulties, providing both a common framework on which the work of diverse policy-oriented scholars could be founded and a perspective through which the role of objective constraints could be properly assessed. Given the foregoing comments about the importance of genuine puzzles, why has not the malaise of small state analysis given way to orderly cumulation? This question can be most easily answered by observing that I have exaggerated the knowledge-building consequences of genuine puzzles. If such queries are not as conducive to cumulation as I have argued, then it is hardly surprising that the conceptual difficulties inherent in small state analyses have inhibited the emergence of viable and widely shared theory.

Admittedly I may be desperately seeking to preserve my own earlier formulation, but I would argue that it is the way in which the small state paradox has been framed, and not an exaggerated view of the importance of genuine puzzles, that explains the persistence of malaise. For reasons elaborated below, puzzlement no longer focuses on the fact of survival as much as on its quality. We have become accustomed to the continued existence of small states and take for granted that their futures as legal entities are assured. The advent of nuclear weapons, the changing role of force, and the fact that most small states have larger allies who will come to their aid in a crisis—to mention but a few of the more obvious factors— have so reduced the probability of troops crossing national boundaries and bringing small states to an end through conquest that the question of physical survival is no longer puzzling. Small states may disappear because of internal division and dissolution, but it is unlikely that they will be militarily overrun. Tibet, Goa, and South Vietnam come to mind as small, postwar states that have yielded to superior force, but these are exceptions that seem to prove the rule[7] and thus do not heighten our curiosity over the fact of survival. In short, to pose the puzzle as a question of why small states survive is to orient us toward an outcome we take for granted rather than one we find challenging to explain. Viewed in this way, it is hardly surprising that the survival question has not been the source of extensive cumulation.

Yet small states continue to fascinate, partly because of a tendency to sympathize with underdogs, but perhaps mostly because they seem so adept at living within their means. Given their limited resources, the deck of international cards appear stacked against small states, and yet many manage to make effective demands abroad and to move toward the realization of goals at home. The quality of their survival, then, is the critical outcome that provokes curiosity, and if major types of survival can be specified as the bases for framing genuine puzzles, orderly cumulation of our knowledge about small states may well follow. Much of the ensuing analysis centers on an attempt to frame such puzzles and to suggest steps that can usefully be taken to facilitate progress toward their solution.

FRAMING THREE PUZZLES

Two general kinds of small state survival, each largely the opposite of the other and yet occasionally interrelated, can be identified as having long been puzzling to analysts. One, what we shall call the "dependency" puzzle, focuses on the qualities of survival that result when the institutions and norms of small states are either locked into international economies (market dependence) or are highly sensitive to and/or penetrated by larger states (power dependence). The other, what we shall refer to as the "defiance" or "autonomy" puzzle, is mainly concerned with the survival consequences for small states that manage to defy or otherwise maintain a high degree of autonomy with respect to larger neighbors and/or distant superpowers.

The first of these types of survival is a major preoccupation of the literature on the new states that emerged out of former colonial empires after World War II and it is also central to works on states in the orbits of superpowers. By what subtle forms of penetration and influence, observers keep asking, do former colonies remain tied to their former metropoles? How does investment, trade, and culture—to mention but a few of the sources of dependency—operate within small Third World countries to incline them to define their survival as forced upon them by the needs and preferences of the states whose colonies they once formed? Or, if they are not former colonies but are located in the orbits of superpowers and are oriented to heeding the latters' dictates, as is the case with many countries of Eastern Europe and South America, by what subtle and not-so-subtle processes of control do the superpowers keep such small states in line? In short, whether it is of the market or power variety, the phenomenon of dependency exhibits the basic criteria of a genuine puzzle: it involves recurring outcomes that observers find both important and challenging to explain, important because of a value that dependence is demeaning and exploitative, and challenging to explain because of an expectation that, other things being equal, no state would accept being demeaned and exploited. And the challenge can be readily framed as a puzzle: why do some small states become and remain so dependent on other states?

Yet, not all small states survive through adjustment to the explicit and implicit demands of former colonial masters, nearby large powers, or superpowers. Some are able to resist, thwart, or otherwise defy the demands of the more powerful while autonomously pursuing policies that allow them to procure from abroad the resources needed to maintain or attain goals at home. What conditions must prevail for successful defiance that permits domestic progress and the maintenace of autonomy? How do small states develop their foreign policies so that contiguous or proximate larger powers define the cost of intervening in their affairs as too great to pay? What compromises, if any, do they have to make to lessen the probabilities of great power intervention? Questions such as these have long been raised in the literature on diplomacy, international bargaining, and military strategy, and they seem to be even more persistently asked in recent years as the passage of time increasingly suggests that Cuba, Albania, or Burma will be successful in their efforts to maintain their autonomy with respect to the United States, the Soviet Union, and China respectively. In effect, small state autonomy also manifests all the characteristics of a genuine puzzle: it is a recurrent outcome that analysts view as important and intriguing, important because of a value that autonomy is far more preferable than submission, and intriguing because of a presumption that, other things being equal, superior powers are unlikely to tolerate defiance and the autonomy it permits. And again the puzzle can be succinctly framed: why do some small states successfully defy or otherwise remain autonomous with respect to much larger states located nearby?

Plainly, dependence and autonomy are opposite extremes of the same continuum. Both forms of survival involve relationships with larger states salient in the external environments of small states, with one founded on an hierarchical authority structure and the other being free of a subordination dimension. Evidence that the two genuine puzzles focus on the quality of survival at the opposite ends of the same continuum is amply available in the efforts of some small states to initiate a transformation which takes them from one form of survival to another, from dependence on a superior power to autonomy with respect to it. Hungary in 1956 and Czechoslovakia in 1968 can be cited as examples of unsuccessful attempts to launch such a transformation, while the recent histories of Albania and Cuba indicate that sometimes such attempts are quite successful.

Indeed, for reasons indicated below, the efforts to achieve greater autonomy and thereby transform links to superior powers have become so pervasive in recent decades that at least the outlines of a third genuine puzzle can be identified. While successful defiance that results in a transformation to the opposite extreme of the dependency continuum does not occur too frequently, substantial movement along the continuum toward substantially greater autonomy occurs frequently enough to seem both important and challenging. Such movement is important because substantial alterations in the degree of autonomy can have significant consequences for the structure and flow of world politics, and it is challenging because, other things being equal, the structure of world politics would appear too fixed to allow for substantial change on the part of small states. How do small states manage to reduce their dependency on larger states and/or international economies, thereby attaining new forms of survival founded on greater autonomy? What strategies do they employ and under what conditions do some strategies prove more effective than others? To what extent and in what ways does substantially greater autonomy depend on and/or foster corresponding alterations in the internal structure of the small state? Such questions are persistently raised when such changes become observable and the literatures on political and economic development are pervaded with them. Thus it is not unreasonable to view these transitional forms of survival and the dynamics that produce them as a genuine puzzle, one that can be called the "transformation" puzzle and that can also be simply framed: Why and how do some small states succeed in achieving substantially greater degrees of autonomy with respect to larger states and/or international economies than they had in earlier eras of their history?

It should be noted that in positing the dependency continuum I have carefully avoided designating its other extreme as the "independence" puzzle. Independence may be the logical and syntactical alternative to dependence, but in the present-day world—and presumably well into the future—the opposite to a high degree of dependence is not so much greater independence as it is a more balanced interdependence. No national state seems presently capable of so fully insulating itself from the rest of the world that it can proceed on the basis of total independence toward the fulfillment of internal goals. To be sure, Cambodia currently appears to have opted for such a posture toward the world, and conceivably it has evolved agrarian goals that allow for domestic progress independent of interaction with the outside world; but one cannot help anticipating that the Cambodian effort will be short-lived, that profound technological change and the subsequent depletion of the world's resources have rendered all national boundaries permeable and all national societies, economies, and polities subject to external influences and at least minimally dependent on external resources. Moreover, even if the Cambodian effort should prove successful by Cambodian standards, it is not likely to be widely emulated and will long stand out as an exception that proves the rule. Why? Because our time is marked by seemingly ever greater interdependence among states, an interdependence in which any state can be either relatively more dependent or relatively more autonomous in its relationship to the outside world—and it is to the distinction between these extremes and the many degrees of dependence and autonomy that lie between them that our three puzzles are addressed.

None of the ensuing discussion of autonomy should thus be viewed as implying the existence of national independence in the full meaning of that term. New states may be achieving statehood and old ones may be gaining more and more sovereignty, but it is a statehood and a sovereignty without full autonomy, whatever top leaders may claim for their achievements of statehood and sovereignty. (After all, neither Cuba nor Albania would have successfully made and maintained the transformation away from dependency without substantial support, respectively, from the Soviet Union and China. Some might even argue that their transformations have come full circle and entered them into new dependency relationships.) In short, our ensuing references to dependent, autonomous, and transformational forms of survival are to relative and not absolute circumstances, relative in the sense that they all are sustained in the context of an increasingly complex interdependent structure of world politics.

A METHODOLOGICAL CANON

In addition to framing the challenge for small states in terms of genuine puzzles, two other steps seem necessary to progress in cumulating knowledge about them. One is the elaboration of a theoretical perspective through which the diverse pieces of the puzzles can be brought together into a coherent whole. The other involves the articulation of a methodological canon that appears central to overcoming the forementioned conceptual difficulties and the subsequent development of viable theory.

The canon can be stated simply: the range of variation of the key variables in the theory needs to be cast as a continuum rather than in dichotomous terms. Most notably, if size is to be used as a variable, it must not be posited in either-or terms, but should instead be conceptualized as encompassing relatively more or less smallness or largeness. Such a formulation not only comes to grips with the problem of defining small states and allows for analyses in which both highly industrial and predominantly agrarian states can be treated as small, but it also encourages creative theorizing. That is, by casting thought in terms of the more smallness or largeness that states exhibit, we do not have to delineate the boundaries of small states, and we also force ourselves to ponder the consequences of each increment or decrement in the attributes or attitudes that are conceived to be associated with relatively more or less smallness. Or at least it is hard to imagine framing a hypothesis in which the dependent variable is posited as increasing or decreasing in relation to larger or smaller states without compelling reflection on how and why the phenomena constituting the dependent variable fluctuate as they do in response to whatever characteristics are linked to variations in state size. If size is treated dichotomously, on the other hand, we need only reflect on differences at the extremes and are not forced to think about the many gradations that lie between smallness and largeness or the dynamics whereby movement along the continuum occurs.

Treating size as a continuum serves to reduce definitional problems because such a procedure obviates the impulse to delineate the common qualities of all small states. In effect, by casting analysis in the context of a continuum, analysts can use whatever definitions of size seem appropriate to their concerns, since any dimensions of smallness they focus on and any observations they make will necessarily involve comparisons with states that are characterized by the same dimensions to a greater degree. The great variety of small states, in other words, need not hinder conceptual clarity. If the foregoing methodological canon is consistently applied, the elusiveness of the size variable may not be a problem. On the other hand, if it proves difficult or impossible to apply, we can usefully wonder whether the range of phenomena encompassed by the concept of size is too great for it to be employed as an incisive analytic variable.

In addition, and no less important, locating the size variable in a continuum minimizes the likelihood of treating size in terms of objective circumstances. Continua compel relational formulations, so that it becomes virtually impossible to view all small states as inevitably constrained by objective conditions in their environments if the differences among them are part of the analysis. For a particular environmental condition of a small state to be posited as an objective constraint, our methodological canon requires that the same condition be treated as somewhat less constraining for somewhat larger states and somewhat more constraining for somewhat smaller states—a formulation which highlights the variability of "objective" realities and the importance of subjective interpretations or environmental circumstances.

The rule that major variables be cast as continua applies equally to those used to assess the quality of survival. As indicated, both dependence and defiance need to be posited in terms of varying gradations of dependence and autonomy even as they are also treated as extremes of the same continuum. Likewise, each of the four types of national adaptation noted below need to be developed in such a way that they are continuous variables.

A THEORETICAL PERSPECTIVE

As previously indicated, the key to overcoming the malaise of small state analysis is the development of viable theory through which work on the genuine puzzles can be creatively and cumulatively organized. Ideally such theory should be broad enough to encompass the dependency, transformational, and autonomy puzzles as well as the more specific questions that preoccupy analysts concerned about immediate policy problems. Given the salience of the transformational puzzle, it also should be dynamic theory, i.e., theory that allows for change through time, including those rare changes in which small states move the whole length of the continuum from a high degree of dependency to a high degree of autonomy. Ideally, too, the hypotheses that comprise such theory should be sufficiently integrated so that the confirmation of one does not negate any of the others.

It would be presumptuous to suggest that what follows meets these ideal requirements for a theory of small state behavior. Time and space limitations do not permit an effort to develop a full-blown theory here and allow only for the identification of some of its main components and the derivation of nine hypotheses relevant to the strategies that small states might employ to move away from the dependency extreme of the continuum. Elsewhere I have developed a theoretical perspective that can serve as a useful starting point for the evolution of theory of small state behavior. Certainly it embraces both the dependency and defiance puzzles as well as allowing for transformations through time to new degrees of autonomy. I call it a theory of the adaptation of national societies,[8] and what follows is an attempt to outline the theory and to suggest some ways that it might be relevant to small states and the genuine puzzles they pose.[9]

Let us first summarize the theory. In its original and most general formulation the adaptation perspective focuses on any state, irrespective of whether it is large or small, developed or underdeveloped, open or closed—to mention only a few of the salient dimensions of states. As long as its sovereignty as an international actor is accepted, every state is conceived to be faced with the problem of adapting to changing circumstances if it is to persist through time and space as a cohesive social unit. The survival of the national state is not theoretically assumed, but is treated as an empirical question. As indicated, few states are likely to be conquered militarily today, but collapse from within is an ever-present possibility. Hence, while most states persist, some go under and those that do point up the delicacy of the mechanisms through which national adaptation occurs. In identifying four types of national adaptation, in other words, I do not mean to imply that the continued existence of any historic nation-state is assured. The theory allows for a fifth alternative: maladaptation that is so severe as to amount to extinction.

National adaptation is defined as a process through which fluctuations in the essential structures of states are kept within limits acceptable to their members. The essential structures are those basic interaction patterns (e.g., the economy, polity, society) that sustain the life of national actors and that undergo fluctuation in response to changing circumstances at home and abroad. These changes are posited as demands with which a nation must cope. Since the demands are both internal and external, the nation is seen as achieving (or failing to achieve) adaptation through the basic orientations whereby the interplay between the demands from at home and abroad is handled.

Built into the theory, in others words, is an internal-external balance which is always present, but which can undergo enormous shifts, depending on the relative potency of the internal and external demands and orientations of the nation's leaders and publics toward these relative potencies. The degree of adaptation and maladaptation at any point in time is conceived to be a function of the discrepancy between the relative strength of the key internal and external variables and the orientations toward the balance between them. If the discrepancy is great, maladaptation will ensue, with either extinction or transformation to a more appropriate set of orientations occurring thereafter. If the discrepancy is slight or nonexistent, then neither extinction nor adaptive transformation will follow.

The theory postulates the nation, like any human entity, as always pursuing one of four basic and mutually exclusive adaptive orientations if it is to maintain its essential structures and survive. It can seek to adjust its present self to its present environment; it can try to shape its present environment to its present self; it can attempt to create a new equilibrium between its present self and its present environment; or it can accept the existing equilibrium between its present self and its present environment. In order to simplify discussion, these four alternative sets of orientations have been designated as giving rise to, respectively, the politics of acquiescent adaptation, the politics of intransigent adaptation, the politics of promotive adaptation, and the politics of preservative adaptation. Present-day Czechoslovakia, Rhodesia, China, and Great

Britain might be cited, respectively, as illustrative of the four types.[10] Table I delineates the four types in terms of the decision-making orientations inherent in each.[11]

TABLE I: THE NATURE OF DECISION-MAKING
IN DIFFERENT PATTERNS OF ADAPTATION

Patterns of Adaptation	Demands and changes emanating from a society's external environment	Demands and changes emanating from the essential structures of a society
Acquiescent	+	−
Intransigent	−	+
Promotive	−	−
Preservative	+	+

+ Officials responsive to changes and demands, either because the changes and demands are intense or because their intensity is perceived to be increasing.

− Officials unresponsive to changes and demands either because the changes and demands are not sufficiently intense or because their intensity is perceived to be decreasing.

It is important to stress that each of the four sets of orientations is conceived to constitute a basic posture from which all policy decisions spring. All four are viewed as stable and enduring as long as the relative strength of the demands emanating from within the national actor and of those from its present environment do not change or are not perceived to have changed. If changes occur and/or are perceived as such, then the national actor is seen as either undergoing a transformation to one of the other three adaptive orientations or failing to survive. This means that the theory allows for twelve possible transformations. It must be re-emphasized, however, that the four types of adaptive orientations are conceived as deep-seated and not transitory in nature, as undergoing transformation only in response to profound social and technological changes, either internally or in the international system. The theory posits an electoral or violent ouster of political leaderships as normally necessary to the initiation of any of the twelve possible transformations, and for some of them (especially the transformation from either intransigent or acquiescent to preservative adaptation), a major societal upheaval would appear to be a prerequisite.[12]

APPLYING THE THEORETICAL PERSPECTIVE:
THE ADAPTATION OF SMALL STATES

The original formulation of the adaptation approach is pervaded with the implicit assumption that the external environment of small states is predominant, locking them into situations from which transformation is unlikely and thus giving rise either to the politics of acquiescent adaptation if their internal demands are perceived as relatively minimal or to the politics of preservative adaptation if the internal demands are viewed as sufficiently great to offset those from abroad. For reasons elaborated below, this assumption now appears untenable. The changing structure of world politics has facilitated, perhaps even encouraged, the emergence of some small states who have managed to lessen substantially their orientations toward their external environments or to raise substantially their orienations toward the needs of their essential structures. That is, some small states have successfully moved their politics from acquiescent to preservative or promotive adaptation (the transformation puzzle), from preservative to promotive adaptation (again the transformation puzzle), or from acquiescent or preservative to intransigent adaptation (the defiance puzzle). In effect, the original formulation was founded on the faulty reasoning (noted earlier) that equates smallness with weakness and that treats objective circumstances as determinative of external behavior. Consequently, dependency was presumed to mark the quality of small state survival, whereas now it is clear that defiance and different degrees of autonomy are also forms of survival available to them.

A number of factors can be cited as sources of the various adaptive transformations experienced by some small states. The breakdown of the bipolar world and the resulting greater tolerance of great powers for the autonomy of small states, the advent of ever greater numbers of small states and the cohesive consequences of the intense nationalism through which many of them came into existence, the relatively lessened importance of military-security issues and the relatively greater importance of socio-economic and scientific issues, the growing number of transnational actors from whom small states can procure assistance, and the dynamism of modern technology and the greater interdependence it has fostered are among the more obvious reasons why the adaptive options open to small states have mutliplied.

Although it is the totality of such factors that comprises the world to which all nations must adapt, one of these changes seems especially salient as a source of the dynamics whereby small states have been able to evolve new adaptive orientations. The shift from a world in which military issues and strategy are predominant to one in which economic conflicts and tactics are paramount—what might be viewed as a shift from foul to fair weather politics—has appeared to have had profound consequences for the way in which small states define their self-environment relationships. When the context of world politics is cast predominantly in terms of military security, with the threat of armed intervention ever present and the demand for adherence to alliance commitments serving as a constant pressure, the officials of small states are likely to perceive their external environments as a series of forces to be deflected, dodged, or otherwise warded off. With the greater prevalence of economic concerns, however, the external environment emerges not as a wellspring of threats, but as a vast reservoir of desired possessions. Instead of being viewed as an ominous source of challenges to be thwarted, the environment comes to be seen as an endless resource from which to procure. To begin to redefine the external environment as a site from which demands emanate to one in which resources are available is, in terms of adaptive orientations, to begin to undergo a transformation from acquiescent to the other three types of adaptation or from preservative to promotive or intransigent adaptation. Such a redefinition of the external environment would appear to be underway among many small states, mainly those in the Third World but also on the part of some in the industrial world. For them the superpowers and other large states are decreasingly seen as armed camps and are increasingly viewed as market-places where goods and expertise can be acquired. And, equipped for the first time with this conception of the outside world as offering procurement opportunities, small states are in the position of considering alternative strategies for coping with their external environment.

There is a curious paradox here. While large states and superpowers, still needing to be attentive to problems of military strategy and for the first time experiencing a substantial degree of dependence on foreign resources, are moving in the direction of preservative adaptation in which a balance is sought between external and internal demands, small states are increasingly able to tip the balance in favour of their internal needs. More accurately, in the case of those small states whose internal structures are basically coherent and not racked by dissension, the external environment is emerging as a place where it is possible to strive for the formation of new arrangements and processes that can yield previously unobtainable benefits. In effect, the small states may be the only ones capable of evolving and sustaining the orientations that underlie promotive adaptation.

Such an interpretation seems especially logical for those small states who are richly endowed with a resource needed in the industrial world. The oil-rich states of the Arab world, once so dependent on the West and so acquiescent in their adaptive orientations, have clearly benefitted from the shift from foul to fair weather politics and been able to evolve perceptions of the world as a vast marketplace in which their oil products can serve as an effective currency with which to promote new arrangements abroad and new dimensions of their essential structures at home. It would be a mistake, however, to conclude that only those small states possessing resources in short supply in the West are capable of redefining their relationship to their external environments. The sight of superpowers becoming increasingly vulnerable and linked to changes abroad, supplemented by the example of small states such as Cuba defying their larger neighbors, would seem to have encouraged other, less richly endowed small states to reconsider their self-environment relationships. In some instances (such as Panama) the reconsideration has been hastened by vigorous demands for greater national autonomy on the part of domestic groups, while in other instances (such as Bahrain) the effort to initiate adaptive transformations has its roots in the calculations of top-level elites. But, whatever the source, a process of emulation would appear to be sweeping the world of small states, encouraging all of them to be much more ready to re-examine whether their dependency form of survival is necessary and to explore strategies for moving toward greater autonomy.

Not all the possible strategies, of course, are equally available to all small states for serious consideration. Even if their officials get swept away by the idea of establishing a new self-environment relationship, several variables can influence the range of alternative strategies they consider, the kind of strategy they eventually pursue, and the probabilities that the chosen strategy will yield the desired results. Three variables are perhaps particularly noteworthy in this regard. One has already been mentioned, namely, the degree to which a resource desired elsewhere in the world is concentrated in the small state. Our previous discussion leads directly to a clear-cut hypothesis relevant to this variable:

> H_1: *Other things being equal, the more of a highly valued resource that a small state possesses, (a) the more are its top officials likely to initiate a search for strategies with which to reduce their dependency on one or more larger states, (b) the wider the range of alternative strategies are they likely to consider, and (c) the more are they likely to be successful in redefining their self-environment relationship.*

A second variable that can importantly influence the framing, initiative, contents, and outcome of adaptive transformations involves the location of the small state in terms of the proximity of large states or superpowers on the one hand and other small states on the other. If, for example, a small state is located astride the lines of defense that large states regard as crucial to their security, then the range of alternative strategies for achieving greater autonomy is likely to be much narrower than if it is located on the periphery of global or regional military considerations. Viewed in this way, for example, it is no accident that Finland's strategy for maximizing autonomy with respect to the Soviet Union is so much less encompassing than Albania's. Much the same can be said about Czechoslovakia in comparison to Rumania, or about the way in which geographic factors enhance the exposure of Tibet and Korea to great power preoccupations in comparison to the way in which Sweden and Switzerland are insulated by their geographic situations. Similarly, the small state surrounded by a number of other small states with comparable adaptive problems is likely to be attracted to strategies for reformulating their self-environment relationships that do not even occur to the small state whose location does not provide it with any "natural" allies. The small states of the Caribbean compared to the situation of Israel could be cited as an illustration in this regard. In short, it seems reasonable to derive the following proposition:

H₂: *Other things being equal, the more the geographical location of a small state places it outside the immediate orbit of great power concerns and inside the immediate orbit of common concerns of the small powers, (a) the more are its top officials likely to initiate and sustain strategies that lead to adaptive transformations, (b) the wider the range of alternative strategies are they likely to consider, and (c) the more are they likely to be successful in redefining their self-environment relationships.*

Still another variable that appears central to the intensity and direction of small state efforts to move away from the dependency extreme of the continuum involves the degree to which consensus and coherence marks their internal structures. This is not simply a matter of whether internal demands are strong, pervasive, and insistent. Rather it is more a matter of whether they are fragmented, divisive, and contradictory demands or whether they spring from shared values and thus seem to speak, in effect, with a single voice, enabling top officials to perceive that their actions enjoy sufficient support to range widely in their efforts to promote new arrangements abroad. If consensus prevails at home and is supportive of basic governmental policies, then the strong and insistent expressions of the consensus are heard by the small states' leaders not as demands, but as support, as license to be innovative and forceful in their attempts to restructure their external environment. The ability to adapt in this fashion, however, is greatly undermined, even thwarted, if division and competing consensuses mark the domestic scene. Hence a third hypothesis can be advanced.

> H_3: *Other things being equal, the more homogeneous the main internal groups of a small state are, (a) the more are its top officials likely to initiate and pursue promotive strategies that reduce their dependency on one or more large states, (b) the wider the range of strategies are they likely to consider, and (c) the greater the probability that they will successfully redefine their self-environment relationship.*

All of this is not to imply that small states who lack a valued resource, a favorable geographic location, and a consensual socio-political structure are incapable of moving away from the dependency extreme of the continuum or that they are unlikely to undertake efforts to make such moves. Nor is it to imply that the smaller states are, the more their efforts to redefine their self-environment relationships are likely to founder. Rather it is to say that the strategies employed are crucial to the adaptive transformations that do and do not occur, so that the self-environment relationships that come to endure seem bound to be significantly shaped by the range, quality, and appropriateness of the strategies that are considered and adapted. Like any state, in other words, those that are small need to maximize rationality in their decision-making even as they need to be imaginative in framing and assessing the viability of the strategies they generate.

ALTERNATIVE SMALL STATE STRATEGIES FOR ACHIEVING NEW SELF-ENVIRONMENT RELATIONSHIP

A number of alternative strategies for defying larger states and achieving a greater measure of autonomy come to mind as possible courses for small states. They are set forth here not in any particular order since, as noted, their consideration, use, and success depends on the resources, location, and consensual foundations of each state. Furthermore, these are not mutually exclusive categories and successful adaptive transformations probably require the development of a combination of several strategies.

One obvious approach might be called the *banding-together* strategy. In it the small state seeks to gain more effective control over its external environment by joining with other small states to get its concerns on the agenda of the larger states and to render more compelling its demands. Banding together in this fashion can embrace a variety of tactics, from a diplomatic convergence for the purposes of pronouncing needs and goods (such as many small states in the Third World did when they aligned themselves with the demand for a New Economic Order) to a pooling of resources and attempts to formulate common policies for their allocation (such as the oil-rich states did in imposing an embargo through OPEC). In some instances, of course, the banding-together strategy has been carried to the extremes of binding treaties or formal federations among small states. But such efforts would appear to create new, even more difficult adaptive problems without necessarily bringing about reduced dependency, and thus often they do not last and are abandoned. Stated differently, the strategy of banding together would seem to be more effective when it is confined to a single issue or problem than when it is expanded to embrace all or most of the matters on a small state's adaptive agenda. To expand efforts at collaboration across a number of issues is to create adaptive problems between small states and thereby to detract from their ability to use their collective clout effectively on single issues of great import.

While the effectiveness of the banding-together strategy obviously depends to a large degree on the number, proximity, and like-mindedness of the small states who adopt it, at least one beneficial consequence would seem likely even if their collective demands on larger states are slow to be appreciated. As noted below, to some extent the quality of survival includes symbolic rewards, a sense of being taken seriously abroad, and it would seem inevitable that the citizens of a small state are likely to enjoy a more favorable self-image to the extent their leaders are able to get their demands on the agendas of larger states through the banding-together strategy. And, if a greater sense of importance on the world stage does develop, presumably it will have moved the small state at least slightly along the continuum away from the dependency extreme. Indeed, it may well be that symbolic gestures which enhance self-images are prerequisites to taking the first steps in the transformation away from acquiescent transformations. Such a conclusion would seem to justify derivation of the following proposition.

H₄: *Other things being equal, the more small states are able to pursue promotive adaptation through a banding-together strategy, the more are they likely to succeed in redefining their self-environment relationships.*

A second strategy, related to all of these, involves actions and policies designed to foster consensus at home and strengthen the ties that bind the society together—what we shall call the *internal coherence* strategy. As previously indicated in Hypotheses #3, homogeneity (or, at least, the absence of widespread dissent) among the main internal groups of a small state frees top officials to move more effectively abroad. To a great extent, of course, the homogeneity of a society's groups is a product of a long history and, if it is minimal and marked by deep-seated racial, ethnic, or class conflicts, the internal coherence strategy is not likely to be very effective. Yet, it is precisely the task of top leaders to fashion wider consensus if internal goals are to be realized, so that such a strategy is constantly being employed in any event. In effect, national adaptation is no less a process of domestic policy-making than it is one of foreign policy-making. Accordingly, it is conceivable that by treating consensus building as an adaptive strategy as well as a domestic policy, the prospects of redefining self-environment orientations are greater than would be the case if the efforts to promote internal consensus are defined merely as a problem of maintaining internal order. To be sure, there is a danger here that repressive domestic policies are adopted and justified as prerequisites to effective adaptive transformation. Modern history is not lacking in cases of top leaders who forced internal coherence on diverse domestic groups in order to effectuate a redefinition of self-environment relationships in which the self was more predominant. [13] It seems doubtful, however, whether the internal-coherence strategy can be as enduring, and thus as effective, when it is founded on repression as when it relies on persuasion and bargaining. Hence an extension of Hypothesis #3 seems in order:

> H₅: *Other things being equal, the more top leaders of a small state are able to promote enduring integration among its internal groups, the more are they likely to be successful in their efforts to initiate and sustain adaptive transformations that lessen their dependency on one or more large states.*

A third approach available to small states under certain circumstances is what might be called the *single-issue* or *limited-issue* strategy. Involved here is an acceptance, even a championing, of dependency on a larger power with respect to a single cluster of issues, while insisting on and retaining autonomy with respect to most matters. In order to preserve freedom of action at home and/or abroad, in other words, a small state may be able to reach a tacit or explicit bargain with a larger neighbor in which it accedes to a high degree of dependence on those issues which the latter views as paramount. Finland's adaptation since World War II is illustrative of such a strategy, even to the point in 1961 when an opposition party invaded the dependency issue-area and was forced to cease contesting a national election when the Russians objected.[14] Outside those matters the Russians regard as inviolable, however, Finland's self-environment relationship closely resembles the configuration of preservative adaptation; or at least it is much further away from the dependency extreme of the continuum than many of the small states in the Soviet orbit of Eastern Europe.

The single-issue strategy is, of course, a very delicate form of adaptation, requiring both an understanding of what constitutes an acceptable range of autonomy for the larger power and a readiness of domestic publics to grasp and acquiesce to the differentiation of issues. The 1967-1968 history of the Dubchek regime in Czechoslovakia, ending as it did with a massive Soviet military intervention, exemplifies the difficulty of maintaining the single-issue strategy and preventing it from encouraging defiant demands from domestic groups for an enlarged range of autonomy. The 1965 U.S. intervention in the Dominican Republic can be easily interpreted in the same way. Indeed, the delicacy of the single-issue strategy is so considerable that the original formulation of the adaptation scheme (Table I) does not make theoretical room for it. To identify it as an adaptive strategy is thus to require revision of the orginal formulation, albeit the fragility of the strategy indicates that theoretical revision need not be extensive in this regard. Perhaps all that is needed is a revision in which the continua from acquiescent to other forms of adaptation are broken down in terms of the number and quality of issues wherein the environment is conceived to prevail over the self. Such a conception allows us to explicate the following hypothesis:

H₆: *Other things being equal, the more top leaders of small states are able to initiate and sustain differentiation among issues in terms of different degrees of dependency on larger states, the more are they likely to succeed in redefining their self-environment relationships.*

A closely related and yet somewhat different approach is what can be labeled the *issue-insulation* strategy. Here the focus is on the way in which small states seek to adapt to the many new international and transnational organizations that have emerged as the world becomes increasingly interdependent. Where the single-issue strategy involves warding off and limiting the dominance of nearby larger powers, the issue-insulation strategy is a means of creatively and yet autonomously becoming tied to common markets, commodity agreements, and other economic international institutions. It is a strategy in which issues are treated as mutually exclusive by the leaders of small states and declared as such whenever they find it expedient to enter economic unions or arrangements with other states. Special trading relationships and fishing boundaries are illustrative of this strategy, as is the Danish declaration that its security policies were unchanged by virtue of its adherence to the E.E.C. or the many instances when the Swiss declare that they are treating important issues as technical questions. Issue insulation is, obviously, an exceedingly complex form of adaptation, dependent on a wide variety of considerations that can render issue boundaries permeable. In general it would seem that issue positions acquire legitimacy the longer they are held, asserted, and acted consistently upon, so that the more a small state can sustain the insulation of an issue area, the greater will be the legitimacy of its claims to acting autonomously within the area and thus the greater will be its ability to maintain high boundaries around the issue. It follows that,

H_7: *Other things being equal, the longer the leaders of small states are able to preserve the insulation of issues in which they have historically acted autonomously, the more will they be able to maintain desired self-environment relationships with respect to such issues.*

A fifth tool available to small states, and one that can be employed in conjunction with all the others, is what might be called the *knowledge-procurement* strategy. As the world becomes more interdependent and issues more technologically complex, knowledge becomes ever more precious, perhaps even more precious than physical resources themselves. For knowledge—technical know-how—is a prerequisite to the acquisition, utilization, and application of resources. Indeed, it might well be argued that physical and social scientific knowledge has come to replace military wherewithal as the basic form of national power as socio-economic issues have increasingly superseded military issues in salience.[15] It follows that whatever the size of a nation's resources, the capacity to cope with external challenges and internal demands autonomously will grow as the technical knowledge base of its citizenry grows. Hence, whatever its size, a state is likely to upgrade the "self" in its self-environment relationship the more it can provide its people with technical training and raise the level of their competence to handle the limitations and opportunities of nature and the dynamics of social, economic, and political organization. The knowledge-procurement strategy may not in itself produce adaptive transformations on the part of small states, but in the long run it can surely facilitate profound change.

A unique feature of the knowledge-procurement strategy is that it does not require small states to interact with other governments. Unlike all the other strategies, this one can be carried forward exclusively through contacts with nongovernmental actors. Whatever transnational entities in the environments of small states possess the requisite forms of knowledge, be they universities, business firms, agricultural associations, labor unions, or political parties—to mention but a few of the types of transnational actors who have become reservoirs of knowledge—they can be approached with a view to entering into negotiations through which their specialized knowledge can be made available to personnel of the small state. My own University, for example, recently signed a two-year contract with the government of Bahrain in which we have, in effect, taken on the obligation of serving as Bahrain's intellectual resource bank, providing guidance, training, and programs in such fields as public administration, education, demography, social services, and whatever other areas of knowledge the leaders of Bahrain deem important and the faculty of the University of Southern California can supply. Along with sending students abroad, bringing specialists in to conduct educational programs, active participation in the congresses of international professional societies, this concrete example suggests that there are a wide variety of ways in which the knowledge-procurement strategy can be implemented. Thus it is reasonable to propose that,

H_8: *Other things being equal, the more innovative and wide ranging the leaders of small states can be in employing the knowledge-procurement strategy, the more will they facilitate their policies designed to redefine their self-environment relationships in the direction of greater autonomy.*

A sixth strategy, alluded to earlier, involves a wide range of possible actions that consist more of symbols than substance. Indeed, it can well be called the *symbolism* strategy, since it encompasses a multitude of ways through which small states can call attention to their growing autonomy, or at least to the appearance of a growing autonomy, thereby enhancing the self-esteem of both their officials and publics. Acquiescent adaptation and the dependency extreme of the continuum requires, by definition, a conception of the self-environment relationship in which the self is felt to be inferior, forever destined to be overwhelmed by the environment. It will be recalled that such assessments are more in the nature of psychological orientations than objective realities. Thus any actions or events which suggest that the self is being taken seriously by other actors in the environment can serve as symbolic rewards through which the balance between self and environmental orientations is tipped in the direction of the former. Obtaining visits from heads of states, especially those that head great powers, is illustrative of how the symbolism strategy can be useful, even if such visits produce no tangible results. Indeed, it might well be argued that since such visits demonstrate the legitimacy of the small state, they provide symbolic rewards and contribute to the process of redefining self-environment relationships even if they yield counter-productive tangible results. External demands may be heightened or hardened as a consequence of the deliberations attending the visit of a head of state from abroad, but at least the visit signifies that the visited small state commands attention on the international scene. The election of a small state's representative to a high office at the United Nations or a regional international organization, domestic policies that promote athletic or artistic triumphs in international competition, and mediating disputes between other states are but a few of the many examples of how the symbolic strategy can be employed. It follows that,

H_9: *Other things being equal, the more top leaders of small states can develop policies to which symbolic rewards attach, the more will they contribute to the potential for a redefinition of self-environment relationships that lessens dependency and heightens autonomy.*

There are, of course, many other strategies small states can follow in order to initiate adaptive transformations, but space limitations prevent their enumeration.[16] Hopefully the foregoing is sufficient to demonstrate that the quality of small states survival can range widely and that their adaptive orientations need not be locked into dependency relationships. And, if it thus seems clearer that environmental constraints are in the nature of manipulable variables rather than objective constraints, then the dependency, transformational, and autonomy puzzles emerge as ever more puzzling. Hopefully, too, this puzzlement will prove sufficiently provocative to lead to tests of the foregoing hypotheses as well as others that can be readily developed, thereby giving rise to the cumulative knowledge through which the pieces of the puzzles can be clarified and fit together.

CONCLUSION: IS SIZE A USEFUL VARIABLE?

Notwithstanding the hope that this discussion of the theory of national adaptation and the various adaptive strategies to which it points will contribute to the evolution of cumulative knowledge about small states, it must be conceded that in one respect the preceding analysis fails to employ one of the criteria set forth as necessary to progress. A close analysis of each of the nine hypotheses will reveal that not a single one of them abides by the methodological canon that requires the location of smallness on a continuum. All nine posit variations on outcomes linked to variations on the possessions of small states or the actions of its officials, but none refers to variations in the degree of smallness or largeness. In effect, size is not treated as a variable.

To point up a failure to proceed by one's own canons is to highlight either one's insufficiencies or the insufficiencies of the canons. I am inclined to opt for the former interpretation, since size is such a predominant concern of world politics. Yet, there may be a lesson in the fact that in working through the analysis I unknowingly strayed from—or at least failed to implement—my own strong and explicit methodological commitment to the use of continua. Even allowing for the limitations of time and talent, this departure from intention at least suggeststhat size may not be a useful independent variable, and that conceivably so many complex and diverse phenomena are encompassed by size that to combine them together is, in effect, to create a constant and not a variable. Not only may it be unsound to dichotomize size as a variable, but it may well be unwise to aggregatively use it at all. The puzzles that are challenging, after all, pertain not to size as an aggregation of variable phenomena; but rather they involve wonderment over several qualities of survival at one end of the size scale.

FOOTNOTES

[1]Niels, Amstrup, "The Perennial Problem of Small States: A Survey of Research Efforts," *Cooperation and Conflict*, vol. 11, no. 3 (1976), pp. 163-182. This article is such a thorough review of the literature on small states that I have relied on it heavily for the introductory section of this paper, rather than undertaking an independent literature search of my own.

[2]These historical periods in the study of small states are summarized in *ibid.*, pp. 163-67.

[3]For a full discussion of the concept of a genuine puzzle and its implications, see James N. Rosenau, "Puzzlement in Foreign Policy," *The Jerusalem Journal of International Relations*, vol. 1, no. 4 (Summer 1976), pp. 1-10.

[4]Amstrup, *op. cit.,* p. 169.

[5]*Ibid.,* pp. 165-167.

[6]*Ibid., pp. 178-179.*

[7]And in one case, South Vietnam, there is considerable controversy as to whether the military outcome can be viewed as a border-crossing conquest.

[8]Thus far I have evolved the theory in five different articles: James N. Rosenau, *The Adaptation of National Societies: A Theory of Political Behavior and Its Transformation* (New York: McCaleb-Seiler, 1970), pp. 1-28; James N. Rosenau, "Foreign Policy as Adaptive Behavior: Some Preliminary Notes for a Theoretical Model," *Comparative Politics,* vol. 2, no. 3 (April 1970), pp. 365-389; James Rosenau, "Adaptive Polities in an Interdependent World," *Orbis,* vol. 16, no. 1, (Spring 1972), pp. 153-173; James N. Rosenau, "Paradigm Lost: Five Actors in Search of the Interactive Effects of Domestic and Foreign Affairs," *Policy Sciences,* vol. 4, no. 4, (December 1973), pp. 415-436; and James N. Rosenau, "Foreign Intervention as Adaptive Behavior," in *Law and Civil War in the Modern World,* John Norton Moore, ed. (Baltimore: John Hopkins University Press, 1974), pp. 129-151. For two other, more empirical applications, see Peter Hansen, "Adaptive Behavior of Small States: The Case of Denmark and the European Community," in *Sage International Yearbook of Foreign Policy Studies,* vol. 2, Patrick J. McGowan, ed. (Beverly Hills, Ca.: Sage Publications, 1974), pp. 143-174; and Patrick J. McGowan and Klaus-Peter Gottwald, "Small State Foreign Policies: A Comparative Study of Participation, Conflict, and Political and Economic Dependence in Black Africa," *International Studies Quarterly,* vol. 19, no. 4, (December 1975), pp. 469-500.

[9]In the analysis I use the terms "national society," "state," "nation," and "nation state" interchangeably, assuming that each designate a political entity that is at least formally sovereign and capable of deciding how to cope with situations at home and abroad.

[10]For a full analysis of each type, see J. N. Rosenau, *The Adaptation of National Societies, op. cit.,* pp. 3-16.

[11]Table 1 has been reproduced from *ibid.,* pp. 5. Several paragraphs of the ensuing summary have also been derived from this monograph.

[12]*Ibid.,* pp. 16-20.

[13]The recent rejection by five Latin American countries of more than $70 million in U.S. military sales credits in protest over President Carter's strong human rights campaign can be readily interpreted as an instance of this negative use of the internal coherence strategy. All five are military controlled and their leaders presumably preferred to forego external resources than risk a heightening of internal demands for greater political freedoms.

[14]For an account of this episode, see David Vital, *The Survival of Small States: Studies in Small Power-Great Power Conflict* (New York: Oxford University Press, 1971), pp. 107-109.

[15]For an elaboration of this argument, see James N. Rosenau, "Capabilities and Control in an Interdependent World, *International Security,* vol. 1, no. 2 (October 1976), pp. 32-49.

[16]Such an enumeration would include resort to bribery of officials in large powers; but as recent events with respect to South Korea illustrate, this strategy is a precarious one that can readily backfire and reduce the probability of successful movement away from the dependency extreme of the continuum.

A Letter to Rosenau on the Three Basic Fallacies Attaching to His Theory of Adaptation of Small States*

Herb Addo

Dear Jim,

I have re-read your (recent) manuscript on "The Adaptation of Small States." I am even more impressed with it now than I was when I first read it in 1977. Within the terms in which you set your arguments, your arguments are very commanding. If I attempt to comment on the manuscript by reference only to your terms—methodological and theoretical—I shall have very little to say against it, but a lot in praise of it. As much as I respect your terms, however, I have to be honest with you by saying that I do not share, or subscribe, to all of them.

You probably know that I have embraced the world-system terms of analysis—both methodological and theoretical. I shall not go into the advantages of the world-system perspective here. It will take too long, and I am sure you are familiar with the claims this perspective makes and the controversy which those claims have precipitated.

What I am about to do here in reaction to your theory of adaptation of small states is in a sense unfair. I am going to do with your theory what I have begun to do with all social science theories which come my way.[1] I am going to use your manuscript to attempt to show how a world-system theory of small states would look like. I am not arrogant and naive enough to think that this will be easy. In fact, I am sure that what will emerge will not be "a world-system theory of small states." At best, it will

*This is a product of the Structural Interpretation Inequality Project (S3IP), a sub-project within the UNU-GPID Project, coordinated by Johan Galtung, c/o UNITAR, Geneva. Thanks to Lily Addo for her editorial and typing services. I am solely responsible for the imperfections and inadequacies in this work.

be what I think should go into such a theory, if there is to be one—a calculus of the world-system-inspired reasons which should inform a theory of small states, their adaptation included.

The apparent unfairness of this exercise notwithstanding, it is *necessary* at this point in time and in this small Caribbean corner of the world-unit, where the theory of small states is a daily occupational encounter and where the very fact of "smallness" itself is a fact of life.

What I find most commendatory about your manuscript in which you attempt to bring your considerable abilities, in the pursuit of cumulation of knowledge in foreign policy generally, to bear on the fascinating subject of small states and the qualities of their survival in the turbulence of world politics, is the tremendous warmth of the inspiration it has given me to put the elements of my thoughts on the subject on paper.

Before I start to comment let me say two things: (1) parts of what I am about to say may sound, in our working language, critical; (2) other parts may sound not critical. I urge you not to take one without the other. The two parts form a dialectical unity. And where I praise your contribution to knowledge in foreign policy studies, I mean every word. This is clear not just to me, but, take my word, to many. Indeed let me ask this: what are the works of senior scholars for, if they are not there to be reacted to by junior scholars?[2]

I shall proceed, then, to comment, more or less, according to the structure of your argument.

1. FROM THE MALAISE OF THE SURVIVAL PUZZLE TO THE QUALITY OF THE SURVIVAL PUZZLE

You begin by calling attention to the fact that this area of scientific enquiry has been caught in a malaise of sorts, even though at the first encounter it would appear as if this area of research is pervaded by a "genuine puzzle." By "genuine puzzle," you mean questions which "are so important and challenging as to sustain the curiosity of successive generations of observers."[3] In order for questions to be really "genuine puzzles," and so contribute to cumulative research, you argue they must concentrate on important and clearly special outcomes which occur with sufficient regularity to be deemed worthy of explanations.[4]

The cause of what you follow Amstrup to call "the malaise of small state analysis" appears to reside in the fact that this area of research has addressed itself to the wrong question. The question in this regard has been: "why do small states survive?" After discussing conceptual difficulties with this question, you come to the conclusion that "why do small states survive?" is really not a suitable question for framing a genuine puzzle, principally because "... to pose the puzzle as a question of why small states survive is to orient us toward an outcome we take for granted rather than one we find challenging to explain." And you add, "Viewed this way, it is hardly surprising that the survival question has not been the source of extensive cumulation."[5]

You suggest that the "puzzlement no longer focuses on the fact of survival as much as on its quality."[6] You argue that so far as small states are concerned "the quality of their survival, . . . is the critical outcome that provokes curiosity and if major types of survival can be specified as the bases for framing genuine puzzles, orderly cumulation of our knowledge about small states may well follow."[7] Your formulation of the genuine puzzle, as a question of the *quality of survival of small states,* in place of the "malaise puzzle," as a question of the sheer survival of small states, appears to be well-reasoned. It seems to suggest that, if it is followed in the proper direction, it could lead a long way toward your aim of contributing toward the cumulation of knowledge. I shall keep this in mind as I proceed.

2. TRANSLATING THE PUZZLEMENT OF QUALITY OF SURVIVAL INTO THREE PUZZLES

If the master puzzle simply deals with the general question of what the qualities of survival of small states are, you conceptualize *quality of survival* along a continuum defined by the extremes of *dependency* and *autonomy,* with the usual conceptual gradations between the two extremes. The point that comes across very clearly in this presentation is that the qualities of small state survival deal not so much with extremes of dependency and autonomy as with the *differences* between the two types of extreme survival. In fact, you say explicitly that "it is to the distinction between these extremes and the many degrees of dependence and autonomy that lie between" that your three puzzles are addressed.[8] The three puzzles, to which your scientific curiosity is attached, are presented in the following forms:

i)   Why do small states become and remain so dependent on other states?[9]

ii) Why do some small states successfully defy or otherwise remain autonomous with respect to much larger states located nearby?[10]

iii) Why and how do some small states succeed in achieving substantially greater degrees of autonomy with respect to larger states and/or international economies than they had in earlier eras of their history?[11]

The general context in which you formulate these three puzzles is an *asymmetric interdependent world-system,* in which small states are deemed to want to change their positions on the quality of survival continuum, but for some reasons, emanating from their very smallness in the real world of politics, these changes are not normal for small states because they are not easy. It is for this reason that, even though you address the first and the second puzzles to the extremes of the continuum, you focus attention on the third puzzle, which is addressed to the conceptual space between the two extremes on the continuum.

Assuming, however, that autonomy is a value in itself, then it is legitimate for one to wonder why all the three puzzles should be presented as *why* questions, rather than *how* questions. Presented in the form of *whys,* the questions which frame the puzzles can be answered in non-puzzling ways by simply referring to your own reasons behind their very formulations. With respect to the first puzzle, the answer could be simply that the small states either cannot do better or that they do not want it any other way. The second puzzle can be answered by saying that the small states concerned want it and, given their *circumstances,* they can do better. Viewed in this way, the first two questions are not only non-puzzling, they are in fact non-questions. The puzzling properties which attach to these questions, to make them *puzzles,* do not reside in their *why* forms. They reside in their *how* forms, because in that form interest does not attach to the questions themselves, but to the "reasoning" behind them which forces attention to focus precisely on the dynamics of transformation—in this context, the politics of movements along the transformation continuum.

Let me explain myself because this is important to my position, which will be clearer soon. In their *why* forms the questions are not addressed to the *system,* the *world-system,* but to the small states, whose very smallness is meaningless outside the precise identification of the *identity* of the world-system. By this I am referring to the historic factor within which the *circumstances* of small states are a handicap. The third puzzle, the transformation puzzle, is presented as a combination of a *why* and a *how* question. Again in its *why* aspect, the puzzle is not a puzzle, for reasons given above. It becomes an interesting puzzle only when it stands in the form of a *how* question. All this becomes clear, and the merit of the criticism becomes obvious, when it is recalled that your own interest is in the dynamics of transformation as such and not in the "comparative statistics" of the maintenance of a quality of survival at the extremes of the transformation continuum, or even along it.

With the puzzles put in the form of *how* questions, one can legitimately wonder further whether there is any real reason to have three puzzles addressed to separate points of the transformation continuum. The question is whether the transformation puzzle, the third puzzle, in its *how* form does not cater for the other two puzzles. I believe it does, in that whatever it takes a small state to move up or down the continuum must be present in its more or less form to keep another small state at the autonomy or the dependence end of the continuum.

I raise the query because, in the theoretical presentation of genuine puzzles, it becomes a little confusing to let multiple puzzles, no matter how genuine they may appear to be, get in the way when one summary puzzle will do. It is even more confusing where hypotheses are expected to emerge to guide empirical research, with the intention of adding to the cumulation of knowledge. Apart from the possible confusion, there is the real danger that analysts will consume precious resources in the course of pursuing multiple hypotheses, which are no more than variants of a basic hypothesis. I am not saying that your hypotheses necessarily run the risk of this danger, but since I understand you to be principally focusing on the politics and the dynamics of transformational adaptation of small states, I would prefer to view your three puzzles as not only genuine, but also that they resolve into a single puzzle when reformulated to read as follows: *how do some small states succeed in achieving substantially greater degrees of autonomy with respect to larger states in the turbulence of world politics where nations—small and large— compete for the same scarce values within a precise world-system which is marked distinctly by unavoidable interdependence in pursuit of a particular historic theme?*

Jim, you will note that I have not only reformulated your third puzzle, I have tampered with it by dropping your reference to "international economies" and "earlier eras of [these small states] history," and in their places I have substituted undisguised references to the "contextual world" as a definite system which pursues a particular *historic theme.*

I now proceed to explain why these latter references are indispensable, if we are to prosecute your chosen subject properly along what could be regarded as probably the right direction. I shall deal with this further in connection with your methodological canon, but please note that our only disagreement here is whether to address the small states or the identity of the total system in which small states find themselves.

3. THE OMISSION OF A CRUCIAL NECESSITY: THE WORLD-SYSTEM CONTEXT

Your acknowledged theoretical mind, which relentlessly pursues cumulation of knowledge in foreign policy, comes out in its full elegance in the section dealing with the methodological canon of your theory of adaptation of small states. No one can possibly disagree with the need for a theoretical perspective, which would gather the diverse pieces of the puzzles into a coherent whole,[12] nor with the necessity for the articulation of a methodological tenet which can transcend conceptual difficulties in the construction of any theory. Indeed, this need and this necessity are imperative for most theories, including the development of a viable theory of small states adaptation in international politics. Further, and as I have indicated above, it is not possible to disagree with you in your preference for casting the range of variation of the key variables as a continuum rather than as a dichotomy. The need to ponder the consequences of each increment, or decrement, in the attributes or the attitudes of states is well taken especially because, as you put it, "if size is treated dichotomously we need only reflect on differences at the extremes and are not forced to think about the many gradations that lie between smallness and largeness or the dynamics whereby movement along the continuum occurs."[13] All this is important because a theory which is sensitive only to the extremes and not the the dynamics of movement along the entire continuum is not much of a theory. Such a theory will only lead us back to a static confusion worse than Amstrup's "malaise of small state analysis."

Following this agreement, however, is a fundamental disagreement with you for omitting the most vital contextual dimension of the world within which your theory will have to owe its eventual viability.

Let me make mention of this serious omission by referring to your conception of the world as interdependent. What I mean here is that it is not enough to merely concede that the world is interdependent, this comes all too easily nowadays; or even to admit that this interdependence is asymmetric, this could be no more than an irrelevant admission. This is not enough to bring out the richness of the *interdependence* idea of the world—its origins, the salient aspects of its development etc.— and its real meaning enough to serve as a context within which to deal with the *historic concept*[14] of small size.

This omission is what deals with the realistic and the precise historic identity of world-history as we have known it unfold over the relevant period. This omission is a gaping omission. It must be filled in, if we are to even pretend that the concepts *size* and *small,* around which your theory revolves, in fact on which your theory hinges, are to have any viable conceptual validity. In this regard the circumstances of small states are subordinate to the *real* history of the world in that they are not merely implied by it but are integral parts of it.

We do not intend to discuss the world-system methodology here at any length.[15] Suffice it to say that without the precise statement of the historic identity of the world-system as capitalist, with the historic theme of accumulating capital in some states (the centre states) and away from others (the periphery states), it is difficult to pin down the utility of size, its assets, and drawbacks; and it will be difficult to know *where* to fit your puzzles and *why*. Even the state conceived of as no more than a legal entity, which moves in no more than legal circles, cannot be properly discussed outside its precise historic referents. The state conceived as an ensemble of attributes and attitudes definitely has a functional utility which relates directly to the historic motive of capital accumulation.[16] Here, I refer to the use to which the state, as an ensemble of attributes and attitudes, has been, and is still, put in the cause of the pursuit of the historic motive of capital accumulation of the world-system within which all states, small or large, exist.

This matter becomes even more crucial if the aim of your elegant formulation is to come to grips with the difficult problem of defining small states to allow for analyses in which both highly industrial and predominantly agrarian states can be treated as *small*. It will amount to very little, if all we can do with your elaborate formulation is to enable us to define both *small agrarian* and *small industrial* states as *small*. This points to a serious flaw in the formulation. The flaw is that the formulation is capable of dealing with *small* as an adjective, but not with the *state* as an ensemble of attributes and attitudes and their utility in the accumulation of capital enterprise. That is, your formulation is capable of dealing with adjectival or *comparative small size*, but not with utilitarian or *instrumental small size*, as they pertain to states in our capitalist world-system.

This distinction within the conception of *small* as it applies to *states* is extremely important, and it must be kept in mind. At the contemporary phase of the world capitalist system, indeed over the last few centuries of the modern world-system, to compare a *small* but highly *industrialized* state and a *small* but predominantly *agrarian* state in terms of the *smallness* of some of their attributes and then proceed to classify the two states as *small*, is to ignore the major *differences* between them precisely because the important attributes which enable each to pursue the accumulation of capital may most likely be different in *size*. The qualities of survival of these two small states will most likely differ, *not because they are not similar in their smallness in some of their attributes, but because they differ in those attributes which compose their capabilities to accumulate capital.* The distinction between *comparative small size* and *instrumental small size* must be recognized, if, as you say, the objective is to "encourage creative theorizing"[17] with the concept of size. Until upon further reflection, or upon your strong objection, I am almost adamant on this point. Or is it that I am just being obtuse?

That this vital distinction between the conceptual dimensions of size is critical, and that it will soon lead to analytic impasse should it be forgotten, is clearly illustrated by you toward the end of the methodological section. This is the section where you say that merely by casting analysis in the context of a continuum, analysts can use *whatever* definitions of size that seem appropriate to their concerns, and that approached as such ". . . the elusiveness of the size variable may not be a problem,"[18] and further that should it prove difficult to apply, we can blame it on the fact that ". . . the range of phemonena encompassed by the concept of size is too great for it to be employed as an incisive analytic variable."[19] The concept of size may very well be a very dull variable, but Jim, is this the best, or the only, way to prove it as such?

This piece of reasoning is dangerous, in any case. It is dangerous to allow that analysts can use *whatever* definitions of size they choose, simply because they seem appropriate to their concerns. This is a sure way to run the risk of *defining away* any analytic incisiveness which the concept of size may have. The real danger is, however, that having defined away the essence of the concept any subsequent analytic difficulties analysts may encounter can readily be blamed on the fact that the concept of size cannot be employed as an incisive analytic variable, in any case. I doubt very much if this approach to the concept of size can be considered a *neat* methodological device. Variables do not come with their own analytic incisiveness. Theorists render them such; and analysts then use them as such to study reality. A theory, which does not endow its variables with realistic analytic properties and dimensions, I would imagine, is not likely to be of much use to analysts in their examinations of reality.

This misconception cannot be blamed entirely on you. Its roots are deep-seated in the liberal school of foreign policy analysis, and they are to be found in this school's ahistoric fascination with the contemporary. Jim, would you agree if I say that this school of thought prefers to look at current affairs as a basis for theorizing, rather than look to theories of international relations anchored firmly in the *history-identified* essence of the capitalist world-system (world-history) for theoretical inspiration? The objective reality of the world-system, within which states interact and fashion their various qualities of survival, exists. This reality, however, differs instrumentally for states and this means that some "small" states are more constrained to move up on the transformation continuum than other "small" states. Given the objective conditions of the world-system, the only other variable left to play with are the subjective circumstances of states *within* the world reality.

You have alerted us to the importance of the variables constituting the particular circumstances of "small" states but not to the precise nature of the objective reality of the world-system in which context alone the differences in the qualities of survival of "small" states, the dynamics of their adaptive transformation, and the very relevance of size in it could combine to claim analytic prominence.

What your methodology should have presented us with, then, is not *why* states adapt differently but *how* they do so in the capitalist world-system. This links with my earlier query about the form of the initial questions; and to show how valid this query is, let me point to how the proper form compels itself on you when you come to formulate your hypotheses.

However, we can seriously claim to be treating *how* "small" states adapt differently only if we do so in terms of their objective and subjective circumstances and their articulation with the objective reality of the world-system in terms of its *historic theme.*

Jim, you do not do this; and yet while you pose your puzzles in terms of *why,* the omissions of this crucial articulation notwithstanding, you end up casting your main hypothesis in terms of *how.* In the course of doing this, you appear to have built too much upon the simple idea that size should be seen in relational terms—as a continuum rather than a dichotomy; and you have completely neglected the differences in the functional utilities of states, as they pertain to capital accumulation, the historic theme of the world-system.

4. THE SLIDE FROM METHODOLOGICAL FLAWS TO THEORETICAL FALLACIES

With this said, let us move on to your "theoretical perspective." Here, as it was in the methodological section, the major device is that the quality of survival is to be conceived as a continuum.[20] What your theory seeks to do primarily is to detect movements along this continuum; but, because of various legitimate limitations, you indicate only some of the main components of the theory. The centrepiece of the theory, as presented in its broad outlines, is "the derivation of nine hypotheses relevant to the strategies that small states might employ to move away from the dependency extreme of the continuum."[21]

Essentially your theory of "the adaptation of small states" is an elaboration of your earlier "theory of the adaptation of national society." In the theory's elaborated form, "small states" is reasoned and substituted for "national societies"; and survival of the states, which was not assumed in the earlier theory, is now more or less assumed and, therefore, what serves as the focus of the theory is the quality of survival.[22] Most importantly, however, is that you do not only heed some of the critics of this earlier theory to include small states, you heed them further by moving the theory in its small state form from the conservative attachment to the fluctuations of the essential structures of states being "kept within limits acceptable to their members" to allow for the changes in these very "critical limits" by the creative use of both internal and external factors.[23] This means, then, that (small) states are no longer condemned to a particular "internal-external balance," but are allowed the possibility of movement "up" or "down" along the quality of survival continuum depending on the changes in the "internal" and/or the "external," keeping in mind the important proviso that the four adaptation orientations of *Acquiescent, Intransigent, Promotive,* and *Preservative* are to be viewed as "deepseated and not transitory in nature. They undergo transformation only in response to profound social and technological changes either internally or in the international." What we have, then, is that smallness is no longer necessarily synonymous with weakness and, hence, does not necessarily allow only acquiescent or dependent adaptation.

The most important innovation, however, is that you no longer consider your four adaptation forms as mutually exclusive with respect to policies of states. Neither do you insist that, at best, a particular adaptation could display only shades of the four types in its bag of adaptation.[24] The important thing now is that, whatever a states's initial adaptation, it is not condemned there, and for this reason scientific curiosity follows the possible changes in this adaptation along the continuum composed by the four adaptation orientations, which serve as convenient observation points for the observer and, at the same time, serve as a "basic posture from which emanate" all policy decisions.

Built into the theory is the indicative value that all states, if they had their way, would want to move toward and stay at the *preservative* end of the adaptation continuum. The movements of small states along this continuum become interesting only because it is easier for "large" states to do this than it is for "small" states. In this context, Jim, we should not forget the reason why states want to move up to, or stay at, the preservation adaptation end of the continuum. Whatever it is, it cannot be considered outside the historic theme of our distinctive historic times—capital accumulation.

As the theory stands there is very little that a critic can object to within the strict confines of establishment foreign policy and international relations. It is when a critic breaks away from these confines and views it from the world-system perspective that the probable weaknesses of the theory stand out.

I have been trying to say that your treatment of small states has two major flaws. The first is that it is *ahistoric* in that it is too concerned with the contemporary circumstances of states. You do not take account of the *historic* reasons which have come to make the distinction between *big* and *small* states of contemporary interest. Not doing this has meant that you have neglected to conceive the concept state, an ensemble of attributes and attitudes, as a modern *historic concept* which has undergone evolutionary motion through this history as it pursues its *historic theme.* This means further that you have ignored to consider *together* the important questions of *why, how,* and *for what* contemporary small and big states came about in the first place. States did not by chance and magic end up being *small* or *big* today. There are clear historic reasons for the smallness or the bigness of states, and until these reasons are specified and identified in their precise *historic* context, the analytic power of any theory of small states adaptation will be impaired.

We shall refer to this flaw as the *fallacy of ahistoric contemporaneity.* For omitting the historic reasons, you are treating the state only, and merely, in terms of its comparative size—big or small, rich or poor, powerful or weak—as it appears at the moment. Until you take the historic *why, how* and *for what* into account, you are not treating small states and the interesting matter of the qualities of their survival in the turbulence of world politics. You are only treating the "smallness of states," a very uninteresting affair by all accounts. What you present to us, then, is a frame for studying small states and why *smallness* need not be constraining, but not a frame for studying the *state* of the *small* kind and the dynamics of the quality of its survival. This latter flaw we shall call *the fallacy of indiscriminate smallness,* because it does not discriminate between smallness. The two fallacies are related. The second derives from the first.

This first fallacy shows clearly through your piece particularly in the few pages which you devote to your reasoned introduction of *small* into the initial theory of adaptation of national societies. You refer to a number of factors which have changed the international environment enough to make the adaptive transformation of some small states possible even in this age and day. Among these factors are: (1) the breakdown of the bipolar world and its consequence of greater tolerance of great powers for the autonomy of small states; (2) the advent of many small states and the relevance of their self-actualizing nationalisms; (3) the lessened importance of military-security issues and the emerging importance of

socio-economic and scientific issues; (4) the growing number of transnationals and their importance for small states in procuring assistance
from them; and finally (5) the dynamism of modern technology. But it is
the lessened importance of military issues and strategy and the predominance of economic conflict and tactics—the changes from foul to fair
weather—that you believe makes the real difference.

A lot can be said on your reference to these five factors. I shall stave
off the temptation to discuss them at length. I shall only state that it is
not entirely correct in the fundamental sense for you to say that the
factors you mention have changed the international environment enough
to make adaptive transformation of small states possible. These factors,
within the methodology of the world system, are no more than mere
changes in the *historic concomitants* and changes in the expressions of
the *historic logical attendants*. These two historic factors change as the
historic force within the *historic theme* changes.[25] The changes which
you refer to, therefore, are not more than intimations of the fact that the
world-system, the world capitalist system, has moved into a new and
different phase which allows, or more precisely commands, the *contemporary* superstructural expressions of the system to undergo changes.
These latter changes occur so that the *constancy* of the historic motive
could be maintained. The constancy of the historic motive is the
sempiternal flow of capital from the periphery (small states) to the centre
of world capitalism (large states). The efficiency of capital accumulation
is affected by the very accumulation itself, and for this reason new levels
of efficiency demand that the *historic concomitants* and the *logical
attendants* change also, if events are to be faithful to the *historic theme* of
accumulating capital in the centre and away from the periphery.

The changes demanded by the new levels of efficiency of capital
accumulation could be far reaching. They could include the notable
changes which you describe so well as the change from "foul to fair
weather." But to really understand the nature of the changes involved,
we must make the distinction between fundamental changes and, for
want of a better word, superficial changes. *Fundamental* changes are
those changes which refer to a change in the historic motive itself.
Superficial changes are those which, no matter how far reaching, leave
the historic theme, as such, intact; or, in more honest words, those
changes which occur so that the historic theme will remain the same.

The changes you discuss are superficial changes and must be seen and
understood as such. They may be significant and far reaching changes
when considered together, or singly; but the real significance of such
changes lies in their consideration with the extent to which they refer to
change in the historic theme. To the extent that this is not the case, to that

extent the changes involved cannot be considered significant in the fundamental sense.

I say the above, in order to be able to say that changes in *historic concomitants* and their logical attendants reflect changes in the efficiency of both human and non-human exploitation, largely due to changes in technology which underly the dynamism of the pursuit of the historic theme. They express the fact that changes in the means of efficient exploitation have occurred, necessitating the need for changes in some aspects of world capitalist life, if the capitalist system itself is to survive and operate efficiently.

To illustrate, your change from "foul to fair weather" simply means that gun boat diplomacy has become a costly and an inefficient way of pursuing the accumulation of capital at this phase of world capitalism. The bipolar structure of world power occupied a very brief period in the long history of world capitalism; and no sooner had the cost this structure incurred for the efficient accumulation of capital been realized, than its breakdown began. The advent of many small states, as a result of the vehemence of their nationalisms, is not be be taken seriously beyond a limit. Elsewhere, I have argued that this is a frivolous argument, because the apparent strength of "small states" nationalisms was indicative of the changing order of world capitalism, which made colonies, as possessions concretely held, obsolete if the meaning of history was to remain the "rational" and efficient accumulation of capital in the centre.[26]

Finally, the dynamism of contemporary technology is not in doubt. But what does this mean for the world and the small states in it? It means first, an increase in the number of transnationals; and second, the spread of the ideology of peripheral capitalism which teaches the importance of the transnational to small states as a source from which to procure assistance.

What do all these changes add up to? They add up to ensuring that at this phase of world capitalism, as in the earlier phases, capital will accrue to the centre from the periphery, except more efficiently than before. Because of the *fallacy of ahistoric contemporaneity*, it is difficult to see the contradiction whereby the world appears to have changed and yet manages to remain the same fundamentally, because it is still a capitalist world in which all changes conspire to make the accumulation of capital in the centre more efficient: and this is the *thesis* of the capitalist world-economy—the unequal incidence of accumulating capital.

This does not mean that the world capitalist system cannot be transcended. It does not mean that these changes do not foreshadow a transformation of the system. The argument here does no more than raise the question: Do these changes constitute a transition phase from capitalism? This question cannot be approached from your framework.

We should be careful not to idealize the present, and the very recent in world-history. Thus, we should pause where you say: "with the greater prevalence of economic concerns, however, the external environment emerges not as a wellspring of threats, but as a vast reservoir of desired possessions."[27] What appears to be true is that the world is still "a wellspring of threats," whether subtle or non-military; and the modern world has always been seen, for better or for worse, "as an endless resource from which to procure."[28] It is therefore simply not true, at best over-stated, to say that "to begin to redefine the external environment as a site from which demands emanate to one in which resources are available is, in terms of adaptive orientations, to begin to undergo a transformation from acquiescent to the other three types of adaptation. . . ."[29] The availability of resources in the environment is not, and has never been, divorced from demands.

The changing nature of these demands do not make them any less of demands. They mainly indicate the rising levels of efficiency in pursuit of capital. This is to say that the rising *levels of efficiency of means* indicate rising *levels of efficiency and subtlety of exploitation* of both human and non-human resources in the external environment. This is not to suggest, however, that there have not been changes in the external environment that are noteworthy. It is not even to say that the severity of the onus of the exploited has not been reduced. It is to suggest strongly that the significance of these changes should not be exaggerated, and in their exaggerated forms be allowed to obscure the existence of the very foundations of the facts of inter-state life. These foundations remain capitalist and are based on the unique, dynamic, and the efficient combination of the inequality and the dependent relations between states, which lead to exploitation of some states by others in aid of accumulating capital in some states and away from others.

Analyses of contemporary foreign policy and international relations, which do not take into account the historico-structural foundations of the modern world-system, will commit the *fallacy of ahistoric contemporaneity;* and this will surely lead them to inflate the difference between the current and the past, at the cost of being insensitive to the challenge inherent in the contradiction that things, while appearing to change, in fact can in essence remain the same.

I am of the view that you commit this fallacy in setting the stage to introduce the hypotheses on the quality of survival of small states, in terms of the framing, the initiating, the contents, and the outcome of their politics of adaptive transformation.

Let me proceed to discuss your nine hypotheses. In doing this, however, let me recall the other fallacy, namely the *fallacy of indiscriminate smallness.* This is the fallacy which does not establish any real differences between small states as such. It does not differentiate between *small* in the sense of *quality* and it is therefore not able to capture the qualitiative difference between a small industrial state and a small agrarian state. This fallacy leads your anlaysis to consider the concept small principally in terms of *comparative quantitative* size, that is, in terms of quantities. This is, however, only one of the two crucial dimensions of the concept small. The other is the functional utility of the state as an *instrument* for capital accumulation. These two dimensions are clearly interrelated, but it is when the *comparative small size* of a state and its *instrumental small size* coincide that the concept small can be said to have come into its own.

In saying this, however, I must add that, in the strict application of the *world-system* methodology and its reference to the all important *historic theme,* as I understand and appreciate it, there is a hierarchy between the two dimensions. *Small,* as *instrumental size* precedes *small* as *comparative size.* This is what explains Japan and England and their dominance in whole eras in history. For this reason, a state is unambiguously small, as for example some of the many Commonwealth Caribbean Islands are, when it is small in "size" on both dimensions. A state is *not necessarily small* even though it may be small in comparative size, if it can hold its own, or perhaps even do more than just that on the dimension of instrumental size. For this reason, a state may not be small in comparative size and yet may be considered *small* if it is small in terms of instrumental size.

We can, therefore, extract from the above the cautious propositions that: *a state which is small only on the comparative size dimension need not necessarily be small, but a state which is small on the instrumental size dimension is most probably a small state in the context of the turbulence of international politics.* So that, as I have indicated above, I would prefer to approach the nine hypotheses from the point of view which suggests that a state is small either because its *comparative small size* and its *instrumental small size* coincide to make it unambiguously small, or that a state is small mainly because its *instrumental size* is small.

I would suggest that this is what could make small states adaptation politics of transformation, at the present phase of the world-capitalist system, interesting. The interest here centres principally on the clever use and the clever manipulation of the attributes and the attitudes of statehoods in their contextual relationships within the objective reality of the world capitalist environment.

The variables which are involved in this "interest" are precisely (at least they include) those variables and variable clusters which you employ in the hypotheses. They fall into two groups, namely self-over-environment variables (the attributes of state variables) and environment-over-self variables (environmental constraints). The main thesis here is that the adaptation politics of transformation is essentially the marshalling of self-over-environment forces to overcome the constraints in the environment. It is for this reason that the interest at this particular level of politics focuses on the quality of survival of small states as they are determined by the conveniently demarcated points on the transformation continuum.

There is nothing contentious about the nine hypotheses as you present them, so long as they are read without reference to the fallacies I pointed out above. We shall get to this, but, before that, let us point out that these hypotheses bear the familiar structure of hypotheses in this kind of work in the social sciences. They are all conditioned on the "all things being equal" crutch; and they then proceed to state that to the extent that small states possess certain transformational variables to that extent is transformational politics leading to possible transformational movements to higher levels of quality of survival probable. The hypotheses are general in that they refer to movements to higher levels of transformation, without linking certain variables, or clusters of them, to specific adaptation points on the transformation continuum. This is all anyone can expect a theorist to do. The specific links between particular variables and particular points on the transformation continuum is an empirical matter, which will have to be approached in that vein.

However, it is when one considers the condition of "all things being equal" that one begins to worry. The worry stems from the fact that generally things in the external environment are not, nor have they ever been, equal for the small states, especially of the kind we describe above as defined by *small instrumental size* and *small comparative size*. When one reasons that things have not been equal for these small states in the past, are not equal for them in the present, and for as long as the world-system remains capitalist things are not likley to be equal for them, one begins to question the plausibility of some of the hypotheses.

Take hypothesis 8 and link the meaning of it to the goings-on in the New International Economic Order and the debate on the transfer of technology problem. It soon becomes clear that at the present "new international division of labour"[30] phase of world capitalism, it is highly improbable that Transnational Corporations of any sort do, will, or even can, serve as effective agents in the knowledge procurement business.

Take another hypothesis, hypothesis 1 this time, where the almost boring example of the Arab and other OPEC countries are supposed to serve as an adaptive example in transformation politics. The question is not that there is not a ring of truth around this example. The question is whether much will be left that is true, when the thin ring of truth is removed by the sheer force of the fact that all things are *not* equal even for these countries. For if things were equal, would the billions of dollars amassed by these oil countries end up in the center countries? Would these dollars not have made a "good difference" to the millions whose lives need such a difference in the oil countries? And would the economy of the many Third World Nations be in so much trouble because of prohibitive oil prices, which have led to severe balance of payments crises? The point is that things are not equal, definitely not in the sense that the structure of your reasoned hypotheses would have us believe. And it is precisely because they cannot be equal in a capitalist world, where whatever benefits accrue favour the few (elites within and among states), that I shall argue that the nine hypotheses call for severe scrutiny, which could lead to the modification and even perhaps the rejection of some of them.

I shall not attempt to do this at the moment. It is enough to point to their probable weakness. I shall rather attempt to conclude by taking a close look at your conclusion, in terms of the fallacies I have pointed out above.

All along, my fears have been that having presented the concepts *size* and *small* in the ways you do, you would most likely end up finding these concepts not very useful for any analyses which lead to the cherished cumulation of knowledge in the field of size (small states) in foreign policy. In all fairness to you, Jim, you did warn us to expect this.[31] I shall recall here that I discussed my fears in terms of my understanding of the world-system methodology, and that I presented them as the *fallacy of ahistoric contemporeneity* and its attendant, or derivative, *fallacy of indiscriminate smallness*.

5. FROM PUZZLES AND PUZZLEMENT TO WONDERMENT

Your pre-emptive warning and our own fears notwithstanding it still comes as very much of a surprise when you begin the conclusion, which asks whether size is a useful variable, with these words: "hopefully the foregoing is sufficient to demonstrate that the quality of small state survival can range widely and that their adaptive orientations need not be locked into dependency relationships."[32]

In the conclusion you say: ". . . and, if it thus seems clearer that environmental constraints are in the nature of manipulable variables rather than object constraints, then the dependency, transformational, and autonomy puzzles emerge as ever more puzzling."[33] This sentence is not clear to understand in isolation or in the context of what you have been saying. What I appreciate from my perspective, however, is why the dependency, the transformational and the autonomy puzzles should "emerge as ever more puzzling." From my perspective, I do not find it puzzling that the puzzles emerged more puzzling. I do not, because I said earlier that by not taking the world context from its *historic* perspective into account, you had committed the *fallacy of ahistoric contemporaneity;* and further that for committing this fallacy, you had omitted to make the vital distinction between *comparative small size and comparative utilitarian size.* The concept *size* will remain and will prove more puzzling than Amstrup's "malaise of small states analysis," which is only irritating, so long as these two dimensions of "small size" and the precedence between them are not recognized.

I take a particular note at the point where you say: "hopefully, too, this puzzlement will prove sufficiently provocative to lead to tests of the foregoing hypotheses as well as others that can be readily developed, thereby giving rise to the cumulative knowlege through which the pieces of the puzzles can be clarified and fit together."[34] That the puzzlement is provocative there is not doubt. But has the nature of the provocation been properly presented? They are worth testing all right, but if one's intention is to remove the puzzlement, then the entire theory of the adaptation of small states, as you present it, will have to be looked at again to remove the two fallacies that impair the formulation. This will mean that we will not only look at the contemporaneous presence of certain attributes of the state and certain internal attitudes of states to construct the theory. It will mean taking these factors in terms of their historic context and observing variations in the quality of survival of small states over the long haul of modern history, in order to understand the real meaning of these variations, if any, in terms of the historic meaning of the quality of survival of small states.

The hypotheses which will emerge from such a theory will address themselves to the persistence of the *historic theme* and its relationship to the ever-changing variations in the *historic concomitants* and their *local attendants.* The quality of the survival of small states will then be understood in terms of the efficiency of means in pursuit of capital accumulation. The hypotheses which will suggest themselves from such a theory will address themselves to a real puzzle: the puzzle inherent in the contradiction that things could very easily appear to have changed while they remain fundamentally the same. These hypotheses will fit themselves together very well under the relationships between the persistence of capital accumulation and the variations in its concomitants and logical attendants.

As the nine hypotheses stand, they cannot distinguish between *appearances* and *reality*. We have no way of testing the appearances and the realness of dependency, transformation, and autonomy as they pertain to the quality of survival of small states. So that, even if all the hypotheses were to be validated, the question as to how they all fit together is not addressed.

You appear to have anticipated the impending collapse of your formulation; and in seeing this happen, you attempt to explain why. You explain that you did not abide by your own methodological canon to locate smallness on a continuum. I said earlier that you had made too much of the "continuum canon," but this is not a prominent part of the problem. The "continuum canon" was employed. It was a built-in part of the nine hypotheses. All we need to do to appreciate this is to read the hypotheses as saying that to the extent that a state *is* small to that extent certain transformational possibilities are not probable, implying, of course, that, to the extent that a state is *not small* these transformational possibilities are more probable. It is, therefore, not true for you to say that, because you ignored your "continuum canon," you had in effect not treated size as a variable.

Our earlier fears are realized to the fullest when you say "... size may not be a useful independent variable ... so many complex and diverse phenomena are encompassed by size that to combine them together ... is to create a constant not a variable."[35] This conclusion would appear to defeat the entire purpose of your brave attempt to theorize on small states. The reasons are, however, not what you suggest. The reasons, as we understand them, are precisely those expressed by the *fallacy of ahistoric contemporaneity* and the *fallacy of indiscriminate smallness*. In addition, your conclusion that size is *a constant not a variable* suggests to us that the two fallacies which we have attributed to your theory of the transformational conditions in terms of the dynamics of the politics of adaptation of small states have merits. Size is a constant and not a variable because the historic motive of the modern world-system which produced the different sizes of states has remained constant. It has been to accumulate capital in large states and away from small states. As the world-system changes its historic character from capitalist to another and different form, then perhaps size will come into its own as an unanalytic variable, a meaningless and, therefore, a useless variable.

In fact, Jim, the two fallacies I have been discussing are precisely what lead you to commit what would appear to be a third fallacy: *the fallacy of creating a constant out of a variable*. In your terms, the conclusion that size may after all be a constant and not a variable is made to appear as if it were a scientific revelation. You hesitate to make this claim for the good reason that you realize that something has gone wrong with your formulation. In the world-system terms, this conclusion, as a matter of fact, is not wrong. In fact it is correct. It is the uses which you make of your assumptions, described by the two earlier fallacies, which make your correct conclusion fallacious. What I mean is that your conclusion is correct but, because it is not "scientifically" valid, it is fallacious.

The sizes of states are integral parts of the development of the capitalist world-system of states. If this is the case, then the interesting question is whether the sizes of states have changed or have more or less remained constant in world-history. In answering this question, we should take into account the origins of every single entity which calls itself a state. Once we do this, it will become clear, very early on, that, up to this point in world-history, by far the greater majority of states have been small and remain small as far as the ability to accumulate and retain capital is concerned. The few exceptions in this regard prove the rule. The point is that most states were created small and are expected to remain small for as long as the world-system retains its capitalist ethos. Any change in the condemned and wretched smallness of small states may be pre-conditioned on change(s) in the very capitalist nature of the world-system itself.

The caveat, then, should be that size, as a probable variable, should not be treated outside the proper historic context. It should not be treated indiscriminately without reference to *comparative small size* and *instrumental small size*. And, above all, it should be realized that dichotomies and continua are not unrelated. The latter derives from the former. Continua are merely stretched forms of dichotomies. The world-system methodology properly used could prove powerful in the scientific analyses of both international relations and foreign policy. It will surely unearth puzzles, but one thing it can probably do is avoid the conversion of scientific puzzles into magical wonderments. This methodology derives its strength from its universal quest to explain the *entire historic world* to the *present world,* not the interests of *part* of the present world to the *entire* present world.

Reading your provocative manuscript very closely, and hopefully correctly, has suggested something radically different to me. Very few works on the concept of size, if any, could have done this. It is that between the *comparative* and the *instrumental* dimensions of size, the instrumental dimension, is the one that is analytically useful to understand the relevance of size in our capitalist world-system. I am inclined to conceive of a small state as one whose "circumstances" mitigate against the accumulation of capital within it, because capital tends to leak from it. I have now the intention of expressing this conception by relating the *imperialist problematique* of the capitalist world-system to its *small state problematique.*

The reasoning is that if the imperialist problematique is conceived as the connections between the domestic circumstances of small and large states within the exploitative capitalist world-system, then the critical examination of these connections may throw some much needed light on the small state problematique, which is the system of problems, or questions, relating to why, in the capitalist world, the many small states tend to remain small, while the few large states remain large or decline only a little, and rarely so.

Sincerely,

Herb

FOOTNOTES

[1] Currently I am working on the theories of capitalism, imperialism, and development.

[2] This reminds me of what Boris Pasternak said in *Doctor Zhivago* to this effect: What are pretty girls for, if they are not there for male students to love.

[3] James N Rosenau, "The Adaptation of Small States," 1977, as in manuscript, p. 2.

[4] *Ibid.*

[5] *Ibid.*, p. 8.

[6] *Ibid.*, p. 7.

[7] *Ibid.*, p. 8.

[8] *Ibid.*, p. 13.

[9] *Ibid.*, p. 9.

[10] *Ibid.*, p. 10.

[11] *Ibid.*, p. 12.

[12] We have already suggested how the first two puzzles can fit under the third puzzle.

[13] Rosenau as in manuscript, p. 14.

[14] A historic concept is a concept the definitional meaning of which is bound by precise historic referents, which relate it to the historic force of a specific historic period. See my "World-System Critique of Euro-Centric Critique of Imperialism," (mimeo, March 1979), especially see notes 2 and 48 of this work referring to Robert Nesbit *Social Change and History*. New York: Oxford University Press, 1969; see also my "Toward a World-System Methodology" (forthcoming) and especially Robert L. Heilbroner, *The Future as History*. New York: Grove Press, 1969, p. 28.

[15] For precise statement of this methodology, see Braudel Centre, "Patterns of Development of the World-System," *Review* 1, 2, Fall 1977, 111-145; *Political Economy of the World-System Annuals*. vol. 1, 1978 and 11, 1979; and my "Toward a World-System Methodology" (forthcoming).

[16] See my "Approaching the Peculiarity of the Caribbean Plight within the Paradox of the Representative State in the Contemporary World-System," (HSDRGPID-24/UNUP-135) where I also discuss these two conceptions of the state.

[17] Rosenau as in manuscript, p. 15.

[18] *Ibid.*

[19] *Ibid.*

[20] See my "Contemporary Adaptation Dialectic of the World Economic System: An Introductory Probing," *Caribbean Yearbook of International Relations*, 1976, 439-463.

[21] Rosenau as in manuscript, p. 16.

[22] It is a minor point, perhaps, but if Survival is assumed and the focus is now in the quality of Survival in the dynamic terms of movement on the continuum from dependency to autonomy, then perhaps what Rosenau is treating is not so much the sheer quality of Survival but the *growth* of Small States. But this will come out and become clear only when the precise context for the identity of the World-System, which makes movement on the continuum possible, is drawn.

[23] See my reference in note 18 above and also B. Korany "Foreign Policy Models and their Empirical Relevance to Third World Actors: A Critique and Alternatives," *International Social Science Journal* 26, 1974, pp. 70-94.

[24] See my reference in note 18 above.

[25] These terms are defined and related in my "Toward a World-System Methodology" (forthcoming), and in my "Informing Visions of Desirable Societies through Dialogue of Civilization," (forthcoming in the 1979 proceedings of the WFSF Mexico City Meeting edited by Eleonora Mansini, Paragon Press). To make for easy reading the reader is referred to sections 1 and 111 of my comment on Kaplan's essay in this book.

[26] Refer to my reference in note 14 above.

[27] Rosenau as in manuscript, p. 21.

[28] *Ibid.*

[29] *Ibid.*

[30] See Folker Frobel, Jurgen Heinrich and Otto Kreye, *The New International Division of Labour.* London: Cambrige University Press, 1980.

[31] See section 111 above.

[32] Rosenau as in manuscript, p. 35.

[33] *Ibid.,* p. 36.

[34] *Ibid.*

[35] *Ibid.*

American Policy Toward the Caribbean Region: One Aspect of American Global Policy

Morton A. Kaplan

There are two world powers today: The United States and the Soviet Union. In addition to being the only two states that can make manifest their presence in a significant way on a world basis, these two countries also are the only countries that possess major strategic nuclear systems. These are the only two states at the present time that could devastate the world. They are the only states with even the potential capacity to intervene in a way that might deter or prevent a catastrophic shift of the structure of international power that might thrust one or the other into the position of world hegemon. There may be matters with respect to which their intervention is either extremely difficult or counterproductive. But there is no matter of political significance in the world that does not affect their security or their ability to protect themselves, their allies, their friends, or those whose interests become tied to theirs for *ad hoc* reasons.

We may regard this latter condition as unjust or as an infringement on the theoretical equality of states. However, it is part of the condition of modern life, a part that for better or worse neither of these two states can abnegate except by passing the mantle of hegemon to the other.

I do not wish to suggest that this role is exercised uninhibitedly or regardless of internal or external considerations, or that international organizations, norms of law or custom, considerations of equity or justice, ties of friendship or feelings of respect play no role in the process. What I do wish to emphasize, however, is that both the United States and the Soviet Union are forced by the structure of world politics, and regardless of wish or transient changes in will, to have global policies within the framework of which a number of matters that are of primary

51

and sometimes urgent interests to smaller states have only secondary or tertiary importance. What might be a matter only of minor importance if considered only within the framework of the relationship between one of the major powers and minor power—perhaps a negligible trifle, "caviar for the general" in Shakespeare's phrase, that might be tossed away as a penny to a beggar—may become transmuted when placed within the framework of global policy and fastened onto as the teeth of the bulldog may clamp upon the neck of his mortal foe.

Without attempting to settle the issue of the possible motivations of the rulers in the Kremlin, both the Russian and the American people experience their world role as a tremendous burden. The more than 100 billion dollars a year that each country spends on its defense department could be put to constructive use at home and abroad. Taxes could be lowered and the conditions of life improved. The threat of war, which is inherent in their world role, and which for these states is omnipresent, invokes the prospect of bodily injury and death for the youth of the country and potential nuclear destruction of the homelands. Superiority of role, at least in the power sense, is more of a burden for those who are forced into that role, by virtue of the fact that they alone have the potentiality for playing it, than their international role is on the whole for those smaller states who occasionally get sideswiped by the after-effects of the collision of the two sets of global policies.

It all depends on the point of view. One might as well ask the political contenders at home to cease their rivalry as to ask the United States and the Soviet Union to cease their global rivalry. The game is not and cannot be played that way, and to ask that is to demand the end of political problems in a world in which conflicts of interests always do require political solutions. The farther from the center of the contest one is, the easier it seems in ideal abstraction for the contest to be foregone. The closer one is to the center, the more one's view changes. The South Koreans are alarmed by the talk of scaling down American ground forces in South Korea and any substantial reduction in American strategic forces would alarm the Japanese, who maintain their peace constitution under the American nuclear umbrella. Western European nations just as strongly resist any scaling down of American forces in Europe and even the Italian Communists regard NATO as necessary.

Therefore, it is in the nature of the beast that the United States and the Soviet Union have global strategies while most other nations have at best regional policies. Quite often resentment is expressed that many Americans have never heard of particular countries or their leaders. But how many Africans could name all the countries in Africa or their leaders? And how many Latin Americans would be familiar with the political situation in

Trinidad? We are familiar with what is at the center of attention; and for most of us that involves either those who have world prominence by virtue of power and position, those whose actions immediately affect us, or those who by virtue of their spectacular horseplay, as in the case of Idi Amin, manage to force themselves upon our attention.

The close attention of the United States is and must be focused on Western Europe, the southern rim of Europe, and the Far Eastern rim. These areas by virtue of geography, population, human skills, and economic and military power are the crucial areas in the contest between the United States and the Soviet Union. But even this limited aspect of the world pattern is far too complex for any group of decision-makers to understand even though their attention be rivetted to the problems of the areas. We have built such a complex world that at best we are idiots in terms of the problems we are required to solve. And whatever individual skills we may possess are watered down by the institutional complexities of the political decision processes. This is small solace for those who are buffeted by policies that are unresponsive to their needs and uninformed by their conditions. But then even within nations if the needs of minorities are satisfied at all, it is only when they are a large minority and, even in these cases, only when they can scream loudly enough to gain attention. I have yet to hear of an affirmative action case in the United States in favor of a Kurd or a Pakistani; and I should be very surprised if any other country, regardless of political system, paid attention to very small minorities.

The center of American global strategy obviously is Western Europe. The population of the Western Europe members of NATO is as large as that of the United States or the Soviet Union. Its economic potential approaches that of the United States and surpasses that of the Soviet Union. Its human skills are as high as anywhere in the world. If it were Finlandized and brought within the Soviet shadow, the Soviet Union would control what Sir Hjalford MacKinder once called the world island. The level of effort the Soviet Union could devote to military matters would far surpass that of the United States. Its population base would be enormous. The pressure it could bring upon China would be overwhelming. This area is, and must be, the very center of American attention and almost everything else must be subordinated to that consideration. Japan's role is secondary to this but still enormous because of the huge economic potential and the human skills of Japan. Were Japan to fall within the Soviet orbit, another element of the Soviet *cordon sanitaire* around China would be filled in. Were China for any reason to fall back within the Soviet sphere, massive Soviet attentions could be reoriented toward Western Europe in a way that it would be very difficult for the United

States to compensate for. Any shift in the Japanese orbit is of immense importance to the United States.

The United States cannot pursue its global policies with respect to Western Europe or the East Asian rim unless it maintains a military establishment that provides at least plausibility for these policies. Because it must operate at a distance, it is necessary for it to have great sea power. This is one reason why American naval leaders are looking askance at recent Soviet naval developments. The role of the two navies is completely different. The role of the American navy is to maintain communications and supply routes to its allies. The role of the Soviet navy is to disrupt American communications and supply routes. Superiority is not needed for the latter role, and perhaps not even equality.

The Soviet Union has a central position on the world island. The United States requires the capability of moving large forces rapidly. It must also retain strategic forces capable of deterring Soviet provocations under most circumstances.

This problem grows more difficult, more complex, and more expensive as weapons technology changes; and it does so constantly. A mere generation ago Western Europe was a potentially huge battlefield with space for maneuver. Even though the distance from the East German border to Paris is less than 300 miles—less than half the width of some of the Eastern European battlefields of World War II—its occupation by military force would have been a vast and time-consuming undertaking until the last ten or fifteen years. Today, however, tank divisions can be expected to advance at the rate of 60 miles a day, even against opposition, and may make as much as 100 miles a day. The Soviet Union is concentrating manpower and modernizing its forces—it places even more emphasis on modern equipment than on manpower—to create an army designed to reach targets in France in less than half a week. Similar changes in technology are transforming the strategic and sea balances. The recent test by the Soviet Union of a submarine-launched missile that travels nearly 6000 miles has made an enormous difference in the strategic balance. The Russian submarine base off Cienfuegos creates enormous difficulties for the United States in terms of shielding the Caribbean and the Eastern frontage of the American system. Changes in cruise missile technology will affect both the strategic and naval balances. These are merely illustrative of the enormously complex issues affecting the strategic balance.

If the strategic balance is largely a bipolar matter, there are other important aspects of global policy that are far from bipolar and that in the long run may have as much or more importance. These involve an entire range of economic issues. It is a mistake to think of these issues as part of a common package as many of the proponents for a new economic order argue. Some of the most important problems involve primarily, indeed almost exclusively, the OECD nations, in particular, Western Europe, Japan, and the United States.

One of the most important of these economic issues is that of the parities of the various currencies. Although the Bretton Woods arrangements had become so dysfunctional that it was necessary at least for the time to move to flexible exchange rates, rapid shifts in the comparative value of the major currencies are highly likely to drive the major states into competitive and restrictive economic practices. On the other hand, those currencies are so strong, and constitute so large a part of the international economic order, that most minor currencies could be permitted to shift regardless of their range of movement without any harm or major restrictive practices. Therefore, there is absolutely no need for arrangements on this issue except among the major industrial states and no need to complicate so difficult an issue by bringing it to a large forum.

A concomitant of this is that the parities of the major currencies cannot be kept within narrow bands of movement for reasonable periods of time unless the major economic states pursue complementary, although not necessarily identical, economic policies that keep inflation and the rate of unemployment within comparable ranges for each of the major countries. If they cannot do this, popular pressure, as well as economic conditions, will force shifts in parity rates. Here again, it is not necessary for minor economic powers to adopt complementary policies. They can be left free to pursue their own paths.

Another set of issues revolves around access to and the development of resources. This issue came to great prominence with the oil embargo. However, even in the absence of an embargo it is an issue that will remain with us for the indefinite future. Part of the problem lies in the fact that resource prices are extremely sensitive to the terms of trade except perhaps under cartel conditions. Thus, many resource-exporting nations experience changes in the terms of trade that are so large in relation to their national economies that these economies are subject to near-catastrophic perturbations that no amount of diligence or wisdom will enable them to avert.

For these reasons, it is important—and it is an element in American global policy—to prevent too rapid shifts in the prices of materials, although just as obviously price indexing would produce economic irrationalities that are indefensible. In general, the cartel solution that the oil producers found will not work for most other commodities. Moreover, such cartels are extremely injurious to those developing nations that do not possess resources in abundance. These cartels impede economic growth and stabilization and are detrimental to the world economy. Furthermore, continued resort to such devices ultimately will result in countervailing measures by the major economic powers that will result in a contraction of the entire world economy. In this case, all nations will be injured, and the small and poor nations devastatingly so. President Carter appears to have taken up the notion of a bank of buffer stocks that will prevent rapid shifts in commodity prices; and this seems a quite good idea to me.

In addition, I think that it would be very important to plan for the development of an infrastructure that will permit the exploitation of the less efficient resources when present resources are used up. Taking inflation into account and introducing a time discount, it is quite clear that it is to the interest of the resource-rich states to sell their resources now, whoever the buyers may be, and to use the funds received for investment and the creation of an economic infrastructure that will permit future production. However, the scale of activity required for developing the infrastructure for the development of less efficient resources is so great, and the time-scale for planning is so long, that the time discount factor properly applicable to individual firms would not warrant it. Moreover, private, or even independent national, investments in developing such infrastructures could so easily be frustrated by cartel price-cutting activities that they are not possible in the absence of intergovernmental planning, contingency plans for reprisals against violators, and agreements on measures designed to sustain income after particular sources of resources are depleted. Because these activities are so monumental in scope and the requirements for them are so different, depending upon the particular resource, it is a mistake to believe that the same set of nations should deal with each and every resource problem.

Still, a further range of activity will involve technological transfers from capitalist systems to underdeveloped areas. In this respect, it is time to stop talking about a redistribution of wealth internationally. Even within nations, redistributions of existing wealth rarely succeed and they usually only undermine the economic structure. Large international transfers of capital would remove capital from areas where it is efficiently used to areas where it would likely be destroyed, and surely inefficiently used. Therefore, although some technological and capital transfers are desirable and should be carried out, the multiplier effect on productivity, both positive and negative, should be taken into account when this is done. Transfers that attempt to redistribute wealth are far less likely to succeed than transfers of capital and technology that occur within the framework of a policy that takes such transfers from wealth increases.

Furthermore, we should be aware that the miracle of Japan, the transformation of Brazil, the frenetic growth of South Korea, Taiwan, Malaysia, and Thailand—all within the last generation—reflect a change that is almost without precedent in human history, including that of the great European industrial powers. It is and should continue to be a component of American policy that such development play a significant role in its global strategy.

We can now turn to specific applications of this global strategy to the Latin part of the Western hemisphere. At least during the first year or two of the Carter adminstration, it will pursue its humanitarian and non-proliferation policies with a missionary zeal. This has already gravely injured relations with Brazil and Argentina, even apart from consideration of smaller states such as Uruguay and of NATO allies such as West Germany. The president is committed to this posture at least temporarily for a variety of reasons. Whether wisely or unwisely, these policies represent deeply felt beliefs. At least until they become far more counterproductive than has been the case so far, the president will not retreat from them.

Moreover, many believe that the enunciation of these policies has as much domestic as international significance for the president. He has watched the disarray of American policy during the last ten years and has concluded that it will be impossible for him to conduct any type of coherent foreign policy in the absence of sustained popular support. This requires that he build among the population at large, and the intellectuals and the media in particular, a supportive frame of mind based upon the belief that American policies are oriented not merely to American interests but to American ideals as well.

In addition to policies that may possibly be counterproductive, President Carter's policy will include elements that should likely prove popular among some of the smaller states in Latin America. The president is likley to move toward a far more substantial compromise on the issue of the Panama Canal than even the previous administration. President Carter will be far less likely than past administrators to encourage the formation of client regimes in Central America. He is far less likely to be offended by nationalizations either from the left or from the right, although his behavior will be somewhat restricted by legislation on the subject of nationalization.

However, it would be a mistake to consider any of the currents mentioned in the previous paragraph as constituting the core of American policy. That core will be far more responsive to permanent and traditional American interests even though these be transformed by technological, political, and economic changes. For instance, the United

States will resist strongly any extension of Soviet basing into the Western hemisphere that goes beyond the Cienfuegos submarine base. This consideration extends beyond the threat of the nuclear weapons that vessels sallying forth from such bases might carry. It involves the entire global naval posture of the United States. The more local basing that is available to the Soviet navy, the greater the potential threat, for instance, to oil shipments from Venezuela or to food shipments to Western Europe. Consequently the greater the threat, the greater the drain upon American global fleet capacity. Extended basing on the part of the Soviet Union sharply reduces the cost of Soviet naval threats and by correlation sharply increases the costs of American defensive operations.

It is virtually impossible to mount a global naval policy without extended bases, for the absence of bases makes costing astronomical. The maintenance of an American base posture in the Caribbean and the exclusion of further Soviet basing involves in a vital way the entire cost structure of the American military establishment. Particularly given the fact that the lion's share of American defense expenditures goes into pensions and salaries rather than into equipment and supplies, the ability of the Soviet Union to transform these cost ratios further by developing its own distant basing, or by encouraging other countries to remove American basing, is one of the least understood but most important aspects of this global contest between the United States and the Soviet Union. Should any such contest over basing in the Central American area break out in a serious way, it likely would lead to a virtual reversal of those policies of the new Carter administration that are responsive to the formal egalitarian demands of smaller states in the Central American region. The reason why it is possible for the United States to compromise as readily with Panama as is likely under the Carter administration is that the Panama Canal is not a vital conduit or base area. However, should Soviet diplomatic offensives further penetrate the American Caribbean screen or place political pressure upon the screen, the incentive to return to a policy of encouraging the growth of client relationships may become irresistable.

Whether a possible normalization of relations with Cuba would permit the relinquishment by the United States of the Guantanamo base depends upon an analysis of alternate available basing. However, I predict that if there is the slightest prospect that Guantanamo might become a Soviet base the issue would become non-negotiable for the United States.

With respect to Puerto Rico, I can be quite brief. The United States does not regard Puerto Rico as a client state. Many Americans, as well as some Puerto Ricans, are less than happy with the current commonwealth status of Puerto Rico and wish that Puerto Rico would choose either independence or statehood. On the other hand, most informed Americans believe that this is a decision that cannot be made by majority vote alone, for the present commonwealth status is clearly preferable to either statehood or independence if either of the latter two positions is opted for by a slim majority, for instance, one of 55 per cent or less. Either option involves a change of such magnitude for the Puerto Ricans that it would be insupportable in the absence of a consensus the size of which guarantees its durability.

In this sense, the United States is the effective client state of Puerto Rico, for it is not in a position where it can influence the choice or even insist upon a choice. The very discrepancy of size in this case ties the hands of the stronger state.

With respect to other states that have at least partial client status, for instance, Haiti or Nicaragua, most Americans wish they knew what could be done about this situation. Many of us feel that the United States would be far better off if these countries possessed vigorous democracies that permitted their substantive independence. Whether past American policies are partly responsible for this state of affairs is a question that goes beyond my competence to answer. I do know that the current situation is one in which the United States does not, and probably cannot, have a policy, for we simply have no idea what we can or might do to transform the situation, although perhaps in the next few years we may learn something about this.

One complication that ought to be mentioned is that some time in the 1980s both Argentina and Brazil likely will become nuclear powers. Even though their nuclear forces would be relatively small and not comparable to that of the United States, this will introduce an enormous change with respect to the entire situation in the Western hemisphere. The problem of client states then might not be one so much vis-à-vis the United States as vis-à-vis Brazil or Argentina. The conflicts that may arise between Argentina and Brazil may have quite untoward consequences not merely for minor states in the Western hemisphere but for the United States as well. This probably is one of the reasons that President Carter places such emphasis on the proposed Brazilian plutonium plant. What he does not seem to recognize is that he cannot stop this development and that he is acting in a manner best calculated to stir resentment and to exacerbate the tendency. For there can be little question that sharp American pressure, without warrant of juridical rule, in a situation in which our influence is minimal will arouse the greatest resentment and the most emotional kinds of responses.

In a very real sense we are returning to our introductory theme: the disjunction between formal and substantive considerations. What in purely formal terms can be expressed as a normative right—the formal equality of all states great and small—can be seen to depend upon the political, military, and economic conditions in the larger world. Every mode of social organization depends upon a set of material conditions. The American republic could not have been produced under the conditions existing in ancient Egypt nor could democratic institutions have developed under the conditions of Tudor England. There is a framework that is required for the approximation of national equality with respect to states both great and small. And military, political, and economic conditions are among the parameters that determine the correlations. Thus, if I am to project what American policy will be, that projection depends not merely upon decisions in the United States but on decisions in the Soviet Union, Western Europe, and Latin America. We cannot predict in any absolute sense. We can only refer to the constraining conditions that permit one line of policy as compared with alternative lines of policy.

We are living in an era in which, despite some of the Carter administration's missionary policies, we may look forward to increased formal equality and greater collegiality in the determination of decisions that affect all states of the hemisphere. However, this development can be threatened. It is not inevitable. For those who aspire to this greater equality and collegiality, sophisticated knowledge of the conditions under which they are possible is essential. Rhetoric will not make it so but only policies that accord with those conditions that are necessary for the development. The prospect is genuine and lies before us, but its fruition depends upon good will, intelligent choice and execution of policy, and good luck; for in the end the goddess of chance can bring us all down regardless of wisdom or virtue.

Morton Kaplan's Bland Re-statement of the Traditional Interpretation of American Policy Toward the Caribbean Region*

Herb Addo

1. THE CONTRAST BETWEEN THE TRADITIONAL AND THE WORLD-SYSTEM CONCEPTIONS OF INTERNATIONAL RELATIONS

Kaplan begins what promises to be an interesting treatment of his subject by stating what we can rightly call the uncontentious appearances in contemporary world power politics. It soon becomes clear, however, that what is missing, which is precisely what should not be missing in the essay if Kaplan is to avoid committing the *fallacy of ahistoric contemporaneity,*[1] is the defining context within which the analysis of these uncontentious appearances in power politics will make interesting and sophisticated reading. Kaplan does not even as much as allude the historic nature of the world in which he situates American policy toward the Caribbean region. For this reason alone, if none other, it will be legitimate to suspect that Kaplan, at best, has not taken precaution against committing the fallacy.

The roots of this fallacy run deep in traditional international relations and are to be found in the highly prized conviction that to understand and analyze the *world* reality one needs only examine super-power relations as they rebound on, and affect, major and lesser powers. The argument here is not that the super-power relations and their tendency to affect all else in world politics are not important. This clearly cannot be the argument.

The argument is that the super-power relations, no matter how dominant

*This is a product of the Structural Interpretation of International Inequality Project (S3IP), a sub-project within the UNU-GPID Project, coordinated by Johan Galtung, c/o UNITAR, Geneva. Thanks to Lily Addo for her editorial and typing services. I am solely responsible for the imperfections and inadequacies in this work.

they may be in the real world, do not, in fact they cannot, constitute the *whole*. There are other analyzable units whose relations and interests within the whole should not, even in a super-power dominated world, be relegated to the secondary and the tertiary. The reason for this is that usually the relations and interests which are so relegated are precisely those which lend understanding to super-power relations in terms of the constancy of the *historic motive* of world-history and alert us to the variations in its *concomitants* and its *logical attendants*.[2]

Traditional perspective of international relations does not neglect a world view entirely, except that, from this perspective, the world is regarded as a unit, as an interdependent "world island," only to the extent that such a conception can provide a convenient but relegated background for the analysis of super and major power activities and interests. How and why this conception of the world, in our particular historic circumstances, explains and justifies activities and interests other than those of super-powers within the genuine *whole* of the world-system is very often not addressed. Because traditional international relations tends to concern itself so much with power, especially super-power, relations, various analyses in this frame tend to be hegemony-stuck. International relations viewed from the traditional perspective can, therefore, very easily be made to appear both bland and barren. It tends to yield only predictable findings and recommendations.

From the world-system perspective, international relations is conceived as a seamless web of relationships between analyzable units whose meanings arise entirely from their relations within the *whole*. It is, therefore, mandatory that in analyzing any aspect of international relations, the exact identity of this *whole* should be clear. It is also for this reason that a world-system methodology for the study of international relations would insist that a sharp distinction should be made between the *historic* and the merely *historical*.[3]

This is necessary to distinguish the *historic motive* from the *historic force*, the *historic concomitants*, and the *historic logical attendants*. The *historic motive* refers to the dominant motive in a historic period which distinguishes this period from other historic periods. The *historic motive* of the *capitalist* world-system is capital accumulation and its unequal incidence in the world by means of rising efficiency of exploitation of both human and non-human resources, which is the system's historic force. The term *historic concomitant* refers to those things which are historical, in the sense of being trans-historic, but which assume radically new relevance, or acquire new meanings, because of new circumstances brought about by the rising level of efficiency of exploitation.[4] And *historic logical attendants* refer to those things which are historic in the sense of being peculiar to the historic period, because they are emergent of the rising level of efficiency of exploitation in pursuit of capital accumulation.[5]

Once the world is approached in this manner, international relations theory then comes to concern itself with the relationships between the constancy of the *historic concomitants,* and the *historic logical attendants.* The point is that while the identity of a *historic period* is principally determined by the constancy of its *historic motive,* its complete identification must take into account the changing aspect of its *historic concomitants* and its *logical attendants,* and how these variations relate to the changing efficiency of the exploitation, the *historic force,* toward the singular pursuit of the *historic motive* at any one time and in any given set of circumstances. So that with respect to the capitalist world-system, world-system methodology, which identifies the *historic motive* as the ever-rising curve of accumulation of capital, would insist that it is the complex inter-relationships between the variations within the *historic force,* and historic concomitants, and the *historic logical attendants* and how they relate to the *historic motive* which should serve as the main focus of analysis in the international relations.

In such an analysis, the main concern, then, will be to attempt to distinguish between superficial and fundamental changes.[6] The contradiction which should guide both theory and research generally, then, will be the contradiction inherent in things appearing to have changed, while in fact things remain *essentially the same, because the historic motive* remains the same. Within the world-system methodology, the key to understanding this contradiction would appear to be the appreciation of the persistence, or the continuity, of the *historic motive* all through a historic period;[7] and how the variations in the other historic referrents play the double role of at once aiding and undermining this persistence. From the above, it should not come as a surprise to say the the world-system approach to international relations, and its sub-part of foreign policy, is ever watchful for the *fallacy of ahistoric contemporaneity.*

The irony of the matter is that, Kaplan, anchored on the Traditional platform in international relations, calls for sophisticated knowledge on the part of those who use any frame other than the traditional big power frame. A critic using the world-system methodology will be very right then, to re-read Kaplan's short essay to see whether this call is justified. In approaching Kaplan's piece with this purpose in mind, it is only fair to state that we believe that sophisticated knowledge in international relations is possible only within the world-system methodology.

2. THE SECONDARY AND TERTIARY IMPORTANCE OF SMALL STATE INTEREST IN WORLD POWER POLITICS

Kaplan's introductory theme deals with the disjunction between formal and substantive considerations in world politics, understood as the world-system of states. His main point is that the U.S. and the U.S.S.R. are hegemony-poised and for this reason intervention by either of these two states anywhere in the world may be difficult or even counter-productive, but it cannot be regarded as "unjust." This is because the structure of international politics makes such interventions a condition of life which cannot be infringed by one of the two super-powers without the consequence of the other super-power assuming the mantle of hegemony. It is this same structure of world politics which, as Kaplan says, regardless of wish or transient changes, forces the two super-powers to have "global policies within the framework of which a number of matters that are of primary and sometimes urgent interests to smaller states have only secondary or tertiary importance."[8]

Kaplan calls attention to two critical matters in this context. The first is that it should not be imagined that the super-power roles are painless. It should be clear to all that uneasy would have to lie the heads that wear the super-power crowns.[9] The second is that it is senseless to ask that the two super-powers cease their global rivalry. Such rivalry is natural to world politics; and therefore, in Kaplan's words, to ask for cessation of this rivalry is tantamount to "demand the end of political problems in a world in which conflicts of interests always do require political solutions."[10]

This is precisely our point of contention with traditional power analysis of *international relations* and *world politics*. There is a built-in false distinction between the two. The *politics* depends upon the nature of the *relations* constituting the *whole* and the ethos of the *whole* cannot be known without specifiying the precise historic categories within it.

The relevant questions in this regard are these: (1) what precisely is the nature of the relations between analyzable units which constitute the *whole?*; (2) what necessitates the rivalry between the two super-powers?; (3) what makes strategic balance largely a bipolar matter, and some other matters the sole preserve of the U.S., Western Europe and Japan?; (4) what precisely are the *interests* involved in these relations which always require *political* solutions?

When we take these four questions together, it becomes clear that we cannot approach the world as a unit, a *whole,* on its own terms without first identifying the interests which *conflict,* require political solutions, and which demand that certain *lesser interest* of certain lesser units be relegated to the secondary and the tertiary. It is imperative that, to proceed toward sophisticated knowledge of the world, we identify the precise content of the interests involved and the ends to which they are aimed. Until we can do this, the concept *interest,* as it pertains to the world as an analyzable whole, will remain bankrupt and empty, as it is within the traditional theory of power politics.

It is in order to avoid this bankruptcy in the analysis of the world reality that the world-system methodology suggests the cardinal necessity of situating analysis within the precise historic context of the capitalist world-economy and insists that this world-economy be understood and identified as motivated by the efficient accumulation of capital. Clearly, matters in the total world situation change for many reasons, but most principally matters change mainly because of the rising level of efficiency in the accumulation of capital enterprise. But then, the system remains essentially capitalist so long as it remains motivated by efficient accumulation of capital. It is to avoid confusing the constancy of the *historic motive* with the super-structural changes that the world-system methodology further suggests the introduction of *historic concomitants* and distinguishes this further from the *historical logical attendants.*

This approach does not allow super-powers and other rivalries to appear as if they are some irrational activities, at best, concerned with some nebulous conception of security for its own sake. It situates, and defines, interest in terms of ability to *accumulate capital,* not in terms of *power* for its own sake, as the power school of thought insists on doing.[11]

The power orientation, which informs Kaplan's analysis, is extremely intolerant of other approaches, because these other approaches are not considered realistic enough in that they seek to *change* things considered unchangeable rather than examine and study things as they *are.* The difference here can be considered minor, if one can only concede that one can analyze things as they are with the intention to change them. The power school of thought, however, tends to frown on this intention. Instead of aiming to change things, this school of thought aims to justify things as they exist. And even when changes begin to occur in the world-system as a result of the rising efficiency in the means of accumulating capital, the power school finds it difficult to incorporate these changes in any systematic way into their stagnant analysis of reality.

Kaplan's treatment of world economic issues illustrates this very well. He disagrees with the proponents of the New International Economic Order on the position that an entire range of economic issues form "part of a common package."[12] Kaplan believes that the most important problem in this respect "almost exclusively involves only Western Europe, Japan and the U.S." These issues include that of the parity of various currencies.

Kaplan's view on this is that "most minor currencies could be permitted to shift regardless of their range of movement without any harm or major restrictive practices."[13] This is bad enough, but then Kaplan follows this curious reasoning to say: "therefore, there is absolutely no need for arrangements on this issue except among the major industrial states and no need to complicate so difficult an issue by bringing it to a large forum."[14]

In all this, Kaplan believes that minor powers can be left free to pursue their own paths. But is there some magnificent virtue in minor powers being left "free" to follow their own paths in a capitalist world-system, where exploitation of one sort or the other appears to be the condemned fate of these powers and where even those among them who really want to be free will be punished at every turn for wanting to be free?

Kaplan's views on access to, and development of, resources are no less justificatory of the existing order. His traditional reading of world problems fly in the face of the emerging awareness that the world is an integrated unit with clear historic explanation as to why some states are *small* and others are *big*;[15] and that for this reason the *small* states have something which they must defend and some things which they must demand of the *big* states, in common.

On the matter of access to and development of resources, Kaplan admits that there are catastrophic fluctuations in resource prices, but he argues that price indexing is irrational and indefensible. In his view, cartels will not work for most commodities because they are extremely injurious to developing nations in that they impede economic growth and stability, and hence are detrimental to the world-economy because they will lead to countervailing actions by the major economic powers, thus resulting in the contraction of the entire world-economy and injuring all nations, "the small and poor devastatingly so."[16]

When one takes Kaplan's argument and reasons it backwards, it points to two things. The first is that whatever the probable evil consequences of resource cartels, cartels are contemplated in the first place because the prices of resource commodities fluctuate rapidly. But this is not all. In addition to the rapid shifts in prices, the main problem is that the prices of these commodities are very low in the first place. So that even if President Carter's "notion of a bank of buffer stocks" materializes, it could only address the fluctuations in prices, but not the initial low prices of these commodities.

Price indexing differs from bank of buffer stocks in that the former addresses both price levels and their fluctuations, while the latter addresses only price fluctuations. The second pointer in Kaplan's argument is that it is the small and the poor among states which will suffer most in any "irrational and indefensible tampering" with the international economy. It has generally been so for small and poor states. The fact that OPEC's gains are most distinguished in their painful impact on the small and poor states simply alerts us to the fact that in a capitalist world-economy where the motive is capital accumulation, at any cost, things easily could appear changed, while in fact they remain the same.[17]

All this notwithstanding, it is still very strange for Kaplan to suggest that to benefit, resource-rich states should "sell their resources now... and to use the funds received for investment [in economic infrastructure] that will permit future production."[18] The suggestion is for the exploitation of less efficient resources in the future when present rich resources are used up. The suggestion is that resources must be sold at their present low and fluctuating prices in anticipation of the costly business of exploiting less efficient resources in the future. This is incredible. Given the highly interdependent nature of the world-economy, given the fact that the "high" price of one resource only shows how "low" others are, and given how high manufactured goods prices have always been, it is nothing short of curious for Kaplan to suggest that "it is a mistake to believe that the same set of nations should deal with each and every resource problem."[19]

On the important matter of transfer of technology, Kaplan advises that "it is time to stop talking about a redistribution of wealth internationally," as this redistribution will only succeed in undermining the international economic structure, and that large transfers of capital are not advisable because they will be "surely inefficiently used." In place of such wasteful transfers, Kaplan suggests "transfers of capital and technology that occur within the framework of a policy that takes such transfers from wealth increases." Some questions are in order here: in which sense does the transfer of capital differ from the redistribution of wealth in a situation where technology is itself capital and where it is costly to obtain, because it cannot be freely prised from its present ownership without payment?; and how does a situation like this lend itself to the generation of increases in wealth, where the problem itself is the generation of this wealth in the first place?

When Kaplan turns his attention to apply his global strategy to the Western hemisphere, it becomes difficult to know what strategy he is referring to. As we read it, Kaplan has presented us not so much with a strategy as an apologia for the existing form of domination of some states by others. But then this is precisely what the traditional frame of analysis does. It justifies the existing order. Kaplan's application of his "strategy" is honest, when he says that Carter's humanitarian and non-proliferation policies are merely a brief departure from traditional American policy and that the moment these policies appear to threaten American interests

American policies will return to their traditional core. His brief references to the Panama Canal and to Cuba tie in well with this interpretation of American policy departures from the traditional norm. It is difficult to appreciate, however, how the United States becomes "the effective client state of Puerto Rico."[20]

It is when Kaplan touches on Haiti of the Duvaliers and on Nicaragua of the Somozas that he becomes unbearably fuzzy and evasive. He claims it is beyond his competence to answer the question of whether past American policies are partly responsible for the situations in those countries. He says on this matter, "I do know that the current situation is one in which the United States does not, and probably cannot, have a policy, for we simply have no idea what we can or might do to transform the situation although perhaps in the next few years we may learn something about this."[21]

One gets this kind of evasive answer, when a defender of the status quo confronts simple problems of this sort; and when honest answers will demand a departure from the traditional terms of reference. Surely, the U.S. is responsible for the situations in Haiti and Nicaragua, to the extent that the U.S. has propped up the sinister dynasties in those two countries. This kind of support of corrupt and illegitimate regimes is nothing shameful in the traditional defence of power in international politics, and so Kaplan should have shown the courage of his traditional convictions by admitting it. In any case, we hope that the peoples of Haiti and Nicaragua will do something about their situation before America *learns* something about it.

When Kaplan touches on the regional giants of Argentina and Brazil—he should have included Venezuela—he touches on a matter which is of extreme relevance to the Caribbean region. These three states may eventually have imperialist ambitions of their own. But if the time referrent is as early as the 1980s, then the problem of clientism is likely to be a complex of *sub-imperialism* and *imperialsm*. This will be the situation where these states act imperialistically on their own behalf and at the same time act imperialistically on behalf of the U.S.

3. CONCLUSION: THE TRADITIONAL FALLACY OF STAGNANT REALITY

In concluding his paper, Kaplan returns to his introductory theme of the "disjunction between formal and substantive considerations." He refers to the dependence of the formal equality of all states, large and small, "upon the political, military and economic conditions in the larger world."[22] To the extent that these conditions distinguish between *small* and *large* states, one begins to wish that Kaplan had departed from the traditional ways of viewing and analyzing this *larger world* to tell us precisely what the nature of it is in terms of its historic referents. As we intimated earlier, it is the variations in the contents of the historic categories which set the context for the precise and specific explanation of the *larger world* within which to understand the nature of the political, economic, and military conditions which disjoin *small* from *large* states and subjects *small* states to *large* states.

The wish grows more intense as Kaplan goes on immediately after recalling his introductory theme to state that "every mode of social organization depends upon a set of material conditions."[23] The question, then, is this: precisely, what is the identity of this set of material conditions, which distinguishes our present *larger* world, our present world's "mode of social organization," from earlier modes in terms of quality and texture of relations? The next question is whether the texture of the relations indicative of, and unique to, the character of our present world can be known without departure from traditional scholarship in international relations, which is intent on obscuring the specific identification of our present world in terms of its historic referents?

It is in pursuit of answers to these questions that the world-system methodology is based firmly, and foursquarely, on the precise identification of the *whole,* Kaplan's larger world. The basic premise of this methodology is exactly as the Braudel Centre has put it: "the arena within which social action takes place and social change occurs is not 'society' in the abstract, but a definite 'world,' a spatio-temporal whole, whose spatial scope is co-extensive with the elementary division of labour among its constituent regions or parts . . . specifically, this arena has been and continues to be the modern world-system, which emerges in the sixteenth century as a European-centered world-economy."[24]

The point in this basic world-system premise,[25] is that while this modern world-system emerged in the sixteenth century as a European-centered world-economy, the history of this world-system, world-history as distinct and different from the history of the world, is larger than the history of Europe.[26] This is because while European history may have been initiating and dominant in world-history, world-history attempts to marry the different and conflicting interests, fates, and involvement of both Europeans and non-Europeans in their world-wide and unitary context. The world-system methodology attempts to study world-history along the singular axis of the development of the modern world-economy, as it is uniquely described by the methodical process of capital accumulation. It is for the sake of analytic versatility within the world-system frame that it is suggested that the *historic motive* should be considered the accumulation of capital, that the *historic force* within this motive be considered the rising level of efficiency of exploitation of both human and non-human resources; and it is for the sake of analytic sensitivity that *historic concomitants* and *historic logical attendants* and their relationships to each other, and to the *historic motive* as it relates to the *historic force* must be respected, if we are going to be able to address the vital contradiction that things can easily appear to have changed, while in fact they remain essentially the same within their historic context.

Usually the adoption of the world-system methodology is not innocent of a conception of a *desirable* world—desirable social actions, and the consequent desirable relations. My adoption and use of this method derive from a deep conviction that a large part of the undesirable aspects of contemporary world can be traced to the historic development of world-capitalism. I, in the company of many, hold world-capitalism culpably responsible, and palpably so, for the state of the world and would like to see the world-capitalist reality transformed into some other form that will not be built on the foundations of irrational exploitation of human and non-human resources, so clearly expressed in the mutually reinforcing relationships between induced dependency and augmented inequality. This desire for change is what informs the historic relationships indicated above.

The changes desired include, among other things, a change toward the approximation of what Kaplan describes so well as "increased formal equality and greater collegiality in the determination of decisions that affect all states of the [world]." On this matter, Kaplan says:

> It is not inevitable. For those who aspire to this greater equality and *collegiality, sophisticated knowledge of the conditions* under which they are possible is essential. *Rhetoric* will not make it so but only *policies that accord* with those conditions that are necessary for the development. The prospect is genuine and lies before us, but its fruition depends upon good will, *intelligent choice* and execution of policy, and good luck; for in the end the *goddess of chance* can bring us all down regardless of wisdom or virtue.[27]

If we may leave the *goddess of chance* out of it for the moment, we can say that we agree with Kaplan that *sophisticated knowledge of conditions* is essential, that *rhetoric* will not help, that *policies that accord* with these conditions are necessary, and that success will depend upon *intelligent choice.* Our agreement is qualified, however, in that we do not think that sophisticated knowledge of "the world condition" is possible within the traditional conception of this world and the traditional analysis of international relations, where rhetoric in the form of worn phrases and envisions justifying reality in its *stagnant concrete* forms lead only to policies which accord with, and so entrench, the very conditions that should be changed. This tradition rules out intelligent policy choices that could lead to the changes we seek.

There may very well be a frame of reference that is required for the approximation of equality with respect to states. But are we ever likely to find this frame, if we persist in the traditional *fallacy of ahistoric contemporaneity* and compound this fallacy by another fallacy, the *fallacy of stagnant reality,* where within the traditional frame the desirable is not allowed to be considered together with the conditions describing the undesirables in reality, thus ruling out any possibilities which the desirable may have in changing the concrete?

In the traditional frame, vital questions such as what motive and what force within it have come to make the whole a "world island," are not raised. The strict application of the traditional frame cannot answer these vital questions, because they are not even raised. We need to search, therefore, for a new frame of reference. This search will have to include all those who believe that answers to these questions could form the basis of the kind of *sophisticated knowledge* which Kaplan calls for. To do this, however, we must endeavour to avoid the twin fallacies of *ahistoric contemporaneity* and *stagnant reality.*

FOOTNOTES

[1] This is the fallacy which treats contemporary issues without due reference to the relevant past in its historic terms.

[2] The meanings of these terms will become clear presently.

[3] For the distinction between the two see Robert Nesbit, *Social Change and History.* New York: Oxford University Press, 1969. See also Robert L. Heilbroner, *The Future as History.* New York: Grove Press, 1969, p. 28; and see my forthcoming "The World-System Methodology." It deals with the distinction we must make between the precisely historical and the historical as merely the past.

[4] Examples will be the changed and the changing conceptions of work, profit, schooling and education in general, hegemony, the role and use of technology, production relations, etc.

[5] Examples will include: independence, modern conception of statehood, sovereignty etc.

[6] We raised this point in the preceding comments on Rosenau's essay, where superficial referred to changes other than in the historic motive.

[7] This is the theme in my "The Continuity of Capitalist Imperialism Theses," forthcoming as an UNU-GPID working paper.

[8] Morton Kaplan, "American Policy Toward the Caribbean Region: One Aspect of American Global Policy," 197, as in manuscript, p. 3.

[9] *Ibid.,* p. 3.

[10] *Ibid.*

[11] This is in broad reference to the third principle of power theory of international politics, as Hans Morgenthau and others, including Morton Kaplan, have developed it.

[12] Kaplan, 1977, as in manuscirpt, p. 8.

[13] *Ibid.,* p. 9.

[14] *Ibid.*

[15] For further development of this theme see my "Approaching the Peculiarity of the Caribbean Plight in the context of the paradox of the Representative State in the Contemporary World-System," (mimeo, July 1979) and see also my comments on Rosenau's essay above.

[16] Kaplan, 1977, as in manuscript, p. 10.

[17] See my "Two Views on Interdependence and Self-Reliance: Politics of De-orientation and Politics of Recreation" a paper written for the UNCTAD Regional Seminar conducted by the ISER, UWI, Mona, Jamaica, March 1979; and also refer to my comments on Rosenau's essay above.

[18] Kaplan, 1977, as in manuscript, p. 11.

[19] *Ibid.,* 12.

[20] *Ibid.,* p. 17.

[21] *Ibid.,* pp. 17-18.

[22] *Ibid.,* p. 19.

[23] *Ibid.*

[24] Braudel Centre, "Patterns of Development of the Modern World-System, " *Review* 1, 2, Fall 1977, p. 112.

[25] For further elaboration, see my "World-System Critique of Euro-Centric Conceptions of Imperialism," (mimeo, March 1979).

[26] By Europe we refer to Europe proper and European-occupied parts of the world.

[27] Kaplan, 1977, as in manuscript, p. 20. Emphases added.

Part II:

Regional Integration

Introduction

Ramesh Ramsaran

The three papers in this section on regional integration address themselves to different, though related, aspects of the question. The paper by Havelock Brewster is concerned with a critical analysis and appraisal of the Caribbean Integration experience. Goodwin and Lake examine the position of the LDCs in the overall integration process, but specifically against the backdrop of the measures designed to assist this group of countries. Vaughan Lewis, on the other hand, explores the prospects for a renewed effort at political integration in the light of new parameters and factors which have emerged to affect the economic and political processes in the region.

Havelock Brewster has long been concerned with matters of economic integration, particularly at the theoretical level. He is co-author of the well-known and widely read *Dynamics of West Indian Economic Integration,* published in 1967, along with a number of other volumes on integration intended to inform strategies on integration being considered in the middle and late sixties. In essential respects there was a fundamental divergence between the proposals put forward in these studies and the approach eventully adopted by Commonwealth Caribbean governments. In the paper "The Theory of Integration and the Caribbean Community Process: Ten Years On," Brewster, using a particular framework, tries to measure the amount and quality of integration achieved under the CARIFTA/CARICOM umbrella. A number of possible approaches to measuring and interpreting the concept of integration are discussed, and their particular merits and elements outlined. The notion of "collective decision-making" was eventually chosen as the standard of measurement. This approach is not free from defects of its own as he rightly points out, but its adoption is dictated by his aim to judge the Community process "by the standard it set for itself and one which it holds in common with other integration groupings around the world."

One may choose to agree or disgree with Brewster's approach and conceptualization, but his results are interesting and often supported by the facts. For example, he concludes "that within the scope of Community issue-areas so far recognized by the Community itself the degree of integration attained is surprisingly low. This is a clear indication that the Community has not been deepened. As the functional scope widens, its degree of integration attained within that scope diminishes." "Evidently," he goes on a little later, "the movement has been toward relatively greater engagement of the Community in issue areas of low-level salience which are themselves now approaching the point of exhaustion."

In his paper "the Architecture of Political Regionalism in the Caribbean," Vaughan Lewis tries to reformulate (though at a high theoretical level) a framework within which the question of political integration in the Commonwealth Caribbean can usefully be approached. The inherent difficulties are not minimized. These, however, are critically put against the historical experience of the insular political and economic model and against certain trends in the larger world system. In the light of recent developments the desire of the pivotal state has attained increasing relevance and is also drawn into the discussion. And, while in certain circumstances the pivot (or pivots) can prove to be potentially disruptive, for Lewis its (or their) existence can facilitate the movement towards integration. His arguments are formulated in the context of a very open system, and therefore a critical consideration may be the desire to counter extraregional influences impinging upon the security and interests of the pivot. The latter's role is by no means perceived to be altruistic, which in effect provides the integration motive. The centrifugal and centripetal forces bearing on integration are very interestingly pitted against each other in this paper.

The paper by Goodwin and Lake focuses on the experience of the LDCs within the Caribbean integration movement. The authors undertake a critical examination of the provision in the CARICOM Treaty intended to assist development in these countries within an integration framework. In so doing, a useful insight is provided into the nature of the problem facing the LDCs and the deficiences in existing strategies.

The Theory of Integration and the Caribbean Community Process: Ten Years On

*Havelock R. Brewster**

INTRODUCTION

Scientific theorizing on integration among states is largely a product of Western schools of thought and is hardly two decades old.[1] The purpose of such supposedly nonnormative theorizing has been to determine if and when and among which nations some observable process of integration will commence; to measure the progress and level attained with respect to such a process of integration; to predict its future development; and to create a system suitable to comparative analysis.

In this paper, I shall present a critical exposition of measurement and predictive aspects of integration theory, and I shall consider those theoretical aspects against the background of Caribbean experience.

The revived process of integration in the Caribbean is now completing its first decade and it seems an appropriate point at which to reflect on the past and speculate on the proximate future, within a stricter analytic framework than has hitherto been used in work on this subject.

CONCEPTUAL AND MEASUREMENT SYSTEMS

Although all concepts of integration are concerned with the broad notion of parts cohering into a whole through noncoercive processes, a variety of definitions of the meaning of integration may be found. Some prominent generic variations of emphasis are[2]

*This paper contains the private opinions of the author and not those of the United Nations Conference on Trade and Development to which he is presently affiliated.

    a) the shifting of loyalties from a national setting to a larger centre;[3]
    b) the attainment of a sense of community;[4]
    c) the recognition of mutual obligations and common interests;[5]
    d) self-maintenance ability in the face of internal and external
       challenges.[6]

From the standpoint of identifying integration as phenomenon measureable at different and marginal levels, these definitional efforts have yielded ambiguous interpretations and empirically unsatisfactory concepts.

In recognizing these difficulties, some researchers have resorted to the use of indirect measures as indicators of integration. Among the variables most often used are the relative growth of transactions (exports, mail, students, tourists), the growth of intergovernmental and trans-nongovernmental organizations, diplomatic interactions, and manifestations for unity efforts (public opinion polls).[7] In the absence, however, of some explained organic linkage of observables to abstract concepts, much uncertainty remains, as it always does with the use of proxies, as to what these indicators ultimately measure and whether they are of any predictive value.

In the case of Western Europe, where mostly these methods have been applied and the variables have generally shown positive trends, even before the establishment of the European Community, a proposition that, correlatedly, these states are progressively shifting their loyalties to supranational government is far from having been satisfactorily established. It seems to me too that the likely presence of an approximate multicollinearity among the variables used reduced them to a unique trade-related indicator.[8] But how this is to be interpreted leaves considerable room for differences of opinion. Is it a measure of an ever-rising level of community among Western European states; or is it, literally, an indication of the increasing alertness of capitalism to profitable opportunities? The conceptual connection between trade and the integration of nations remains unexplained.

A directly measureable concept of integration is the scope and level of collective decision-making.[9] One useful aspect of such a concept is that all integrating groupings of countries in the world, with the possible exception of the Council for Mutual Economic Assistance, seem to define their arrangements and aspirations in terms of collective decision-making. It sets union among states as the norm or terminal state of integration. Another merit of this concept is that artificial distinctions between economic and political integration are unnecessary. In fact, it harmonizes well with those concepts which define economic integration in terms of a neat progession of collectively made decisions relating to the removal of barriers to trade and factor movements and to the formation of economic policy.[10] While it may not embrace all the qualities inherent in the other definitions of integration mentioned above, these qualities, in most cases, presuppose operationally, some collective decision-making capacity. As such therefore it would seem to constitute the conceptual core of most notions of integration.[11]

The possibilities of greater clarity and more precise scoring do not, however, diminish the difficulty of actual measurement. Decision-making is a complex concept, involving, at the level of authority alone, such multiple dimensions as functional scope, the range of decision stages, and the relative decisiveness of the collective issue-areas. This poses a problem not only of the cardinal measurement of each dimension but of the aggregation of the scores of the separate dimensions in terms of some common abstraction.

The definition of discrete stages in the progression of integration in terms of the scope (functions) and level (authority) of collective decision-making offers some possibilities of overcoming measurement problems associated with the use of a more continuous empirical interpretation of that concept. Analytically, the stages may be differentiated by three modal responses: revision of the scope and level of obligations; maintenance of the *status quo;* and retreat on the scope and level of obligations. Thus, an heuristic typology of the progression of integration may be defined at such discrete levels as:[12]

a) increase in the scope and level of collective deision-making (spill-over);

b) increase in decision scope only (spill-around);

c) increase in the level of decision-authority without entrance into new areas (build-up);

d) retreat from certain areas while increasing the level of joint deliberation (retrenchment);

e) expostulation by regional bureaucrats on a wider variety of issues while decreasing their actual capacity (muddle-about);

f) decrease in both scope and level of decisional authority (spill-back);

g) marginal modifications within zones of indifference (encapsulation).

However, such a typology appears to be useful only insofar as it is felt that the developments are clearly unambiguous, cross-sectional and over time, or where the answers are already known intuitively. This may be the case at some times and in some integrating groupings of countries. In those cases, such a system could permit a clearer identification of the pattern of integration evolving. Where however there is uncertainty, as, for example, in the case of changes occurring in different directions in many or all of the categories, the need remains for a more refined and numerate dissection of the content and dimensions of collective decision-making. Evidently, the theoretical generality of the methodology is limited.

THEORETIC PREDICTIVE SYSTEMS

The uniting of nations as the terminal state in a noncoercive process of collective decision-making has never actually occurred in the history of the world. Integration, if it may be so called, has occurred only through the force of arms and the force of transnational capitalism. Hypotheses on integration have therefore been formulated around a nonexistent phenomenon and, as such, this cannot be, as it pretends to be, the subject of nonnormative scientific theory. In reality, the theoretical edifice collapses into a set of value-constrained propositions. These, on the one hand, reveal a concern for the painless creation of monolithic, authoritarian states and, symmetrically, for the expansion of transnational capitalism; on the other, they mask the possibility of integration through antithetic, decentralized, institutionally different processes, and its actual emergence through forces which bypass, override or render redundant national and regional decision-making centres.

Concepts of integration of the genus discussed above raise problems of theory formation for those, like myself, who would insist that integration is a substantive process, interpretable in terms of what actually takes place in the social and economic life of societies; not simply a matter of the morphology of decision-making. When understood substantively, different macrohypotheses emerge and a different predictive apparatus becomes relevant. Whether or not a scientific theory of integration can be shaped with reference to the substantive content of integration depends on whether phenomena recognized as such can actually be found in the real world. Alternatively, the task is to create explicitly normative theories of integration.

Theoretical models of integration require the specification of the predictive variables and the formation of hypotheses governing their behaviour.[13] For both purposes, researchers have recognized the value of differentiating between different, actual or potential cycles in the integration process, from initiation through priming, to transforming and transcending cycles.[14] The priming or accelerating stages are mainly of concern to us at this stage of our experience with integration among states. A sample of the prominent so-called independent variables common to the principal analyses include: structural homogeneity, transactions (intraregional flows of trade, capital, labour, communications), elite value complementarity; pluralism and extraregional dependence.[15]

These variables are operationalized in the models in terms of marginal rates of change.

The principal macrohypothesis is that tensions or crises are generated by the initial collective decisions which give rise to a variety of possible solutions or outcomes to the integration process ranging, as was noted before, from various forms of upgrading, stagnation or downgrading. The tensions or crises created are the product of conditions which characterize the process of integration. These process conditions are thought to be changes in the balance of political power among benefiting and losing groups within states; welfare and status redistribution among states; reduction of alternatives open to sovereign states; and externalization of activities.[16]

In the absence of sustained attempts to satisfactorily operationalize and use the determining variables, it is difficult to judge the power of the predictive models created. Variables tend to multiply, although there is no evidence of what they individually or together add or subtract from the explanatory power of the assumed relationship. Indeed, it is not known whether the predictive systems as a whole are valid since they have not been amenable to any rigorous tests of falsification. While taking on the appearance and using the language of empirical science, the calculus of the relationships remains of doubtful precision, and the actual attempts to use them have been an anticlimax in the thin commonsensical conclusions drawn out of an elaborate intellectual web.[17]

In the inital stages of all sciences, the predictive system will be the product of collections of random information, commonsense, intuition, imagination, guesses, and so on, empirical methods progessively falsifying the pre-theories drawn out of them. Given widely different social conditioning, it is inevitable then that predictive systems will reflect the subjective values of their authors, in terms both of what they recognize and what they do not.

Thus, as noted before, Western schools of analysis have recognized integration essentially as a process of collective decision-making, not as a matter of people's social and economic reality. Decision-making itself is viewed as a superficial phenomenon: who proclaims decisions rather than what forces determine them; what issues are legislated on rather than the relevance of the decisions to those issues.[18]

Likewise, such a perception of reality offers a predictive system which is mostly concerned with surface observables, themselves unlinked to the phenomena to be explained: are the units becoming more equal in size; are trade and capital flowing at a greater rate; is the elite socializing more closely; are extraregional imports and exports increasing, and so on. The absence of ontological methodology results in the reflection of such variables as 'independent,' capable of determining the process of integration, even taking integration as a limited collective decision-making concept. In my view, these are distorted images of reality.

In recognizing integration as a substantive concept, the need at once arises, in devising a predictive system, to isolate the forces manipulating the configuration of economic and social relationships which make up society: who are they; what are their interests and who benefits; what dynamic conditions are produced by the coalitions; and what tensions, contradictions, and alternatives are generated to explain the evolving process. I believe that such a matrix of experiential observations, even conflictive ones, may provide a simpler methodology of prediction and a more lucid vision of the future than the attempts to operationalize an infinite series of conceptually ambiguous and organically unlinked variables with the aim of compressing them into neat simulations of linear or parabolic single-equation functions.

NEW PERSPECTIVES ON THE CONCEPT OF INTEGRATION

As far as I have been able to judge, Third World scholars have not yet contributed a great deal to conceptual thought on integration among states, though in many cases their economic writings betray a dissatisfaction with notions of integration as they have evolved in American and European literature. My own contribution has been at a highly abstract level, defining integration in terms of its organic functioning: the diffusion of attributes of strength and weakness throughout the parts of a system, so that the potential of the integrated system becomes greater than that of the summation of the individual unintegrated components.[19] Such an abstraction obviously needs to be decomposed and I wish now to add some elements in that connection.

Firstly, in a state of disintegration, the economic and social transactions which make up society are highly concentrated, being locked into a rigid enclave pattern by the structure of power (external and internal). This limits the development potential of the system as a whole. Secondly, the dynamic force for the destruction of such concentrated power structures, and for the construction of diffuse patterns of participation in decision-making, derives from an egalitarian instinct in man. Thirdly, the ensuing process of integration is manifested in the progressive creation of interlinked structures of economic as well as social relationships.

Egalitarianism nowhere seems to have been recognized as basic to the notion of integration. Yet, going back to elemental units of society, it seems to me to be the primal source of a sense of community.

Equality is the transcendence of self, the putting aside of notions of what separates one from another, the overcoming of disuniting tendencies. A higher state of self-realization derives therefrom and is experienced through attainment to community. Individuals cohere freely through equality and equality is the source of community. Thus, equality would seem to be the conceptual core of the notion of integration at any level of association.

Such a perspective leads to two important propositions. First, integration may not be relevant to and may not be achievable by capitalist societies (state or private entrepreneurial) since the principles of such societies are founded on and lead to the creation of divisions among people: divisions of labour, class, status, wealth, and race. Second, integration may not develop among states without the simultaneous equalizing process occurring within national societies.

This second proposition requires further that integration should be conceptualized, as I have tried to do, at a high level of generality: one that could be applicable at the global, international, and national levels. The present state of affairs whereby different notions of integration prevail at these levels is not only theoretically untidy, but highly selective in its recognition of abstract phenomena in the real world. The contradictions are starkly revealed, for example, in the disconnected thought processes of the Western School when it comes to defining national integration (with reference to African, Asian, and Latin American states): centralized political structures, decentralized political structures, compliance with government directives, popular legitimacy, national identity, adpatation to pluralistic loyalties, agreement on values, conflict resolution capacity.[20] This schizophrenia seems to betray an uncertainty about how the subjective values of the authors could best be pursued in the national context.

It follows from the above perspective that the manifestations of integration could be measured in terms of three properties: power concentration (p), concentration of economic transactions (e), and concentration of social communications (s). These are interconnected phenomena. For example, concentrated structures of power produce a high concentration in intersectoral transactions, and this in turn necessarily leads to a highly functionally stratified pattern of social relations, and so on in a circular quagmire.

The operationalization of the concept being proposed might be undertaken through the use of a statistical measure of concentration (or dispersion) for each property, described either, simply, in a single vector space[21] or, more elaborately, in a multi-vector matrix.[22]

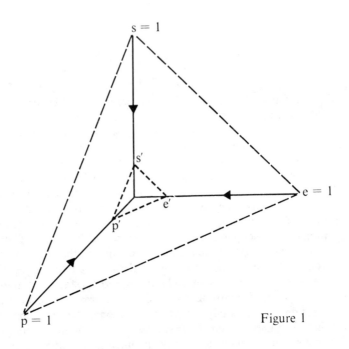

Figure 1

Such a coefficient is calculated to approach the limits of concentration (disintegration) at unity and the limits of diffusion (integration) at zero. The coefficient for each of the three properties, for different time-periods, could be located in a three-dimensional space, as shown in Figure 1.

Here, the vector p e s(p, e, s = 1) locates the limits of disintegration(d) and the origin, the limits of integration (n = 0). p' e' s' is an intermediate stage attained in some point of time. Thus positive and negative movement in the process of integration between time-periods can be expressed conceptually in terms of a common abstraction, referred to as concentration, and quantitatively in terms of the relative magnitude of the vector space[23] (even where, p, e, and s move in different directions). Similarly, cross-sectional comparisons can be made.

The relative degree of disintegration in Figure 1 is

$$d = \frac{p'\,e'\,s'}{p\ e\ s} \qquad \text{Lim} \text{---} \blacktriangleright 1. \qquad (1)$$

and the relative degree of integration is

$$n = (1 - d) \qquad \text{Lim} \text{---} \blacktriangleright 0. \qquad (2)$$

MEASURING THE LEVEL OF CARIBBEAN COMMUNITY

I will not attempt in this paper to apply the concept and methodology outlined in the previous section to Caribbean community. For one thing, empirical data are not available. For another, that conceptual framework is enough to reveal the nature of Caribbean community and what has been occurring. Here, power is highly concentrated in centres comprising externos and the local burgeoisies (politicos, technicos, and entrpreneurs). This is the locus of practically all decision-making relating to community issues (from security to calypso contests). Economic transactions are, symmetrically, highly concentrated; pure plantation economy with virtually zero inter-industry linkage. Social communications flow preponderantly within the boundaries of the functional enclaves of status—on the whole, a highly disintegrated community. In terms of equations (1) and (2), illustrative concentration values of the three properties might be $p' = 0.95$; $e' = 0.90$; $s' = 0.85$. The level of integration $(1 - d)$ would therefore be nine per cent.

Developments over the last few years have not done a great deal to alter this situation: independence, nationalism, nationalizations, Caribbean community, socialist governments. If anything, power has become more concentrated with the widening scope of government directives, and the increasing entrenchment of the postindependence black bourgeoisies. The economic system has become less cohesive as domestic supply diverges wider from domestic demand.[24] The pattern of social communication is essentially unchanged from that of the colonial period: different actors in the same play; while an ever-increasing number of people are consigned to zero status. The Caribbean community has contributed positively to this process. It has facilitated the increasing concentration of power; the lowering of domestic inter-industry transactions through an open origin system for internal free trade; and the strengthening of the status of the national bourgeoisies: the conception of its aims are in no way qualitatively different from those of the national governments.[25]

Primitive statements about the Caribbean Community abound. They are made by those who are closely involved as well as by distant observers. It is said, for example, that the Caribbean Community has been deepened; that it is in the vanguard of integration groupings; that we shall sink or swim by it; that it is moving toward a new federation and encroaching upon the prerogatives of states. On the other hand, it is claimed also that it is a useless imperialist device; that it has contributed little or nothing to real Caribbean unity and prosperity; that only businessmen and foreign corporations have profited; and that it is so conflict-ridden that it is on the verge of collapse.

I intend now to undertake a fairly elaborate empirical analysis of the community process, judging it by the standard it set for itself and one which it holds in common with other integration groupings around the world. This is, as discussed previously, collective decision-making, a notion of integration I considered inadequate. The Community Secretariat, as may be expected, although often presenting a Community problem in vivid substantative language, never fails to assess the potential solution and evaluate its performance strictly and purely in terms of collective decision-making instruments.[26]

The model is as follows:

The horizontal range of issue-areas in the decision-making matrix is x, and

$$x = (1.s) \tag{3}$$

where s is a measure of the salience of issue-areas. The vertical range of decision-making is y, and

$$y = (v.s) \tag{4}$$

where v is a measure of decision stages. The spatial range of decision-making is z, and

$$z = (t.v.s) \tag{5}$$

where it is a measure of the depth of applicability of decisions within the Community. Measured in terms of degrees of salience, issue-areas ($N = a_1, \ldots, a_n$) are scored

$$a_1 = (1.s) + (v.s) + (t.v.s)$$

that is,

$$a_1 = s(1 + v + tv) \tag{6}$$

and

$$N = \sum_{i=1}^{n} s(1 + v + tv) \quad n \quad i = 1 \qquad (7)$$

The maximum integration attainable within the existing scope of issue-areas is therefore

$$U = \text{Max.} \sum_{i=1}^{n} s(1 + v + tv) \quad n \quad i = 1 \qquad (8)$$

The degree of integration attained within the existing scope of the Community is

$$N' = N/_U \qquad (9)$$

As U approaches the potential limit of integration,

$$F = \text{Lim } U.$$

And the actual degree of integration is

$$n = N/_F \qquad (10)$$

In vector space the model may be expressed as

$$N = \begin{bmatrix} x \\ y \\ z \end{bmatrix} \qquad F = \begin{bmatrix} x' \\ y' \\ z' \end{bmatrix} \qquad (11)$$

Certain characteristics of this model need now to be discussed, and some comments made on the pertinent literature. Issue-areas are identified, to the extent convenient, as they are treated by the Community itself and not necessarily in preconceived general policy categories. Such apparently neat categorizations are a feature of the literature on integration and decision-making,[27] but it is evident that the range and complexity of the individual components of such categories vary so widely from one category to another and one group of countries to another that it would be incorrect and probably impossible to assess the specific salience of issue-areas in such an indiscriminate fashion. For example, import policy is an area of the highest salience in Caribbean policy but it is only one aspect of trade policy. Its salience is much greater than that of the intraregional tariff regime or intraregional agricultural marketing which are also part of trade policy. It would therefore introduce a strong bias if the rank of trade policy as a general policy category were to be assessed in relation to, say, fiscal policy. Within the group of countries itself, it has been necessary to make some allowance, in the overall assessment, for the fact that the salience of an issue-area may vary widely from one country to another, for example, tourism in Barbados and Guyana. The most objective procedure appeared to be to take the issue-areas as given and described in Community deliberations, to the extent possible. As a result, the range of areas identified may be, to a good extent, peculiar to the Caribbean Community[28] and a somewhat different identification of issue-areas may be relevant to other integration groupings.

I have ranked decision-making in three dimensions, referred to as horizontal, vertical, and spatial range. Horizontal range is the functional scope of the issue-areas. Vertical range refers to the stage decision-making has reached. And spatial range is the depth at which decisional choice is collectivized. These three dimensions seem to capture the most important properties of decision-making *per se*. Other dimensions of decision-making could include the 'animators' and the 'consequences' of decision-making.[29] These, however, go beyond the notion of the collectivization of decision-making as a conceptual description of integration, though they may be useful, if they could be satisifactorily operationalized, in a predictive system based on the notion of decision-making.

The explicit hypotheses used in determining the salience[30] of an issue-area are that (a) the primary aim of political parties in power is to maintain and consolidate their power, and consequentially, (b) governments assess the salience of an issue-area according to the political opportunity cost entailed in transferring responsibility in that area to the Community. This political opportunity cost is measured in levels in terms of the loss of potential power to influence the electorate, ranging from minimal to substantial.[31] Obviously, salience could be ranked by many other standards and some are suggested in the literature, for example, intensity of actors preference, powers of actors affected, anticipated deprivation, proportion of government revenue devoted to particular issue-areas, and so on. In none of these instances is it possible to judge their merit since they are not accompanied by an explicit hypothesis linking the arithmetic calculus to the concepts used. I prefer to use my own hypotheses and ranking system in determining the horizontal range of collective decision-making. In enumerating the range of issue-areas in Table I, a distinction is made between those in which there is some recognized decision behavior at the Community level and those in which there is none.

The vertical range or stage of decision-making is measured between the extremes of no engagement at the Community level and full implementation, administration, and enforcement at the Community level.[32] The spatial range or depth of collectivized decision-making is measured between the extremes of all decision-making activity taking place at the national level and all decision-making activity taking place at the Community level.[33]

The vertical and spatial dimensions are related to the horizontal dimension and to each other through the common abstraction of salience. The specific form of the relationship postulated may be derived from equations (3) to (5).[34] This connection, which appears to be absent, even conceptually, in the literature, is rationally necessary if (a) the three elements are to be differentiated according to their dimensionality, as they are in reality, and (b) they are to be aggregatable.

The engagement of the Community in any particular issue-area is essentially a decision of low-level salience, whatever be the issue-area. What matters a great deal more is the stage at which collective decisions are taken and the depth at which decisional choice is collectivized. The horizontal range will therefore be much smaller in magnitude than the vertical range which, in turn, will be a great deal smaller than the spatial range. Thus, the general shape the integration vector $(x', y', z',)$ will take in this conceptualization of integration will be as shown in Figure 2.

The data presented in Table I yield the following results:

$$N' = 12.82$$
$$n = 8.05$$

That is, the level of integration attained within the existing functional scope of the Community is in the thirteen percent range and the level of integration attained in relation to the limits of integration is in the eight percent range. Illustratively, the latter corresponds to the shaded area of Figure 2. I will now offer a few observations on the Caribbean Community process.

The degree of integration attained in the Caribbean Community is as yet minor. The apprehensions entertained by some national bureaucrats are quite unfounded. What is even more revealing is that within the scope of community issue-areas so far recognized by the Community itself the degree of integration attained is suprisingly low. This is a clear indication that the Community has not been deepened. As the functional scope widens, the degree of integration attained within that scope diminishes. Thus, the Caribbean Free Trade Association probably attained a much higher degree of integration within the scope set for it than the Caribbean Community shows signs of attaining.

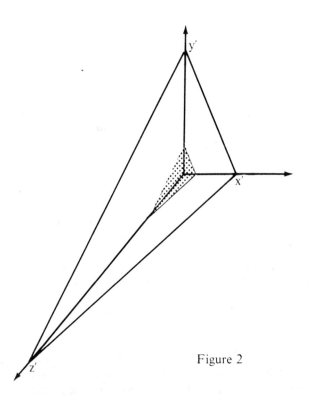

Figure 2

Within the eight percent level of integration attained, well over one-half the degrees of salience is accounted for by only nine decision areas, those relating to the free trade regime, the common external tariff, the scheme for the harmonization of fiscal incentives to industry, the agricultural marketing protocol/scheme for guaranteed markets, the balance of payments mutual support interim facility, joint participation in the European Economic Community commodity marketing/stabilization scheme, the Caribbean Development Bank/Caribbean Investment Corporation, the University of the West Indies, and the West Indies Shipping Corporation. When it is further taken into account that the first seven of these instruments function ineffectively, inadequately, or not at all, and that the last two were inherited from the colonial period, the substantive level of integration achieved in terms of decisional consequences is much lower than the apparent eight percent level.

A notable feature of the Community process is the wide scope of its engagement in issue-areas. It seems that this is in the range of 62 percent of the limits of integration. This is greatly in contrast with the twenty percent level of engagement with respect to the stage of collective decision-making and the seven percent level of engagement with respect to the depth at which decisions are collectivized.

More remarkable is the fact that within the range of issue-areas of high-level salience, those ranked 5 and 4, the level of integration attained is miniscule, being only at the level of three percent of the limits of integration, while that attained in issue-areas of low-level salience, those ranked 3, 2, and 1 is nineteen percent. Symmetrically, among the issue-areas in which there is as yet no recognized decision behaviour at the Community level, a disproportionate number, some seventy percent, are located in the range of high-level salience. Evidently, the movement has been toward relatively greater engagement of the Community in issue-areas of low-level salience which are themselves now approaching the point of exhaustion.

The generalization that I would make with regard to this situation is that the political power structure of Caribbean societies has been quite effective in containing the community process, on the whole, to the 'zone of indifference.'[35] At the same time, regional bureaucrats, conscious of their own technocratic interests, have been fairly adept in securing community legislation within the 'zone of irrelevance,' a zone characterized by the presence of highly visual Community instruments which allow practically unlimited national discretion.

PREDICTING THE PROCESS OF CARIBBEAN COMMUNITY

I remarked earlier in this paper that integration as a substantive concept requires a predictive apparatus which is different from that used by the formal theorists. Ontologically, we need to identify the power-centre and its interests, relate the decisions taken to that centre and those interests, and isolate the dynamics of the process. The predicted pattern of behaviour will then depend on the nature of the contradictions generated by the coalition of power-centre actors, the kinds of tensions produced by the process dynamics, the national alternatives which become feasible, and the entry into the system of qualitatively different variables. The outcome in terms of subsequent integration actions is determined by the manner in which all these forces are resolved.

Issue-areas of some recognized decision behavior at community level	X Horizontal range (l.s)		Y Vertical range			Z Spatial range			Brief description of behavior at community level
	s	Max Points	v	(v.s) score	Max Points	t	(t.v.s) score	Max Points	
1 Industrial Planning and Development	5	5	1	5	30	0	0	180	Preliminary research, limited *ad hoc* feasibility studies, a limited number of unconnected joint venture decisions.
2 Agricultural Planning and Development	5	5	1	5	30	0	0	180	Preliminary research, limited *ad hoc* feasibility studies, a limited number of unconnected joint venture decisions, Caribbean Food Corporation decision.
3 Marketing Primary Commodity Exports Extraregional	5	5	4	20	30	3	90	180	Joint negotiations and participation in Lomé Convention (European Economic Community and the African Caribbean Pacific Group of countries) primary commodities stabilization scheme.
4 Monetary Policy	5	5	1	5	30	0	0	180	Information, research
5 Fiscal Policy	5	5	1	5	30	0	0	180	Tax administration organ for training and technical assistance, double taxation agreement between more and less developed member countries.
6 Development Finance	5	5	6	30	30	1	30	180	Caribbean Development Bank and Caribbean Investment Corporation
7 Foreign Investment and Ownership	5	5	1	5	30	0	0	180	Problem recognition, preliminary research on the problem
8 Import Policy Extraregional	5	5	1	5	30	0	0	180	Problem recognition, meeting of an expert group on bulk procurement.

									Description
9	Labour Movements	5	5	1	5	30	0	0	180	Simplification travel documentation, Community recognition national decision on dual nationality within Caribbean.
10	Social Security	5	5	1	5	30	0	0	180	Problem recognition
11	Mass Communications	5	5	1	5	30	0	0	180	Regional news agency, broadcasting union, training exchanges, technical assistance.
12	Tourism Planning and Development	4	4	1	4	24	0	0	144	Regional centre, information, preliminary research.
13	Energy	4	4	1	4	24	0	0	144	Problem recognition, short-fall guarantee by regional producer.
14	Exchange Rates	4	4	1	4	24	0	0	144	Problem recognition, information.
15	Prices	4	4	1	4	24	0	0	144	Problem recognition, decision on regional commission.
16	Incomes	4	4	1	4	24	0	0	144	Problem recognition
17	Labour/Industrial Relations	4	4	1	4	24	0	0	144	Problem recognition
18	Public Service Administration	4	4	1	4	24	0	0	144	Intraregional pension rights transfer.
19	Extraregional Trade Régime	3	3	5	15	18	4	72	108	Common external tariff.
20	Exports other than Primary Commodities	3	3	1	3	18	0	0	108	Research.
21	Fiscal Incentives to Enterprise	3	3	5	15	18	3	54	108	Harmonization of fiscal incentives to industry.
22	Foreign Policy other than Economic	3	3	1	3	18	0	0	108	Problem recognition, ad hoc exchange and information.

23	External Representation	3	1	3	18	0	0	108 Problem recognition
24	External Security	3	1	3	18	0	0	108 Problem recognition.
25	Economic and Monetary Aid to other Policies	3	1	3	18	0	0	108 Problem recognition.
26	Balance of Payments	3	6	18	18	1	18	108 Balance of payments mutual support interim facility, limited central banks clearing.
27	Education Primary	3	1	3	18	0	0	108 Textbook preparation activity.
28	Education Secondary	3	1	3	18	0	0	108 Regional curricula and examinations preparatory activity.
29	Education Tertiary	3	6	18	18	4	72	108 University of the West Indies, common legal education and training.
30	Intraregional Trade Régime	2	5	10	12	6	72	72 Free trade régime.
31	Agricultural Marketing Intraregional	2	6	12	12	5	60	72 Agricultural marketing protocol and guaranteed market scheme, oils and fats agreement.
32	Maritime Transport Intraregional	2	6	12	12	3	36	72 West Indies Shipping Corporation.
33	Maritime Transport Extraregional	2	1	2	12	0	0	72 Problem recognition, research, coordination of negotiation on terms.
34	Air Transport Intraregional	2	1	2	12	0	0	72 Problem recognition, financial support for Leeward Islands Air Transport, intergovernment expert committee of two member countries.
35	Air Transport Extraregional	2	1	2	12	0	0	72 Problem recognition, joint representation in International Civil Aviation Organization.

36 Health	2	2	1	2	12	0	0	72	Problem recognition, survey of problem, establishment of regional nursing body.
37 Culture and sports	2	2	4	8	12	2	12	72	Regional arts festivals, combined cricket teams, recognition of principles applicable to racism in sport
38 Legal System	2	2	1	2	12	0	0	72	Research on harmonization of company law, industrial property systems, status of women, exchanges on Law of the Sea.
39 Standards and Quality Control	1	1	3	3	6	0	0	36	Regional commission decision, drug testing arrangements.
40 Meteorology	1	1	1	1	6	0	0	36	Regional meteorological organs—information, training, advisory.
41 Hurricane Insurance	1	1	1	1	6	0	0	36	Problem recognition, preliminary research.
42 Export Credit Insurance	1	1	1	1	6	0	0	36	Ministerial endorsement scheme applicable to some member countries.
43 Technical and Financial Assistance Intraregional									Community fund of limited size, special emergency fund for programme assistance to less developed member-countries.
Sub-total	—	139	—	274	834	—	588	5,004	
Issue-areas of no Recognized Decision Behaviour at the Community Level									No behavior at Community Level
44 Land Resources Policy	0	5	0	0	30	0	0	180	
45 Land Distribution	0	5	0	0	30	0	0	180	

46 External Reserves	0	5	0	30	0	180
47 Wealth and Income Distribution	0	5	0	30	0	180
48 Capital Movement Extra-regional/Exchange Control	0	5	0	30	0	180
49 Employment	0	5	0	30	0	180
50 Housing	0	5	0	30	0	180
51 Town and Country Planning and Development	0	5	0	30	0	180
52 Constitutional and Electoral System	0	5	0	30	0	180
53 Human Rights	0	5	0	30	0	180
54 Internal Security	0	5	0	30	0	180
55 Sea and Ocean floor Resources Policy	0	4	0	24	0	144
56 Foreign Aid	0	4	0	24	0	144
57 External Debt and Borrowing	0	4	0	24	0	144

58 Insurance	0	4	0	0	24	0	0	144
59 Capital Movement Intra-regional/Exchange Control	0	3	0	0	18	0	0	108
60 Technology Transfer and Development	0	3	0	0	18	0	0	108
61 Export Credit	0	2	0	0	12	0	0	72
62 Caribbean Overseas Communities	0	2	0	0	12	0	0	72
63 Postal Service	0	1	0	0	6	0	0	36
64 Environment	0	1	0	0	6	0	0	36
Sub-total	0	83	0	0	498	0	0	2,988
Grand Total		222		274	1,332		588	7,992

In Figure 3, I have attempted to illustrate, in a highly simplified abstract form, how this constellation of power, process dynamics, and contradictory forces are interrelated and determine integration behaviour. Its explanation in terms of the Caribbean situation follows.

The regional capitalist class are the comprador and branch-plant agents of the international capitalist system, the external force. Their combined interests are to expand and penetrate markets through regional free trade with minimal origin restraints. Regional political power structures, while having allied economic interest, in some degree, also have other substantial interests of a political character, to be pursued, at least partially, through integration. In combination therefore with the alliance between the local capitalist class and their external patrons, they take integration step 1, the establishment of an open-origin free trade area. It is a fact that the only interest-groups allocated participation in the decision-making process, from beginning to end, leading to the establishment of the Caribbean Free Trade Association were the national political power structures and their technocratic agents and the national and regional Chambers of Commerce and Manufacturers Associations.[36]

The conjunction of interests of the national power-centres which I have identified and which will be an element in the predictive operation are as follows:

Guyana	Counterbalance internal racial insecurity
	Countervail possible external territorial aggression
	Dipomatic cover for "socialism"/power concentration
Trinidad and Tobago	Markets[37]
	Egocentric 'Williams' Pan-Caribbeanism
Jamaica	Markets
	Countervail opposing political party
Barbados	Markets
	Improve relative attractiveness for foreign capital
Belize	Alternative diplomatic/military cover for independence
West Indies	
Associated States	Improve relative economic status
	Diplomatic/economic backstopping for transition to independence.

The free trade process creates a dynamic of its own: uneven distributions of costs and benefits within states and between states. It also preempts some possible national alternatives such as nonmarket directives

Figure 3

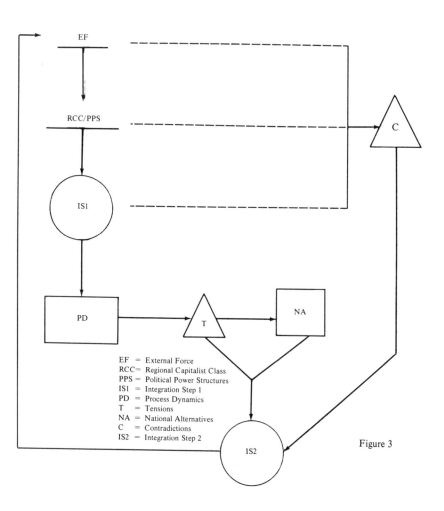

EF = External Force
RCC = Regional Capitalist Class
PPS = Political Power Structures
IS1 = Integration Step 1
PD = Process Dynamics
T   = Tensions
NA = National Alternatives
C   = Contradictions
IS2 = Integration Step 2

Figure 3

for determining the source and quantity of imports. These have certainly been a feature of the Caribbean free trade process, generating internal tensions through the adverse redistributive effect on consumers and through the consequences of customs revenues foregone; and interstate tensions through the medium of envy. In fact, the nongainers (all member-countries except Jamaica, Trinidad and Tobago, and Barbados, to a lesser extent) had no reason to expect free trade gains and never really did. To the extent that the tensions have come to be described in terms of a maldistribution of trade benefits, they were in reality an expression of dissatisfaction over the failure of their, sometimes unstated, expectations to materialize through the symbolic umbrella of an elementary economic connection.

At this stage, which marks the half-way mark in the deveploment of the integration process, there are no viable national alternatives since national power-centres still expect to secure their interest, in part at least, through the regional cooperation vehicle. At this stage, too, the contradictions are muted since the free trade process is essentially in harmony with the interests of the external actors, the regional capitalist class, and the still-expectant regional political power structures. The resolution of the tensions described above are therefore sought in: (a) Caribbean Development Bank finance to balance out the unevenness in the distribution of trade benefits; (b) a special regime for the less developed countries to bolster their flagging expectations; (c) the harmonization of fiscal incentives to industry to restrain the emergence of new imbalances in the attraction of industry and in the accrual of benefits (not, it may be noted from the terms of this agreement, to put a stop to or effectively curtail the abuses of the incentive system); (d) a common external tariff to expand the capacity of the capitalist class to make better use of the free trade system and, in lagging countries, for it to catch up on the benefits distribution.

This development in the process of integration is achieved through the design of a carefully balanced package intended to neutralize the tensions created by integration step 1 by simultaneously offering something extra to the laggards in exchange for an inducement of the other participants. They reflect the presence of tensions but not, at this stage, of contradictory forces or the play of feasible national alternatives.

Such a development is described by the theories reviewed as "upgrading" or "spill-over." In fact, it is revealed for what it is: the creature of negotiation, intended to preserve the basic and original power-centered inspiration of integration through an imaginative system of self-sustaining redistribution, at essentially the same functional and conceptual level of integration. Far from being spill-over, it is drain-off.

This is the stage of the inauguration of the Caribbean Community integration, step 2. Via Bank financing, the dependence of the common external tariff for its productive consequences on the technological reservoir of transnational capitalism, and the continued mediation of their regional agents, we return to the source.

This time round, however, profound contradictions appear: (a) political power structures in the drive to power concentration through the search for mass legitimacy find themselves transparently propping up the very antithesis of such legitimacy, the external force and the local burgeoisies; (b) these political allies when the latter are constrained by the compromises that the political power structures must make to ensure the *status quo* (some of the concessions made in integration step 2) and to attract mass legitimacy (nationalization, subsidies, house-feed-and-clothe-the-nation programmes, restraint on the use of foreign exchange, state trading, and so on); (c) the political power structures are likewise on a collision path with the external system as a result of some of the tendencies described in (b), while ultimately deriving their economic legitimacy from that very source; and, finally, (d) the regional capitalist class, having tasted of the first fruits, begin to clash with their metropolitan patrons over the division of the bigger spoils, forthcoming through the possibilities of regional protection and industrialization, even as they are locked into a more vicious technological dependence.

The process dynamics of this second step are essentially of the same nature as those of the first step. They are, however, more pronounced because the community Stage-two package is unable to drain-off the effects of the tension-producing genesis. Caribbean Development Bank finance, even if disbursed at a sufficiently high rate, cannot significantly alter the relative situation of the nongainers because the ratio of the Bank's resources to total capital formation requirements is miniscule. The special regime for the less developed countries cannot work because it presupposes the operation of competitive market forces which are only very faintly in evidence; the harmonization of fiscal incentives to industry is inoperable because industry location is not finally dependent upon such incentives and the scheme is applicable within a range which allows wide enough latitude to national initiative. Common external tariff protection is, effectively, neither common nor protective.

At this stage, political power structures are in a better position to take stock of the balance of their expectations and to begin to chart their national options. In Guyana, it becomes apparent that Caribbean community is too abstract a relationship to perform the counterbalancing and protective internal and external role required, and too internationally insignificant also. Visible participation in nonalignment has been an alternative and parallel strategem. Now, with the dramatic demise of nonalignment as a credible, coalescent, aggressive Third World force, under the conservative twin pressures of Islam and petrodollars,[38] the move is to the Soviet sphere of Eastern Europe, China being an eccentric and ineffectual voice on Third World interests.[39]

In Trinidad and Tobago, the shadowy dreams of an old man[40] lie broken, emitting brief but faint signals over the Caribbean Sea; now through the stillborn Caribbean Development Cooperation Committee.[41] The *démarche* of hemispheric Latins, rich in dollars if not in discretion, and the far-flung and alien alliances[42] of his partners must be enough to convince him that some men do live by bread alone. The national options for Trinidad and Tobago are clearly to be seen in the prime ministerial search for transnational corporation partners, across the sea, from Japan to the United States.[43]

In Jamaica, the flippant bogey of the opposing political party has vanished. Regional cooperation neither scores nor loses points at this juncture, and whither Jamaica goes in terms of national options, no man knows.[44] Barbados has witnessed sadly the disappearance of its vision of becoming the Hong Kong of the West as its partners recklessly dispel all confidence in the region as a haven for foreign investment.

Belize can scarcely entertain an expectation of anything more than rhetoric, as the partners stand aside in the Anguilla secession, in the Trinidad and Tobago army revolt, and as they fail to exhibit any military or diplomatic capacity to withstand even the gentler varieties of so-called destabilization. The West Indies Associated States must surely have lost all hope of improving their relative economic status and securing some tangible backstopping for the transition to independence through the Community. However, the alluring twilight attractions of the demi-monde await them.

In short, the original conjuncture of interests has all but evaporated, leaving a tangle of contradictions, tensions, and wayward nationalism. In projecting the Community's future, I shall (a) assume neutral external exigencies in order to detect the possible direction of the internal momentum; and (b) reimpose these external forces to determine the possible difference they could make to the basic outcome of the unconstrained process.

The initial assumption of neutral external forces implies simply that these forces are satisfied, at the present time, with the free trade regime, the maintenance of which is purchased at the cost of some of the other provisions of the Community (such as development finance, the common external tariff, and the harmonization of fiscal incentives to industry). My hypothesis is that the tensions and contradictions which characterize integration step 2, that is the Community, are not resolvable at the existing or at a higher level of integration. The reasoning behind this hypothesis is that

(a)   the resources that would be needed to buy off the nongainers in this nonzero sum game simply to maintain the *status quo* at the Community's second-order equilibrium is far beyond the gainers' assessment of fair compensation and even beyond their ability to pay measured in terms of political opportunity costs;

(b)   the national alternatives now appearing on the scene, evaluated in terms of their capacity to satisfy the national objectives of nongainers and gainers, seem not only to be superior to the maintenance of the *status quo* but also to be inconsistent with it;

(c)   the tensions and contradictions of the present stage of integration are systematic. They inhere in the nature of Caribbean polity and economy. They are not functional crosscurrents, as they seemed to be at integration step 1, amenable to solution simply by technocratic bargaining devices and tricks;

(d)   there are no new internal sources of Community dynamic.

The short-range rational outcome therefore would probably be some lowering of the degrees of integration, achieved, to be sure, through some visible Community instruments which purport to advance the Community process. Nonrational occurrences, as was the dissolution of the Federation, are not the subject of scientific prediction. The following specific occurrences are predicted:

(a)   a halt to the engagement of the Community in an ever-widening range of issue-areas (e.g., nonengagement in issue-areas 44 to 64 of Table I). In any event, outstanding issue-areas of low-level salience are nearing exhaustion and a continuation of this process would have to involve engagement in highly contentious areas of high-level salience. In addition, the process would be halted by an increasingly nonviable ratio of sources to demands;

(b)   issue-areas at the initial decisional level of 'problem recognition' remain there (e.g., foreign investment, exchange rates), while retrenchment to a lower level of obligation takes place with respect to those issue-areas at the level of research (e.g., industrial and agricultural planning and development) or at the level of Community—formation of policy guidelines for national action (e.g, fiscal incentives to enterprise, primary commodity marketing, noneconomic foreign policy, transport);

(c)   nonimplementation of joint venture projects agreed on (e.g., aluminum, Caribbean Food Corporation projects) and avoidance of decision on additional projects of this kind;

(d)   renegotiation of the free trade regime, providing for different origin rules, reintroduction of some tariff-related device by the less developed member-countries, Community framework for the operation of nontariff barriers and state trading practices and for the wider application of balance of payments safeguard and national infant industry protection clauses;

(e)   inoperability of decisions on Community institutions (e.g., those relating to prices, standards and quality control, balance of payments facility);

(f)   separation of existing Community service institutions into autonomous national units connected through some loose regional framework (e.g., University of the West Indies, West Indies Shipping Corporation);

(g)   marginal or zero reduction of the slack within the non-preemptive zone of irrelevance (Caribbean Development Bank finance, the common external tariff, harmonization of fiscal incentives to industry, special regime for the less developed countries, including the agricultural marketing protocol/guaranteed markets scheme);

(h)   maintenance of the *status quo* within the low salience zone of indifferenece (e.g., culture and sports, meteorology, technical and financial assistance).

In reimposing the external parameters, two recent occurrences may seem relevant: the persisting economic crisis in the world economy (the oil price increase and the recession with inflation in the Western capitalist countries) and the socialist declarations of the governments of Guyana and Jamaica, including their stated desire to seek some form of association with the Council for Mutual Economic Assistance. Official and some academic analyses[45] trace a good deal of the tensions within the Community to the world economic crisis.

I do not, however, regard this so-called crisis as a qualitatively different variable in the integration equation. It is a little more or a little less exaggerated characteristic of the capitalist system, depending on one's perspective, and, as such, accounts for degrees rather than the nature of things. The crisis, essentially an increase in import prices and reduction in export earnings, explains little about the tensions inherent in the integration process adopted by the Community and less about the contradictions which this process, Caribbean polity, and transnational capitalism together excite. Indeed, looking at the crisis *per se* a case could be made, equally well and as easily, that it provides a good stimulant toward greater and more intensive collective efforts at economic cooperation.

Scanning the world at large, we find little connection between world economic crises and the fate of integration in the Third World. During the present crisis, the Association of South East Asian Nations has taken a small step forward, the Bangkok Agreement was signed, and the giant Economic Community of West African States was inaugurated. The Latin American Free Trade Association, the Central American Common Market, and the Regional Cooperation for Development (Turkey, Iran, Pakistan) ground to a halt at the height of the Western boom in the early 1970s. The Council of Arab Economic Unity and the East African Community have been in the doldrums through the thick and thin of the Western economic cycle, and so on. Evidently, basic explanations must be sought in the nature of systems and processes rather than in import and export price trends.

The socialist declarations of the governments of Guyana and Jamaica raise, first, the question as to whether socialism is actually developing in those societies and, secondly, speculations about the reaction of the hemispheric Power. Regrettably, the first enquiry is obscured by rhetoric and counterrhetoric, by simplistic interpretations (nationalization, dictatorship of the proletariat, trading with Eastern Europe) and by academic references to Marxism-Leninism. Without intending to undertake an evaluation of the announced trends, suffice it to say that when judged empirically against the grand precepts of socialist philosophy—egalitarianism, moralism, rationalism, and libertarianism—clear tendencies toward authentic socialism are not discerned. What may be more in evidence are mass legitimizing techniques of power concentration such as those previously referred to. Techniques of power concentration are not, however, unique to the "socialism" of Guyana and Jamaica. They have been perfected through other means elsewhere in the Community, notably through a fusion of pantomime with monomythical heroism. Whether or not socialism is actually developing in Guyana and Jamaica is, however, less relevant to the hemispheric Power than its implications for world power politics. The internal economic organization of states *per se* is evidently a matter which has receded in importance in United States foreign policy, and more so should it be in resource-redundant regions such as the Caribbean. What really matters is whether the socialism of Guyana and Jamaica will actually involve a significant, material increase in Soviet influence in the Caribbean, and whether the United States views the strengthening of the Community and its nonsocialist members as a useful tool in the conduct of its foreign policy in this region.

Neither of these questions is answerable at the present time. The first is not answerable by reference to a fragile linkage to the ineffectual Council for Mutual Economic Assistance in Moscow or to the normal diplomatic and economic intercourse among independent nations. This may even be a tactical political precondition or justification for a continued or more intensive courtship of Western markets, transnational corporations, World Bank and International Monetary Fund loans, and grants from the European Development Fund. The answer to the second question might be extrapolated from United States policy toward individual states since it has no experience itself in dealing with such a matter at the level of a Community of states outside the special case of the North Atlantic Treaty Organization. The nature of the response possibly might be foreshadowed by United States policy toward the Andean Group where expected investments for a large-scale regionally integrated industrial development programme have failed to materialize, and toward Peru and the Allende government of Chile within it. Whatever happens then, the possibilities for maintaining the Community at the present level or for upgrading the level of integration are traceable uniquely to the source.

FOOTNOTES

[1] Pioneering works are: Karl W. Deutsch, *Political Community at the International Level: Problems of Definition and Measurement* (New York: Doubleday, 1954); Ernst B. Hass, *The Uniting of Europe—Political, Social and Economical Forces, 1950-1957* (London: Stevens, 1958); Leon N. Lindberg, *The Political Dynamics of European Economic Integration* (Stanford: Stanford University Press, 1963); Ernst B. Haas, *Beyond the Nation State: Functionalism and International Organization* (Stanford: University Press, 1964); Ernst B. Hass and Philippe C. Schmitter, "Economic and Differential Patterns of Political Integration: Projections about Unity in Latin America," *International Organization*, vol. 18, no. 4 (Autumn 1964); Joseph S. Nye, "Patterns and Catalysts in Regional Integration," *International Organization*, vol. 19, no. 4 (Autumn 1965).

[2] These are critically discussed in J. K. De Vree, *Political Integration: The Formation of Theory and its Problems* (The Hague: Mouton, 1972).

[3] Ernst B. Haas, *The Uniting of Europe—Political, Social and Economical Forces, 1950-1957* (London: Stevens, 1958), p. 16.

[4] Deutsch, *op. cit.*, p. 33 and Karl W. Deutsch *et al.*, *Political Community and the North Atlantic Area* (Princeton: Princeton University Press, 1957), p. 5.

[5] Joseph S. Nye, *Pan-Africanism and East African Integration* (Cambridge, Mass.: Harvard University Press, 1965), p. 84.

[6] Etzioni, Amitai, *Political Unification—A Comparative Study of Leaders and Forces* (New York: Holt, Rinehart and Winston, 1965), p. 330.

[7] Among the many works discussing or using these methods see Hayward R. Alker and Donald J. Puchala, "Trends in Economic Partnership: the North Atlantic Area, 1928-1963," in *Quantitative International Politics*, ed. David Singer (New York: The Free Press, 1968), pp. 287-316; Donald J. Puchala, "International Transactions and Regional Integration," *International Organization*, vol. 24, no. 4 (Autumn 1970); and "Patterns in West European Integration," *Journal of Common Market Studies*, vol. 9, no. 2 (December 1970); Bruce M. Russett, "Transactions, Community and International Political Integration," *Journal of Common Market Studies*, vol. 9, no. 3 (March 1971).

[8] For example, the conclusions drawn by Puchala could perhaps be reinterpreted along these lines. See Donald J. Puchala, "Patterns in West Europe Integration," *Journal of Common Market Studies*, vol. 9, no. 2 (December 1970) p. 141.

[9] The most systematic expositions of this concept are: Leon N. Lindberg, "Political Integration as a Multidimensional Phenonemon Requiring Multivariate Measurement," in *Regional Integration: Theory and Research*, eds. Leon N. Lindberg and Stuart A. Scheingold (Cambridge, Mass.: Harvard University Press, 1970), pp. 45-127; and Leon N. Lindberg and Stuart A. Scheingold, *Europe's Would-be Polity: Patterns of Change in the European Community* (Englewood Cliffs, N.J.: Prentice-Hall, 1970). Other researchers have also made considerable use of collective decision-making interpretations of integration, for example: J. S. Nye, "Comparing Common Market: A Revised Neofunctionalist Model," and Philippe C. Schmitter, "A Revised Theory of Regional Integration," in Leon N. Lindberg and Stuart A., Scheingold *op cit.*, pp. 194-195, 239-240.

[10] Bela Balassa, *The Theory of Economic Integration* (Homewood, Ill.: Richard D. Irwin, 1961), p. 1.

[11] On this point see DeVree, *op cit.*, p. 325.

[12] Philippe C. Schmitter, *op cit.*

[13] For a review of the state of theory formation on regional integration see Ernst B. Hass, "The Study of Regional Integration: Reflections on the Joy and Anguish of Pretheorizing," in Linberg and Scheingold, *op cit.*, pp. 3-42.

[14] Schmitter, *op cit.*, and Nye in Lindberg and Scheingold, *op. cit.*

[15] Schmnitter, *ibid.*; Nye, *ibid.*

[16] Nye, *ibid.*

[17] For example, the conclusions of Nye, *ibid.*, pp. 224-225.

[18] Some researchers, for example, have referred, in certain instances, to integration groupings advancing to, for example, common external tariffs and the harmonization of fiscal incentives to industry. A substantive knowledge of the decisions would have revealed them to be essentially nondecisions; that is legislation within the sphere where national discretion remains virtually unlimited. The integration arrangements or nonarrangemnts themselves are not always truly noncoercive. In one case it is suspected that heavy financial pressures were generated; in another, that large sums of money were offered to the presidents concerned; in a third case, that it was a necessary military survival tactic, and so on.

[19] Havelock Brewster, and Clive Y. Thomas, "Aspects of the Theory of Economic Integration," *Journal of Common Market Studies*, vol. 8, no. 2, (1969), p. 112.

[20] A brief survey is given in Fred M. Hayward, "Continuities and Discontinuities between Studies of National and International Political Integration," in Lindberg and Scheingold, *op cit.*, pp. 313-337.

[21] For example, single vector measures could be:

p = relative power of decision-making on community issues (investment, production, budget, infrastructure, education, housing, health, social welfare, . . .) allocated to interests groups $a_1, \ldots, a_n$ (external, central government, capitalist, peasant, trade union, student, cooperative, municipality, village, . . .).
e = relative use of domestic output in economic sectors $x_1, \ldots, x_n$ (agriculture, manufacturing, construction. . .). s = relative incidence of social communication of power-centre actors (externos, local burgeoisies, politicos, technicos, entrepreneurs) with other functional groups of society $y_1, \ldots, y_n$ (peasants, labourers, service proletariat . . .). A revealing indicator of social communication could be social contact (e.g., social mixing). this would require sample surveying.

[22] A multi-vector matrix records the quantitative relationship between each one of a series of entities, $p = (a_{ij})$; $e = (x_{ij})$; $s = (y_{ij})$.

[23] The magnitude of a vector space $v = (x, y, z)$ is

$$\sqrt{x^2 \ y^2 \ + \ z^2}$$

[24] This concept is explained in Havelock Brewster and Clive Y. Thomas, *Dynamics of West Indian Economic Integration* (Kingston, Jamaica: Institute of Social and Economic Research, 1967), p. 78.

[25] It is perhaps not accidental that the Community has never sponsored any joint activity by alternative political groups, trade unions, peasants, consumers, or unemployed workers.

[26] Good examples are the Secretariat publications: *From CARIFTA to Caribbean Community,* (Georgetown, Guyana: Caribbean Community Secretariat, 1972); *The Caribbean Community: A Guide,* (Georgetown, Guyana: Caribbean Community Secretariat, 1973).

[27] See Lindberg, (1970) *op. cit.;* Nye, *op. cit.;* and J. S. Nye, *Peace in Parts,* (Boston: Little and Brown, 1971), pp. 21-54.

[28] In the absence of annual published Community reports and access to the minutes of the Councils of Ministers there could be a margin of error in my data. If so, I believe this would be relatively small.

[29] See Lindberg (1970), *op. cit.;* Harold A. Lasswell, and Abraham Kaplan, *Power and Society—A Framework for Political Inquiry* (New York: Yale University Press, 1963); Harold D. Lasswell *The Decision Process: Seven Categories of Functional Analysis* (College Park, Md.: University of Maryland, 1956).

[30] Ultimately, it is impossible to measure such nonphysical phenomena in exact cardinal units. Nonetheless, the ranking methodology to be adopted seems to make for greater precision than simple judgmental observations, particularly in making comparisons over time and cross-sectionally.

[31]

Political Opportunity Cost	Level
Minimal	1
Minor	2
Moderate	3
Considerable	4
Substantial	5

[32]

Stage of Decision-making

Level	Decision Stage	Description
0	No collective decision behaviour	—
1	Collective problem recognition	Information, research, training, assistance, consultative and advisory groups, coordinating and harmonizing instruments
2	Collective definition of specific action alternatives	Some policy options defined as acceptable, not acceptable.
3	Collective decision on choice of policy as guidelines for national policy	Intergovernmental bargaining and choice of a type of policy.
4	Collective decision for legislative implementation by national authorities	Policy chosen limits national authorities to legislate and implement.
5	Collective legislation and national enforcement	National discretion only in enforcement.
6	Collective legislation implementation, administration and enforcement	National discretion only in enforcement. No national discretion; supranational organization.

[33]

Depth of Decision-making Activity

Level	Decision Depth
0	All activity at national level.
1	Preponderant at national level, small at Community level.
2	Majority at national level, moderate at Community level.
3	Roughly equal at national and community levels.
4	Majority at Community level, moderate at national level.
5	Preponderant at Community level, small at national level.
6	All activity at Community level.

This scale as well as that in note 32 are simplifed and adapted from the work of Lasswell and Lindberg, *ibid.*

[34] For example, $x = s$; $y = s(t)$; $z = s(t^2)$. It is not possible, of course, to prove that this is the correct quantitative function for the relationship. The principle of a relationship is established and alternative postulates are possible.

[35] They reinforce this by an increasingly nonviable ratio of resources to demands. The community Secretariat has about 2/10 of one professional man-year per unit of issue-area salience, a situation which is absurdly untenable for undertaking an effective, innovative role.

[36] Apart from a few academics of the University of the West Indies, who wrote some largely unread papers stressing the need for action in the productive sectors.

[37]This includes Trinidad and Tobago's interest in the national airline becoming the regional carrier.

[38]Forty percent of the membership of the Non-Aligned group of countries is now Islamic, not to count those of wavering faith and empty coffers who may be converted through the medium of Saudi Arabian and Kuwaiti petrodollars.

[39]The positions taken by China on Bangladesh, Angola, Mozambique, and Zaire are suggestive of its priorities.

[40]Eric Williams, *Inward Hunger: The Education of a Prime Minister* (London: André Deutsch, 1969) p. 289.

[41]An Intergovernmental Committee Prime Minister Eric Williams was influential in having set up at the Sixteenth Session (1975) of the United Nations Economic Commission for Latin America. To date it has outlined certain areas in which research would be desirable.

[42]The governments of both Guyana and Jamaica have recently announced their intention to seek some form of association with the Council for Mutual economic assistance (Moscow).

[43]Toward the end of 1974 Prime Minister Williams undertook a voyage of discovery which resulted in his personal sketches to Parliament of a number of possible large-scale joint venture projects with transnational corporations.

[44]The place of Caribbean Community in Jamaican Foreign policy is discussed by Prime Minister Michael Manley in his *The Politics of Change: A Jamaican Testament,* (London: André Deutsch, 1974), p. 126: "The perception that leads one to the conclusion that economic regionalism is a logical pre-condition of accelerated national development must now be applied to the world situation."

[45]For example, Vaughan A. Lewis, "Problema y Posibilidades de la Communidad del Caribe," *Nueva Sociedad,* (January/February 1977), pp. 52-66.

The Architecture of Political Regionalism in the Commonwealth Caribbean

Vaughan A. Lewis

This paper is a response to the concern with whether a reasonable possibility of political unification of the countries which constitute the Commonwealth Caribbean area can be said still to exist. Such a response should, for completeness, take into account to what extent political unification can be considered technically feasible at the present time, in terms of its being a mechanism for coping with political relations among a number of countries concerned with the optimal elaboration of a set of social goals. But it should also consider the extent to which the *idea* of political unification still possesses normative legitimacy among *at least* those whose responsibility it might be to implement it (at a minimum the political actors), even if it should be technically feasible, given that any such schema must be sustained by popular support.

Political unification is a concept and system which is, in the literature, generally subsumed under the concept and process of "political integration." This latter is assumed to be capable of taking a variety of forms. This paper, therefore, given the type of response which the writer makes to the question of the possibility of unification also, as will be seen, examines the relevance of this larger notion of political integration to relations between the Caribbean states. And integration is, in turn, taken to be an aspect of those political relations which tend to be assumed to have a special character about them, because the states are said to exist in a particular "region." The politics of regional integration, therefore, constitute necessarily, a part of the politics of regionalism; this latter suggesting the nature of diplomatic relations taking place in some circumscribed geographical-cultural area.

In the contemporary literature, political unification is usually taken to refer to two types of government of entities previously having a separate

111

political or administrative existence: first, the subordination of the entities to one single centralized government or administration, this being generally known as a *unitary* system. The second is the system known as *federalism,* which is intended to give international significance and recognition to the structures which regulate the relations between entities that wish, while cooperating with each other in certain agreed spheres, to retain each in its domestic (national) sphere a large measure of political autonomy. The extant forms of such federal systems exist mainly in the Western world.

Increasingly, federalism has been recognized not simply as system, but as process in which both centralizing and countercentralizaing tendencies exist in constant tension. This is especially the case where, as the modern history of Canada demonstrates, there exist unequal levels of resources among the constituent units and such resources become dominant stakes in the cooperation-competition system; or where one or other entity perceives itself to be unduly subordinated to the centralizing aspects of federalism.

As is well known, the Anglophone countries of the Caribbean archipelago undertook a short-lived experiment in federalism. While it is true to say that the federation, like those encompassing units in other regions of the British Empire, was colonially-inspired, and indeed existed under colonial "tutelage," it can also be said to have had a certain local legitimacy. This is in the sense that the system came into existence on the basis of universal suffrage; and in the sense that it was in some measure the culmination of demands for some form of political integration among the territories, in the pre- and postwar periods, from the indigenous labour and middle-class leadership.

The story of the life and demise of the federation has been adequately told,[1] and is part of a general trend characterizing the colonial federations constructed by the metropolitan authorities. Evident during the life of the system were the controversies about its centralist or countercentralist character (this taking the form of an ongoing debate between the Governments of Trinidad and Jamaica). And the end of the federation actually saw the formal offer made, by Trinidad, to other territories, of support for the establishment of a unitary state. The offer was accepted by only one territory, Grenada.

But what is instructive in this regard is that the Commission set up by the Government of Trinidad and Tobago to consider the mechanics for establishing the unitary system came to the conclusion that a period of accommodation or harmonization of institutions and processes was necessary, this suggesting for an initial period a system of politial relations somewhat less than unitary.[2] This recommendation appears not to not have been acceptable, and was certainly not implemented.

In consequence, the political leadership of the various territories have proceeded to exercise the option of *insular independence*. This process has proceeded, as each succeeding territory exercised the option, to a chorus of doubts from within the region itself about the capacities of the insular territories for effective independence—while at the same time perceiving formal independence as inevitable in the modern world. Proposals have been myriad, as the prospect of the separate independence of the Windward and Leeward islands has appeared, for encompassing the countries of the Eastern and Southern Caribbean within some form of political integration system which might, at a minimum, meet the requirements of recognition by the international community as a sovereign entity. Some of these have recently been reviewed elsewhere.[3]

It is, then, presumably fair to say that the option of political unification has been rejected by the contemporary political leadership as a viable mechanism for the foreseeable future. On the other hand, it tends to be argued, even by the current political authorities, that some form of political integration is necessary, if the unit Governments are to be capable of providing themselves with an effective "size," for coping with economic and political processes of the contemporary environment. What this effective size might be is increasingly a subject of contention. Nevertheless, the general argument does allow both academic and political protagonists of the ideology of political integration to maintain that, while immediate implementation of some system of political integration is not presently possible, some alternative mechanism must be devised for ensuring that it is arrived at, in some unspecified future.

Thus, following European Economic Community precedents, a process of economic integration for the Commonwealth Caribbean countries has been articulated as a necessary prelude to political integration. As with other Third World countries, the literature and practice of European integration has had an influence on Caribbean political authorities which should not be underestimated. This applies in particular to assumptions about what in the literature is called the "expansive logic" of the integration process; and to assumptions about the development of political cooperation and integration mechanisms to match the development of increasingly coherent economic harmonization mechanisms. Political integration has, therefore, tended to be seen as "following" economic integration, "political" and "economic" being seen as separate and separable modes.

It is true to say that recognition has been given among technicians of the region to critiques of the applicability of theories of economic integration among industrialized countries to the States of the ex-colonial world. But what is also valid is that the assumed distinction between the economic and the political, which is institutionalized in mechanisms such as the

Caribbean Free Trade Area (CARIFTA) and the Caribbean Common Market and Community (CARICOM), represents a misreading of the actual process of elaboration of the European Community system. This misreading arises as a consequence of the laissez-faire ideological veil that legitimized the organization of the system.[4]

A variety of arguments can be found legitimizing the option towards insular independence and against any commitment to immediate political integration. First, given small geographical size and what are perceived as the limited resources deriving from such size, it tends to be assumed that the political and economic costs of an integrated organization of territories that are not geographically contiguous, in the sense of being on one landmass, would outweigh the, particularly short-term, benefits to be derived. The short-term calculus is important because most of the territories still subscribe to the five-year electoral cycle based on universal suffrage and the multiparty system. The perception has been that accountability in terms of producing meaningful benefits for local (island) populaces existing at low levels of income would be difficult. Underlying this perception is that in a political integration system with multiple levels of government, control over the direction of the integration system is more difficult than control over the local system. In fact, it is in turn assumed that the 'politics' of the local system is likely to be made more complex through intervention from the integration system in the course of the process of integration. A certain institutional inertia in favour of the insular therefore tends to prevail.

A second argument legitimizing insular independence has tended to be that, given the existence of a variety of international institutions devoted to the economic sustenance of the new states, it might be possible to seek bilateral solutions to insular problems, unencumbered by prior necessity for negotiation or justification at regional levels. This argument was assumed to have some utility particularly during the period of economic expansion among the industrial countries, in the course of which a reasonably coherent ideology of economic assistance prevailed. In effect the argument simply recognizes the possibility of relatively small countries attaining "free rides" in an international system devoted to some level of economic cooperation, and in which larger countries bear the major costs of such cooperation.

A third rationale for the insular option rests on the perception, particularly among the smaller countries of the area, that there is no country of sufficient size (and therefore predominance) which might have the capacity to bear the short-term costs of the political integration process. Observations relevant to international economic cooperation have a similar relevance to the operation of regional systems:

The direct incentive that countries have to go along with their international obligations—and besides this to shore up the obligations of others—will tend to be increased by their relative size. For size, in effect, gives them a larger proportion of the collective benefit, and thereby makes it worth their while to incur substantial direct costs—and perhaps even the whole cost—to assure that the collective benefit is provided. Here then is a structural reason why international cooperative benefits are more difficult to organise when the international system becomes less dominated by a single great power—which again appears paradoxical at first sight.[5]

Caribbean political leaders have always recognized this principle in a negative way, even the larger countries tending to take the view that none of them was of a sufficiently predominant weight to bear the costs of integration. Some Jamaican political leaders (in particular those of the Jamaica Labour Party which won the referendum held on federation) propagated the view, for example, that too large a portion of the resources of Jamaica would be used to provide the small units with "free rides." The Prime Minister of Trinidad and Tobago suggests the problem in recent remarks:

> Without being arrogant or crude, the fundamental fact of the matter is that this is an association in which the economic power, such as it is—we are all poor, poverty stricken, etc.—the economic power, such as it is, rests with Trinidad and Tobago. It always has. . . . But if you are going to spend any money on buying something from outside, and you come to Trinidad and Tobago for finance, there can be only one law laid down—that if you have to buy anything from outside and it is produced by Trinidad and Tobago, Trinidad and Tobago has the first choice, otherwise give that country that you buy from the first claim to supply you with the money.[6]

The history of customs unions arrangements is replete with discussions of this problem, one of the prime examples being the place of Prussia in the establishment of the Zollverein.[7] What we might call the 'pivotal state' feels itself capable of sustaining short-term losses, or alternatively with providing the system with more than a 'normal' share of resources; the assumption being that it stands to gain from the maintenance of the collective system as a whole more than it would, over the long term, if the system were not to exist. Difficulties arise, as we have suggested earlier, where (unlike the Zollverein system for example) political authorities are accountable within the electoral cycle; and where the pivotal state, though of some economic predominance, cannot provide itself with sufficient political and economic weight in the system to ensure control over the direction of a process in which it has invested substantially.

In the Commonwealth Caribbean region both of the difficulties can be said to exist. They have been exacerbated by the 'open' character of the countries' economies, in a situation in which the rules of the common market regime are sufficiently flexible (or nonexistent) to permit countries to evade them without being subject to the constraint of punitive action; or to seek extraregional solutions on the assumption that regional solutions are either unavailable or too costly.

It is the openness of the national systems, constituted as they are of a number of segments (enclaves) each linked, as Caribbean historians and economists have demonstrated, to some segment of metropolitan economy in an asymmetrical relationship that has, in fact, inhibited progress within the Common Market regime on the question of harmonization of policies in respect of foreign investment along the lines, for example, of the Andean Pact. And the very failure of the Andean Pact initiatives has reinforced arguments which suggest that the Commonwealth Caribbean area, as presently defined, is of insufficient weight in the international economic system to be capable of protectionist initiatives. Such arguments can be derived implicitly from the practices of various Governments in respect of incentives to foreign investment.

And insofar as there have been, recently, any tendencies to consider the utility of protectionist measures, these arise from pragmatic considerations: that is, mainly as responses to increasing policies towards protectionism in the world economy as a whole; and to shortages of foreign exhange consequent upon the world inflation of the post-1973 period.[8]

As a fourth, more recent, justification of the insular option, arguments have tended to be advanced that ideological differences as between the ruling regimes, particularly those of the larger countries, make even the experiment in customs union difficult. While it is true of Guyana in particular that the regime there has adopted the ideology of Marxism-Leninism and has brought under state ownership the major areas of production of the economy, it seems fair to this writer to say that policies adopted in respect of import restrictions, quotas, restrictions on capital outflows, are as they appear to be also in Jamaica, responses to balance of payments difficulties, made pragmatically, rather than in response to ideologically-based policy lines. In none of the Caribbean countries is there yet the effective and deliberate planning of foreign trade (along lines characteristic of the European socialist economies or Cuba, for example) that would make the national regime incompatible with the common market regime.

THE VIABILITY OF THE INSULAR OPTION

The national sovereignty model having been chosen for the island territory (and for Guyana), a genuflection to the notion of nonviability of the units has been made by way of adherence to the economic integration regime. Over time, the factor of harmonization of international negotiating positions has been added to the common market system proper, as it has become clearer and clearer that open island economy is heavily influenced in its domestic oragnization and behavior by international processes. This has particularly been the case as preferential systems have become regional rather than international (in the sense of extended imperial relations).

Nevertheless, as is well known, the trading regime which encompasses the area does not relate to those areas of production from which is derived the substantial portion of the national income of each territory. In any event, it ought to be remembered that the common market system has existed for a relatively brief period of time, even in terms of the period of life of the sovereign states themselves.

The central proposition that we would wish to advance here is that the insular model, in terms of the demands made upon, or expected of, it has not up to now proved a viable one. The arguments in support of this can be made from two directions.

First, in terms of the political economy adopted, the insular option has been accompanied by an adherence to the essential maintenance of the 'open' economy based on the so-called industrialization by invitation model. In what appeared to be a persistent period of expansion among the industrial economies, this seemed to be an attractive option. In most of the economies the option recognizably depended on the existence of some 'enclave product' attractive to foreign investors, and provided with steady market demand in one or other metropolitan country. In theory the returns provided from the product, in addition to foreign inflows taking advantage of attractive conditions for light manufacturing, should have permitted increasing levels of economic organization, income, and absorption of labour. The model, however, while admittedly producing new areas of economic and commercial activity, has been unable to cope with rising population levels, and with a substantial rural-urban drift itself encouraged by possibilities suggested by the model. The result has been mounting unemployment, either because of international recessions or by a diminution in the reserves of the local enclave product. With unemployment, therefore, there occur periodically situations of absolute limitations of foreign exchange. But foreign exchange has become completely critical to the persistence of the model at levels of domestic market demand that are increasingly costly as time goes on, and whose costliness is, in fact, a *consequence* of the character of employment and (this being skewed) generated by the model itself.

The nature and, more importantly, the relative weighting of the social groups developed in this model comes to have a specific relation to the political system. This latter being a competitive, multiparty one, it becomes susceptible to the influence of the higher-income sectors (high being relative to the minimum wage, for example, and these sectors therefore possibly including part of the 'working class'), both in terms of finance and organizational skills. The political elite is constrained to manipulate the political economy of the country, therefore, in terms of the life of the electoral cycle to an inordinate degree. And even where deprived sectors of substantial numbers seek to have an influence on the manipulation of the system, the burden of servicing those sectors for any reasonable period of time, exerts pressure on the balance-of-payments position of the country.[9]

This phenomenon has been most visible in Jamaica in the period since the 'windfall gain' derived from the imposition of the bauxite levy in 1974. It, however, characterized the political economy of Trinidad in the middle 1960s, when diminishing reserves of petroleum led, not only to diminishing foreign exhange reserves and increasing lack of attraction in the international financial markets, but to retrenchment from the enclave and consequent unemployment. One of the consequences of the behaviour of the model in this way is that it gives rise to increasing administrative costs, particularly in the area of the development and maintenance of efficient 'security' services—even where these costs are sometimes shared between the country and the major metropolitan power in the hemisphere.

This model therefore tends to move in cycles of upswing and downturn, and is increasingly seen as not being permissive of economic development. The model is, to put it crudely, stuck.

The second argument suggesting the nonviability of the sovereignty model adopted in the Commonwealth Caribbean relates to countries which have partially ceased to function in terms of the open economy, politically-competitive model. This alternative is visible mainly in Guyana, not an insular polity, but one in which assertions of the nonviability of the territory as an economic unit have also been evident.[10] Guyana is, as is known, characterized by a racially bifurcated social system which reflects itself in the political organization of the country. The ideology of Marxism-Leninism, the philosophical and organizational principle of the People's Progressive Party, the national movement of the 1950s, served to mute the effects of the bifurcated social system by focussing on working class unity. The movement having been dissolved for reasons which are well recorded, after the imperial suspension of the country's Constitution and government, the subsequent adoption of Marxism-Leninism as the ideology of the present Government of the country has not served to induce any degree of sociopolitical unification along previous lines.

Nevertheless, given the economic bases on which the two substantial racial groupings rest, and their separate political representation, national economic organization and development is impeded. And this, in spite of the fact that the competitive party system does not function in the conventional liberal democratic manner, cannot therefore be said for that reason to give undue weight to sectoral groups in the sense of that model, and cannot then be said to distort the capacity of the system for systematic policy-making and implementation. The fact is, of course, that this bifurcated political model acts through different mechanisms to impede effective policy-making, and to incline the system to stasis.

The import of the discussion in this section is that while there has been a rejection of some form of political integration or unification system as an immediate possibility, there is also a perception of the lack of capacity of the territorial sovereignty form as adequate to present demands. The attempt to weld insular or territorial sovereignty with an economic integration process has not sufficed in negating the deficiencies of the sovereignty model. And the dubious normative character of this model, at least from the public point of view of the political leadership and particularly in the Eastern and Southern Caribbean, is hinted at in numerous statements to the effect that economic integration is a mechanism for attaining some future state of political integration. But experience has shown that the very mechanisms of the national model inhibit in turn the development of any 'expansive logic' of the integration process. This has been particularly the case in the contemporary period of international economic dislocation.

Now, at the level of metropolitan scholarship on the subject, the relevance of regional integration theory and current practice, even to the European Economic Community's development, is being placed in doubt, such doubts being led by one of the original and main protagonists of the theorizing, Ernst Haas.[11] At the same time, in addition to ongoing critiques linking the failure of integration experiments in various Third

World regions to their location within the international capitalist system,[12] a developing critique of current integration models, and proposition of an alternative strategy of development is noticeable, particularly in the recent work of Clive Thomas,[13] from the Marxist point of view.

The fundamental orientation of Thomas' model rests on the establishment of a worker-peasant alliance. At the same time, his recommendation is for a national approach in which the gains from integration are to be derived from linkage with other, some more-developed, socialist countries. The strategy might be called a "simple transition" model in the sense that the transition problem does not speak to the situation of states with politically plural systems still linked to the capitalist system.

Nevertheless, within the terms of Thomas' model itself, the trajectory is against *regional* integration, this being only possible where the states involved are of a similar ideological (socialist) orientation:

> . . . when evaluating the possible contributions of political and economic union to increasing the effective size of nations, it seems to us that the real issue is whether existing states are more likely to be able to forge meaningful integration arrangements among themselves, as opposed to the prospect that historical circumstances may require these states to go it alone in their attempts at socialist transformation. It seems to us far more likely that many of the small underdeveloped areas will have to advance toward socialism in relative isolation from their neighbours. . . . Of course, as the numbers of these states increase, and socialism advances in a broad front, the scope for the effective integration of neighbouring states will be broadly enhanced.[14]

Going it "alone" is meant to refer to neighbours.

POLITICAL INTEGRATION
AND THE DEFINITION OF THE REGION

Not even the smaller territories (the Windward and Leward Islands or West Indies Associated States) have deemed it possible to operationalize the commitment to political integration which many have asserted to be necessary. Most recent proposals commissioned by some Associated States leaders indicating possible integration formulas, other than the orthodox ones of federalism and unitary statehood,[15] have been followed by a new thrust towards insular independence. The post-1973 effects of the world recession and commodity inflation on the other, larger Caribbean countries have, in a paradoxical way, served to lessen the strength of the arguments emanating from the larger countries that the

Windward-Leeward economies were specially small and specially vulnerable. All countries have had to subscribe to emergency funding provided by the country currently pivotal in the Region. And some of the smaller countries, in spite of assertions of unwillingness, fell prey to the demonstration effect of formal sovereignty.

We have already suggested that the perceived costs of integrated organization, in addition to nature of the openness of the economies, which directs the flow of resources away from the different segments of the insular system, leaving those segments unintegrated in an economic sense, both have the effect of negating commitments to integration. This is most likley to be the case where, as in the case of the Windward and Leeward Islands, no single unit possesses the resources or stakes to induce or constrain others to come into some alliance with itself; or where it is perceived that resources derived from the international environment through some form of bilateral negotiation are not likely to be less than those derived from negotiation through collective representation.

Now in the first instance, integration can be considered a form of protective device, intended to constrict the losses arising from the current characteristics (segmentation and small economic size) of the insular units. What needs to be recognized is that such characteristics, especially those relating to segmentation, themselves tend to become stakes and sources of dispute in the intergration process itself. This is because the processes of international economy into which the segments of insular systems are already integrated tend, initially, to be almost as strong as the stakes that induce regional cooperation, and therefore as powerful or even more powerful than the structures that are designed to underpin regional coherence. That this particular tension is an ongoing and long-term process, given the countries' current mode of international economic integration, can be illustrated from an example not drawn from the Caribbean at all:

> The Canadian economy is integrated on East-West lines only to a limited degree. It remains, to a large extent, a collection of regional economies, some of which are bound by closer links to a southern metropolis than to other parts of the country. This condition is easily demonstrated by figures on major provincial exports. . . . This regionally-differentiated economic structure with regionally-specific external links is a fundamental cause of many federal-provincial disputes in Canada. . . . Moreover, as provincial governments increasingly see resource exports as a primary basis for provincial development, the stakes can only become greater.[16]

What all this suggests is that for proposals for integration systems to be persuasive, the boundaries of the proposed systems have to be demonstrated to be viable in the sense that they contain stakes and resources that possess a capacity to produce sufficiently strong counter-incentives to match the assumed incentives from the international environment to continue segmented (systemic) integrations. These boundaries must also be stable in the sense that the capacity of those outside to penetrate and offer incentives with facility must not be greater or unrestricted.

Both of these prerequisites are more easily provided in a situation in which there exists a *pivotal state* within the proposed system: one which has the interests (development and maintenance of markets, protection of its own security through 'extended' boundaries) and the resources, which its domestic structure permits it to expend as a form of initial investment. The pivotal state will then have sufficient capacity to induce adherence to boundaries over time.

An alternative mechanism for drawing boundaries might be that in which two states with resources and interests for pivotal status exist, but whose resources are not substantially greater in the one case than in the other. But boundary-drawing is in this case likely to be enhanced and an accommodation reached if the two pivotal countries have an interest in excluding some third party, stronger than each of them, from penetration and domination of the particular geographical area.

What this leads up to is the following proposition, enunciated elsewhere somewhat more abstractly:[17] that for any proposed integrated system to have the stability characteristics alluded to above, the geographical area of which it is a part must, prior or concurrently, be agreed upon as a relatively stable diplomatic zone or "theatre," whose introduction of unwanted influences into the integration area is neither autonomatic nor unpredictable. The definition of a geopolitical space as a relatively stable diplomatic theatre is what in turn allows for the definition of that space or a circumscribed part of it as an autonomous—in the sense of substantially self-sustaining—integration area.

By a diplomatic zone or theatre, we mean (following Aron and Hoffmann) one in which certain norms of behaviour, underpinned by such incentives as the constituents of the zone have the resources to supply and exchange, are accepted in the definition and resolution of disputes.

The central characteristic of the Caribbean, however defined, is that there has as yet been no definition of any relevant space as a diplomatic zone, and thus no definition of indigenous diplomatic community. Hence, the fact, for example, that the basic terms of discussion among the members of the geographical area towards the resolution of disputes or problems arising within the area are incapable of being arrived at. The members of the geographical area are part of no consensus on what modes of behaviour are to apply, to whom they should apply, who has legitimate rights of entry or intervention in what are deemed to be local disputes, or what types of problems and disputes might be qualified as "local." These lacunae in the proper management of relations between independent states claiming some cultural affinity among themselves have been visible among the Commonwealth Caribbean countries at least since the period of assumption of national sovereignty (1962). The attempts of the Prime Ministers of Trinidad and Jamaica at resolution of the political problems of then British Guiana, and Dr. Williams' subsequent admission of failure in this regard; the failure of the attempts at indigenous resolution of the St. Kitts-Nevis-Anguilla dispute; still unexplained difficulties in the Trinidad position at the Santo Domingo Conference on the Law of the Sea; the legal and diplomatic confusion arising out of the bombing of the Air Cubana aircraft, bear adequate testimony to the problem here: the lack of basic norms for defining a relevant zone and for defining behaviour within it.

The problem is exacerbated because, if the geopolitical definition of the Caribbean is taken at its widest, there can already be said to exist a notion of diplomatic community (and therefore an international law underpinning it) pertaining to the South American countries, and to which the Spanish-speaking members of the archipelago and littoral might be said to subscribe. Such is the strength of this tradition, as Commonwealth Caribbean countries functioning within the Organization of American States have found, that the Commonwealth Caribbean countries might, as they become independent, be expected, through force of circumstances, to adhere to it. And this tendency might be strengthened if OAS norms, into which the United States has a substantial input, come to be increasingly defined as nonlegitimate.

It is this deficiency in the area of the definition of diplomatic theatre and community (we use this latter term while accepting Stanley Hoffman's strictures in relation to it) that in this writer's view is at the base of the current and continuing disputes among Caribbean leaders that have been brought to light by Dr. Williams' strictures on Jamaican behaviour in relation to Venezuela, and that country's "role" in the "Caribbean" defined by different people in different ways. The initiative of Trinidad and Tobago in attempting to foreclose the substantial discussion needed to remedy the basic deficiency, by successfully seeking to institutionalize the Caribbean archipelagic presence (the CDCC) within the Economic Commission for Latin America indicated a perception of, but can hardly resolve (for reasons to be discussed below) the problem. And what is referred to as the "reintegration" of Cuba into the area, can be seen as, through the resumption of diplomatic relations with her, only a minor part of the problem of defining the norms that should apply to all Caribbean countries falling within particular institutions.

This discussion takes us towards the proposition that the norms of behaviour applying to participation in economic or political integration processes are, then, only *an aspect* of the norms of diplomatic community agreed to for the particular area. For acceptance of norms for a particular diplomatic theatre suggests some prior consensus (or notions at a minimum) as to the relationship between that theatre and the remainder of the international environment, and as to modes of response to changes in that environment. Where, conversely, changes in the international environment are of such strength as to substantially affect this relationship, then the internal behaviour of the integration area will also be affected, and the consensus on modes of behaviour in that area will be distorted.

It is, to take an example, precisely because in recent years both the economic parameters of the North Atlantic system, of which the European Economic Community, have been subject to change; and the political parameters in terms of East-West security relations have also been amended, that distortions have arisen within the EEC which had the effect of halting the assumed automaticity of that system's processes.

Now it is then as the orthodox integration process attempts to move from its free-trade/customs union stage to the stage involving integration of basic sectors of production that the interconnection of economic and political processes becomes most evident. For this stage involves major decisions about the long-term orientation of basic structures of the *national* systems, and the elaboration of collective institutions to monitor the effects of implementation of such decisions. It is here that we move, in this writer's view, from processes that can perhaps be described as the "politics of regional integration" to processes of "political integration" defined as occurring, following Lindberg,

> when the linkage [between nations] consists of joint participation in regularised, ongoing decision-making. ... the essence of political integration is that governments begin to do together what they used to do individually; namely, they set up collective decision-making processes that in greater or lesser degree handle actions, engage in behaviours, and make allocations of goods and values that used to be done (or not done) autonomously by their governments or their agencies.[18]

And it is precisely the underpinning of prior agreed norms of general diplomatic behaviour for the prescribed area that permit the establishment of norms and institutions for collective decision-making, and modes of behaviour that allow for *systematic* "allocations of goods and values."

Regional political integration therefore which, from the point of view of the development of economic resources, necessarily accompanies the long-term, systematic integration of production systems among geographically contiguous countries, is an aspect of stable regional diplomatic arrangements; what might in a shorthand way be referred to as political regionalism. The architecture of an integration system therefore requires consideration of which units have the resources to participate in the definition of the diplomatic theatre that will allow for the functioning of the integration zone.

PREREQUISITES FOR THE CONSTRUCTION OF POLITICAL REGIONALISM

This issue has been raised in a variety of ways in the 1960s and 1970s, most vocally in the Prime Minister of Trinidad and Tobago's assertion of a Venezuelan "Threat to the Caribbean Community." Though it can be shown that there are a number of existing conceptions as to the status and role of the various Anglophone Caribbean countries in relation to the non-Anglophone ones and to the countries of the South American mainland.[19] In addition, persistent complaints by the larger independent Anglopone states about the remaining "metropolitan presence" in the Region, this referring to the states of the Windward and Leeward Islands, have suggested that whatever the merits of the ongoing economic integration process, no meaningful transformation of this process, such that it involves the harmonization of foreign policies, can as yet take place.

But most regional systems tend to be composed of States of unequal sizes and endowments, and even among the Commonwealth Caribbean countries these are marked. The disparities in this regard are even more substantial if one extends the area to include the mainland countries washed by the Caribbean Sea. Where such disparities exist, and there is a concern with economic and social development, the competition to attract developmental resources will be severe. This is well known to be the case in respect of Third World-metropolitan country relations. But as certain countries in regional areas come to acquire substantial resources (whether through windfall gains or otherwise), then they will naturally tend to be seen as being or having the potential for being pivotal states from whom resources might be derived.

A regional system is, of necessity, a competition-collaboration system. The same applies to an integration system. In such systems, especially where based on consensus, as distinct from domination arrangements, balance of power considerations continue to be present as part of the process of cooperation. The character of the balance of power relations, and the extent to which they introduce contention into the system, is a function of the nature of the "stakes" available to the constituent members of the system; and secondly, the relationship between those stakes and others available from interested parties outside of the proposed system. The relevant questions about the stakes of the system refer to (a) whether they are in scarce supply and therefore the objects of intense competition; (b) the extent of their capacity to produce additional resources in the future; (c) their 'value' in terms of their capacity to induce cooperation at particular, desired levels.[20]

In the Caribbean area, and more particularly, in terms of the verbalized contention between Trinidad and Venezuela on the definition of the area, answers to these questions are likely to indicate the pattern of subsequent arrangements. They must be analyzed in conjunction with what we have called the other elements of competition-coherence — the character of cultural relations, and the power of extra-region units to provide inputs which aid or constrain particular members of the region.

Insofar then, as one or other country of the geographically-defined region wishes to impose a particular diplomatic definition upon it, or part of it; and insofar as such a country wishes to proceed to circumscribe that defined area, or a part of that, as a political integration or unification area, then the first step in the process must take the following form: elaborate the stakes or resources which might be transformed into capabilities that induce cooperation. But the capacity of a country seeing itself as pivotal party because it possesses certain material resources is also to be determined by the character of its domestic structure. Significant elements of that domestic structure must perceive the geographic zone as capable of behaviour which is likely to positively affect the organization of that structure over time. Such elements must therefore perceive themselves to have an interest in a particular form of political coherence of that zone. This is the dialectic that will determine the character of future Commonwealth Caribbean political relations. And if our assumptions as to the nonviability of the insular model as currently practised should be correct, then the Commonwealth Caribbean area will be subject to extra-area penetration and attempts to exert influence therein. In that context the question of achieving greater political coherence will consistently reassert itself.

FOOTNOTES

[1] See particularly J. Mordecai, *The West Indies: The Federal Negotiations* (London: Allen & Unwin, 1968). The applicability of the theory of federation to the West Indies is well discussed in L. Bobb, "The Federal Principle in the British West Indies," *Social and Economic Studies,* vol. 15 (1966).

[2] See *Report of the Economic Commission Appointed to Examine Proposals For Association Within the Framework of a Unitary State of Grenada and Trinidad and Tobago* (Port of Spain, G.P.O., January 1965).

[3] See *Report of the Constitution Commission on the West Indies Associated States and Montserrat* (Chairman: Professor Telford Georges), June 1976, pp. 6-11.

[4] See S. Warnecke, "American Regional Integration Theories and the European Community," *Integration* no.1 (1971). See also V.A. Lewis, "The Evasion of Size: Regional Integration As an Avenue Towards Viability," paper presented at the IPSA Congress, Edinburgh, August 1976.

[5] F. Hirsch, "Is There a New International Economic Order?" *International Organization,* vol. 30, no. 3 (1976), pp. 521-32, at p.529.

[6] *Trinidad Guardian,* April 10, 1977.

[7] See W.O. Henderson, *The Zollverein, 2nd ed. (London: Frank Kass and Co., 1968).*

[8] I have considered some of these questions in V.A. Lewis, "Problems and Possibilities of Caribbean Community," *Social Studies Education,* vol. 2, no. 8 (October 1976), Proceedings of the Commonwealth Caribbean Social Studies Conference.

[9] See, in general, N. Girvan, and O. Jefferson, *Readings in the Political Economy of the Caribbean* (Jamaica: New World, 1971).

[10] The Government of Guyana was one of the main protagonists of the Grenada Declaration of 1971, proposing a sovereign unit encompassing the territories of the Eastern Caribbean.

[11] See E.B. Hass, "Turbulent Fields and the Theory of Regional Integration," *International Organization,* vol. 30, no. 2 (1976), pp. 173-212. For a discussion, see my IPSA paper referred to in *Social and Economic Studies* (forthcoming 1977).

[12] For a recent discussion see W. Axline, "Underdevelopment, Dependence, and Integration : the Politics of Regionalism in Third World," *International Organization,* vol. 31, no. 11 (1977), pp. 83-106.

[13] His main work here concerning Third World countries being *Dependence and Transformation* (Monthly Review Press, 1974).

[14] *Ibid.,* p. 276.

[15] See the Report of the Commission referred to at Note 3 and the Report of the Technical Sub-committee of the Commission, *The Political Economy of Independence for the Leeward and Windward Islands* (March 1975).

[16] J. Levy, and D. Munton, "Federal-Provincial dimensions of state-provincial relations," *International Perspectives* (March/April 1977), pp. 23-27 at p. 25.

[17] See my "The Evasion of Small Size. . ." *loc. cit.*

[18] L. Lindberg, "Political Integration as a Multidimensional Phenomenon Requiring Multivariate Measurement," in *Regional Integration,* eds. L Lindberg and S. A. Scheingold (Cambridge, Mass.: Harvard University Press, 1971), pp. 45 and 59.

[19] I discuss some of these in my "Problems and Possibilities of Caribbean Community," *loc. cit.*

[20] See for elaboration, my "The Evasion of Small Size. . ." *loc. cit.*

The LDCs in Integration Schemes: The CARICOM Experience

*George Goodwin and Yolande Lake**

INTRODUCTION

Movements at economic integration are featuring more and more prominently in the relations between the so-called "relatively less developed countries" of the globe. The records have shown, however, that the development of these relations has not been free of crisis periods. One such period of crisis that appears with a degree of regularity relates to the proportionate sharing of the benefits which should come with participation in integration movements. As is common, not all the participating countries are at comparable levels of development. There-fore, these crises can tend to assume the nature of a conflict situation between the countries at relatively lower levels of development *vis-à-vis* those at higher levels, the latter seemingly gaining disproportionately. In attempting to avoid or reduce these conflict situations, it has become standard practice for integration schemes to devise special mechanisms for ensuring that all participating countries share proportionately in the gains from integration.

This paper is an analysis of this problem in the experience of the economic integration movement of the Commonwealth Caribbean. This movement embraces twelve territories, eight of which have been officially designated as the Less Developed Countries or the LDCs.[1] We shall identify the special arrangements for this subgroup of countries, assess their performance, and then their relevance given the constraints on the economies of the subgroup. Before looking specifically at the experience

*The authors are on the staff of the Secretariat of the East Caribbean Common Market. The views expressed in the paper are those of the authors and not necessarily those of the Council of Ministers or the Secretariat.

of the Commonwealth Caribbean, we shall examine, albeit briefly, the theoretical foundations of the mechanisms for equalizing the distribution of benefits in integration groupings.

The exercise suffers from two sets of limitations, both relating to the unavailability of data. Firstly, as is known, countries such as these under review here do not produce statistical data of the quality and frequency that would be desirable to the serious researcher. Macroeconomic data are at best rudimentary indicators of the direction of the economies, and their use in this paper should be seen merely as such. We use the figures published by the United Nations Economic Commission for Latin America (ECLA) Caribbean Office, which in the opinion of the authors are the most reliable. Secondly, the latest available year for which comparable data is available is 1974. Finally, a great deal of the information available on the integration movement exists in documents that are classified as 'official' and thus cannot be quoted. In the last two cases, the authors have had to rely on their personal knowledge to supplement the lack of sources.

THE NOTION OF BENEFITS IN INTEGRATION THEORY

A. The Objectives of Integration Schemes

Havelock Brewster and Clive Thomas have argued that an organic interpretation of the theory of economic integration implies that the theory must be an integral element of a theory of economic and social transformation, and not simply an adjunct of the microeconomics of static location theory.[2] Raul Prebisch and the UN/ECLA group of economists have consistently advocated such an approach to integration.[3] The ECLA thesis as summarized by Aldo Dadone and Eugenio Di Marco, reads thus: "Economic integration should serve as an instrument of national development by helping *inter alia*, to settle the balance of payments deficit, overcoming difficulties arising from the size of national markets, raising productivity and the efficient use of regional resources, and serving as a strong stimulus for the incorporation of technical progress."[4]

Integration schemes come in different forms and their precise objectives vary according to the form which they each assume. It therefore means that the objectives as enumerated above are neither absolute nor all-embracing. In fact, economic integration schemes can range from loose cooperation arangements to a tightly knit group where several sectors of the national economies are integrated. As the level of integration increases upwards from loose cooperation agreements, the more objectives are encompassed.

The free trade area is considered as being among the lowest levels of integration since only the markets of the individual countries are integrated. The objectives here are limited to the creation of a single larger market and its attending benefits. At the other end of the scale is the economic community where the participating countries, in addition to integrating their markets, protect that market behind a common external tariff, free the movement of factors among themselves, and harmonize their economic, financial, and monetary policies. At this level, the objectives as stated in the UN/ECLA thesis might be expected to obtain.[5]

In economic groupings of underdeveloped countries the case has been made for the countries to seek the higher levels of integration. One view is that for such integration schemes to generate dynamic effects, they cannot afford to rest with the creation of an expanded market; instead, they must seek to break down other barriers to economic development.[6] This point of view is shared by Miguel Wionczek who states that the removal of these barriers to economic development cannot be left to the movement of free market forces; for, bearing in mind the disparate levels of development that exist among underdeveloped countries, the mere liberalizing of trade would only result in a centre-periphery type relationship.[7]

B. The Determinants of Benefits[8]

From the outset it must be recognized that participation in integration schemes implies both benefits and costs to the countries involved. The same factors which will determine the benefits to be received also determine the costs to be borne. Any discussion of the one has of necessity to include the other.

Each level of integration confers its own benefits and incurs its own costs. At the level of the free trade area the elimination of the obstacles to free trade will inevitably alter the patterns of trade that existed prior to the integration of the markets. The factors determining benefits and costs originate in this first step. They will be determined by the extent to which markets for the particular goods produced by each country expand, and protection affecting other products is reduced as a result of the removal of the trade barriers. In the customs union, where the market is protected by the common external tariff, other determinants are introduced. The relation between the pre-union tariffs of the individual countries and the new tariff will determine the relative possibilities for trade expansion. It would also have some influence on the costs of trade diversion.

At higher levels where the schemes become more *dirigiste* or policy-oriented, the policies themselves or lack thereof, are additional determinants. In a common market, the free movement of factors can have both desirable and undesirable effects depending upon the state of a particular economy. Similarly, in an economic community, common policies on fisal incentives, prices, and exchange rates might favour some countries more than others. The absence of such policies could very well produce the same result.

Two final sets of determinants can be mentioned. The first is where the countries integrate certain segments of their productive sectors; and secondly, where the group decides to establish common services. In the first instance, the creation of new industries or the expansion of existing plants produces benefits from the increased activity. At the same time these benefits have to be set against the higher costs of the products. In the second instance, the location of the common service headquarters could be seen as a benefit to the host country and its loss as a cost to the other partners.

The conclusion to be drawn at this point is that at successively higher levels of integration, where the schemes encompass a broader range of objectives, the factors giving rise to benefits are increased. Inversely, the costs of participating in such schemes increase proportionately.

C. The Nature and Distribution of Benefits

The experience of integration groupings where the integration process is limited to the removal of trade barriers suggests that benefits will not be distributed proportionately. The Secretariat of UNCTAD has observed that in such schemes the tendency has been for investments to concentrate in the more advanced countries or areas.[9] The polarization effect from such a situation produces benefits to the particular countries or areas that can become cumulative and self-reinforcing. The relatively higher level of development of the economic and social infrastructure and services which served to attract the investments in the first place can only develop further. So that, especially in the early stages of the integration process, additional investment and technical and entre-preneurial skills can be expected to gravitate towards this locale producing at the same time increased tax revenues.

On the other hand, the relatively less well-off countries would stand to lose from such a situation. Firstly, their industries might well cease to be competitive once protection is removed, and be forced to close. Secondly, the revenue from customs duties foregone because goods which were previously imported from outside of the area are now imported from within might be significant. (It must be remembered that revenue from customs duties contributes significantly to overall revenue in most underdeveloped countries.) In addition, to the extent that goods traded within the area are more expensive than similar goods from third country sources, those countries that are unable to take full advantage of the new trade opportunities could see a worsening of their balance-of-payments position and an increase in their cost of living.

In those schemes where a common protective policy is adopted, the benefit to be gained lies in the protection offered to existing and future operations. The level of protection is obviously of major importance. The weaker economies and fledgling industries would need a relatively higher level of protection. Where this differential is not included in the policy, or where the differential is not wide enough to reflect the different levels of economic development, then the stronger economies and more established plants would tend to gain more. Also, if the tendency towards polarization is not checked early enough, then the adverse effects on these economies mentioned earlier will be reinforced by the protective policy. In the specific case of the common external tariff, the rate structure, especially on capital goods, can be an additional source of benefits for some. If the rates of these goods are set at high levels, it could mean that those countries industrializing after the establishment of the scheme would be doing so at relatively higher costs.

In more *dirigiste* type integration schemes the task of identifying where benefits and costs may arise is more difficult. These schemes do acknowledge the need for the harmonization of economic policies and a greater degree of government intervention as a means of correcting the imbalances caused by trade liberalization.[10] In the final analysis, however, the particular policy instrument or the absence thereof, will determine the nature and distribution of benefits; and each has to be looked at in relation to the countries' economic characteristics and circumstances.[11]

D. Measures for Distributing Benefits Proportionately

Measures for distributing the benefits of integration proportionately form the basis of the special arrangements for the LDCs in integration schemes. There is no prescribed formula for combining an ideal package of special arrangements. Instead, the range of employed measures tend to be based more on experience and geared towards pragmatic solutions.[12] This is no doubt due to the fact that in many instances the maldistribution of benefits was not foreseen at the outset of the integration movement, or it became more pronounced as the movement progressed. In spite of this, it is possible to arrive at a classification scheme for the range of measures that can be employed.

Lizano in his study prepared for the UNCTAD Secretariat suggested the use of either of two classification schemes. The one used here

classifies the measures according to the effects they are designed to have
on the economies at which they are directed.[13] Thus, some measures may
be designed to expand the market of some member countries; others are
designed to improve the quantity and quality of production factors; and
yet others will simply be to permit the direct or indirect transfers of
income. Similarly, the measures may be designed to solve pressing short-
term problems, such as imbalances in the balance-of-payments position
and problems relating to public finance; and others may be designed to
bring about desired changes, such as increasing production capacity and
improving the competitive position of some countries by making
production factors and wider markets available to them.

The measures that can be taken by integration groupings to expand the
market of some of the member countries include:

— allowing these countries longer transitional periods for opening
  up their markets to intraregional trade while allowing them full
  access to the markets of their partners;
— where a common external tariff exists, these countries may be
  allowed a longer period for aligning their national tariffs with the
  common external tariff. This means that they can continue to
  import from third countries for a longer time;
— the grouping may give priority to the liberalization of trade in
  commodities of special export interest to these countries;
— the grouping may on the other hand exclude certain products
  from tariff cuts as a means of protection for the infant industries:
— finally, the criteria for goods to enjoy area-origin status may be
  less stringent for goods originating in these countries.

The net effect of these measures should be to give the recipient
countries a wider market and, at the same time, enable them to protect
their own domestic market. The scope of the measures would depend
first of all on the length of the grace periods; secondly, on the real
expansion of the market; and thirdly, on the availability of production
factors to enable them to fully exploit the expanded market.

The second category of measures, which are those designed to
improve the quantity and quality of productive factors, should have as
their net effect the opportunities for the recipient countries to expand
plants and/or establish new ones in order to take full advantage of the
new market. Some such measures are:

— allocating to these countries a disproportionately larger share of
  the foreign financing and technical assistance available to the
  area; and

— establishing development banks and other institutions for mobilizing finance capital which give priority to projects submitted by these countries.

The final category of measures basically constitute an admission that some countries will not obtain as large a share of benefits as some others. Therefore, mechanisms are employed for transferring income either directly on a government-to-government basis or indirectly through, for example, subsidized contributions to regional institutions or common services.

As stated above, there is no prescription for achieving a desirable distribution of benefits in integration schemes. For that matter, none of the above measures, or category of measures, is mutually exclusive for this purpose. The objective can best be achieved through a

> ... judicious combination of several policy instruments appropriate to the severity of the problems faced, the institutional particularities of the countries involved and the practical possibilities at the time such measures are taken.[14]

In summary, it can be said that economic integration schemes come in various forms and are desiged to achieve certain specific objectives. Whatever the form they take, they are seen as means of fostering the development process. At the same time a problem that seems to be endemic in all integration schemes is a real or perceived unequal distribution of the benefits which are expected to flow from the integration process. In the light of this problem most schemes have adopted certain special arrangements aimed at those members which stand to gain less as a result of their participation. The Caribbean Community and Common Market (CARICOM) is no different to other integration groupings. This problem has been ever-present. CARICOM has also adopted a series of special arrangements for the LDCs in the scheme. The balance of the paper will be given over to discussing the CARICOM experience against this theoretical background.

THE INTEGRATION MOVEMENT IN
THE COMMONWEALTH CARIBBEAN 1968

The history of the Commonwealth Caribbean[15] is fraught with attempts at integrating the scattered islands and the two mainland territories. The formation of the Caribbean Free Trade Association (CARIFTA) in 1968 had proved to be the most viable in the series of efforts and false starts. CARIFTA has since been superseded by a closer form of integration in the presence of CARICOM.

CARIFTA, as the name implies, was primarily a free trade area. With a few exceptions, there was the immediate removal of all barriers to trade in goods which met the qualifying criteria for area origin. The exceptions were a list of commodities falling under sixteen heads of the Standard International Trade Classification (original) (SITC 'O') scheme and which formed the substance of ANNEX 'B' of the Agreement establishing the Association.[16] This annex provides "special arrangements for the progressive elimination by Member Territories of import duty" (para. 5) on the products listed. Also included here were longer periods for the "less-developed Territories" to eliminate the import duties. It is instructive to note in this connection the existence of Article 39 *Promotion of Industrial Development in less-developed Territories* in the body of the Agreement. This Article sought to give protection to industries sited in the LDCs. In other words, from the earliest days of the integration movement, official recognition was given to the existence of a subgroup of LDCs and attempts were made to accord them special arrangements.

In July of 1968, shortly after the inception of CARIFTA, the LDCs, with the exception of Belize, came together to form the East Caribbean Common Market (ECCM). The primary consideration behind the formation of the ECCM can be said to be the recognition of the need at that time for the subgroup to enjoy a higher degree of integration among themselves; and secondly, to form a group which through acting jointly could take advantage of the concessions offered them in the wider grouping.

At the Seventh Heads of Governments of the Commonwealth Caribbean Conference at Chaguaramas, Trinidad, in October 1972, a decision was taken to

> Deepen and strengthen CARIFTA and to convert it into the Caribbean Common Market. At the same time, the decision was taken to create a Caribbean Community which would include, but not be limited to, the Caribbean Common Market.[17]

Pursuant to ths decision, the Treaty establishing the Caribbean Community was signed at Chaguaramas on July 4, 1973, among the four MDCs, and came into force on August 1, 1973. By August 1974, the LDCs had all acceded to the Treaty and CARICOM had fully superseded CARIFTA.

William Demas, the first Secretary-General of CARICOM, was to write afterwards that

CARIFTA would have to move on to a deeper form of economic integration in order to promote more effectively regional economic development and to give greater opportunities for the Less Developed Countries to benefit from economic integration.[18]

Accordingly, the scope of activites of the new integration arrangements was expanded to include other areas of cooperation. The activities of the Caribbean Community can now be divided into the following areas:

— Economic Integration through the Caribbean Common Market;
— Common Services and Functional Cooperation; and
— Coordination of Foreign Policy among the independent Member Countries.[19]

An improvement over the former arrangements is a defined set of mechanisms for conferring benefits on the LDCs.

THE SPECIAL ARRANGEMENTS FOR THE LDCs

The special arrangments for the LDCs in CARICOM are to be found within the provisions of the Treaty of Chaguaramas, in subsidiary instruments to the Treaty, and some exist outside the Treaty altogether. The Treaty provisions are crystallized in Chapter VII, *Special Regime for the Less Developed Countries,* of the Common Market Annex to the Treaty, and are intended to cover the main areas of activity of the Common Market. The measures which exist outside the ambit of the Treaty are included in the following at the appropriate times.

The classification scheme outlined previously (see *D* above) will be applied against the CARICOM measures. In the category of measures designed to expand the market, the CARICOM Treaty includes a longer phasing-in time into the common external tariff (Article 55); at the same time the LDCs are allowed to reserve a list of products from trade liberalization (Article 52); in order to protect their domestic markets these territories are allowed to impose restrictions against goods from the MDCs (Article 58); and lastly, the origin criteria for LDC goods to qualify for Common Market treatment are less stringent (Article 53). The foregoing measures apply only to manufactured goods. Marketing arrangements for agricultural products are to be found at Schedule VII to the Treaty, *Marketing Arrangements for Selected Agricultural Products,* and in the Guaranteed Market Scheme (GMS). The former constitutes an attempt to restrict imports into the Region of certain goods by ensuring that Regional Demand is satisfied from Regional

Supply before the imports are allowed in. The Schedule does not specifically mention any special provisions for the LDCs, but in the actual operation of the arrangements preference is supposed to be given to supplies from these territories. The GMS is specifically aimed at the LDCs, and provides for the MDCs to import specific quantities of six of the products included in Schedule VII.

In the second category of measures—those for improving the quantity and quality of the productive factors in the LDCs—the following exist in CARICOM: the LDCs can obtain temporary protection for their industries by closing off their markets to competing MDC products (Article 56); they are allowed to give more generous incentives to industry (Article 54); the MDCs "agree to co-operate" in encouraging investment and loan capital into the LDCs, negotiate double taxation agreements in respect of income earned from these investments, and the Member States agreed to establish an "appropriate investment institution" to promote the development of industries in the LDCs (Article 59). In accordance with the final provisions of article 59, the Caribbean Investment Corporation (CIC) was established in 1973 with both public and private funds. The essential role of the Corporation is the promotion of industrial development, including agro-based industries, in the LDCs.[20] In addition, the MDCs undertake to make their technological and research facilities available to the LDCs (Article 60). There is one measure dealing with agriculture which is not contained in the Special Regime. Article 49, *Rationalisation of Agricultural Production,* in the Common Market Annex states that as a general principle, the rationalization scheme is to provide "special opportunities for the development of agriculture in the Less Developed Countries" (paragraph 1). The Article further states at paragraph 2.(g) that one of the specific objectives of the scheme is

the provision of greater opportunities to the Less Developed Countries for the expansion of agricultural production for export to markets within and outside the Common Market.

The final measure in this category is the Caribbean Development Bank (CDB). The Bank was established in 1969 with all the countries of the Commonwealth Caribbean being among its membership.[21] Although it was established outside of the formal integration arrangements, the Agreement establishing the Bank states specifically that one of the objectives is "promoting economic co-operation and integration having special and urgent regard for the needs of the less developed countries of the region."[22]

Of the third and final category of measures, those which transfer income, only one of the CARICOM measures can be said to be of the direct government-to-government type. In 1976, the four MDCs agreed to the establishment of a fund for Emergency Programme Assistance to the LDCs to assist them with their budgetary difficulties.[23] All the other measures are of the indirect type and consist of subsidized contributions to the institutions and common services of the integration grouping.

THE EXPERIENCE OF THE LDCs
OVER THE INTEGRATION PERIOD

It seems more relevant to the exercise to attempt to determine the effects of the special arrangements for the LDCs by looking at their peformance over the integration period and by assessing their present relative position within the integration movement. This method of analysis also provides a necessary introduction to the final chapter where the relevance of the CARICOM arrangements to the LDCs is examined.

The structural characteristics of all the economies of the Member Countries of CARICOM are as a result of their historical development in a context of imperial and colonial domination. These countries were made adjuncts of the metropolitan countries with economic activity centering around a single crop which was produced within a framework of protection and preference arrangements. The most highly developed sectors were the export agriculture subsector and the service sector directly connected to export agriculture. Whatever manufacturing activities developed were cottage-type operations geared to domestic import substitution. Domestic agriculture remained in a state of underdevelopment while the countries continued to import larger and larger quantities of food to satisfy the growing domestic demand.

By the beginning of the sixties, the MDCs, Jamaica and Trinidad and Tobago in particular, were already taking positive steps to diversify their economies. The mineral deposits in the presence of bauxite in Guyana and Jamaica and petroleum in Trinidad and Tobago were already attracting inflows of investment capital some of which were able to penetrate the rest of the economy. Also, through the policy of "industrialization by invitation" they were able to attract some manufacturing activity. Initially, the manufacturing sector was aimed at domestic import-substitution. It was not long, however, before they began to make in-roads into the markets of the LDCs. By the mid-sixties, imports into the LDCs from the MDCs had doubled over an eight-year period, and a significant portion of the increase was in the form of manufactured goods especially from Jamaica and Trinidad and Tobago.[24]

During this same period the majority of the LDCs continued to exist with their monoculture still intact, but declining. In some of the territories, Antigua, Grenada, and St. Lucia in particular, tourism as a dynamic form of economic activity was appearing and was given active support by the respective governments. Whatever manufacturing activity had appeared was still the cottage-type operation.

In 1968 when the free trade area was formed, therefore, the MDCs had already achieved a comparative advantage in manufacturing. The industries that had been erected to satisfy local demand were in many cases able to expand production and thus seize the opportunities offered by the creation of CARIFTA. The UN/ECLA was thus able to conclude in its 1973 assessment of the impact of CARIFTA that the manufacturing sector had indeed expanded, but

> In looking at these increases, however, one must bear in mind the fact that the less developed countries of CARIFTA account for less than 2 per cent of the area's manufacturing GDP. Inevitably, the initial response of manufacturing to the consolidated CARIFTA market was to expand output by the utilization of excess capacity.[25]

There is evidence that here has been some flow of investment into the manufacturing sector in the LDCs. The sources of these investments have been extraregional, regional and domestic. It is not possible to arrive at the quantum of either the total inflow or to identify the recipient activity. It does seem, however, that domestic and regional investment are to be found mainly in such activities as garment manufacturing and foreign investment into assembly operations. It would also seem that up until 1975 manufacturing had not had any significant impact on the overall economic activity of the territories. All that the UN/ECLA could find to say in its survey of the economies for that year is that "Economic Activity in the manufacturing sector remained at a low level during 1975."[26] The following indicators bear out this observation:

TABLE I
ESTIMATED CONTRIBUTION OF MANUFACTURING TO G.D.P.

(EC $ mill)

	1968	% of Total	1974	% of Total	Growth Rate % 1968/74
LDCs	9.3	4.2	19.8[1]	4.3	112.9
MDCs	445.4	15.4	1438.7[1]	14.7	223.0

[1]Includes authors' estimates.
Source: See Table II in Statistical Appendix.

The agricultural sector has always been more problematic, and, probably because of this, the most neglected sector. The export subsector producing bananas, sugar, and spices for the metropolitan markets had developed alongside a stagnating domestic subsector which is supposed to produce food for domestic and regional consumption. The Report of the Tripartite Economic Survey of the Eastern Caribbean (January–April 1966) concluded that while possibilities for growth existed for some of the export crops, "taken as a whole these will not generate the necessary rate of growth in the economy." The Report then continues:

> It is impossible to exaggerate the importance of a determined intelligent attack on the development of the long neglected foodcrop and livestock sector.[27]

The CARIFTA arrangements were unable to get the LDCs to make this "determined and intelligent attack" on the development of the domestic subsector. In 1972, four years after the establishment of the Association, the Regional Secretariat bemoaned that

> . . . the domestic agricultural sector . . . is in poor shape in all the CARIFTA countries and this is manifested in the large and growing volume of imports of food for domestic as well as for tourist consumption.[28]

The situation in the agricultural sector is now not as bleak as it was in the early seventies. National governments faced with steeply rising food imports have had to pay more attention to the food producing subsector. There is evidence that, at least in some crops, the production of the LDCs as a subgroup has increased to a level where there are now exports both to regional and extraregional markets. In spite of the fact that

TABLE II
ESTIMATED CONTRIBUTION OF AGRICULTURE TO G.D.P

(EC $ mill)

	1968	% of Total	1974	% of Total	Growth Rate % 1968/74
LDCs	59.5	26.9	92.5[1]	20.1	55.5
MDCs	325.5	11.2	842.2[1]	8.6	158.7

[1]Includes authors' estimates.
Source: See Table II in Statistical Appendix.

there may be cause for cautious optimism in some areas, the overall performance of the sector is still far less than could be desired. The dual nature of its organization still remains; production is still not properly organized, so that periods of gluts and scarcity are still common and the existing marketing arrangements seem incapable of ensuring a steady trade in agricultural commodities within the CARICOM area.

The lack of dynamism in the productive sectors is manifested in the pattern and composition of the trade of these territories. In 1967, the subgroup exported a total of EC$51.6 million. Of this total, EC$36.2 million went to the United Kingdom and was comprised mainly of bananas and sugar. Exports to other Commonwealth Caribbean territories totalled EC $7.3 million or was equal to 14.2 percent of total exports. The composition of the trade with their Caribbean partners was, with the exception of one single large item, petroleum products from Antigua, overwhelmingly agricultural products. In this year the estimated trade balance between the LDCs as a group and the MDCs was a negative balance of EC$2 million in favour of the MDCs.[29]

Over the integration period there has been some change in both pattern and composition of trade. The increases in production recorded in the productive sectors have registered themselves in the trade figures also. In 1970, total domestic exports had increased to EC$66.8 million. At this time the share of agriculture and food items was approximately 57 percent and manufactures accounted for 0.9 percent. By 1974 when total domestic exports were EC$163.9 million, 32 percent was taken up by agriculture and food and manufactures had increased to 3.7 percent.[30]

Some shifts were also recorded in the direction of trade over this period. Between 1970 and 1974, the MDCs were the only traditional partners to record a positive growth in their exports into the subgroup. Of total imports of EC$266.1 million, EC$46.6 million or 17.5 percent came from the MDCs, and in 1974 of a total of EC$418.9 million the corresponding figures for the MDCs were EC$73.5 million and 17.6 percent. Comparative percentage figures for the other traditional trading partners are: for the United States and Canada combined 25.8 and 21.5 percent respectively, and for the United Kingdom and other European Economic Community countries combined, it was 39.6 and 29.6 percent respectively.[31] The following figures summarize the picture in tabular form:

TABLE III
PATTERN OF LDC IMPORTS 1970 AND 1974

(EC $ mill)

Imports from	1970	1974	Growth Rate % 1970-74
Other LDCs	1,970	8,153	313.9
MDCs	46,619	73,484	57.6
Canada & USA	68,755	90,224[1]	31.2
EEC Countries	105,245	124,146[1]	19.1
Rest of the World	43,536	122,860	182.2
TOTAL IMPORTS	266,125	418,867	57.4

[1]Includes authors' estimates.
Source: ECCM Digest of External Trade Statistics 1976—Table 4.1

Although not directly related to the integration experience, some mention has to be made of the contribution of tourism to the economies of the LDCs. In the absence of any other form of vibrant economic activity, it is this sector that has shown the greatest potential for growth.

By the mid-sixties tourism was already developing as a significant contributor to the overall economic activity of the LDCs. By the early seventies it had become the most dynamic sector, stimulating the growth of such other sectors as construction and services. It had also become a major earner of foreign exchange. The tourist industry has been suffering since the international economic crisis of 1973-74, but in spite of virtual stagnation it is still significant to economic activity.

TABLE IV
ESTIMATED CONTRIBUTION OF TOURISM TO G.D.P.

(EC $ mill)

1968	% of Total	1974	% of Total	Growth Rate % 1968/74
10.4	4.7	20.0[1]	4.4	92.3

[1]Includes authors' estimates
Source: See Table II in Statistical Appendix

Notwithstanding the importance of tourism to the economies in terms of overall activity, the full benefits are lost, both to the individual economies and to the Region. The sector is dominated by foreign ownership and control; the hotels operate behind a wall of incentives and concessions; in general they operate as enclaves importing practically all of their requirements and thus exporting most of the income. The weak linkages between this sector and the productive sectors mean that even though the economies may gain through dollar receipts, leakage reduces the net gain and consequently worsens the external position of the economies. Finally, the individual governments undertake a large amount of the promotion for the industry, and when this is coupled with the amounts spent on providing infrastructure and services at the expense of other sectors of the national economies, the net gains are reduced further.

Finally, it might be instructive to look briefly at the performance of the public sector alongside these other developments. The government sector is the single largest contributor to overall economic activity.

This should not appear strange when it is realized that each of the individual LDCs has to maintain its own public service, plus provide a given level of services for its population, as well as develop its infrastructure. Also to be taken into consideration is the fact that in the absence of adequate and sufficient levels of investment, governments, for reasons that are not always economic, feel bound to generate a certain amount of activity. All of these things have only served to increase the spending of these governments and at a rate that they can ill afford.

During the period of classical colonialism, the individual territories could look to the United Kingdom to make up the short-falls on recurrent revenue and still provide funds for capital projects. Since 1969, however, budgetary assistance has been on the decline. This has come at a time of rising costs and rising expectations on the part of the populations. Thus, whereas in that year the governments were able to meet their recurrent expenditure of EC$69.9 million from their own resources, [32] in 1975 when expenditure was estimated to be EC$156 million, revenue from domestic sources was estimated as being EC$136 million thereby producing a deficit of EC$20 million. In the absence of increased budgetary assistance, and since the monetary arrangements of the territories do not permit them to print more money at will, the short-fall had to be met through increased government borrowing. It also means that these governments are not left with very much for capital projects such as development of infrastructure.

What the foregoing really shows is that the economies of the LDCs have hardly been transformed, and although there has been modest overall growth, the contribution of the productive sectors has not been significant.

When their record is set alongside that of their MDC partners over the same period, their relative significance to CARICOM as a group appears negligible. The crucial question of why this is so after over eight years of economic integration begs an answer. The next section attempts such an answer.

THE RELEVANCE OF THE CARICOM ARRANGEMENTS TO THE LDCs

It should be evident from the preceding section that the greatest constraint on the economies of the LDCs is their structural organization. The comparable levels of development reached at the inception of the integration movement meant that the MDCs were already in a position to exploit the new arrangements. In the absence of effective measures to reverse these divergencies, the polarization effects could be only reinforced.

The mechanisms for expanding the market available to the LDCs— those relating to the common external tariff, the less stringent rules of origin, aid to exporters, the freedom to impose quantitative restrictions, etc.,—although theoretically very correct could not be expected to achieve much. Marketing arrangements are basically supportive in nature. They presuppose that a level of production already exists with the capability for satisfying demand. They may further act as stimuli to production. When the level of production does not exist and the sectors are not organized to react to the stimuli, the marketing arrangements are fundamentally academic. These were the problems facing the LDCs in their agricultural as well as their industrial sectors. What was, therefore, urgently needed in the integration arrangements were measures capable of transforming the productive sectors of the LDCs which would have enabled them to seize the new opportunities.

The measures that were designed to achieve this transformation are all dependent upon the forces of the market place. The two principal measures are the Caribbean Development Bank and the Caribbean Investment Corporation. There can be no doubt that since the CDB started active operations in 1970 that the bulk of its funds has gone to support projects in the LDCs. The total amount disbursed as of December 31, 1976, was US$50.7 million.[34] Our estimate, which is based on the breakdown offered by the Bank, is that approximately US$30 million went toward projects in these territories. It is important to note here that it was only after 1974 that the disbursements of loans exceeded approvals by over 20 percent.

To realistically evaluate the performance of the Bank the figures must be disaggregated on a sectoral basis. An examination of the CDB's Annual Report for 1976 suggests the following breakdown:

LOAN APPROVALS TO ECCM STATES 1970-1976

	(US$)
Industry (including industrial estates)	6, 818,296
Agriculture (including agricultural infrastructure, meat packing and marketing facilities)	10,451,508
Hotels	1,722,433
Infrastructure and Services (including Student Loans)	24,177,793
Estimated Total Approvals	43,170,030

Using the percentage of cumulative disbursements to approvals which at 1976 was 45.6%, it means that actual disbursements were no more than US$20 million with approximately one-half going towards the productive sectors.

The figures are quite revealing. They reveal, first of all, that governments are the single largest borrowers; and that secondly, they are borrowing for projects that are in themselves nonproductive. That is not to say the infrastructure projects are not necessary. At that level of development in the LDCs they were and probably still are so. It must be remembered, however, that infrastructure is developed to service the other sectors, it is not a substitute. The reasons behind this pattern of loans undoubtedly lie in the nature of the institution—its operations are prescribed by its very nomenclature. As a bank, it is obliged to conform to certain standard banking procedures with respect to dispensing its money. The procedures for approving and disbursing funds, the terms and conditions of its loans are not tailored to suit its borrowers, but merely reflect the terms and conditions under which the Bank raises its capital for financing the projects submitted to it.

The CDB has now set its minimum loan at US$100,000 up from US$50,000 where it had stood until 1975. Until this time also, the Bank had required that private sector borrowers cover their loans by security valued at not less than twice the amount. They are apparently now prepared to be more flexible with respect to loans for agricultural and tourism projects.[35] The borrower's contribution to projects is now 60 percent of projects costing up to US$375,000 and 40 percent for projects above this amount.

The interest rates on ordinary operations are as follows:

	(old)	(current)
Government Financial intermediaries	7.25%	7.5%
Government (Infrastructural and Public Utilities)	8.00	8.5
Industry and Hotels	9.00	10.0
Agriculture	8.00	9.0

The paper has gone into some detail on the CDB for a reason. The CDB represents the principal institution for mobilizing financial resources into the LDCs. But the weight of the procedures and the terms and conditions under which loans are dispensed effectively precludes the typical LDC borrower, that is, the small entrepreneur whose prime need is for risk capital. The Government Financial Intermediaries, through which the Bank channels its small loans, hardly ease the situation. When dispensing CDB's money their procedures and terms and conditions are basically no less stringent.

The other institution for mobilizing finance capital has had a shorter history. The CIC only started disbursing funds in 1974. At the end of the 1975 fiscal year, the cumulative total for approved investments was EC$1,292,040 of which it had already disbursed EC$549,000 and had committed EC$622,000.[36]

The distribution of these investments was as follows:

Industry	8 projects	EC$ 681,040
Agro-Industry	3 projects	456,000
Tourism	2 projects	155,000
Total 13 projects		EC$1,292,040
Average size of investment		EC$ 99,388

It would not be entirely fair to the Corporation to critically evaluate its performance in the short span of time that it has been operating. What can be said is that the CIC ideally should bridge the gap between the small entrepreneur needing risk capital and the CDB. Since its establishment, however, the resources which would enable it to properly function in this role were not made available. Two statements from the two annual reports are instructive. The 1974 Report states:

> It is now apparent that the architects of the CIC grossly under-estimated the needs of the LDCs for equity capital. Apart from the CIC, there is virtually no other source of risk capital available to the LDCs.[37]

The 1975 Report continues in the same vein:

> ... the Corporation came to the realization at a very early date that based on the formula laid down in its Charter for the call-up of its Share capital, its rate of investment approvals, disbursements and the volume and quantum of applications pending, its available resources would be insufficient to enable it to function effectively.[38]

Thus, even with the best of good intentions, the CIC could not have had the desired impact on the economies of the LDCs.

Of the other measures that are designed to improve the quantity and quality of the productive factors, the undertaking in Article 59 by the MDCs to assist the flow of both investment and loan capital into the LDCs is similar in intent to the CDB and the CIC. The underlying wisdom seemed to have been that the MDCs encourage members of their private sectors to invest in the LDCs. In practice this could not have been very successful. There is no surplus of investible capital in the MDCs, except perhaps in Trinidad and Tobago. In fact, it is known that the MDCs are themselves trying just as hard as the LDCs to mobilize their domestic capital. Secondly, even if there were this surplus, the currency and foreign exchange regulations being enforced in these territories would have militated against its success. Without a CARICOM policy on currency and foreign exchange regulations, there will always be a hesitancy to encourage such investments for fear that they are used as means for circumventing the stricter regulations. The Harmonization of Fiscal Incentives to Industry Scheme is another of the CARICOM measures that is undoubtedly very sound theoretically. As it applies to the LDCs, however, its success was bound to be limited. The Scheme offers a single element in the whole range of elements making for a choice of location to establish an industry. The other elements which give the MDCs a comparative advantage in this respect—size of the domestic market, the relatively more developed social and economic infrastructure among them—most definitely seemed to have outweighed the differentials in the Scheme. The same conclusion can be applied to the MDC—LDC Double Taxation Arrangements. As an incentive for MDC entrepreneurs to invest in the LDCs it is certainly not enough when all other considerations are included.

All the other measures in this category are dependent upon the success of the others above. Once the measures for encouraging the establishment of industries perform, then the protection being offered becomes functional. The same reasoning can be applied against the use of research and technological facilities. The measure can only be activated when there is the objective need to use the facilities, and this in turn will come when the industries are established.

The success of the agricultural measures is more dismal. Serious efforts at rationalizing the Region's agricultural production are yet to be made. The establishment of the Caribbean Food Corporation (CFC) in the context of a Regional Food Plan is the closest the Region has come to seriously tackling the problem of developing the food producing subsector. According to the original proposal, the CFC would produce, process, and market foodstuffs. The Corporation is to be a jointly-owned, commercial enterprise which will concentrate in the short-term on those food items with the highest import content—milk, fish, animal feed, and fertilizers.[39] It would not be fair to pronounce on this venture at this time.

The measures designed to transfer income from the MDCs to the LDCs have all worked with a high degree of success. The amount transferred under the Fund for Emergency Programme Assistance in 1976 was in the order of EC$10 million. This has been able to maintain such common services as the university and the shipping service which the LDCs enjoy at subsidized costs. Their contributions to the Regional Institutions are also subsidized.

The lack of success of the measures, other than the last set, is to be found in the contradiction between the nature of the measures and the nature of the integration scheme. It was recognized quite early in the integration movement that given the economic characteristics of its membership, the integration arrangements had to be strengthened. The movement therefore moved away from the *laissez-faire* arrangements of the free trade area and into a more *dirigiste* form of integration, but the special arrangements for the LDCs still remained essentially *laissez-faire* in nature.

The level of development which existed in the LDCs at the inception of the integration movement, coupled with the constraints of the lack of financial and human resources, effectively meant that a development bank and an investment corporation passively waiting for projects to be submitted to them could not be expected to achieve much. What was, and still is, needed is an industrialization policy which would guarantee the LDCs some minimum level of investment without them having to compete on the open market for the limited investment opportunities. It is instructive to note that Article 46 of the Common Market Annex makes provision for such a policy. A necessary complement to such a policy would be one relating to foreign investment and the transfer of Technology. Only in these circumstances would the CDB, the CIC, and the Harmonization Scheme produce the benefits they are designed to confer.

As far as agriculture is concerned, it is unfortunate, to say the least, that in place of a policy for rationalizing the agricultural production in the Region, a corporation to operate along commercial lines is substituted. It does not matter that the corporation is owned by Regional Governments. What was, and still is, needed is a comprehensive rationalization policy which, among other things, would remove the competition between the farmers in the MDCs and the farmers in the LDCs; would make financing available at rates and conditions that the individual small farmers in the LDCs, who produce the bulk of the produce, can afford; and would integrate the system of production into the system of marketing.

Another notable omission from the arrangements is a policy on tourism. Given the emphasis that is put on tourism by some CARICOM Member Governments, both MDC and LDC, Article 50 of the Common Market Annex which simply states that the Member States " agree to collaborate in the promotion and development" *et cetera* of the industry, is shallow. In the meantime the Member States individually expend scarce hard currency promoting their individual markets, each competing against the other for the same body of tourists.

Finally, the realities of CARICOM make it clear that the LDCs' trade balance will always be in a deficit position *vis-à-vis* their MDC partners. A compensatory mechanism addressed to what would seem to be a permanent imbalance would very likley go a long way to minimize tension between the two subgroups.

What all of this means is that, given the special characteristics of the economies of the LDCs, their participation in a scheme that is policy-oriented without special arrangements that are similarly policy-oriented, the only result would be a polarization pattern that works against them.

If from the beginning of the integration movement these types of measures were devised with suitable mechanisms for ensuring their effective functioning, it is more than likely that they would have provided the LDCs' economies with tougher insulation against the international economic crises of the post-1973 era. In the absence of proper measures, these economies had to bear the full force of the shocks with the result that their position only deteriorated further, thus making their relative position in CARICOM worse than it would normally have been.

CONCLUSION

Economic integration, it must be remembered, is an attempt at a political solution to economic problems. The effectiveness of the integration arrangements and the effectiveness of their functioning will, in the final resort, rest upon the political development and cohesiveness of the grouping. The political element becomes all the more important when the integration scheme is heavily policy-oriented.

The types of policies that we claim are absent in the CARICOM arrangements are neither new nor revolutionary. In fact some already exist, albeit in vague terms, in the CARICOM Treaty. They can only be successfully implemented, however, when the member states of CARICOM cease to see each other as competitors for the limited resources. What, therefore, is needed most in CARICOM is a set of policy instruments that meaningfully distributes resources, and not the set of measures that regulates competition as is now the case. Only then can the LDCs expect an effective package of special arrangements. In the final analysis, the political dynamics will still be the deciding factor.

STATISTICAL APPENDIX
TABLE I

AREA AND POPULATION OF CARICOM REGION 1970 AND 1974
(Showing percentage growth rate)

| CARICOM Region | Area | Population | | Growth Rate % | Av. Annual Growth Rate |
	sq. mi.	1970[1]	1974	1970-1974	% 1970-74
Antigua/Barbuda	170.0	65,525	69,750[2]	6.45	1.61
Dominica	289.5	70,513	76,188[2]	8.05	2.01
Grenada	120.0	93,858	104,177[2]	10.99	2.75
Montserrat	37.5	11,698	12,981[2]	10.97	2.74
St. Kitts-Nevis-Anguila	104.0	45,608	47,400[2]	3.93	0.93
St. Lucia	238.0	100,893	109,000[2]	8.04	2.01
St. Vincent	150.0	87,305	97,500[2]	11.68	2.92
ECCM	1,109.0	475,398	517,896	8.94	2.24
Belize	8,866.0	120,936	132,456	9.53	2.38
LDCs	9,975.0	596,334	650,352	9.06	2.27
Barbados	166.0	237,701	264,000[3]	11.06	2.77
Guyana	83,000.0	701,885	833,000[3]	18.68	4.67
Jamaica	4,411.0	1,848,512	2,162,00[3]	16.96	4.24
Trinidad/Tobago	1,980.0	940,719	1,143,000[3]	21.50	5.38
MDCs	89,557.0	3,728,817	4,402,000[3]	18.05	4.51
CARICOM	99,532.0	4,325,151	5,052,352	16.81	4.20

[1] 1970 Census
[2] Mid-year Estimates
[3] Rounded to the nearest thousand
Source:
1. 1970 Population Census of the Commonwealth Caribbean
2. Digests of ECCM Statistical Offices
3. East Caribbean Common Market Secretariat—Annual Digest of Statistics 1974 (LDC Countries)
4. Latin American Development and the International Economic Situation—Second Regional Appraisal of the International Development Strategy—Part three—Indicators of Economic and Social Development in Latin America. (MDC Countries).

TABLE II
ESTIMATED G.D.P. AT FACTOR COST OF CARICOM COUNTRIES
1968 AND 1974
AND PER CAPITA G.D.P. 1970 AND 1974
(Showing contributions of productive sectors)

(E.C. $ Million)

| | | | | | Growth Rate % | |
	LDCs[1] 1968	LDCs[1] 1974	MDCs 1968	MDCs 1974	LDCs 1968/74	MDCs 1968/74
Total G.D.P.	221.1	460.1	2902.3	9775.7	108.0	236.8
Agriculture	59.5	92.4[2]	325.5	842.2[2]	55.5	158.7
% of total	26.9	20.1	11.2	8.6		
Mining/Quarrying			517.9	1764.4		240.7
% of total			17.8	18.1		
Manufacturing	9.3	19.8[2]	445.4	1438.7[2]	112.9	223.0
% of total	4.2	4.3	15.4	14.7		
Construction	26.1	49.6[2]	209.9	819.5	90.0	290.4
% of total	11.8	10.8	7.2	8.4		
Distribution	30.1	87.7[2]	467.6	1490.6	191.4	296.7
% of total	13.6	19.1	16.4	15.3		
Transport	10.4		101.9	401.9[2]		294.4
% of total	4.7		3.5	4.1		
Government	39.2	87.0	313.6	1145.4	121.9	265.2
% of total	17.7	18.9	10.8	11.7		
Services	30.0		302.6	1138.8[2]		276.3
% of total	13.6		10.4	11.7		
Hotels	(10.4)	(20.0)[2]			(92.3)[2]	
% of total	4.7	4.4				
Others	16.6	123.4[3]	208.9	733.7[2]	357.4[4]	251.2
% of total	7.5	26.8	7.2	7.5		
	1970	1974	1970	1974	1970/74	1970/74
Per Capita G.D.P.	656.5	888.4	1329.1	2220.7	35.3	67.1

[1]Data excludes Belize
[2]Includes authors' estimates
[3]Included in others
[4]Includes Transport
Sources:
1. Economic survey of Latin America 1970 and 1973.
2. CARIFTA Countries overview of Economic Activity 1972 (ECLA).
3. Economic Activity 1975—Caribbean Community Countries (ECLA POS 76/6).

TABLE III
PATTERN OF TRADE OF THE ECCM MEMBER STATES 1970-74
(Showing percentage growth rate)

(E.C. $'000)

	1970	1971	1972	1973	1974	Growth Rate % 1970-74
Imports						
Intra ECCM	1,970	1,634	4,794	2,947	8,153	313.86
Rest of CARICOM	46,619	53,063	54,201	57,827	73,484	57.63
Rest of World	217,536	255,218	254,245	269,056	337,229	55.02
Total	266,125	309,915	313,240	329,830	418,866	57.39
Exports						
Intra ECCM	3,519	4,897	7,339	5,796	11,131	216.31
Rest of CARICOM	6,253	6,016	7,453	13,058	15,890	154.12
Rest of World	65,920	70,312	78,081	118,461	153,315	132.58
Total	75,692	81,225	92,873	137,315	180,336	138.25
Balance of Trade						
Intra ECCM	+1,549	+3,263	+2,545	+2,849	+2,978	92.25
Rest of CARICOM	−40,366	−47,047	−46,748	−44,769	−57,594	42.68
Rest of World	−151,616	−184,906	−176,164	−150,595	−183,914	21.30
Total	−190,163	−228,690	−220,367	−192,515	−238,530	25.43

This Table represents the total trade pattern of the ECCM States, broken down to show:
(a) Trade among ECCM Member States;
(b) Trade between ECCM States and the Rest of CARICOM; and
(c) Trade between ECCM States and Rest of World.
Source: ECCM Digest of External Trade Statistics—1976.

FOOTNOTES

[1] The LDCs are Antigua and Barbuda, Belize, Dominica, Grenada, Montserrat, St. Kitts-Nevis-Anguilla, St. Lucia, and St. Vincent. The More Developed Countries (MDCs) are Barbados, Guyana, Jamaica, and Trinidad and Tobago, cf Article 3 of the Treaty establishing the Caribbean Community, Chaguaramas, July 4, 1973. In this paper, however, because of the unavailability of sufficient data, Belize is *not* included in the analysis.

[2] Havelock Brewster and Clive Y. Thomas, "Aspects of the Theory of Economic Integration," *Journal of Common Market Studies,* vol. 8 (1969-70), p. 113.

[3] S. Miguel Wionczek, "Introduction: Requisites for Viable Integration," in *Latin American Economic Integration—Experiences and Prospects,* ed. S. Miguel Wionczek, (New York: Praeger, 1966), p. 3.

[4] Dadone Aldo Antonio and Luis Eugenio Di Marco, "The Impact of Prebisch's Ideas on Modern Economic Analysis," in *International Economics and Development—Essays in Honour of Raul Prebisch,* ed. Luis Eugenio D. Marco (New York: Academic Press, 1972), pp. 27-28.

[5] For the various stages of the integration process and a simple characterization of each stage, cf Caribbean Community Secretariat's *The Caribbean Community—a Guide* (Georgetown, Caribbean Community Secretariat, 1973), Chap. 5.

[6] Ya-min Chou, "Economic Integration in Less Developed Countries, The Case of Small Countries," *Journal of Development Studies,* vol. 3 (July 1967), p. 255.

[7] Miguel Wionczek, *op. cit.,* p. 8.

[8] This section is heavily indebted to two Reports released by the Secretariat of the United Nations Conference on Trade and Development (UNCTAD). *The distribution of Costs and Benefits on Integration Among Developing Countries.* Report of the Group of Experts, Geneva, July 1972. (TD/B/413) and *Trade Expansion and Economic Integration Among Developing Countries.* Report by the Secretariat. (TD/B/385/Rev. 1 New York, 1967).

[9] UNCTAD. *Trade Expansion and Economic Integration Among Developing Countries. op cit.* p. 20.

[10] Andrew W. Axline and Lynn K. Mytelka, "Dependence and Regional Integration. A Comparison of the Andean Group and CARICOM," paper presented at the annual meeting of the International Studies Association, Toronto, February 28-29, 1976, p. 6.

[1] Eduardo Lizano, "The Distribution of Costs and Benefits in Economic Integration Among Developing Countries," study prepared at the request of the UNCTAD Secretariat. (TAD/EI/CBI/1 22 June, 1972) p. 24.

[12] UNCTAD. *Trade Expansion and Economic Integration Among Developing Countries, op cit.,* p. 23.

[13] Eduardo Lizano, *op. cit.,* p. 24. The balance of this section draws heavily from this same source cf pp. 24-28; also from *The Distribution of Costs and Benefits of Integration Among Developing Countries, op cit.,* cf pp. 9-13.

[14] UNCTAD. *The Distribution of Costs and Benefits of Integration Among Developing Countries.* Report of the Group of Experts. *op cit.,* p. 9.

[15] The Commonwealth Caribbean refers only to the present members of CARICOM. See note 1.

[16] The agreement establishing the Caribbean Free Trade Association (1968) is taken to mean the principal agreement and the supplementary agreement negotiated by the participating governments.

[17] William Demas, *West Indian Nationhood and Caribbean Integration* (a Collection of Papers). (Barbados: CCC Publishing House, 1974) p. 31.

[18] *Ibid.*, p. 31.

[19] Caribbean Community Secretariat. *The Caribbean Community: A Guide, op cit.*, p. 25.

[20] Caribbean Investement Corporation. *Annual Report and Statement of Accounts for the Year Ended 31st December, 1975.* p. 8.

[21] In addition to the countries of the Commonwealth Caribbean, the original membership included the British colonies in the Caribbean, the United Kingdom, and Canada.

[22] *Agreement Establishing the Caribbean Development Bank* (1969) Article 1.

[23] Caribbean Development Bank's Press Release No. 1/77, Janaury 7, 1977.

[24] Carleen O'Louglin, *Economic and Political Change in the Leeward and Windward Islands* (New Haven and London: Yale University Press, 1968), p. 139 also *Table 21*, p. 135.

[25] UN/ECLA. "The Impact of the Caribbean Free Trade Association (CARIFTA)," *Economic Bulletin for Latin America*, vol. 18, nos. 1 and 2 (1973), p. 148.

[26] UN/ECLA. *Economic Activity 1975—Caribbean Community Countries* (ECLA/POS 76/6) Part IX. p. 1.

[27] *Report of the Tripartite Survey of the Eastern Caribbean* (January-April, 1966) (London: Her Majesty's Stationery Office (1967) p. 11.

[28] Commonwealth Caribbean Regional Secretariat, *From CARIFTA To Caribbean Community* (Georgetown, Guyana: Commonwealth Caribbean Regional Secretariat, 1972), p. 12.

[29] Figures extracted from UN/ECLA. *CARIFTA Countries—Overview of Economic Activity, 1972.* (ECLA/POS 73/3) Tables III, p. 155; V, p. 157 & VI, p. 158.

[30] Figures extracted from East Caribbean Common Market Secretariat. *Digest of Statistics 1976 (External Trade)*, Dutchman Bay, Antigua: (ECCM Secretriat, (October 1976), Table 5.6.

[31] Figures extracted from *Ibid.*, Table 4.1.

[32] Figures extracted from UN/ECLA. *CARIFTA Countries Overview of Economic Activity, 1972, op cit.* Table VII, p. 159 and Table VIII, p. 160.

[33] Figures extracted from UN/ECLA. *Economic Activity—1975—Caribbean Community Countries, op cit.*, Tables VI and VII, Part V pp. 17 and 18; and Tables III and IV, Part IX pp. 16 and 17.

[34] All figures relating to the CDB are extracted from its accounts in Caribbean Development Bank. *Annual Report 1976*, unless otherwise stated. cf pp. 44-45.

[35] Caribbean Development Bank. *Annual Report 1975.* pp. 19-20.

[36] All figures relating to the CIC are extracted from Caribbean Investment Corporation. *Annual Report and Statement of Accounts for the Year ended 31st December, 1975*, unless otherwise stated.

[37] Caribbean Investment Corporation. *Annual Report and Statement of Accounts for the Year ended 31st December, 1974.* p. 13.

[38] Caribbean Investment Corporation. *Annual Report and Statement of Accounts for the Year Ended 31st December, 1975.* p. 13.

[39] *The Agricultural Sector in the Economic Integration Systems of Latin America.* Report prepared by ECLA/FAO Joint Agriculture Division, Santiago, August 1975, p. 107.

BIBLIOGRAPHY

1. W. Andrew Axline and Lynn K. Mytelka, "Dependence and Regional Integration—A comparison of the Andean Group and CARICOM," (paper presented at the Annual Meeting of International Studies Association, Toronto, February 25–29, 1976).
2. Havelock Brewster and Clive Y. Thomas, "Aspects of the theory of Economic Integration," *Journal of Common Market Studies,* vol. 8 (1969-70).
3. Caribbean Community Secretariat. *The Caribbean Community—A Guide* (Georgetown, Guyana, Caribbean Community Secretariat, 1973).
4. Caribbean Development Bank. *Annual Report 1975.*
5. Agreement Establishing the Caribbean Development Bank (1969).
6. C.D.B. Press Release No. 1/77, 7th January, 1977. (Georgetown, Guyana: Commonwealth Caribbean Regional Secretariat).
7. *CARIFTA and the New Caribbean.* (Georgetown, Guyana: Commonwealth Caribbean Regional Secretariat, 1971).
8. Caribbean Investment Corporation. Annual Report and Statement of Accounts for the Year Ended 31st December, 1975.
9. Annual Report and Statement of Accounts for the Year Ended 31st December, 1974.
10. Commonwealth Caribbean Regional Secretariat. *From CARIFTA to Caribbean Community* (Georgetown, Guyana: Commonwealth Caribbean Regional Secretariat 1972).
11. Ya-Min Chou, "Economic Integration in Less Developed Countries, the Case of Small Countries," *Journal of Development Studies,* vol. 3 (July 1967).
12. Aldo Antonio Dadone, and Luis Eugenio Di Marco, *The Impact Prebisch's Ideas on Modern Economic Analysis,* in *International Economics and Development—Essays in Honour of Raul Prebisch,* ed. Luis Eugenio Di Marco (New York: Academic Press, 1972).
13. William G. Demas, West Indian Nationhood and Caribbean Integration (A Collection of Papers) (Barbados: CCC Publishing House, 1974).
14. East Caribbean Common Market Secretariat, Digest of External Trade Statistics, 1976 (Antigua ECCM Secretariat, 1976).
15. Annual Digest of Statistics, 1974. (Antigua: ECCM Secretariat, 1975).
16. Dermot Gately, "Sharing the Gains From Customs Unions among Less Developed Countries—A game theoretic approach," *Journal of Development Economics* (1974) 213-233 (c) North Holland Publishing Company.
17. Eduardo Lizano, *The Distribution of Costs and Benefits in Economic Integration Among Developing Countries.* Study prepared at the request of the UNCTAD Secretariat (TAD/E1/CB1 Add. I and II, 22 June 1972).
18. A. V. McIntyre, A. Lewis and P. Emmanuel, *The Political Economy of Independence for the Leeward and Windward Islands.* Report of Technical Committee of the Commission established to review the constitutional status of the West Indies Associated States and Montserrat. Bridgetown, Barbados, 23 February, 1975.
19. Charles Pearson, "Evaluation Integration Among Less Developed Countries," *Journal of Common Market Studies.* vol. 8 (1969-1970).
20. Carleen O'Loughlin, *Economic and Political Change in the Leeward and Windward Islands* (New Haven and London: Yale University Press, 1968).
21. John Sloan, "The Strategy of Developmental Regionalism; Benefits, Distribution, Obstacles and Capabilities," *Journal of Common Market Studies,* vol. 10 (1971-1972).

22. United Nations. Economic Commission for Latin America. *Economic Activity— 1975—Caribbean Community Countries* (ECLA/POS/76/6).

23. .... *The Agricultural Sector in the Economic Integration Systems of Latin America.* Report prepared by ECLA/FAO Joint Agricultural Division, Santiago, August 1975.

24. .... *Latin American Development and the International Economic Situation.* Second Regional Appraisal of the International Development Strategy. Parts one (Vol. 1) two and three. CE/CEPAL 981 2 April 1975.

25. .... *Current Problems of Economic Integration. The role of Institution of Regional Integration among Developing Countries.* Prepared by Dr. Dusan Sidjanski New York: TD/B/422 1974.

26. .... *Trade Expansion, Economic Co-operation and Regional Integration among Developing Countries.* Regional and Sub-Regional Groupings and Agreements in Latin America, Africa and Asia. UNCTAD/TE/67 13th April, 1973.

27. .... "The Impact of the Caribbean Free Trade Association (CARIFTA)," *Economic Bulletin for Latin America.* vol. 18, nos. 1 and 2, 1973.

28. .... *Economic Survey of Latin America 1973.* New York, United Nations, 1975.

29. .... *Economic Survey of Latin America 1972.* New York, United Nations, 1974.

30. .... *The Distribution of Costs and Benefits of Integration among Developing Countries.* Report of the Group of Experts. Geneva: TD/B/413 July, 1972.

31. .... *CARIFTA Countries Overview of Economic Activity, 1972.* ECLA/POS/73/3.

32. .... *Economic Survey of Latin America 1970.* New York, United Nations, 1972.

33. .... United Nations Conference on Trade and Development. *Trade Expansion and Economic Integration among Developing Countries.* New York: TD/B/385/Rev. 1, 1967.

34. .... *Economic Survey of Latin America 1949.* New York, United Nations, 1951.

35. .... University of the West Indies Census Research Programme. 1970 Population Census of the Commonwealth Caribbean, 1973.

36. Miguel S. Wionczek, "Introduction: Requisites for Viable Integration," in *Latin American Economic Integration—Experiences and Prospects,* ed. Miguel S. Wionczek (New York: Praeger 1966).

Part III:

Negotiation

Introduction

Basil A. Ince

These two articles, "In whose Interest? Nationalization and Bargaining with the Petroleum Multinationals: The Trinidad/Tobago Experience" by Trevor Farrell, and "The Third World and Modern International Negotiations: The Case of the Third United Nations Conference on the Law of the Sea (With a focus on Commonwealth Caribbean Positions) by Winston Extavour, both fall within the bailiwick of negotiation. However, Farrell's article is different from Extavour's in that the negotiations described by the former take place within a bilateral environment, while Extavour deals with negotiations within a multilateral setting. Additionally, in Farrell's article negotiations are conducted between a state and multinationals, and in Extavour's, between developing countries and developed countries. Students of modern international relations and, more particularly, students with a special interest in the international relations of Third World countries cannot afford to ignore these forms of interaction between developing and developed countries, and between developing countries and the multinationals of developed countries, if they are to comprehend the international interaction of Third World countries. In Farrell's article a Third World country negotiates with petroleum multinationals (British Petroleum Oil Company [BP] and Shell Trinidad Limited), while in Extavour's article, Third World states negotiate with developed states over a variety of aspects of the law of the sea. Strictly speaking, all states are negotiating on the law of the sea, but the Third Law of the Sea Conference (LOS III) turns out, like so many other U.N. conferences on economic issues, to be a competition between the developing and developed countries. Economics, however, is not the only issue involved in LOS III, the military and strategic use of ocean space is also of prime importance.

It has already been noted that the LOS III negotiations took place in a multilateral environment, while the negotiations between Trinidad/Tobago and the multinationals occurred in a bilateral setting. Regardless of the different environments involved in both types of negotiations, two relevant and related questions may be posed, namely, when are negotiations needed and what are the elements for negotiation? One scholar writes that "There is no simple rule as to when negotiation is needed. . . . For certain arrangements negotiation clearly cannot be dispensed with; for others it is optional; and there are some issues which are better settled without it."[1] It seems to me that in both case studies negotiation could not be avoided. In the case of the LOS III, virtually all of the nations of the world are involved. In short, these nations have sufficiently common interests in the sea to force them to sit in conference rooms to discuss how these interests, often conflictual, can be resolved. In the case of the nation-state and the multinationals, negotiation was the only way out since the nationalizations involved were betweeen a friendly host country and multinationals of friendly states. The matter of expropriation was out of the question.

Although Professor Ikle has made the point that there is no simple rule as to when negotiation is needed, it is evident that nations negotiate, or nations and multinationals negotiate, when they have conflicting common interests which they prefer to resolve by means short of force. In many cases resort to negotiation becomes necessary when transactions involving monetary compensation are the order of the day. Monetary compensation was involved in Trinidad/Tobago's negotiations with both multinationals, and negotiations between developing and developed states in the LOS III discussions involved the sharing of economic benefits among states. Negotiations in both cases under study were entered into with little difficulty since the situations did not contain the traditional impediments to negotiation. Professor Lall itemizes them as (a) disparity in power levels between the parties to a dispute or situation; (b) when the power disparity exists and the more powerful party has international commitments that would preclude resort to negotiation; and (c) when there is personal animosity between heads of states.[2] None of these situations existed so as to prevent negotiations in the Trinidad/Tobago cases or in the LOS III dicussions. Although there was disparity in the Trinidad/Tobago cases (for, make no mistake, the home country of the multinationals invariably support them), both B.P. and Shell had already begun to find their ventures in Trinidad/Tobago uneconomic. The LOS III negotiations were a matter of continuing discussions that had already been started.

After these general remarks on some of the elements involved in negotiations, including factors facilitating negotiations, something should be said on the environments in which these negotiations were undertaken. We have already mentioned the bilateral and multilateral environments in which the negotiations were conducted, and are aware of the positive and negative elements of conducting negotiations in these environments. Under normal circumstances, the greater power would have an advantage in bilateral negotiations, but, in the Trinidad/Tobago case, both BP and Shell were already prepared to move out and had already begun to liquidate. In the LOS III situation, developing countries found themselves in the situation most congenial to them, in that they could band themselves to collectively negotiate with the developed nations. While this multilateral situation, found often in various UN fora, assists the negotiating strength of developing nations, it is not unusual to find that developing nations do not derive the sort of advantage that they should because of disunity within the group. The LOS III situation proved to be no exception to the rule on account of the various cross cutting relationships that place some developing nations in the camps of developed states and vice versa.

THE BILATERAL ENVIRONMENT

Taking over the commanding heights of the economy has been a major preoccupation of Third World countries since their emergence as sovereign entities in the world community. One strategy employed to achieving command over the economy has been nationalization. This strategy has been utilized by various Third World countries, including those in the English-speaking Caribbean, which began to become independent in the sixties. Some Third World countries that have nationalized foreign concerns have discovered that nationalization does not, *ipso facto,* bring the commanding heights of their economies under their full control, while others that eventually nationalize, do so under less than propitious circumstances.

Farrell's article discusses the case of Trinidad and Tobago and its nationalization of two petroleum multinationals, British Petroleum (BP) and Shell Trinidad Ltd. The former is a case of nationalization cum joint venture, while the latter is an outright nationalization with the subsequent creation of a wholly state-owned company. The central point that this article makes is that both these nationalizations did not serve the public interest but the interests of the multinationals themselves. The author arrives at this conclusion after analyzing both the BP and Shell cases in their context of a check-list of variables for evaluating a nationalization. Among the salient questions posed to evaluate a nationalization are: the object of the nationalization, the motivation for acquisition, the terms of nationalization, in whose interests was the settlement made, did the government achieve effective direct control and, if so, in whose interest was control exercised, and, finally, the economic success or failure from the viewpoint of the public.

The paper is well-organized and divided into three sections. The first relates to the general problems and issues involved in nationalization and bargaining, and the second and third sections treat the case studies of BP and Shell respectively.

Section One is, without doubt, the most important section of the paper since it provides criteria for judging whether any nationalization has been successful from the public's viewpoint. Any studies other than those of BP and Shell could have been analyzed in the second and third sections. After a discussion of nationalization, the author concludes what it should mean, namely ". . . the compulsory, state-initiated and state-executed acquisition of effective direct control over properties, with or without compensation, and with such control once achieved being exercised in the public interest." Control is the important factor of nationalization and not necessarily ownership, since it is possible to have the latter without control. Even with ownership, control can be frittered away via management contracts or technological and marketing agreements. Modified nationalizations, such as joint ventures, can only be successful if they provide for not only access to technology, markets, etc. but, in addition, national control. After indicating the difficulties involved in creating a theoretical framework for the evaluation of nationalizations, the author identifies nationalizations by categories, in this case three, namely, 'rescue,' 'cosmetic,' and 'reasoned' nationalizations. The first is usually undertaken to prevent some impending economic dislocation; the second where political capital is the primary motivation of the state at the expense of effective control; while the third focuses on an economically substantive target important to the development objectives of the state concerned. While Odle, in his "Towards Understanding the Dynamics of Nationalization in the Caribbean,"[3] does not employ identical terminology in his description of the nationalization in the Caribbean, it is evident that the nature of the nationalizations he discusses are similar. The rescue and cosmetic catgories can easily be identified in the following statements: ". . . a just as important explanation for the series of nationalizations in the post-independence period is the continuous state of economic and social crises" (p. 104).[4] Odle continues further: "The nationalizations . . . were designed to tackle the immediate crises situation, by making it appear that the government was serious about change, and so take the steam out of the rebellion" (105).[5]

After discussion of the terms of settlement and in whose interest such a settlement is made, Farrell applies his check-list to both the BP and Shell cases. The major conclusion to be drawn in each case follows:

B.P.   (i)   a 'crisis management' decision and consequently a rescue nationalization (p. 183); in addition, not genuine but a psuedonationalization (pp. 190, 192).

(ii)   'cosmetics' involved to appear to keep in step with progressive developments (p. 185).

(iii)   A joint-venture arrangement where the government surrendered direct control to Tesoro (p. 189).

(iv)   In addition, Trinidad/Tesoro gained no technical or commercial success as a result of Tesoro (p. 191).

(v)   In accordance with (ii) above the political elite had been served.

(vi)   The government felt itself to be bargaining from a position of weakness (p. 193).

(vii)   The government's failure in the negotiations was attributed to:

     (a) its fears about foreign capital

     (b) its lack of confidence in its people

     (c) haste in negotiations

     (d) ignorance about the oil industry internationally and about local capabilities with respect to the oil business.

SHELL (i)   No governmental forethought in planning nationalization (pp. 194, 199, 203).

(ii)   Climate favourable for nationalization (p. 199).

(iii)   Lack of government's information about Shell's operation in the country (p. 200).

(iv)   Government's negotiating team weak but onus of blame must fall on government (p. 203).

(v)   Unlike the BP experience, effective direct control was achieved (p. 204).

(vi)   Political leadership's interests served but not public's.

(vi)   Government's failure in negotiations similar to those as in BP case (see vii above).

In both cases, certain constants with respect to the government's failure to get the better of the negotiations are evident. They are (1) lack of expertise among the government's negotiating team and (2) the psychological weakness of the government especially with respect to the fear of foreign capital leaving the country. While the first is an objective factor, many of the psychological constraints in government's bargaining position are subjective. While psychology plays a major role in the bargaining powers and may necessarily inhibit a negotiator from acting in a positive and confident fashion, the attitude to foreign capital flight would seem to be one based on objective factors. Since the role of foreign capital is so focal a point of debate in the English-speaking Caribbean, the reader might have been better informed if the author had expanded and clarified the "apparent ignorance of, or naivete about certain fundamentals of the motivations and operations of foreign capital," and the ". . . naive conceptions about foreign capital, what attracts it and what repels it, its importance and its necessity." The author, however, makes the point very well that a nationalization is not a panacea for foreign exploitation or the economic ills of a country. The call for nationalization must carry with it precise terms, which will make for control by the state and in the public's interest. This requires long term planning, not only about the nationalization but also about the developmental objectives of the economy as a whole.

THE MULTILATERAL ENVIRONMENT

The aim of Extavour's paper is three-fold. In examining LOS III, it focuses on (a) the major issues before the Conference; (b) the positions of Third World states as they act collectively in pursuing their interests or individually as sovereign entities in advancing their special interests; and (c) a particular segment of the developing countries, the Commonwealth Caribbean countries and their positions on various issues. In order to carry out his plan, the author discusses (a) the main issues before LOS III, (b) the negotiating structure of the conference, and (3) the positions of the Commonwealth Caribbean states. Of all the issues that found their way on the agenda of LOS III, six receive the author's attention. They are an International Regime for the Sea Bed and the Oceanfloor beyond national jurisdiction; the territorial sea, straits for international navigation, the continental shelf, the exclusive economic zone, and landlocked and geographically disadvantaged states. These major issues demonstrate in sharp relief the differences between the developing and developed nations. Re the international regime for the Sea-bed and the Oceanfloor beyond national jurisdiction, the developing countries would like to rest full control of operations in the seabed area beyond national jurisdiction in an International Authority to be established. On the other hand, the developed countries would like to institute a licensing or registration system according to which the Authority would contract out certain parts of the seabed area to states or companies which would then exercise exclusive control over that part of the area and its activities for a specified period of time. The negative implications of this position for the developing countries is evident.

On the subject of the breadth of the territorial sea, the developed states, also the major maritime states, would like to preserve the narrowest breadth as possible, while the developing countries see the advantage of securing the exercise of sovereignty or at least exclusive jurisdiction over as wide an expanse of the adjacent seas as possible. With respect to straits used for international navigation, the developed states believe that the rights of transit passage should apply, while the developing states, to whom this position is partially acceptable, would like a formula that would guarantee their sovereignty over those territorial straits at all times. The dichotomy between the developed and developing countries again presents itself over the issue of the exclusive economic zone. While the developed states, possessing superior technology and technological skills, favour freedom for scientific research in the exclusive economic zone, the developing states prefer to have exclusive control over all scientific research in the exclusive economic zone. But while the rivalry between the developing and developed countries hold the center stage in LOS III, there are cross cutting relationships that at times pit developing countries against one another. For example, there is competition between developing coastal states and those developing states that are geographically disadvantaged and landlocked. In fact one scholar has written that the Group of 77 was captured by the coastal states.[6]

The section on "The Mechanics of Negotiation" is brief and more descriptive than analytical. It describes the three committees which have been entrusted to deal with various topics of the Conference and the other informal organs, which are myriad, and work alongside the formal organs of the conference. Among these informal groups are the Group of 77 (consisting of some 116 states), the Latin American Group, the Asian group, the Group of Socialist States, the Group of Western European countries and Others. In addition, there are other groupings with common interests and positions which cut across the above-mentioned groups. The names of some of these groups are self-explanatory, for example, the Coastal State Group and the Group of Landlocked and Geographically Disadvantaged States. Negotiation between these two groups is facilitated from time to time by the formation of the 'Group of 21,' which is constituted by members from both the coastal states and the geographically disadvantaged states. Negotiation amongst all these groups do not facilitate the negotiating process and, in addition, the decision to negotiate the various aspects of the LOS simultaneously was an error.[7] As a result the negotiations of the LOS Conferences can be expected to be protracted over a number of years. While we have already been warned by Professor Lall that international negotiation should not be expected to succeed in one, two, or three rounds of discussion, and that most issues require years of consideration, we can safely state that the LOS Conferences will be held for many years to come.[8] Edward Miles has already written that "negotiations will be constant, detailed, technical and onerous. . . ."[9]

The final section of the article treats the Commonwealth Caribbean states, a subgroup of the Latin American group which, in turn, is a sub-group of the Group of 77. The author has remarked that these new states have played an active role in the progessive development of the international law of the sea and this could be expected since they are a sub-group of the larger Latin American group which has been in the forefront in the development of the law of the sea. In addition, it should be pointed out that, save Guyana, they are small states surrounded by the sea, and their interest in the development of the law of the sea would flow naturally from this geographical circumstance. At LOS III, the Caricom states arrived at their positions on issues via two approaches namely: (i) regional and (ii) national. Employing the regional approach, the Caricom states coordinated their efforts to arrive at a common position based on regional solidarity. When national interests predominated and the regional approach was unsuccessful in bringing about a common position, the national approach prevailed. Thus it proved possible for the Caricom states to harmonize on such issues as coastal states regulating marine scientific research and the elaboration of an international regime for the seabed beyond national jurisdiction. When national interests prevailed, it usually meant a split amongst the group. There were two issues where cleavages obtained. One was on the matter of the exclusive economic zone where Jamaica championed the concept of the matrimonial sea while Guyana, Trinidad and Tobago, and Barbados expressed a differing viewpoint. While all three states saw the exclusive economic zone as a useful instrument for allocating the resources of the adjacent seas, they all differed in detail. On the question of the continental shelf Trinidad and Tobago, on account of its exploitation of hydrocarbons, found itself the odd man out among the Caricom states as it sided with those states that possess a continental shelf beyond 200 nautical miles. On this issue, the three other Caricom states sided with the group of landlocked and geographically disadvantaged states. However, all four Caricom states were able to support landlocked states on questions of the rights of equitable participation in exclusive economic zones of states belonging to a region. For Caricom states to be influential, they had to work with the Latin American group, which in turn sought to bring its influence to bear on the Group of 77. This is the sole *modus operandi* open to a handful of small states in a huge conference where there are myriad groups, a number of cross-cutting relationships and where horsetrading is prevalent.

CONCLUSION

Both articles are concerned with negotiation in different environments and a conclusion has been reached in the bilateral negotiations between

Trinidad and Tobago and the multinationals. In those cases it is less difficult to draw conclusions as to which of the parties receive the better deal. It is not possible to do so in the LOS negotiations because such negotiations will be continuing over a protracted period. Even if observers find difficulty in assessing the outcome of the negotiations in both cases, it is certain that the principals in both sets of negotiations have made their assessments of one another. The assessment that one party has made of another is important in terms of bargaining strength in the future. A party that has demonstrated decided weakness or weaknesses in any area can be certain that the other party will not forget to exploit such weakness in future negotiations. In short, bargaining is an important factor for states. Perhaps Farrell will conclude that Trinidad and Tobago's bargaining reputation has been sullied. It is more difficult to fault the Caricom group since it is bargaining where it has strong reinforcements in the Latin American group and the Group of 77. It is only when the final LOS Conference is about to be held that a better assessment can be made of what the Caricom countries have gained or lost.

In the first case study, the author believes that government's failure stemmed from its lack of confidence in itself and in its bargaining representatives. Elsewhere, it is pointed out that there were outstanding personalities from the Caricom states in the LOS III negotiations.[10] On the other hand, it was stated that in the nationalization of the multinationals that the government's team was weak. This may or may not have been the case but one point can be made about personalities and proximity to power. The nearer the bargaining personality is to power, the better for his side. If a negotiator is in direct touch with, or can approach, the sources of authority in his government, this is likely to have a significant bearing on his effectiveness as a negotiator and therefore on the result that he obtains. This proximity to the source of authority seems to be more important in the case of bilateral negotiations, since in the multi-lateral setting it is possible to look to a sympathetic group as a source of strength.

Finally, the role of domestic opinion is important if it is brought to bear on the bargaining process. Without doubt Third World determination to change the tenor and past trends of international law has been a source of strength for developing countries and perhaps a source of dismay for developed states. One observer, commenting on the LOS III Conference, has stated that the 'good old days' for the developed states have ended. It is more difficult to whip up domestic opinion on a foreign policy issue unless the people perceive the survival of the nation is at stake. In the Trinidad and Tobago cases, the issues may have been of importance to the Government, but the people were not mobilized in such a way as to make the issue one of national survival. Consequently, domestic opinion played a minimal role.

Negotiation between developing and developed countries is becoming much more prevalent as East-West issues fade into the background. So, too, is negotiation between new states and multinationals, as the former attempt to gain control over the commanding heights of their economies. These two developments will provide a host of material for research for scholars of the Third World who have lost interest in issues such as arms negotiations between super-powers.

FOOTNOTES

[1]Fred Ikle, *How Nations Negotiate,* (New York: Harper and Row, 1964), p. 4.

[2]Arthur Lall, *Modern International Negotiation: Principles and Practice,* (New York and London: Columbia University Press, 1966). Chapter 10, pp. 132-150.

[3]Maurice Odle, "Towards Understanding the Dynamics of Nationalization in the Caribbean" in Basil A. Ince (ed.), *Contemporary International Relations of the Caribbean,* (St. Augustine: I.I.R., UWI 1979), pp. 102-120.

[4]Maurice Odle, "Towards Understanding the Dynamics of Nationalization in the Caribbean," *op. cit.* p. 104.

[5]*Ibid.,* p. 105.

[6]See Edward Miles, "The Structure and the Efffects of the Decision Process in the Seabed Committee and the Third U.N. Conference on the Law of the Sea," *International Organization,* Vol. 31, 1977, p. 233.

[7]This is one of the major conclusions of Edward Miles. See his "The Structure and the Effects. . . . . *op. cit.* p. 159.

[8]Lall, *op. cit.* p. 3.

[9]Miles, *op. cit.* p. 234.

[10]Miles, *op. cit.*

In Whose Interest?
Nationalization and Bargaining
with the Petroleum Multinationals:
The Trinidad and Tobago Experience

Trevor Farrell

INTRODUCTION

International relations has traditionally emphasized the interaction between nation-states. In today's Third World, however, foreign policy tends to be primarily concerned with development issues. As such, it turns out that a great deal of these countries' international relations involves directly or indirectly the large, foreign, multinational companies. Because of the size, spread, technological sophistication and power of these companies, their relations with some nation-states have tended to take on more of the character of the interaction between formally equal sovereign states, than the relation between superordinate state and subordinate company. Further, some of the relations between the economically developed home countries of the multinationals and host underdeveloped countries are related to issues involving the Third World State and the corporations. Modern international relations can therefore hardly ignore the interactions between nation-state and multinational company without running the risk of becoming irrelevant to an understanding of much of the Third World's international interaction.

A key area of this interaction is the issue of nationalization. Several factors, including actual experience, have combined to make the previous era of unquestioned accommodation to foreign capital give way to a new era of economic nationalism, the rejection or rigorous control of foreign capital, and widespread nationalizations. But at the same time, foreign capital and the MNC still exert an appeal by the lure of their technology, market access, etc. The result is frequently ambivalence. This leads in some cases to modifed nationalizations. It leads to attempts in some cases to promote joint ventures. These seem to provide the best of both worlds—access to technology, markets, etc., plus national control.

Significant questions arise about the new trends. Does nationalization in fact serve to achieve the state's presumed goals—for example, more and faster economic development? Do joint ventures in fact provide the best of both worlds? Are nationalizations really resulting in local control? Or are they being perverted somehow to serve the MNCs' interests? Do nationalizations benefit the mass of people? In whose interests exactly are they? What is the decision-making and bargaining process behind a nationalization like, and who really benefits?

In the present paper, we seek to explore these issues through the medium of two case studies based on Trinidad and Tobago's recent experience in oil nationalization. The first case is a combination of nationalization cum joint venture. The second is a straight nationalization with the subsequent setting up for a wholly state-owned company. The first is the 1969 purchase of the B.P. Oil company and the formation of a joint venture company, Trindad-Tesoro, with a U.S. Oil company, Tesoro of Texas. The second is the 1974 nationalization of Shell Trinidad Ltd.

These two cases are both significant and instructive. Petroleum is the most important resource in Trindad and Tobago. It provides the vast bulk of government revenues and exports and is regarded as the prime mover of the domestic economy. Further, petroleum as the world's most important industrial commodity and the petroleum multinationals as some of the oldest and most sophisticated of all the multinationals are critical to an understanding of the nature of the game being played globally today.

The two cases chosen are Trindad and Tobago's major oil nationalizations to date. One involved one of the oldest and most sophisticated petroleum multinationals—Shell. The other involved another old oil multinational B.P., and a small U.S. company (Tesoro) which became a multinational by entering Trinidad. The analysis of the two cases is based on financial data on the acquisition, interviews with some of the key negotiators and actors on the country's side and, unusually, actual internal memoranda relating to the negotiations. The unusual wealth of data on these cases permits some interesting insights to be gained into negotiations between underdeveloped countries and the MNCs and into nationalizations.

NATIONALIZATION AND BARGAINING: PROBLEMS AND ISSUES

Before attempting to discuss and assess Trinidad and Tobago's two major ventures into petroleum nationalization, it is necessary to set up a framework within which the available material can be properly analyzed.

The Meaning of Nationalization

Nationalization is one of those frequently used terms which, like 'socialism,' has come to be applied in loose and imprecise fashion to a heterogeneity of situations. It is increasingly difficult to discern the elements of commonality in these situations which justify the use of the same term to cover them all. The semantic problems associated with the term nationalization are, at least in part, a clear sign of theory badly lagging behind practice.

From popular usage and from an examination of actual experiences, it is possible to distil certain elements of an action which are necessary for it to be termed a nationalization.

(a) Nationalization implies the acquisition of properties by the state. The term is therefore not applicable to the acquisition of previously foreign-owned properties by local private interests.

(b) The action is usually initiated by the state.

(c) There is some element of compulsion or force involved. At a minimum, the state makes it clear that it intends to use its sovereignty to acquire the properties. The exact terms and timing are left open to negotiation but the basic issue of a state takeover is not left in doubt. At a maximum, the state dictates unilaterally all terms and conditions related to the acquisition. There is no negotiation.

(d) Nationalization usually implies the acquisition of ownerhsip rights by the state.

This last condition requires some clarification and qualification. Ownership is usually felt to be a condition not for its own sake, but because it is thought to imply control. Control is what is important. Ownership, however, is neither a necessary nor a sufficient condition for control. It is not necessary since control may be achieved without it. For example, a management contract may confer effective control over an operation without the contractor having any equity ownership. Similarly, since control may be either direct or indirect, the state may effectively control a venture through indirect means. Its battery of legislative and regulatory powers may be used to leave a company only the freedom to exercise the option preferred by the state.

Theoretically, direct and indirect control can have exactly the same result. In practice, indirect control through the use of legislative and regulatory power is frequently vitiated by the active, overt or covert, maneuvering and manipulation by the affected companies. Lobbying, corruption, and plain human ingenuity at discovering loopholes are among the weapons used to thwart the effective exercise of indirect control. It is for this reason that direct control is felt to be a superior option in certain circumstances. After all, indirect control could theoretically be as effectively applied to foreign as to locally owned enterprises.

Ownership is also not a sufficient condition for control, since its mere possession need not result in active control or, indeed, in any control. There are many examples. State ownership need not mean active control, especially in joint ventures. The state may act as a 'sleeping partner' (e.g. in the case of British Petroleum). Again, the modern large capitalist corporation is 'owned' by a plenitude of shareholders who have neither the opportunity nor the interest in controlling it. In yet other cases, state ownership may exist but effective control be surrendered to other parties (perhaps foreigners) through management contracts or technological and marketing agreements.

Therefore, while nationalization is popularly felt to imply state ownership, it is better in defining the term to specify 'effective control' as a condition rather than (or if one likes, as well as) simple state ownership. There are two other points to be noted here. The issue of nationalization is not usually thought to be predicated on whether compensation is paid or not paid. The nonpayment of compensation is therefore not a necessary condition for an action to be deemed a nationalization. The term 'expropriation' is better reserved for this 'extreme' case.

Likewise, few observers look back to see in whose interests effective direct control is exercised—whether it is in the interests of the bureaucrats, the local elite, or the public interest. It seems to be implicitly (and erroneously) assumed that acquisition by the state naturally means the exercise of control in the interests of the people as a whole. This assumption ignores completely the class character of the state, and the fact that the state is responsive to certain interests and not to others.

We may therefore sum up this discussion on the meaning of the term 'nationalization' by saying that nationalization 'should' mean the compulsory, state-initiated, and state-executed acquisition of effective direct control over properties, with or without compensation, and with such control once achieved being exercised in the public interest.

Evaluating a Nationalization: The Problems

Nationalizations of one sort or another have been occurring with considerable frequency among Third World States in the recent past. There is a clear need for some sort of theoretical framework within which particular actions termed nationalizations might be evaluated to permit analytical judgements to be made on the social, political, and economic usefulness of particular nationalizations and even on nationalization in general. This need is heightened by the confusion and misrepresentation which so frequently surrounds the practical application of the term.

There are several difficulties that arise in the attempt to construct such a framework. Nationalizations involve politics and political judgement, and usually involve bargaining. A nationalization may be effected from a variety of political motives. A government may pay obviously extortionate prices for worthless or insignificant assets either because this is in the personal pecuniary interests of politicians or their agents, or because a purely symbolic and cosmetic act of defiance or aggression against foreign interests will deceive and satisfy local demands. Can such a nationalization be deemed incompetent? After all, a 'successful' or 'sensible' nationalization formed no part of the state's objectives.

Again, a state may pay high, and even exorbitant, prices for a property, because its decision-makers deem this prudent in terms of avoiding or minimizing the risks of retaliation. Other people may have quite different assessments of the risks associated with paying the same, a larger, or a smaller sum.

Nationalization is not a panacea for a country's or an industry's economic ills. Nationalization simply provides an opportunity—to redirect the use of certain properties to the service of the public interest. This opportunity may or may not be seized. Failure to seize it may be blameable on the action or inaction of the state, or it may be ultimately due to external, uncontrollable factors—for example, an embargo, the loss of markets, the decline of a particular industry relative to competing industries, etc. Therefore, before adjudging the socioeconomic success or failure of previousy nationalized properties, it is necessary to carefully investigate the attendant circumstances.

The fact that nationalizations involve political judgement, complex and varied motivations and bargaining means that we have essentially three options in seeking a framework for evaluation. The first is to refrain altogether from attempting to evaluate and adjudicate on nationalizations on the ground that since action may proceed from all sorts of motives it is difficult or impossible to pass on the competence or incompetence of a government in terms of what it agrees to. After all, an apparently incompetent nationalization may be due simply to the fact that the negotiators or politicians were bribed to settle where they did, and that from that point of view their behaviour was eminently rational and competent. Similarly, if cautious decision-makers judge the risks of retaliation as high, how can one prove that they were wrong without being able to rerun history and perform simulation exercises with it?

The second option is to evaluate nationalizations simply in terms of the decision-makers' own objectives, and the extent to which they were successful in achieving them. The third option is to set up criteria for a proper or genuine nationalization—one which maximizes the gains to the people of a state. Then actual nationalizations may be judged against these standards. Naturally there may be deviations—precisely because the state may have been operating on the basis of a complex of motivations, or on its judgement of the political risks.

The analyst must then exercise his judgement as to whether the variances or shortfalls of the actual as compared to the desirable can be justified by the value of the other objectives and motives of the decision-makers. The analyst must also be prepared to make his own evaluation of the political risks involved in the nationalization, and in this context judge the implicit or explicit evaluation of these risks by the state.

The first option is unacceptable. There are obviously well-done and badly-done nationalizations. The citizens of a state have every right to call for an account of their government's stewardship in this matter, as in any other. This means that it is necessary to be able to judge where a particular nationaliztion falls. The second option is also unacceptable. It threatens to lead into a cul-de-sac where a reluctant imprimatur would have to be helplessly applied to the worst kinds of sell-outs simply because this successfully achieves the goals of some group of decision-makers. These decision-makers could be totally corrupted and their objectives socially and morally unacceptable, yet we would be obliged to adjudge their actions a 'success.'

While the third option may seem a little like playing God, it is the one that we have to settle for. In any event, the requirement for omniscience is more apparent than real. This option really implies only that the analyst be required to make explicit his own value-judgements. Since these value-judgements enter analysis anyway, it is better, as Myrdal has argued, that this be done openly and therefore be challengeable.

Evauating a Nationalization: The Criteria

The criteria for evaluating a nationalization stem from the definition of nationalization arrived at above plus certain subsidiary issues. One can ask a series of questions which form the basis for the criteria to be set up:

(1) Was the action state-initiated and state-executed, and did it involve the minimum degree of compulsion? (i.e. a clear understanding that ultimately acquisition would be effected?)
(2) What was nationalized and why? Were the properties economically substantive or insignificant? What were the motives of the state?
(3) How was the nationalization effected—what were the terms of acquisition?
(4) In whose interest was the final settlement—the foreign company's, some local elite's or the public interest?
(5) Was effective direct control achieved?
(6) In whose interests was this control exercised—foreign interests, some local elite's, the public interest?
(7) Was the nationalization economically successful or unsuccessful, and why?

From these questions the basic criteria may be distilled. The first question relating to the initiation of the action, the agent of its execution, and the existence of at least minimum compulsion follows straight forwardly from the definition of nationalization. This requires no real elaboration and is essentially a factual matter depending for its answer on empirical research.

Nationalization: The Motivation

The second question—what was nationalized and why—needs further elaboration. From the point of view of motivation one may distinguish between different (not mutually exclusive) types of nationalization. For our purposes in this paper, three types are of interest. There is first of all the 'rescue' nationalization. This is essentially pure crisis management, undertaken to prevent some immediate, threatened economic dislocation. It is often a genuine nationalization in the sense defined above. Sometimes, however, these nationalizations have in the long run proven to be a heavy drain on the public purse.

Secondly there is the 'cosmetic' nationalization. Here the primary motivation of the state is to make political capital out of the move. In some cases this is a 'pseudo-nationalization' as well, with effective control left, more or less clandestinely, in foreign hands. In other instances, cosmetic nationalization is focused on some insignificant aspects of a company's operation, or on a largely symbolic, as opposed to an economically substantitve, target.

Thirdly, there are 'reasoned nationalizations.' These focus on some economically substantive target and are effected because they would fit in with, and may be absolutely necessary to, the furtherance of the country's development objectives.

Terms of Acquisition

The third question relates to the terms of acquisition. There are perhaps four major issues here: (1) The valuation placed on the properties acquired and the recompense to be paid; (2) The Time Horizon over which compensation is to be paid, the timing of payments within that horizon and the interest rate on upaid balances—i.e. the cost of payment deferral. (3) The form of compensation—currency, bonds, product, or a combination. (4) The source of finance or compensation for the acquisition.

With respect to valuation, there are in turn two basic questions—(1) What is to be valued? (2) How is the valuation to be arrived at? The first question here relates to such issues as what is to be treated as assets up for purchase and acquisition. Every asset has a 'referent.' That is, it is an asset to somebody. But it may not be an asset to someone else. It could even be a liability. Next, it is often the case that a country can deny that certain assets of a company in fact belong to it in the sense that it may sell them freely. One well-known example in the petroleum industry is oil in the ground which is the patrimony of the country, though it may appear on the balance sheet of a foreign company.

After a decision is made on what is to be bought, the next issue is the method of valuation to be applied. There are several possibilities here: (a) Assets may be valued at replacement cost—i.e. how much it would cost to provide alternative assets capable of providing the same stream of output. (One problem here is that the dynamic of technological change and obsolescence frequently preclude exact replacement.)

(b) Assets may be valued at their 'market value'—i.e. the price they would fetch if placed on the market and sold to the highest bidder.

(c) Alternatively, the opportunity cost or economic value to the seller of the assets may be used. This is the discounted stream of net benefits the seller may reasonably have expected to obtain from the continuation of his investment over some acceptable time horizon. This method raises manifold difficulties with respect to the time horizon to be used, the discount rate, assumptions about future prices, and whether the cost accounting should reflect social costs such as pollution.

(d) Valuation may also be on a net book value basis. One version of this is net book value (historical). This method values properties at their historical cost of acquisition as carried on the books, less accumulated depreciation and outstanding liabilities.

(e) Finally, one may use the economic value to the buyer. This relates to the point that every asset has a referent. Some plant may be very valuable to a foreign company but of little economic value to the state, just as a motorcar may be worth little in roadless jungle.

These different methods will usually result in different valuation figures. It is in the seller's interest to choose the method which he believes will provide him with the largest compensation. Equally obviously, it is in the country's interest to minimize the compensation it pays. Thus the country will likely argue for a net book value approach, or in some cases, economic value to the buyer. The foreign company will likely suggest replacement value, market value, or an opportunity cost valuation.

Similarly, the longer the time horizon over which compensation is to be paid, the lower the interest rate, and the more deferred the payments, the better for the country. The higher the interest rate, the shorter the time horizon and the more immediate the payment, the better for the company. For the company, payment in convertible foreign currency or, in some cases, product is most desirable. For the country, payment in local currency, local securities or, in some cases, product would be most desirable.

Finally, the source of payment is a factor of considerable importance. Cash payments in convertible foreign exchange out of the nationalized enterprise's profits can cause serious cash flow problems. Payment from the local treasury has to be evaluated in terms of the opportunity cost of this use of the country's funds. The exact terms of a financial settlement can be analyzed in terms of these four broad areas. (This does not mean that other aspects of the settlement may not in some cases warrant as much attention—for example, technological and marketing arrangements where the previous foreign owner retains some connection with the business.)

The Settlement: In Whose Interests?

The terms of the settlement may be in the interests of one party, the other party, or both parties. Many multinationals for instance have learnt how to make nationalization serve their interests. They may do so in several ways: (a) Nationalization can help the company's cash flow through the compensation it receives. This may be very useful depending on the company's investment plans. (b) This boost to the cash flow is especially useful if at the same time it is possible to maintain its essential interests intact—for example, continued access to raw materials, effective operational control, choice of technology, and the maintenance of the enterprise's technological dependence. (c) Continued control plus a boost to the cash flow is further sweetened by the advantage that a settlement on attractive terms now reduces or eliminates the risk of a more unattractive nationalization from a tougher and more competent government sometime in the future. (d) Nationalization may also be cleverly guided over the course of negotiations so that the company gets the government to 'prune' its operations for it of unwanted, unprofitable, and increasingly unattractive properties at a high price to the state, while the company retains control or even ownership of the useful properties. (e) Nationalization, if it is pseudonationalization, also has the attraction that it reduces the company's visibility and defuses local criticisms while its essential interests are maintained intact.

On the other hand, the nationalization may serve the interests of one or other or all of the local elites. Given these alternative possibilities, the important test is whether it serves the public interest. This can in principle be assessed on the basis of whether (a) the nationalization is of economically substantive properties; (b) the terms of acquisition maximizes the gains to the country; (c) the nationalization is genuine, with effective direct control achieved.

Effective Direct Control

The fifth question in our list of criteria is related to whether effective direct control is achieved. This needs to be defined. Put simply, it means the acquisition of the ability to determine directly—i.e. at the operational level by means of direct orders such economic matters as (a) the quantity and composition of output; (b) its disposition; (c) the choice of technology used; (d) the disposition of the surplus; (e) the financing of operations; and (f) the disposal of the net assets of the enterprise. If the power to determine these matters is possessed and actively exercised by the state, effective direct control may be said to have been achieved. This is one of the key characteristics of a genuine nationalization.

There are 'fake' or 'pseudonationalizations' as well. Here only the semblance of effective direct control is provided. So ownership is formally acquired but control is left with the same, or given to another group of foreigners.

The Use of Control: In Whose Interest?

Even where effective direct control has been gathered up firmly in the hands of the state, it is necessary to go further in the analysis and ask the question of in whose interests effective direct control is being exercised. It may be exercised in the interests of an elite group in the society. This is a 'Leopoldian' nationalization—so termed after the Belgian king who treated the Belgian Congo as his personal fief.

If control is being exercised in the public interest, then this can in principle be adjudged by studying the contribution of the enterprise to the society's development.[1] There are several elements that are involved here. They may briefly be summarized as:

(i)   The basic material welfare of the people.
(ii)   Education.
(iii)   The development of an indigenous technological capability.
(iv)   The proper utilization of the country's resources—including
        its human and natural resources.
(v)   Greater equity in the distribution of income and wealth.
(vii)   Contribution to structural transformation.
(viii) Contribution to the 'quality of life.'

Naturally, an enterprise may not contribute to all of these, and its
contribution may be in some cases indirect. Nevertheless, this checklist
of developmental variables provides a basic framework within which a
judgement can be made as to whether a nationalized enterprise is
performing in the public interest. By going further and asking 'why?' with
respect to its performance, it would also be possible to deal with the last
of our questions on the economic success or failure of a nationalization.

This, of course, involves certain problems such as when should such
an evaluation be made, how does one weight disparate performance in
various categories. Space precludes a thorough discussion of these
problems. It is now possible to summarize this approach to evaluating a
nationalization in the form of a checklist of variables. This appears
below:

CHECKLIST FOR EVALUATING A NATIONALIZATION

Question	Factors Involved
(1) Are the properties acquired by the State?	
(2) Did the State initiate the acquisition?	
(3) Was there the minimum degree of compulsion—i.e. that acquisition was definitely going to be effected?	
(4) What was nationalized?	— Economically substantive assests — Economically insignificnt assests
(5) What was the motivation for acquisition?	— Rescue Nationalization — Cosmetic Nationalization — Reasoned Nationalization

(6) What were the terms of Nationalization?	(a) Valuation
	    — Replacement Cost
	    — Opportunity Cost to seller
	    — Market Value
	    — Net Book Value
	    — Economic value to the buyer

Question	Factors Involved
	(b) — Time Horizon— No. of years
	— Interest Rate
	— Payments Stream
	(c) Form of Compensation
	— Convertible Foreign Exchange
	— Local Cash or Securities
	— Product
	(d) Source of Compensation
	— Nationalized Enterprise
	— Treasury
	— Other
(7) Settlement: In Whose Interests?	— Foreign Company
	— Local Elite
	— Public Interest
	— Some Combination
(8) Was effective direct control achieved?	
(9) In whose interest control exercized?	— Foreigners
	— Local Elite
	— The Public Interest
(10) Was/Is Nationalization economically successful or unsuccessful from the point of view of the public interest?	— Yes. Why?
	— No. Why not?

Actual Evaluation

The checklist above cannot provide a quantitative or mechanical evaluation of a nationalization. No weights are assigned to the various factors, nor is any scoring system attached to the answers in each category. This checklist helps in two ways. First, using the checklist in conjunction with our definition of nationalization permits a definite judgement to be made as to whether a particular action is or was a nationalization. Second, by setting out systematically the major factors of interest, it aids in forming a *judgement* about a given nationalization and aids in making the bases of that judgement explicit and therefore challengeable.

As stated earlier, variances are to be expected between actual nationalizations and what can be argued to be desirable. In examining these variances, three further issues or questons arise:

(1)   The motivation and objectives of the state—can these be adjudged valid or invalid as justification for observed variances?

(2)   The State's assessments of the Political Risks—Acceptable or unacceptable, and why?

(3)   The particular settlement arrived at may be a function of the bargaining process. This needs to be looked at explicitly.

Obviously, the bargaining process plays a crucial role in the final settlement arrived at. What is actually agreed on depends in part on the bargaining strength and bargaining skill of the participants. Bargaining strength is related to three factors:

(a)   Objective factors—the resources available to a given party, the alternatives or options available, the need for or intensity of desire for an agreement, and the expected benefit-cost ratio accruing from a given settlement.

(b)   Subjective Factors—Perceptions of self, the other party and the environment; psychological factors.

(c)   Information—the quantum of information possessed by each party relevant to the bargaining situation.

Bargaining skill is quite complex. However there are two basic dimensions here. First, proper planning of the negotiation and one's interests, fall-back, and minimum positions.[2] Second, that actual skill of the negotiator—the timing and use of charm, threat, propaganda, warnings, bluffs, etc. The choice of items to be placed on the agenda and the order in which agreement is sought on them is also another aspect of skills.[3]

These three factors can be used as useful preliminary tools for evaluating the reasons for any deviation of actual from desirable in the settlement of a nationalization.

The 1969 B.P. Nationalization and the Creation of Trinidad-Tesoro

The Trinidad and Tobago government's first major venture into oil nationalization came in 1969 with its decision to purchase British Petroleum's Trinidad holdings. B.P. had come to Trinidad after the 1956 Suez crisis in an apparent attempt to diversify its sources of supply into a 'safe' area of the British Empire. B.P. was very dependent on Middle East crudes at the time, especially its 50% share of Kuwait's production and reserves. The crisis with Egypt in that period and Nasser's threats to and actual closure of the canal posed a grave problem for the company.

In the 1960s, however, with the reduction of overt tension in the Middle

East, the erosion of oil prices, and the comparatively high cost and marginal nature of its small Trinidad production, Trinidad became increasingly unattractive to B.P. It consequently began to liquidate its Trinidad operations. In 1962-63 it retrenched some 250-300 workers precipitating a long and bitter strike. In 1967, after considerable public agitation by the company, it was given the green light by the state to retrench even more. Despite this victory, B.P. declared that its operations were unprofitable, its properties were uneconomic to produce oil from, and that it was going to discard its Trinidad holdings in 1969.[4]

This decision threatened to throw over 1500 workers out of work and with the multiplier effects thereof to cause a major economic crisis in South Trinidad, and worsen an already serious unemployment situation nation-wide. The government moved to intervene directly in the crisis. It attempted to persuade both Shell and Texaco to take over the properties. Both refused. This left either the option of seeking to attract (or passively allowing) another foreign investor from outside to take over the properties, the option of taking them completely over itself, or a compromise between the two—a joint venture with a new foreign investor. It was finally decided to seek a joint venture, but one in which the government would insist on having majority ownership.

This was a 'crisis management' decision. There was no independent, unilateral government initiative to nationalize. The decision that the state would use its sovereignty to take over the properties, and preclude them simply being sold to any foreign investor B.P. might find, was essentially a response to a confluence of circumstances the government had had no hand in engendering. While the state did finally decide that it would bar the sale of the properties to an outside investor and take them over itself within a partnership arrangement, this only came after B.P. decided to sell out and Shell and Texaco declared their disinterest.

Thus, while it may conceivably be termed a nationalization in the sense that the state ultimately used its authority to foreclose certain options, it is at best a very reluctant nationalization.

The government was apparently motivated principally by fear of the political and social implications of the increase in unemployment that B.P.'s abrupt departure presaged. The decision to nationalize but within the framework of a joint venture seems to have been the result of two factors. On the one hand the failure of the Lewis strategy of indiscriminately welcoming any and all foreign capital was increasingly clear to many people. The Oilfield Workers Trade Union (OWTU)), Caribbean academics and other observers, both regional and international, were increasingly questioning the exploitative nature of the operations of foreign capital. There was, too, the immediate and concrete evidence of B.P.'s callous unconcern with the interests of the country and its tender solicitude for its own. This meant that simply allowing another foreign investor to come in was somewhat distasteful.

On the other hand, the government, and especially the politicians,[5] felt afraid of the 'complexities' of the oil business. Without any real analysis, but at some primal, 'gut' level they did not believe local black men and women could run an oil company. A joint venture in which the government would have majority ownership and where foreign 'white' expertise would be available to actually take charge of things seemed to be overall the best policy.

There was no plan for organizing the petroleum industry or even any part of it in the service of the nation's development properly defined. The first concern was 'crisis management.' There was secondarily some concern for 'cosmetics'—appearing to be in step with progressive developments internationally by taking majority ownership in an oil company. Therefore, one can sum up the motivation for this reluctant nationalization as being a mixture of 'rescue' and 'cosmetic' nationalization, with the former predominating.

Let us look now at what was to be nationalized and the terms of acquisition. B.P. in 1969 was the second largest oil producing company in Trinidad. It was producing from its own fields about 8.4 million barrels of oil annually—13% of the country's total crude production. In addition, it obtained another 8 million barrels of oil annually from its one-third share of oil producing operations offshore in the Gulf of Paria. It owned these operations jointly with Shell and Texaco. B.P. had in all a crude availability of some 16½ million barrels of oil a year—roughly 25% of Trinidad's crude production. In 1967, its reported proved reserves amounted to some 75 million barrels of oil, and it employed 1517 workers, mainly in the Deep South of Trinidad. It possessed a small, worthless refinery with a throughput of less than 40 barrels a day. Its land holdings were about 8% of the total land under oil lease. Overall, however, its operations were of considerable economic significance to the whole country, and especially to the Southern region where it was based.

Though B.P. had declared its properties to be uneconomic, it nevertheless demanded compensation for them. In fact, it demanded compensation of more than double the book value which was US$14.3 million. It even demanded compensation for the oil in the ground and counted its refinery as part of its properties for sale. Oil in the ground could hardly be regarded as an asset of the company since it is widely recognized that mineral reserves in the ground are the patrimony of the nation, and that the mineral bearing lands are merely leased to an enterprise. The refinery in question represented an asset to neither the company nor to the country.

Given all the circumstances, the government could have quite justifiably settled the issue peremptorily in its favour. However, it feared to take any strong action against B.P. despite the circumstances, because such action might have upset foreign capital generally, and damaged the country's 'image' internationally. The government was, and is, very exercised to maintain a welcoming and favourable 'climate' for foreign investment. Therefore it called in a firm of American consultants, and despite the clear contradictions between B.P.'s statements and its demands eventually agreed to pay B.P. US$22 million— a sum far higher than the book value of what were supposedly 'worthless' properties.

The government apparently accepted B.P.'s demand for a valuation related to the 'market' value of its properties including the oil in the ground. Payment was to be made partly in cash (convertible foreign exchange— sterling) and partly in oil. B.P. was paid off within a year. Part of the payment was in the form of product from the nationalized company and the cash portion came from the proceeds of a loan raised by the newly nationalized company (of which more anon). With respect to valuation, time horizon, nature of compensation, and timing of payment, B.P. was clearly far and away the winner in the negotiation.

The settlement certainly was in B.P.'s interest. The company was able to enter Trinidad when it suited it, leave when it suited it, suck its operations dry, and then receive prompt and handsome compensation for the shell it left behind. B.P. had a very weak case on which to argue for compensation at all, far less for as much as it did, given its operating record and its own public pronouncements. Its home government, Britain, was hardly likely to attempt any intervention on its part, and most certainly not military intervention. Trinidad was so marginal to B.P. that the company was unlikely to resist a hard line by the government on the question of compensation. One suspects that B.P. was surprised at how much it was able to get. The hair-trigger fear of damaging the country's 'image' with the international community and adversely affecting its 'climate' for foreign investment is based on an apparent ignorance of, or naivete about, certain fundamentals of the motivations and operations of foreign capital.

We can turn now to the issues of whether effective direct control was achieved, in whose interests this control, if achieved, has been exercised, and whether the nationalization can be deemed to be economically successful or not. With respect to the first two issues here, what turns out to be key is the nature and operation of the joint venture set up.

The company chosen as a joint venture partner was Tesoro of Texas, USA. It was decided that the government would own 50.1% of the shares of the new company (the barest minimum needed to advertise local majority ownership) and Tesoro of Texas would own the remaining 49.9%. Tesoro was a fledgling oil company at the time. It had never been out of the USA before. In fact, it became a multinational with its entry into Trinidad.

In 1969, its assets amounted to a paltry US$69 million, and its net earnings were only $3.6 million. By contrast, Texaco reported assets of US$8.6 billion, revenues of $6 billion and net earnings of $702 million the same year. Tesoro produced a miniscule 3,250 barrels of oil a day in 1969, had a refinery throughput of less than 13,000 barrels a day, employed no more than 470 people, had little in the way of marketing outlets, no technology to speak of, was heavily in debt and financially weak.

Tesoro's rate of return on invested capital in 1969 (without its Trinidad venture) was only 5.6%. It had debt of $33.4 million compared to a stockholder's equity of only $21.3 million. The so-called 'current ratio' is widely used as an indicator of financial solvency. It is computed as Current Assets ÷ Current Liabilities. Time honoured rules of thumb suggest that it should be at least 2. For Tesoro in 1969, it was 1.6. Another ratio widely used as an indicator of a company's ability to carry its debt burden is the earnings coverage ratio. This is calculated as 'net income before the payment of bond interest and extraordinary items ÷ Bond Interest Expense.' This should be at least 5. For Tesoro in 1969, it was 4.5. The company's pre-tax operating rate of return (i.e. Income before taxes and Interest Payments ÷ Average Total assets) was only 5.94% in the same year.

This financial analysis of Tesoro's shakiness as a joint-venture partner is corroborated by the evaluation of professional investment analysts. As late as 1972, Financial World rated Tesoro as C+ in terms of investment quality. C+ means 'semi-speculative.' Texaco by contrast drew an A+ rating. In Moody's Industrials of 1971, Tesoro's bonds were rated 'B.' B means 'generally lacks characteristics of the desirable investment. Assurance of interest and principal payments or of maintenance of other terms of contract over any long period of time may be small.'

Desite all this Tesoro was chosen as a joint-venture partner. According to some senior government officials interviewed, Tesoro sold itself on the basis of having special expertise in secondary recovery. Given the declining nature of Trinidad's land production, this was felt to be a valuable asset.[6] According to one key Board member of the new company, the reason for the choice was that Tesoro was regarded as having special access to finance and as led by some 'very dynamic' individuals. Whichever of these rationalizations was more important, Tesoro was chosen.

As stated previously, Trinidad and Tobago was to own 50.1% of the new company and Tesoro 49.9%. This would seem to give the Trinidad government effective direct control. In fact, it did not. First of all, Tesoro got a management contract giving it control over finance, technology, and marketing. Next, it succeeded very cleverly in nullifying the supposed superordinate control the board of directors was to have exercised.

Trinidad as the majority shareholder was naturally to have the majority of the directors and so control the board. There were to be nine directors, of whom Trinidad would appoint five and Tesoro, four. One of the five appointed by Trinidad would be the Chairman of the Board. However, this Chairman had to be approved by Tesoro, and could only cast a vote in the event of a tie. Most importantly, the bye-laws of the board stipulated that on important matters, including the issuance of new stock and major investment decisions, a two-thirds majority on the board was necessary. Since two-thirds of nine is six, this meant that Tesoro, the supposedly minority shareholder, as well as having effective operating control through its management contract, obtained veto power on the board. Thus Trinidad and Tobago did not obtain effective direct control.

In whose interests has control been exercised? Who has benefited, and who has benefited most from the deal? Tesoro of Texas did very well indeed. In addition to capturing effective direct control to a considerable extent, it did so at very little cost to itself. The B.P. properties were being bought for US$22 million. Tesoro was to own 49.9% of the new company. Far from Tesoro bringing half (at least) of the cost of the acquisition, it came to Trinidad with only US$50,000. This was about the annual salary of a middle-level U.S. executive.

How did it 'swing the deal?' It got the Trinidad government to put up US$50,000 too and with this US$100,000 of paid-up capital the new company Trinidad-Tesoro was formed.

Virtually the first act Tesoro made the fledgling company perform was to go the the Eurodollar market and borrow US$25 million there and from local banks. Part of this was used to pay off the cash part of B.P.'s compensation package. Of this amount, Tesoro stood guarantor for only $7.5 million, the government and the assets of the new company—i.e. Trinidad's oil—standing guarantor for the remainder. Tesoro thus not only brought no capital to the deal, but it also cleverly held down its own share of the risk. In fact, given that it was in partnership with the Trinidad and Tobago government which was in no danger of bankruptcy, it stood virtually no risk at all.

With virtually no capital investment Tesoro found itself owning assets valued US$13.8 million in 1969. By 1975, this had increased to $80.9 million—i.e. by 486%.[7] Tesoro's net equity in Trinidad-Tesoro by 1974 had come to represent 26% of the parent company's net equity, and by 1975 this had grown to 28%. (See Table I.)

Between 1969 and 1974, Tesoro USA did not receive any dividends from its investment in Trinidad-Tesoro. This was because of an agreement to declare no dividends for the first five years and plough profits back into the Trinidad company. Nevertheless, Tesoro still received a cash flow from Trinidad-Tesoro in two ways at least. First of all, it received management fees.[8] Secondly, it was able to use Trinidad-Tesoro to some extent as a captive customer for equipment from some of its subsidiaries (e.g. winches and pumping jacks).

By 1974, however, at the end of the five-year moratorium period on dividend payments, Tesoro's share of Trinidad-Tesoro's net earnings amounted to 43% of the parent company's global net earnings. By 1975, this had grown to 48%. (See Table II.) Tesoro also benefited financially from its share in Trinidad-Tesoro in other ways. For example, by bolstering its accounts with the Trinidad contribution, regardless of actual cash flow, the company was able to dramatically improve its credit standing and its industrial rating. It had a generous assistance from the boom in oil prices after 1974.

By 1975, out of Tesoro's global crude reserves of 112.4 million barrels, its share of Trinidad-Tesoro's reserves (72.8 million barrels) represented 65%. By contrast, its reserves of crude in the USA accounted for only 9.1% of its reserves. Similiarly, of its average daily crude production globally of 25,563 barrels, 17,464 or 69% were attributable to the contribution of Trinidad-Tesoro.

By 1975, Tesoro of Texas had become a real multinational with operations in Indonesia, Bolivia, and Trinidad, and with footholds in Canada and the North Sea. It has accumulated 27 wholly-owned subsidiaries. Also, apart from its 49.9% of Trinidad-Tesoro, it acquired 37.6% of CORCO (Commonwealth Oil Refining Company)—a Puerto Rican based company engaged in oil refining and petrochemicals production with 26 subsidiaries of its own and rather shaky finances. Tesoro has also diversified into coal, tanklines, and even a finance company incorporated in a tax haven. By 1975, too, it had become the 238th largest U.S. corporation in Fortune's famous list of 500. Much of this expansion had been directly or indirectly fueled by Trinidad and Tobago and its joint venture there.

What has the country gotten out of all this? It surrendered effective direct control to Tesoro. This control was achieved by Tesoro through

TABLE I
COMPARISON OF THE NET ASSETS OF TRINIDAD-TESORO
AND TESORO (U.S.A.) 1972-75 ($US)

Year	Shareholder's Equity (Net Assets) in Tesoro Texas	Tesoro's Share of Net Assets of Trinidad-Tesoro	(2) as of % of (1)
	(1)	(2)	
1972	94,154,000	12,690,619	13.5
1973	114,269,000	18,691,759	16.4
1974	180,348,000	47,455,500	26.3
1975	223,055,000	62,212,000	27.9

Source: See Table III.

TABLE II
COMPARISON OF THE NET EARNINGS OF TRINIDAD-TESORO
AND TESORO (U.S.A) 1970-1975 ($US)

Year	Tesoro Texas Net Earnings	Trinidad-Tesoro's Net Earnings	(2) as a % of (1)	Tesoro's Share in Net Earnings of Trinidad-Tesoro	(4) as a % of (1)
	(1)	(2)	(3)	(4)	
1970	5,994,000	4,988,238	83.2	2,489,131	41.5
1971	7,672,000	8,743,553	114.0	4,363,033	56.9
1972	13,047,000	10,197,242	78.2	5,088,424	39.0
1973	19,874,000	12,026,333	60.5	6,001,140	30.1
1974	66,938,000	57,453,000	85.8	28,726,500	42.9
1975	42,926,000	40,847,000	95.2	20,423,500	47.6

Sources: Tesoro Petroleum Corporation, *10k Reports to the S.E.C.* (various issues).

TABLE III
PRODUCTION AND RESERVES OF TRINIDAD-TESORO 1969-1975
(mm. barrels)

Year	PRODUCTION				Crude Reserves
	Trin-Tesoro	Share of T.N.A.	Total	% of Nat'l Prod.	
1969	7.4	8.4	15.8	27.5	
1970	7.1	8.0	15.1	29.6	
1971	7.5	7.3	14.8	31.4	
1972	8.1	6.3	14.4	28.1	
1973	8.2	6.3	14.5	23.9	186.7
1974	7.9	6.3	14.2	20.9	153.2
1975	6.5	5.8	12.3	15.7	145.5

Sources: T.T. Ministry of Petroleum and Mines *Annual Reports* and Monthly Bulletins (various issues)
Tesoro Petroleum Corporation *10k Annual Reports to the S.E.C.* (various issues).

the management contract, through its power on the board of directors, perhaps most importantly through its exercise of quiet, subtle but very real influence among the Trinidad directors on the Board and in the corridors of governmental and ministerial power. Perhaps the most dramatic example of Tesoro's effective control was when in 1975 it was able to have Trinidad-Tesoro supposedly majority-owned and controlled by the Government balk at paying taxes on the basis of tax reference prices, on the grounds that the prior agreement with Tesoro had provided for paying taxes on a realized basis. This was despite the fact that the Trinidad and Tobago legislation explicitly overrode any previous agreements, and despite the fact that as a sovereign state it had the legal right to do so. Trindad-Tesoro, a supposedly government-controlled company, protested the application of the government's law to it at the behest of Tesoro Texas and won.

What did Trinidad and Tobago gain from the Agreement? Tesoro brought no capital. It brought no technology. It brought no markets. As it turned out, it in fact possessed no special expertise in secondary recovery. The actual day to day work of the company was and is done by nationals. In fact up until very recently, Tesoro maintained no more than three expatriates in Trinidad, only one of whom was employed on the production side. Nor was it the case that the important technical work was really carried out abroad, or serviced by itinerant trouble-shooters. Nationals have in fact, from all reports, done it all. Engineers with the company were, in interviews, loud in their derision of the idea that Tesoro had contributed anything technologically to local operations.

As far as markets went, initially more than half the oil was sold to Shell in Trinidad. The rest was sold to Amerada Hess in the Virgin Islands. The Trinidad government's own oil legislation (1969 Petroleum Law and the 1970 Regulations, Sec. 43 [U]) obliges local refiners to give preference to indigenous crude. Thus it had the legal means to insist that Shell and Texaco buy and refine Trinidad-Tesoro's crude. Instead, Shell and Texaco were allowed to continue importing 57% and 77% respectively of their throughput. Recently, virtually all the Tesoro production has been going to the now nationalized Shell refinery. Thus Tesoro provided no markets that Trinidad could not have provided for itself with a modicum of effort.

As far as the economic success of the nationalized properties goes, it can hardly be claimed that Trinidad-Tesoro has enjoyed any particular technical or commercial success as a result of Tesoro. On the financial side, the company seems to be doing well. But this is due simply to the external factors of the 1973-74 energy crisis and the dramatic increase in oil prices. Thus net assets jumped from US$37.3 million in 1973 to US$94.9 million in 1974 and US$124.4 million in 1975. After tax earnings rose from US$12 million in 1973 to $140.8 million by 1975.[9]

But when one looks at basic factors such as production and reserves, it is a far different story. As Table III shows, it has been a constant struggle to maintain the level of production and reserves. In fact, total production has slipped more or less steadily from 1969 to 1975. With a reserves to production ratio of just 12 years in 1975, the company could hardly be said to be in a good position. More tellingly, there has been no significant diversification into new areas (e.g. petrochemicals), no evidence of any steady growth in technological capability, and no evidence that the company is making significantly increased contribution to the utilization of the country's resources—e.g. significantly expanded employment, new uses for natural gas, etc. And whatever little has been achieved, it has had little to do with the association with Tesoro of Texas.

Evaluation

The acquisition of the B.P. properties by the government of Trinidad and Tobago and the creation of Trinidad-Tesoro cannot be claimed to be a genuine nationalization, in the sense in which that term was defined in Section II. It falls down in several important respects. Firstly, it requires considerable stretching of one's interpretation of the events to consider the acquisition state-initiated. More clearly, effective direct control was not achieved. Furthermore, the exercise of this control has benfited more significantly the interests of the joint venture partner, rather than the public interest. The interests of the governing political elite has been served in that it has been able to hold up Trinidad-Tesoro as an example of the progressive nature of its oil policy and its determination to participate in the commanding heights of the company.

The surrender of effective direct control to Tesoro marks this as a pseudonationalization. It also falls into the categories of 'rescue' and 'cosmetic' nationalizations as defined earlier. The terms of acquisition, it was seen, were clearly to B.P.'s advantage just as the terms of the joint-venture agreement have worked to Tesoro's advantage. Economically, the nationalized properties would appear to have enjoyed success when measured financially. However, a deeper examination of the situation suggests an indifferent or fair performance at best and certainly little in the way of the kind of dynamism one would have desired to see. Given all the facts and setting them against the checklist of Section II, it would be our unequivocal judgement that this acquisition does not merit the term nationalization, and that the country and the public interest have clearly had the worst of the deal.

The next issue is whether the deal made could be justified in terms of the state's other objectives and motives and in terms of its assessment of the political risks. With respect to the state's ostensible motives, five factors appear to be relevant. One was its fear of the politically and socially explosive nature of the situation B.P.'s departure might have precipitated. A second factor was its concern not to sully its international image. Third was its anxiety to reach a quick settlement of the issue—the usual pressures of a crisis-management situation? Fourth, we may note a desire to make some political capital out of the move—i.e. by appearing to be progressive and to be nationalizing. A fifth factor was its feelings of insecurity with respect to local ability to run an oil company without foreign participation.

The government, according to one senior official interviewed, felt itself to be 'weak' at the time. A review of the economic situation at the time offers little evidence to support such a feeling. While the economic situation was not particularly healthy, neither was it deteriorating. As far as the actual bargaining went, a study of the objective factors suggest the government had considerable elements of strength on its side. B.P.'s record, its public statements, the marginality of Trinidad to it, and the fact that its home country was virtually certain not to intervene was one element of strength. Similarly, Tesoro was obviously in a weak position to negotiate for as much as it did. There was also considerable local, popular support for the idea of nationalization.

It seems clear that the government's failure was due primarily to certain subjective, psychological factors—its fears about foreign capital, its lack of confidence in its people's ability, and its anxiety to make a deal and get over the immediate crisis. Another important factor was its serious ignorance about the oil industry internationally, the companies it was dealing with, and local capabilities with respect to the oil business. It made serious miscalculations with respect to all these factors as well as with respect to the nature and operations of foreign capital generally.

This psychological failure has its roots in deeper factors such as class, the colonial mind, and the political and technological unsophistication of a young nation. This cannot be pursued here. Suffice to say, an examination of the motivations, objectives, and risk assessment of the state hardly justifies the significant variance of the deals it made from what would have been desirable.

THE 1974 NATIONALIZATION OF SHELL TRINIDAD

In 1974, five years after the B.P.-Tesoro deal, the Trinidad and Tobago government effected its second major oil nationalization with the take over of Shell Trinidad Ltd. This move coincided with the period of the 1973-74 energy crisis and the Arab oil embargo.

In this period, there was a wave of oil nationalizations throughout the major Third World oil-producing countries. Countries such as Libya, Algeria, Iran, Iraq, Venezuela, Nigeria, and Kuwait began to take over or to control their petroleum industries. These moves were stimulated and lubricated by (1) vastly increased financial reserves which both provided funds for the payment of compensation and a shield against economic retaliation; (2) a new awareness of the bargaining strength arising out of concerted, collective action; and (3) a new political determination to act forcefully against decades of exploitation. These factors combined with economic and political disarray in the West to provide an extremely favourable climate internationally for nationalization of mineral resources.

The Trinidad and Tobago government felt it could hardly ignore this new trend. The existing situation gave it little excuse for failing to move to control its own oil industry, which has been a classic example of neocolonial control and dependent underdevelopment. The question was in which direction to move.

There were (and are) four major producing companies in Trinidad and Tobago. Texaco and Amoco are the two most significant, dominating refining and production respectively. While Texaco in 1974 accounted for only 23% of total crude production, its refining capacity of nearly 364,000 b/d represented 80% of refining capacity in the country. Amoco, who refines none of its crude domestically had an output of 29.5 million barrels of oil in 1974—43.3% of total production. By 1975, this had risen to 45.5 million barrels—57.9% of total production. Furthermore, according to Amoco's figures, its declared proved reserves of 177 million barrels of oil and 243 billion cu.ft. of gas in 1974, and its holdings of large acreage off the country's East Coast gave it control of the most significant and potentially most lucrative aspect of crude producing operations in Trinidad and Tobago to date. It is obvious that any serious attempt to bring the Trinidad oil industry under local control would have to deal with Texaco and Amoco. These are the prime targets.

The other two major companies were Trinidad-Tesoro and Shell. Trinidad-Tesoro was the third largest of the four, accounting for 22% of Trinidad's 1974 crude production and with gross reserves of 153.2 million barrels of oil and 178 billion cu.ft. of gas. Shell was the smallest and least significant of the four companies. In 1974 it accounted for 8.7 million barrels of oil (13% of total crude production). Of its oil (6.3 million barrels), 72% came from the joint-venture operations in the Gulf of Paria (T.N.A.). Shells's own land fields then produced only 2.4 million barrels of oil in 1974. It had crude reserves of 67.7 million barrels of oil at the end of 1973. Two-thirds of these reserves were located in T.N.A.'s reservoirs. In 1974, then, Shell had a reserves to production ratio of only eight years.

Shell also owned a refinery of 100,000 b/d nominal capacity. This refinery was old, simple, and primitive by modern standards. About 70% of its output consisted of relatively low value residual fuel oil. Shell's operations in Trinidad had been organized by its parent companies as one link in the Shell chain. Thus much of the refinery's throughput (over 55% after 1970) was crude brought in from Shell Nigeria through Shell organized tanker transportation. The major part of the refinery's output was either marketed through the Shell organization in the USA (e.g. the residual fuel oil), or consisted of unfinished products sent to Shell's major Caribbean refinery in Curaçao. The Shell Trinidad refinery was little more than an adjunct to the Curaçao refinery.

The Trinidad operations were also dependent on the parent network for essential technical services, customized spare parts (for the refinery's hydro-treater for example), and additives for the manufacture of lubricating oils. Shell Trinidad then (like Texaco Trinidad) was a specialized segment of a highly integrated operation, and the local operations viewed in isolation from the rest of the network were highly irrational. Shell Trinidad made sense only as part of Shell's international system. Despite all of this, the Trinidad and Tobago government chose to nationalize Shell.

It must be emphasized that this decision was not part of any carefully thought out, well-worked out plan for controlling and reorganizing the entire Trinidad petroleum industry in Trinidad's interests. It is only in such a context that the Shell nationalization would have made sense. As we shall see, the failure to do this was responsible for many of the problems the nationalized company has faced and the difficulties and failures of the negotiations themselves. Apparently, there were two key factors in the decision to nationalize Shell.

The first was simply that Shell was the only one of the four companies which was willing to leave. For Texaco, Amoco, and Tesoro, their Trinidad operations are all currently very important to the global companies. Any attempt at truly effective nationalization and local direction of the operations of these companies in local interest is certain to be strongly resisted. This was not the case with Shell.

Shell had entered Trinidad in 1913. The reason for its entry at that time was to produce oil for the British Navy. (Trinidad's oil from Shell and other British companies played an important role in Britain's victory in World War I.) Over time, this initial rationale evaporated and by the early to mid-sixties Shell had come to have little further use for Trinidad.

Trinidad as a source of crude was extremely minor to Shell. In 1972, for instance, when the Shell Group's global production of crude amounted to 4,526,000 b/d, the contribution of Shell Trinidad was 26,000 barrels. In the same year Shell Trinidad refined some 67,000 b/d compared to refinery runs of 5,022,000 b/d for the global organization. Shell's Trinidad reserves were miniscule compared to its alternative sources. Trinidad was insignificant as a market, and Shell's Caribbean market could be effectively serviced from its Venezuela-Curaçao operations if necessary.

Furthermore, as the Shell Group discerned the rise in militancy of oil-producing countries elsewhere, it began to quietly develop and operationalize a new strategy—withdrawing from some areas of the underdeveloped world, concentrating effort on the safer areas of the developed world, for example, the North Sea and the U.S. offshore, and diversifying rapidly into areas such as nuclear energy. Trinidad played no part in this new strategy.

Thus the available evidence suggests that from the mid-1960s or thereabout Shell began to quietly liquidate its Trinidad operation. This was effected with respect to both its producing and refining operations, though more ruthlessly with the former. The essence of Shell's liquidation scheme seemed to center, as liquidations usually do, on the non-reinvestment of any significant capital into ongoing operations. In manufacturing operations, the failure to spend money on preventative maintenance—the non-replacement of worn-out equipment, etc.,—and instead the practice of break-down maintenance and 'patch-up' jobs, is sometimes (not always) a sign of a deliberate decision to disinvest.

In crude production the failure to undertake exploration and development activity and the reliance on proved reserves for production is sometimes a comparable clue. This practice effectively amounts to liquidation of existing oil inventories. After some time the effects of this practice are manifested in falling reserves/production ratios, higher costs of production (as reservoirs are drained), and ultimately, absolute falls in production.[10]

From mid-1967 to February 1970 (a period of 32 months), Shell Trinidad did absolutely no drilling. When it began again in 1970, it drilled only 29 developmental wells between 1970 and 1972, compared to 162 for Texaco and 222 for Tesoro. (See Table IV.) In 1974, Shell had not opened a new oilfield, land or marine, for over ten years. Its newest oilfield dated back to 1963. It refused to take over B.P.'s properties in 1967 and also reportedly refused Amoco's offer in the 1960s to share in the exploration off the East Coast. Between 1960 and 1974, Shell's annual crude production from its own wells fell steadily from 7.2 million barrels to 2.4 million barrels. By 1974, Shell's 346 wells were averaging crude production of only 22-23 barrels a day, less than half the (low) national average of 53 barrels per day per well.

TABLE IV
DRILLING ACTIVITY OF MAJOR OIL-PRODUCING COMPANIES
IN TRINIDAD AND TOBAGO 1970-1972

	No. of Development Wells Drilled		
Company	1970	1971	1972
Amoco	n.a.	—	28
Texaco	29	79	54
Tesoro	52	86	84
T.N.A.	21	16	14
Shell	9	20	0

Source: T.T. Ministry of Petroleum and Mines
        Monthly Bulletins December 1971 and 1972.

The government was well aware of the situation. A 1974 Ministry of Petroleum and Mines memorandum stated, inter alia:

> The view has long been held by the Petroleum Inspecting section, that the general condition of the fields operated by Shell Trinidad Ltd. is deplorable. In particular, reports from this section to the Development Engineer from as far back as 1970 indicate that this section is thoroughly dissatisfied with the company's policy in the matter of proper maintenance. Inspectors indicate the Gathering Stations are improperly kept, and in some areas, e.g. Balata West..., the conditions are horrible.[11]

The document goes on to cite lack of equipment maintenance, the failure to maintain access roads to producing wells, the creation of pollution problems and the (illegal) neglect of the company to report these. It also noted that local staff's proposals for exploration and development programs had been turned down by headquarters, and terms the practices reported on "apparently planned neglect."

Though Shell spent some money on its refinery in the late 1906s, this too was in poor condition. Again, Ministry of Petroleum and Mines reports indicated an awareness of the unsatisfactory nature of Shell's refining operations. One report clearly identified the problems besetting the refinery as resulting from the fact that "for a long period, Shell has been carrying out break-down maintenance rather than preventive maintenance which is necessary for a high degree of reliability."[12] It was recognized that the refinery would require heavy maintenance expenditure to bring it up to standard and that its major processing plant, the distillation unit, might have to be replaced within ten years.

In addition to all this Shell had since 1967-68 embarked on a well-organized program to reduce its labour force as much as it could. The company seemed to have no further use for Trinidad though its operations were still providing a high degree of profitability. (Ignoring the added profitability through the processing fee arrangement and other transfer pricing devices, Shell Trinidad showed an annual average after tax rate of return on net assets of 25.4% between 1964 and 1973.)[13]

Shell's willingness to leave (or, at the very least, indifference to leaving) was one factor behind its choice as a nationalization target. Another factor was the instigation of Tesoro who had been urging the government for some time to nationalize Shell and turn the properties over to Trinidad-Tesoro. In a 1974 memorandum written by a key director of Trinidad-Tesoro, Trinidad-Tesoro is credited with persuading the government to nationalize Shell:

> At the end of the first quarter of this year (1974) presumably to thwart Trinidad-Tesoro's insistent demand that something be done about their gross neglect, Shell offered government a small interest in the refinery only and on our advice Government rejected that minimal participation and demanded a complete surrender of all producing and refining and marketing facilities.[14]

Tesoro proposed a merger of the two companies and offered the government a larger equity (60%) in the merged operations. Tesoro's motivation was perhaps two-fold. One factor might simply be a compulsive bureaucratic urge to empire building on the part of some senior Tesoro executives. The second, more Machiavellian, factor is that the addition of Shell's reserves and other assets to Trinidad-Tesoro's accounts and through this Tesoro U.S.A.'s accounts would have boosted Tesoro's credit rating and enhanced its ability to further fuel its general expansion.

Given that the government chose to ignore Amoco and Texaco as nationalization targets and instead to tackle Shell, it would appear to have had certain strengths in its bargaining position. First of all, Shell had a very poor operating record. Secondly, the dramatic rise in oil prices gave the government the financial resources to nationalize, compensate, and reorganize the company's operations and to withstand any ordinary economic dislocation. Thirdly, the international climate in 1974 was extremely propitious for nationalization.

On the other side of the table, Shell had some strengths of its own. When analyzed, these turn out, ironically enough, to derive from the government's lack of planning, its perception of the world, its weakness in dealing with foreign capital, and its perception of Shell's strength and its own weakness.

First of all, the government was unwilling to offend foreign capital generally. It felt that any strong action against foreign capital would hurt its international image and jeopardize the inflow of foreign capital to the country. This has been a persistent characteristic of its dealings with foreign investors. Thus it began by making it clear that it would not expropriate Shell unilaterally but was anxious to reach a negotiated settlement giving assurances to Shell that the acquisition would be "on terms and conditions acceptable to both parties." In fact the Trinidad and Tobago Prime Minister wrote to the British Prime Minister, inter alia, "You may wish to know that as an earnest of good faith, we were prepared to deposit a sum of money in Barclays Bank, London, to finance the purchase, if Shell had queried our intentions."[15] Shell therefore began the negotiations with the considerable advantage of knowing that there were limits beyond which the government feared to go, and a 'floor' to the settlement it could bargain for.

A second source of Shell's strength in the negotiations derived from the government's lack of prior planning, its unwillingness to deal wth the local oil industry as a whole, and its negotiating team's consequent perception of the difficulties the nationalized company would face. Shell's Trinidad operations as pointed out earlier were one link in the Shell chain and made little sense apart from the rest of the chain. Its refining operations depended heavily on crude from other Shell subsidiaries, principally Nigeria. The finished products of the refinery were handled through the Shell marketing network. The unfinished products went to the Curaçao refinery for finishing. Transportation was arranged through the Shell Group.

The nationals in the Shell Trinidad operation, while knowledgeable about Shell's Caribbean markets, knew little about international marketing and transportation. To attempt to buy crude for the refinery from abroad would have most likely been highly uneconomic given the refinery's output mix and the predominance of relatively low valued residual fuel oil. The new company would also have to find markets and would have trouble even in the Caribbean, it was felt, since the distribution facilities were all owned by the oil companies including Shell.[16]

The government team was aware of these problems and agonized over them at length. The team was also aware of the technological 'lock-ins.' These were of four kinds—proprietary technology in the production equipment, Shell's monopoly in spare parts for custom-built equipment, specialized inputs for certain processes, and Shell's brand names and trade marks.

In the negotiations Shell cited 13 patents covering refining processes—either its own or licensed from Universal Oil Products. These patents were all registered between 1960 and 1973.[17] Certain equipment, notably the hydro-treater, relied on the Shell organization for spare parts. Without Shell's cooperation, maintenance could be difficult. Also, Shell's lubricating oil business depended on its special additives and the negotiating team did not know if these could be substituted for.

There was only one way these problems could have been eliminated—through long and careful prior planning and through a willingness to deal with the local oil industry as a whole. This would have solved the problems of crude feedstocks, dependence on Shell's spare parts and additives, and permitted the obtaining of markets through a more attractive output mix, a political solution to controlling CARICOM markets and the well-worked out development of international transportation and marketing.

As it was, the negotiating team felt constrained to urge an accommodation with Shell and a continued relationship after nationalization, hoping to obtain access to crude, markets, and technology, as well as to certain personnel. In fact, reading through the records of the negotiations, the most arresting feature perhaps is the negotiating team's sense of weakness, rather than strength, and the way in which this, combined with the government's almost tropismatic fear of offending foreign capital and frightening away foreign investors, eroded the government's real bargaining strength.

Another noteworthy feature of the negotiations was the dependence of the government's negotiating team on Shell for information. The list of data requested from Shell included its balance sheets, details of its structure and internal organization, including the names and nationality of senior appointees, details of its patents, management and service contracts, and details of its organizational links with other Shell companies. The full list of information requested suggested an extremely high degree of ignorance on the part of the government about foreign companies operating on its soil. Furthermore, it provided Shell with yet another negotiating advantage since, given the time constraints in the negotiations, the data provided could hardly be thoroughly verified.

The negotiations began in London and then shifted to Trinidad. The government's team for the major negotiations (in Trinidad) comprised some of its most senior civil servants with experience in matters of oil, finance, and law. The six-man team was aided by a four-man squad of advisers, including a well-known foreign consultant. Against this, Shell sent a team of three of its foreign executives.[18]

The government team took the view that valuation should be based on net book value (historical). Some members even argued that this formula should be adjusted to reduce reported assets because of Shell's recovery of capital through special tax concessions such as the permission to expense intangible drilling costs for tax purposes though capitalizing it on the company's books and the recovery of capital through the submarine depletion allowance. The team was also well aware of the run down condition of Shell's properties, though no serious valuation of these was made.

The team did not, however, view the valuation of the properties from the point of view of the economic value to the country (e.g. of residual fuel oil production.). Nor did it apparently consider liabilities to the state due to Shell's accounting practices. Two of these were of especial significance. First, Shell (like Texaco) refined its foreign crude under a processing agreement according to which the foreign affiliate simply paid Shell Trinidad a 'fee' for refining crude for it. Profits on foreign crude refining were therefore not calculated in the normal fashion—i.e. Value of refined products – Cost of refining – Cost of crude feedstocks. Instead revenues were simply the processing fees received and profits were calculated as Processing fees received – Cost of refining.

The processing fee was nothing more than a transfer price which could be, and was, used to transfer profits tax-free out of the country. Data for 1970 for example show that the processing fees were set at 22¢ TT per barrel, while processing costs were 45¢ TT per barrel. Shell thus showed a paper 'loss' of 23¢ a barrel on every barrel of foreign crude it refined.[19] This was 55% of its throughput. This 'loss' was charged off againt the profits from the refining of indigenous crude not subject to the processing agreement and resulted in a massive loss of tax revenues to the government.

Furthermore, Shell made use of low transfer prices on the export of refined products from Trinidad crude thus again reducing its tax liability. The government had negotiated rather ineffectively with Shell between 1972 and 1974 seeking to obtain a revaluation of the prices and recoup some of its due taxes. Both of these practices could have been the source of large claims for liabilities to the state.

Shell by contrast started by arguing for an opportunity cost (market) valuation for its producing and marketing operations, a replacement cost valuation for its refining business, a return of the signature bonus it had paid to government for exploration rights off the South-East Coast, and an independent valuation of its unused land. This gave a figure of TT$201 million compared to a net book value (historical) of TT$56 million in 1973.

The government team rejected the Shell approach and pointed to its deplorable operating record. Shell professed ignorance af any malfeasance and in turn argued that the government's net book value approach based on precedent elsewhere was inapplicable in the given context. It claimed that such a valuation method was usually accompanied by an arrangement for the selling company to 'buy-back' some of the crude from the nationalized properties at concessionary prices thereby recovering some of its capital through this means.

The actual settlement arrived at was highly favourable to Shell. Another factor apparently intervened—the impatience of the political leadership to get a settlement which would permit a formal take-over by the country's Independence Day (August 31st). The negotiating team lost its argument for a net book value (historical) approach. Thus while the 1973 net book value was TT$56.6 million, Shell finally obtained TT$93.6 million, without any valuation of its rundown assets and no claim for liabilities to the state pressed.

With respect to the timing, time-horizon, cost of deferral, and currency of payment, Shell got payment in convertible currency (sterling, though it was willing to settle for oil), with 75% of the compensation paid immediately and the balance within a year in two installments, and at a 7% rate of interest (net of tax). Interest was to be compounded monthly and the source of the payment was to be the Treasury.

Shell received compensation of $758,400 for its proprietary know-how against the issue of licenses to the new company. In addition, it was contracted to provide a range of technical services to the new company plus its additives at an undisclosed price. Furthermore, Shell, who from the very first meeting in London had asked that certain aspects of its operation important to it be exempted, obtained permission to set up a new local company to continue its chemical operations.

Shell had therefore much the better of the bargain. The company had successfully liquidated its operations and been paid handsomely for the shell that was left. It was able to retain aspects of the operation it was interested in and stood to benefit further from the technical services it contracted to provide the new company.

Shell bargained throughout with considerable skill. The fact that at the first meetings in London (on the 9th and 10th May, 1974) Shell asked that chemicals, bunkering, the supply of aviation fuels, lubricants, and its research testing station be excluded from nationalization suggests careful prior consideration of its interests and careful planning.

Shell also made good use of the government's concern for maintaining amicable relationships with foreign capital by implying when it suited it that the government was exerting 'pressure' upon it and claiming that an application of net book value was a departure from the principles laid down in London where it had been emphasized that negotiations would be "free," on "commercial terms," and "non-pressurized." Shell, it appears, was well aware of the government's psychological weakness and cleverly exploited it.

Trinidad and Tobago by contrast came off much worse than Shell. The country ended up overpaying for poorly maintained, badly rundown oil fields, and an old inefficient refinery producing an economically irrational slate of products. The new company was born to problems—marketing, distribution, refining, and producing. By 1975, the refinery's throughput had fallen to 47% of capacity—far below an economic level as it faced problems finding crude for feedstocks. A massive effort would clearly be needed to put the company on a sound footing. Currently, its nonfailure is attributable simply to continued high oil prices.

The Trinidad side in the negotiations can be faulted on several counts. Firstly, they chose a target for nationalization which would have made sense only if the policy had been carefully planned and had been related to a programme for the reorganization and rationalization of the Trinidad oil industry as a whole.

Secondly, the government fenced in its team from the start by fore-closing certain options for dealing with Shell through its fear of offending Shell and foreign capital. What was even worse, it telegraphed its psychological weakness to Shell who did not fail to take advantage of it.

Thirdly, the failure to conduct a proper valuation of Shell's properties and equipment, and near total reliance on Shell for the information necessary for preparing the government's position led to considerable weakness and opened the door to sharp practice by Shell.

Less blame attaches to the team perhaps and more to their political masters. The team, it is true, suffered from certain weaknesses. They shared the politicians' naive conceptions about foreign capital, what attracts it and what repels it, its importance and its necessity. One suspects too that the team was rather weak with respect to its understanding of the technological problems that would confront a nationalized industry and consequently unimaginative in finding solutions for the problem (for example, on matters such as the significance of Shell's additives). It could be that the most crucial problem here was lack of time to thoroughly investigate the problems and feasible solutions.

The team however had a fairly good grasp of the fundamental issues— for example, on approaches to valuation and which approach would have been in the country's interests. They also made a point of bringing up Shell's record though not as forcefully or as centrally as they might have done.

In the final analysis, the technocrats were undermined by their political masters. The psychological weakness of the politicians with respect to foreign capital, their disinclination to really tackle the major oil companies in Trinidad, their tactical negotiating errors (for example, telegraphing their anxieties), and finally, their impatience to conclude a deal all significantly weakened the country's position at the bargaining table, and enabled Shell to emerge with the better of the deal.

Evaluation

Unlike the B.P.-Tesoro case, effective direct control was achieved in the Shell nationalization. One cannot be certain that this control will be retained given Tesoro's interest in taking over the running of Trintoc—the newly nationalized company.[20] The nationalization once initiated did involve the minimum degree of compulsion that marks a genuine nationalization. The available data suggest, however, that the initiative for the nationalization was not wholly from the State. As we have seen, certain Tesoro memoranda boast of the role Tesoro played in instigating the government to nationalize Shell.

There is little doubt, however, that part of the initiative at least was from the politicians, primarily because they saw political capital to be gained from the nationalization. This then was a clear case of a cosmetic nationalization. This judgement is further reinforced when we stop to note that the properties involved were not economically substantive in the context of Trinidad oil, and that the nationalization did not take place with any serious prior planning either of the acquisition itself, or of the role to be played by the properties in overall development strategy.

The actual terms of the acquisition were highly favourable to Shell. It had the better of the deal with respect to the valuation of the assets, the time horizon over which payment was to be effected, the timing of payments within that horizon, the currency of compensation, and the rate of interest. The actual settlement was clearly in the interest of Shell first of all, and the local political elite secondarily. Shell received prompt and generous compensation for the properties it surrendered, it was able to carry out a successful liquidation of these properties prior to nationaliza- tion, it was able to maintain the parts of the business it was still interested in free from nationalization, and it stood to profit further from selling technical services and other inputs to the new company.

The political leadership was able to satisfy its interests in claiming publicly that it was pursuing progressive politicies in oil and bringing the oil industry under greater local control gradually, sensibly, and prudently. Given the price paid for the properties, the nature of the assets bought and the ignoring of the real targets in the local oil industry, it seems reasonable to conclude that the actual settlement did not adequately serve the public interest. It is still too early to make a judgement on the economic success of the nationalization, or in whose interests effective control is being exercised.

Finally, when one attempts to explain the actual settlement in relation to the desirable, it is interesting to observe the same factors operating in the case of the Shell nationalization as in the B.P.-Tesoro deal. Once again, subjective, psychological factors stand out—the fear of offending foreign capital, the sense of weakness and feelings of inability with respect to the oil industry, the anxiety and haste to arrive at a settlement (in this case for purely cosmetic reasons). Objectively, the government seems to have been in a strong position. There was the favourable international climate for nationalization, there was Shell's deplorable operating record, no pressing domestic crisis existed to warrant haste in arriving at a settlement, the properties were marginal to Shell and to its home country, finance was available not only to pay compensation but to service the country's other needs. There need be little fear that an economic failure with respect to the nationalized company would threaten the country with serious economic dislocation.

The political risks involved in driving a harder bargain would seem to have been negligible given all the attendant circumstances, domestically and internationally. A perusal of the records of the negotiations suggests that while the government team suffered from some informational weakness, and did not seem to be as highly skilled as their opponents, neither information nor bargaining skills were in the final analysis the critical factors in the State's failure. Failure can be laid rather at the door of the politician's psychological weaknesses, in the haste to arrive at a settlement and in the poor planning that preceded the negotiations. None of these factors would seem to extenuate the deviation of the actual settlement from the desirable.

CONCLUSIONS

The canons of sound methodology sharply constrain the nature and extent of the conclusions one can presume to draw from a couple of case studies. Generalizations can only be based on the study of a wider range of actual experiences. Nevertheless, there are a few points that the material analyzed does serve to point out or illustrate.

The two cases studied do illustrate the point that multinational corporations have increasingly learnt to make nationalizations and joint ventures work for them. Joint ventures in fact may not provide the best of both worlds for the host underdeveloped country. In the case of Tesoro, the joint venture did not provide access to any significant technology, nor did it mean national control because of majority ownership. It might be noted here too that experience elsewhere also shows that 100% national ownership need not result in effective, local control. This may be vitiated through management, marketing, and technology agreements.

It is also clear that nationalizations need not serve the public interest. The general presumption that simple nationalization is necessarily and always in the public interest is quite false. Nationalization can easily be perverted to serve other interests—the interests of foreigners or of some local elite. It is therefore not enough to call for nationalization as a cure-all for foreign exploitation or economic ills. Other conditions must be laid down. In fact, at best nationalization is simply an opportunity to redirect the use of certain properties in the public interest. The opportunity may or may not be grasped. If grasped, it may or may not succeed for all sorts of internal and external factors.

Our final conclusion is that those who call for nationalization need to be much more rigorous and precise in terms of what they seek. Nationalization cannot be touted as a cure-all—it is simply to provide an opportunity. The translation of this opportunity into success requires the fulfillment of several other conditions. Next, nationalization must result in effective direct control—control over the fundamental economic variables outlined in Section II. Finally, a genuine nationalization must serve the public interest. It must be reasoned, planned, and the public interest in the specific case needs to be carefully defined in terms of the society's general developmental goals and objectives.

FOOTNOTES

[1]For a fuller discussion of these developmental criteria see Trevor Farrell, *The Economics of Discontent* (Port of Spain, Trinidad: Vanguard Publishing Company, 1975).

[2]Sidney Verba, "Assumptions of Rationality and Non-Rationality in Models of the International System," in *International Politics and Foreign Policy,* ed. James Rosenau (New York: The Free Press, 1969).

[3]Fred Iklé, *How Nations Negotiate* (New York: Praeger, 1964), Chs, 5, 9 and 11.

[4]It should be noted that analyses of the company's operations quite contradicted its claims of unprofitability. See Extracts from the Evidence of Dr. Charles Feinstein in O.W.T.U. pamphlet entitled *O.W.T.U.-B.P. Case* (San Fernando, Trinidad: Vanguard Publishing Company, n.d.).

[5]O.W.T.U. "Oil in Turmoil" and Memorandum on the formation of a National Oil Company (San Fernando, Trinidad: Vanguard Publishing House, n.d.) The statements attributed to Cabinet Minister J. O'Halloran are especially instructive.

[6]This was questionable logic. It is evident that Trinidad's future as an oil province is in the offshore, and that this is the area of expertise most important to acquire. Land production is inexorably being exhausted. In any event, land production and secondary recovery on land turns out to be one of the areas where Trinidad's nationals are strongest and have had the most experience. And as it turned out anyway, Tesoro did not in fact have any 'special' expertise in secondary recovery.

[7]Tesoro Petroleum Corporation *10k Annual Reports to the Securities and Exchange Commission (S.E.C.)* (Washington D.C.) various issues.

[8]My own estimates based on a study of the company's accounts are that these could have come to something near to US$17 million between 1971 and 1975. This estimate, however, is unconfirmed.

[9]Tesoro Petroleum Corporation, *ibid.*

[10]An important piece of financial evidence of liquidation would be of course the funds statements of the enterprise. Unfortunately, these do not form part of the financial data on Shell which is currently available.

[11]Ministry of Petroleum and Mines Memo. dated 27/3/74.

[12]Ministry of Petroleum and Mines. Internal Memo. 1974.

[13]Shell Trinidad Company Accounts (unpublished).

[14]Trinidad-Tesoro memo. 1974.

[15]Unpublished Government documents.

[16]One example of the kind of difficulties the nationalized company faced when cut off from the Shell system was with respect to the handling of its major product, residual fuel oil. This is a seasonal product, in demand in winter and fetching higher prices then, in lesser demand in summer and with lower prices then. Summer sales tend to be relatively uneconomic. However, Shell produced fuel oil in Trinidad all year round and could dispose of it through its global marketing system. The new company found that it made little economic sense to sell fuel oil in summer, but given the refinery inherited it was locked into its production. Nor could it store it for the brisk season since it lacked sufficient storage capacity. Shell hadn't needed it. The decision taken was to expand storage capacity for the fuel oil.

[17]Between 1956 and 1967 Shell took out 131 patents in Trinidad and Tobago. Between 1968 and 1973 it took out 13 more.

[18]This in itself provides another interesting commentary on the operations of the MNCs. However 'high' locals may seem to rise in the local organization, when critical matters are involved, it becomes clear who the real decision-makers are. Though Shell Trinidad was locally incorporated, had a local board of directors staffed by its most senior local executives and with nationals in most of its top posts, when the time came to transact the company's fundamental business, it was the foreign executives who came in.

[19]Peat, Marwick and Mitchell, Unpublished Accounting Study on the Trinidad oil industry.

[20]There is some confusion apparently over exactly what role Tesoro has played in the management of Trintoc. Trintoc managers unanimously and vehemently denied in interviews that Tesoro was involved in running the company. However Tesoro has been stating publicly that they are, or were, involved. In its 1974 annual report, Tesoro U.S.A. stated it had been 'assisting' the management of Trintoc, and the report goes on to say that "Trinidad-Tesoro commenced negotiations with the government for the possible combination of the assets and operations of Trinidad-Tesoro with certain assets and operations of Trintoc." See Tesoro Petroleum Corporation, *Annual Report 1974*, p. 10.

BIBLIOGRAPHY

1. Martin Bronfenbrenner, "The Appeal of Confiscation in Economic Development," in *The Economics of Underdevelopment*, eds. A. N. Agawala and S. P. Singh (London: Oxford Univ. Press 1958).
2. R. L. Curry, and D. Rothchild, "On Economic Bargaining between African Governments and Multinational Corporations," *Journal of Modern African Studies*, vol. 12, no. 2 (June 1974).
3. Norman Girvan, "The Question of Compensation: A Third World Perspective," in *The Valuation of Nationalized Property in International Law*, ed. R. B. Lillich (Virginia: University of Virginia Press, 1975).
4. _____ , "The Guyana-Alcan Conflict and the Nationalization of Demba," *New World Quarterly*, vol. 5, no. 4 (1971).
5. _____ , *Corporate Imperialism: Conflict and Expropriation* (White Plains, N.Y.: M. E. Sharpe, Inc., 1976).
6. Fred Iklè, *How Nations Negotiate* (New York: Praeger, 1964).
7. Raymond Mikesell, *Foreign Investment in the Petroleum and Mineral Industries*, (Baltimore, Md.: John Hopkins Press, 1971).
8. Oilfield Workers' Trade Union, *OWTU—B.P. Case* (San Fernando, Trindad: Vangaurd Publishing House, n.d.).
9. Edith Penrose, "Ownership and Control: Multinational firms in less developed countries," in *A World Divided*, ed. G. K. Helleiner (Cambridge: Cambridge University Press, 1976).
10. James Rosenau, ed. *International Politics and Foreign Policy* (New York: The Free Press, 1969).
11. P. Semonin, "Nationalization and Management in Zambia," *New World Quarterly*, vol. 5, no. 3 (1971).
12. Tesoro Petroleum Corporation, Annual Report, 1974.
13. _____ , 10k Annual Report to the S.E.C., Washington D.C.
14. T.T. Ministry of Petroleum and Mines, Monthly Bulletin (various issues).

The Third World and Modern International Negotiations: The Case of the Third United Nations Conference on the Law of the Sea (With a Focus on Commonwealth Caribbean Positions)

Winston Extavour

INTRODUCTION

Modern-day international negotiation may be effectively dated from the end of the Second World War and the creation of the United Nations Organization. This statement is not intended, of course, to be interpreted as discourteous or diluting the invaluable role played by the League of Nations, and the many important international conferences and institutions which preceded the Versailles Peace Conference[1] in the development of the mechanisms and techniques of conference diplomacy. The emphasis is here being placed on the effects of the establishment of the Organization upon the evolution of the international society and the implications which this evolution has held for the postwar developments in multilateral diplomacy.[2]

The most crucial element, perhaps, of the effects of the establishment of the Organization—and one which is of immediate relevance to the question of the evolution of multilateral diplomacy—has been the numerical increase in the size of the international community of States resulting from the consecration of the principles of self-determination of peoples and the sovereign equality of States in the Organization's Charter. In furtherance of these principles, the international Community has tripled in size by the addition of some one hundred new members in the postwar period. It was inevitable, therefore, that the modes and importance of multilateral diplomacy would undergo significant changes with the emergence of this so-called 'Third World' group of States especially as this group of 'new' states, in spite of certain affinities existing among them based on common historical experiences, did not always manifest an identity of national goals and aspirations.

The area of international activity for the advancement of cooperation among States which has perhaps most attracted the attention of the States of the 'Third World' during the last two decades has been the improvement of the institutions which constitute the field of international law. The recurrent theme of publicists from these countries and elsewhere during this period has been the need to restructure the international legal system so as to make it correspond more realistically to the present stage of the international community of States. The perennial argument has been that international law still unduly reflects its Western European origins in that it continues to cater for that small group of European nations which were responsible for its early development and does not sufficiently take into account the need and interest of the majority of the members of the international community.

Efforts to renovate the structures of international law have indeed been made on the basis of Article 13 of the Charter of the United Nations, which gives the General Assembly the power to initiate studies and make recommendations of a character which would promote the progressive development and codification of international law. The newly independent States by their participation have assisted in the elaboration of important international conventions and other multilateral instruments which respond more realistically to realities of contemporary international life.[3]

Within the last two decades, the branch of international law which has most consistently held the attention of the developing countries of the Third World has been the international law of the Sea. The economic condition of the majority of these States has served as a national catalyst for their developing interest in elaborating new rules, which would govern the use and disposal of the considerable store of mineral and biological wealth which the oceans are purported to contain.

The Geneva Conferences on The Law of the Sea of 1958 and 1960 unfortunately did not benefit from the participation of the great majority of these developing countries owing to their improved second-class status on the international scene. In the latest attempts to modernize the rules of the law of the sea, however, the developing countries constituting the majority in the United Nations system have in fact taken the initiative and are currently playing a vital role in the negotiations at the Third United Nations Conference on the Law of the Sea.

It is not only economic considerations, however, which have dictated the positions adopted by the developing States of the 'Third World' at the Third United Nations Conference on the Law of the Sea. Considerations involving military and strategic use of ocean-space, for instance, also find a place among the factors which determine the stand taken by these countries in their negotiations with the countries of the developed world on the one hand, and with their developing counterparts on the other hand.

The aim of this paper is to isolate the major issues which are before the Third United Nations Conference on the Law of the Sea and to examine the positions adopted by Third World countries, either as a single pressure group at the Conference or in their individual capacity as independent sovereign States advancing their own special interest irrespective of the demands of growing solidarity in the confrontation with the more powerful developed countries. Attention will be drawn, in particular, to the positions which have been adhered to by the Commonwealth Caribbean States members of the Caricom subregional organization. Section I shall be devoted to a presentation of the principal issues which are before the Conference for negotiation; in Section II the negotiating structure of the Conference shall be dealt with showing the various bodies which have been created to deal with the problems involved; finally, in Section III we shall view the positions which the Commonwealth Caribbean States have formulated with regard to the problems of the Conference and the considerations which have dictated these positions.

SECTION I
ISSUES BEFORE THE THIRD UNITED NATIONS
CONFERENCE ON THE LAW OF THE SEA

Resolution 2750 (XXV) of December 17, 1970, adopted by the General Assembly of the United Nations, stated in its relevant portion that the General Assembly:

Decides to convene in 1973 in accordance with the provisions of paragraph 3 below a conference on the law of the sea which would deal with the establishment of an equitable international regime—including an international machinery for the area and the resources of the sea-bed and the ocean floor and the subsoil thereof, beyond the limits of national jurisdiction, a precise definition of the area, and a broad range of related issues including those concerning its regions of the high areas, the continental shelf, its territorial sea (including the question of its breadth and the question of international straits) and contiguous zone, fishing and conservation of the living resources of the high seas (including the question of the preferential rights of coastal States), the preservation of the marine environment (including *inter alia,* the precaution of pollution) and scientific research.[4]

The foregoing citation from the General Assembly Resolution, by which the decision was taken to convene a third United Nations Conference on the Law of the Sea, indicates immediately that the convocation of a comprehensive conference on all the problems of the law of the sea was intended by the Resolution. For those familiar with the work of the two previous United Nations sponsored Conferences on the Law of the Sea and the four Conventions adopted at the first of the two conferences held at Geneva in 1958, the Third UN Conference was intended to review all aspects of the law of the sea including the four aforementioned Conventions. In addition to a review of the four existing international conventions on the Law of the Sea, certain issues representing developments in the field since the 1958 Geneva Conference had to be dealt with, including, particularly, the question of the establishment of a territorial machinery to govern the exploration and exploitation of the seabed and subsoil situated beyond the limits of national jurisdiction. In this process of reexamination of the law of the sea, the interests of all countries, whether landlocked or coastal, had to be considered, and this explains the comprehensive form in which the decision to convene the Third United Nations Conference on the Law of the Sea was couched.

More specifically, the agenda of the Third Conference comprises a list of twenty-five topics[5] which were adopted by the preparatory SeaBed Committee in 1972.

International Regime for the Seabed and the Ocean floor Beyond national jurisdiction. The effort to elaborate an international regime for the seabed and the ocean floor beyond national jurisdiction results from the designation, within the United Nations in 1970, of the submarine areas lying outside the jurisdiction of coastal states as the common heritage of mankind.[6] Prior to this development within the United Nations Organization, the submarine areas which lay beyond the limits of national jurisdiction would have been considered as being subject to one of two regimes according to interests of the claimant. On the one hand, it was believed that the concept of *res communis omnium,* that is communal property subject to appropriation by no state, would apply, on the other hand, certain countries held that the area in question must be considered to be *res nullius,* and, therefore, subject to appropriation by the first comer. The decision taken by the United Nations to regard henceforth the area and its resources as the "common heritage of mankind" brought an end to the debate and gave rise to the necessity to elaborate rules to govern the administration and use of the seabed and subsoil of the submarine areas lying beyond national jurisdiction.

The importance of this issue before the Conference lies in the potential wealth of the resources of the ocean floor, in the form particularly of the manganese nodules which are known to exist in greater or lesser quantities throughout the ocean floor. These nodules will be the source of various metals including nickel, copper, cobalt, and manganese, and although it is estimated that to date only three percent of the ocean floor has been extensively surveyed, it is believed that exploration to date justifies the commencement of commercial exploitations. The extent of the prize which awaits those bodies, either States or juridical persons, which are to undertake exploitation of the nodules of the ocean floor are indicated by figures of estimated metal production of high-grade nodules. It is estimated, for instance, that the approximate metal production of a million tons of dry nodules would be in the vicinity of 230,000 tons of manganese; 15,000 tons of nickel, 13,000 tons of copper, 2,000 tons of cobalt, and 2,500 tons of other metal. In terms of prices, it is estimated that the gross revenue for a mining operation of 1 million tons per annum producing manganese metal would be approximately US$170 million.[7]

The significance of these figures has not escaped the countries with vital interests in this area of seabed activity, namely the developing countries and at least certain developed countries. Those developed countries which possess the necessary finance and technology to make the projected estimates ordered above a reality have a vital interest in the regime which would eventually be elaborated to govern the use of those resources. On the other hand, the developing countries have a stake in the use which is to be made of these resources either in their capacity as producers of minerals (and thus may be prejudiced by the exploitation of seabed minerals), or as developing countries who see in the vast store of mineral wealth a bonanza which would stimulate and advance their own economic development.

On this issue, the positions before the Conference have been clearly defined between the two groups of States: the developed and the developing countries. Depending partly upon their numerical strength within the Organization and partly also upon the "Declaration of Principles" adopted by the United Nations General Assembly in 1970,[8] the developing countries have made proposals before the conference which are aimed at vesting full control of operations in the seabed area beyond national jurisdiction in the International Authority which is to be established. One of the most important position papers presented at the Caracas Session of the Conference by the "Group of Seventy-seven" in the name of 116-odd members of the Group,[9] for instance, ensures the direct and effective control of the Authority at all times, through appropriate institutional arrangements. Proposals emanating from the developed countries, on the other hand, sought to institute a licensing or registration system, according to which the Authority would contract out certain parts of the seabed area to states or companies which would then exercise exclusive control over that part of the area and its activities for a specified period of time, for instance 30 years.

Generally speaking, the positions of the developing and developed countries on this issue have remained constant throughout the negotiations to date. It is clear, however, that if the principle of the "common heritage of mankind" is to be respected, The International Authority, which is expected to be created the machinery of that body, must be permitted to function in such a way as to ensure equitable participation and returns for all the members of the international community from the exploitation of the resources of the international seabed area.

The Territorial Sea

The problem of the territorial sea at the Third United Nations Conference on the Law of the Sea may be regarded as being restricted to two items: the breadth of the territorial sea and the definition of the concept of innocent passage on the territorial sea. The final solution of the first problem, which has so far evaded the attempts of the two major international conferences on the law of the sea of 1958 and 1960, is dependent, however, upon the resolution of other problems which face the conference.

The solution to the second problem ought to present less difficulties in that all the definition attempts to do is to fill one of the deficiencies of the 1958 Convention on the Territorial Sea and the Contiguous Zone which had not gone far enough in defining the true nature of innocent passage through the territorial sea. The draft proposal before the conference, which is contained in the Revised Single Negotiating Text presented by the Chairman of the Second Committee of the Conference,[10] entails an enumeration of the various activities which, if undertaken by a foreign ship in its passage through the territorial sea, may be considered to be prejudiced to the peace, good order, and security of the Coastal State. Such passage would, therefore, cease to be qualified as innocent passage.

As regards the question of the breadth of the territoral sea, the distance which appears to be generally favoured among delegates at the Conference is twelve nautical miles. This distance corresponds to that which today is practised by the majority of coastal States around the globe,[11] and for decades has been a distance favoured by States either for the exercise of sovereignty over the territorial sea, exclusive jurisdiction over fisheries or more limited jurisdiction for specialized purposes in a zone contiguous to the territorial sea.

Final acceptance of a number of developing coastal states of the distance of twelve miles is dependent, however, upon the reception which is accorded the concept of the exclusive economic zone by the major maritime states, in the form in which it has been elaborated in the Revised Single Negotiating Text. The reason for this state of affairs is that in addition to those States[12] which actually claim in their legislation the distance of 200 nautical miles as their territorial sea, many other developing coastal states have expressed their intention to establish a territorial sea of a similar breadth if exclusive economic jurisdiction is not recognized by the Conference in a zone extending up to 200 nautical miles from the territorial sea baselines.

On this question of the territorial sea also, the divergent interests are those of developing countries on the one hand, and of the developed countries on the other, including particularly the major maritime States. The interest of the latter lie in preserving the narrowest possible breadth of territorial sea, so that by so doing the sovereignty of coastal States would not extend to any considerable distance into the seas. Once the seas remain free in its widest possible expanses, few obstacles would arise for the freedom of navigation. The developing countries, on the other hand, perceive their interests as lying in securing the exercise of sovereignty or at least exclusive jurisdiction over as wide an expanse of the adjacent seas as possible, motivated mainly by economic interests but also in the interests of national security. Such objectives would best be served by the extension of the territorial sea to a reasonably wide distance, but failing this they would be disposed to accept a limited breadth of territorial sea of twelve nautical miles coupled with exclusive resource jurisdiction up to the 200-mile limit.

Straits Use for International Navigation

It is estimated that the establishment of the breadth of the territorial sea at twelve nautical miles would automatically draw within the territorial sovereignty of coastal states some 16 international straits situated around the globe. The development in itself does not create any problems for the expanses of water which will be affected. The problem which arises, however, relates to the effects which the development can have on freedom of navigation through these international waterways which formerly would have been considered as high seas. In short, it is a problem in which the major maritime States, and particularly the naval powers, and the Strait States themselves—but for different reasons— have vital interests.

In broad terms, the situation which will result is that since waters which were formally high seas, subject to freedom of navigation for the ships of all States including warships, would now be transformed into territorial waters within which only the right of innocent passage would be recognized, ships of those States which have important interests in international navigation of all kinds would be constrained to observe the rules governing the right of innocent passage through the territorial straits of the strait States.

Once again on this issue the confrontation at the Third United Nations Conference on the law of the Sea is between the major maritime States, including the naval powers, and the developing countries which are in the majority of the riparian strait States.[13] The developed States have proposed at the Conference that in these international straits the right of transit passage should apply, that is, "freedom of navigation and overflight solely for the purpose of contiguous and expeditious transit of the strait between one area of the high seas or an exclusive economic zone and another area of the high seas or an exclusive economic zone."[14]

In short, what is being sought under that formulation is the maintenance of freedom of navigation and overflight through those international straits, except that such freedoms shall be exercised as expeditiously as possible therein. On the other hand, the preference of the strait states is for the maintenance of the reprise of innocent passage within those international straits. They seem prepared, however, to accept some formula which would guarantee their sovereignty over those territorial straits at all times, and so give them the right to enact rules and regulations for the use of the strait which would avoid any undue impediment to navigation and overflight and, at the same time, protect their interests with respect in particular to security, protection of the marine environment and economic rights.

The Continental Shelf

The outstanding problem in relation to the continental shelf is that of arriving at a more precise definition than that contained in the 1958 Continental Shelf Convention of the external limit of the shelf. The rapid development of ocean technology since the adoption of the 1958 Convention on the Continental Shelf has made the deep ocean floor more accessible for purposes of exploring and exploiting the natural resources thereof. Consequently, the dual criteria contained in the definition of the continental shelf (Article 1 of the Convention) had the effect of pushing gradually seawards into the area of the ocean floor beneath the high seas the external limit of the continental shelf. The two criteria involved were the depth of 200 metres and the so-called "exploitability" criterion.

The alarm which was created by this state of affairs prompted the Maltese Ambassador to the United Nations to raise the question in that forum of defining in a more precise manner the external limits of the shelf and, consequently also, the internal limits of the international seabed area which would be reserved exclusively for peaceful purposes and for the benefit of all mankind. The initiative of the Maltese Ambassador has today blossomed into the Third United Nations Conference on the Law of the Sea.

At the Conference itself, efforts are being made to find a stable definition of the external limits of the shelf which would prevent further encroachment of coastal state jurisdiction upon the international seabed area and, at the same time, take account of the rights which States presently enjoy on their continental shelves on the basis of the 1958 Continental Shelf Convention.

The relevant draft article of the Revised Single Negotiating Text (RSNT)[15] accordingly contains a definition of the continental shelf which proceeds on the basis of a distance criterion in the first instance, and attempts at the same time to safeguard the natural prolongation principle which is germane to the concept of the continental shelf,[16] when this natural prolongation extends beyond the stipulated minimum distance of 200 nautical miles. The external limit of the natural prolongation of the continental shelf beyond the distance of 200 nautical miles is to be coincident with the outer edge of the continental margin.

It is not to be reasoned, however, that all the difficulties inherent in arriving at a precise and unambiguous definition of the continental shelf will be removed with the application of the definition outlined above. The problem remains of locating with a reasonable degree of precision the centre edge of the continental margin in every case. In this regard, it seems that the geological techniques have not been developed which could determine in any satisfactory manner the boundary line between the continental and oceanic coastal structures. Moreover, the practical methods which have been suggested as an alternative have not been found acceptable in many quarters, including particularly those States which because of their unfavourable geographical location stand to benefit more from a limitation of the full extent of the continental shelf to 200 nautical miles. These methods include the use of the thickness of sedimentary rocks in relation to the distance from the foot of the continental slope seaward.

Apart from this problem, there is the proposal before the Conference which seeks to provide some compensation to landlocked States and "geographically disadvantaged" States for their loss of benefits which they regard themselves as suffering on account of the exercise of exclusive jurisdiction by certain coastal States over that part of their continental shelves which extend beyond the 200-nautical-mile limit. This proposal involves a profit-sharing arrangement based on the proceeds accruing from exploitation of natural resources located in the submarine areas beyond the 200-nautical-mile limit. The details of the profit-sharing arrangement are still, however, to be finally worked out, although the principle seems to be acceptable to all the parties concerned with the possible exception of one or two States.[17]

The Exclusive Economic Zone

It was pointed out earlier that the acceptance of the concept of the exclusive economic zone at the Third United Nations Conference on the Law of the Sea is regarded by the bulk of States participating at the Conference as a *sine qua non* for the recognition of the twelve-mile breadth of territorial sea as the maximum permissible breadth under the law. The concept is, in short, a compromise arrangement arising out of two separate and competing claims: a twelve-mile territorial sea claim and a 200-mile territorial sea claim.

The essence of the concept is that States which might otherwise be drawn toward the establishment of a 200-mile territorial sea would enjoy in an exclusive economic zone, which would extend to a maximum distance of 200 miles from the territorial sea baselines, certain rights which, taken together, would fall short of the exercise of territorial sovereignty in the zone. At the same time, the international community of States would continue to be recognized as being entitled to exercise certain prerogatives in the zone, including particularly the freedom of navigation and the freedom of overflight.

The rights which the Coastal State would be entitled to exercise in its exclusive economic zones relate mainly to the economic uses of the zone, for instance, the exploration and exploitation of all the resources of the zone, both living and nonliving, but would also include jurisdiction, exclusive or otherwise, over activities of scientific research and pollution control, these being activities which can have a bearing upon the effective benefits which the coastal States may achieve from their exclusive economic zone.

It seems safe to state at this stage that the principle of establishing an exclusive economic zone extending up to a distance of 200 nautical miles from the territorial sea baselines has been accepted by the majority of delegations at the Conference. The outstanding areas of differences relate to the regions which are being worked out to govern scientific research and pollution control activities in the zone and the safeguards which would be provided for the exercise of the freedoms of navigation and overflight in the exclusive economic zone.

As regards the question of scientific research, the developed countries, which possess the necessary capacity to undertake intensive marine scientific research, are seeking to maintain the freedom of scientific research in the exclusive economic zone which before its establishment would have been part and parcel of the high seas and thus subject to such freedom. The developing countries on the other hand have insisted on reserving for themselves exclusive control over all scientific research activities in the exclusive economic zone. The argument is that since such activities may be prejudicial to the economic interests of the coastal State, full control over such activities must be vested in that State. Moreover, the experience of certain developing countries appears to have been that researching states have at times used scientific research activities as a guise for more clandestine activities which have been regarded as potentially harmful to the security interests of the coastal States.

In response to these arguments, the researching States maintain that a distinction must be made between the different kinds of marine scientific research: pure scientific research which is aimed at advancing mankind's knowledge of the marine environment, and applied scientific research, the results of which would normally be used for commercial benefit if used in the context of exploitation of the economic resources of the exclusive economic zone.

On the question of activities related to protection of the marine environment against the hazards of pollution, the interests which appear to be susceptible of being affected by the draft provisions relating to pollution control in the exclusive economic zone are those of the major shipping States. These States fear that if exclusive control over these activities are vested in the wide range of divergent rules and regulations which may be emanated by coastal states in relation to pollution-control activities in the exclusive economic zones, it may greatly affect their exercise of freedom of navigation in the exclusive economic zone. For instance, it is argued by the shipping States that the regulations which may relate to design, construction, and manning of ships may differ so greatly from one State to another that it may become virtually impossible for the ships of these States to operate effectively on the seas.

The two questions of scientific research and preservation of the marine environment are being treated together in greater detail in a separate part of the draft convention, and it is likely that accommodation of divergent positions would be arrived at in the content of the Committee of the Conference which has the mandate to deal with these questions.

The final difficulty, which we must evoke here in relation to the concept of the exclusive economic zone, is the interpretation which is to be placed upon the provision governing the exercise of freedoms of navigation and overflight and other freedoms related to international communication in the exclusive economic zone.

According to Article 46 of the RSNT, which deals with "Rights and duties of other States in the exclusive economic zone,"

> ... All States, whether coastal or land-locked, enjoy, subject to the relevant provisions of the present Convention, the freedoms of navigation and overflight and of the laying of submarine cables and pipelines and other internationally lawful uses of the sea related to navigation and communication.

It is to be noted that although the intention in establishing the exclusive economic zone is to attribute mainly economic rights to the coastal State and to maintain certain freedoms of the high seas in the zone, the formulation cited above places certain added restrictions upon what would otherwise have been relatively unlimited freedoms of the high seas. The exercise of the freedoms indicated above are made subject to the relevant provision of the draft Convention. In short, the sovereign rights of the coastal state in the exclusive economic zone are paramount.

The reference in Article 46 of the RSNT to "other internationally lawful uses of the sea related to navigation and communication" is intended, in particular, to exclude the possibility of interpreting the provision to mean that States are entitled to indulge in activities which may have no bearing upon the passage through the exclusive economic zone, for example, military activities or upon other kinds of activities related to communication. The intention of the sponsors of this text, namely the developing countries, is also to correct what was regarded in some quarters as a deficiency of the corresponding provisions relating to the freedoms of the high seas in the 1958 Convention on the High Seas. Under those provisions,[18] the major powers sought to justify, for example, their nuclear-testing activities upon the high seas or the emplacement of nuclear weapons on the seabed of the high seas.

Landlocked States and Geographically Disadvantaged States

The final issue of particular importance to the developing countries which we shall discuss here relates to the claims of the landlocked and the "geographically disadvantaged States to equal treatment with other States in the allocation of the resources of the seas, and, in particular, to equitable participation in the exploitation of the resources, both renewable and nonrenewable, of the exclusive economic zone."

Of the twenty-nine landlocked States situated on the various continents, twenty are developing countries in Asia, Africa, and Latin America. The claims of this group of States, however, taken as a whole is that in the first place, the Geneva Convention of 1958 had perpetrated an injustice, in failing to take into account their geographical situation in allocating exclusive rights to coastal States over the continental shelf. These countries, while perhaps not insisting that the present state of affairs in relation to the continental shelf be reversed, are intent upon forestalling any such eventuality in the proposed allocation of new rights over the living resources in the exclusive economic zone to coastal States.

Proposals have, therefore, been placed before the Conference in the form of draft articles of the RSNT which would ensure that equitable participation is secured for these states, and especially the developing members of the Group, in the exploration and exploitation of the living resources of the exclusive economic zone. Certain difficulties exist, however, in relation to these provisions in that the landlocked States do not regard the draft provisions as responding adequately to their claims. In effect, an objective analysis of the relevant provisions reveals the existence of certain inconsistencies in the text which may lead in practice to the dilution of rights of participation which are being proclaimed for the landlocked States.[19]

With regard to the nonliving resources of the exclusive economic zone, the claims which are being made by the landlocked States to participation therein are not beng seriously addressed by the States which are expected to benefit from the establishment of exclusive economic zones. In many, if not most, instances the mineral resources present within the 200-mile zone already belong as of right to the coastal States involved, and claims to participation by landlocked States could hardly be justified. The position of these States on this question could only be regarded perhaps at this stage as a negotiating position aimed at finally securing acceptance of their other demands.

The position of the "geographically disadvantaged" States[20] in respect of participation on an equitable basis in the exploration and exploitation of the resources of the exclusive economic zone of other coastal States are similar to that of the landlocked States. In fact, those two groups of States constitute a single negotiating unit at the Conference.

Draft provisions have also been included in the draft convention relating to participation by these States in the exploration and exploitation of the living resources of the exclusive economic zones in the same region on bases which are to be worked out with the States involved. The degree of participation which is anticipated under these provisions closely approximate those which have been proposed for the landlocked States, and the observation made earlier with respect to the inconsistency between intent and reality holds equally good in the context of the "geographically disadvantaged" States.

The Draft Convention on the Law of the Sea contains other provisions which touch directly the interests of the developing countries but which, on account of the fact that they sometimes affect only a handful of States, need not be discussed here. Our intention in surveying in this section the crucial issues before the Conference, insofar as the interest of Third World countries are concerned, has been to emphasize those areas in which the majority of these countries have a direct interest. We shall now proceed to consider the mechanisms which the Conference has adopted in order to achieve its goal of arriving at solutions to the above-mentioned problems, solutions which it is hoped would attract the support of the majority of States represented at the Conference, and the tactics which have been employed by the developing countries in their capacity as members either of the broader groupings or of special interest groups to achieve their objectives.

SECTION II
THE MECHANICS OF NEGOTIATION
AT THE THIRD UNITED NATIONS CONFERENCE
ON THE LAW OF THE SEA

The magnitude of the topics to be negotiated at the Conference has necessitated the separation of the twenty-five topics on the agenda and their numerous subitems into three categories, each of which has become the responsibility of a separate Committee.[21] Accordingly, each of the three main Committees of the Conference has the following topics mandated to it: Committee I has been entrusted with the negotiation of the regime governing the uses of the seabed and subsoil of the submarine areas beyond the limits of national jurisdiction; committee III is dealing with the regions which are to govern the conduct of marine scientific research and the preservation of the marine environment; while Committee II has been entrusted with the negotiation of all the other items on the agenda of the Conference, that is, all the other substantive questions relating to the law of the sea.

Alongside the formal organs of the Conference, consisting of the three Main Committees and the General and Drafting Committees and the Plenary of the Conference, there are the traditional political groupings operating within the United Nations system, namely the Group of 77 (consisting of 116 States), the Latin American Group, the Asian Group, the Group of Socialist States, and the Group of Western European Countries and Others. However, there emerged at the Conference various other groupings of States based on common interests and common positions *vis-à-vis* the issues for negotiation by the Conference. These groups included the Territorialist Group, the Coastal State Group, and the Group of Landlocked and Geographically Disadvantaged States.

The existence of these many groupings of States at the Conference has not served to facilitate the negotiating process, but perhaps has had the effect of hardening the positions of the group of States which have been formed in order to defend some specific interest. The Coastal State Group has been formed, for instance, as a counterfoil to the Group of Landlocked and Geographically Disadvantaged States to uphold and defend the interests of the former group. True negotiation on specific issues has perhaps become possible only with the formation of the so-called "Group of 21" which is constituted by members chosen from both the Coastal State Group and the Group of Landlocked and Geographically Disadvantaged States.

Moreover, the existence of the political groupings has also served to enhance confrontation on certain sensitive topics between the developed and the developing countries, for instance, the question of international straits and the right of innocent passage of warships on the territorial sea and the exclusive economic zone.

The group of 77, on the other hand, by far the largest grouping of States at the Conference, has the potential to serve as the forum from which important decisions can emerge and subsequently direct the work of the Conference. Possessing an automatic majority, the Group of 77 has the capacity to direct the Conference along any path it may choose. The difficulty has been, however, that external influences have often succeeded in eroding the solidarity of the Group and, moreover, the perceived interests of many members of the Group on specific topics have not coincided, so that what in fact results is a grouping of countries with an ideological commitment to defend the interests of the developing countries against the demands of the developed countries, but who in practice found it difficult to agree on common positions on many of the crucial items before the Conference.

In terms of negotiating strategy, one of the curiosities of the Conference is the assemblage of States designated the Group of Landlocked and Geographically Disadvantaged States. This group, described elsewhere as a "coalition of misfits," is constituted by developing and developed countries, landlocked and coastal countries, and countries of differing ideological persuasions, and possesses the single aim and intention of securing access to resource exploitation in the exclusive economic zones of coastal States. At the same time, the developing members of the group are committed by their membership in the Group of 77 to oppose the positions of the developed members of their group on many important items before the Conference, including especially the question of the International Seabed Authority and Marine Scientific research. In short, the effectiveness of such a grouping in the negotiations at the Conference would depend upon the relative importance of the various topics to the individual developing State.

SECTION III
THE POSITIONS OF THE COMMONWEALTH CARIBBEAN STATES

The independent Commonwealth Caribbean States, with the exception of Grenada,[22] have all played an active role in the process of the progressive development of the international law of the sea. This development was inevitable in the sense that being a subgroup of the wider grouping of the Latin American States, which for decades had been instigating movements for the development of the law, the Commonwealth Caribbean States would naturally be called upon to play their role in this development. Despite this fact, however, the Commonwealth Caribbean States themselves early awoke to the realization that the Caribbean sea which washed their shores represented an important instrument in their economic development and that it was crucial that activities in that area must be closely monitored in order, for instance, to obviate the effects of marine pollution arising from intemperate uses of the sea.

If all four independent Caribbean States were not directly involved from the outset in the movements of the United Nations towards the present Conference, these countries quickly livened to the momentum which had been created in the Latin American region and within the United Nations System and have since that time continued to play a most active and sometimes pioneering role.

In fact, it was Trinidad and Tobago which blazed the trail in the United Nations, in conjunction with a handful of other States, in taking up the initiative which had been made by the Maltese Ambassador to the United Nations in 1967. This country was also one of the sponsors of the General Assembly Resolution 2574A(XXIV) of 1969 requesting the Secretary General of the United Nations to seek the views of member States of the United Nations on the feasibility of convening a comprehensive conference on the law of the sea. Finally, Trinidad and Tobago was the first of the independent Commonwealth Caribbean States to be named a member of the Seabed Committee, which served as the preparatory body of the Third United Nations Conference on the Law of the Sea.[23]

In 1970, when according to General Assembly Resolution 2750(XXV), it was decided to convene a Conference on the Law of the Sea in 1973, the Seabed Committee was expanded to eighty-six members and Jamaica was included as one of the new members while Barbados was admitted as one of the observers at the Sessions of the Committee. Subsequently, in 1971, Guyana was appointed a member of the Seabed Committee.

These Caribbean Countries, in pursuance of their national interests, have participated fully in the work of the Seabed Committee in its preparation of the Conference and have submitted, either individually or jointly, many important proposals and draft articles relating to various aspects of the law of the sea. At the Conference itself, certain proposals advanced at the preparatory stage in the Committee have continued to gain the support of many participating delegations, and new proposals put forward at the Conference have also attracted respectable support.

The positions which have been adopted by the Commonwealth Caribbean States on various issues which we have discussed above in Section I may be placed into two categories. These are those positions which have resulted from efforts to coordinate a common Commonwealth Caribbean position on the basis of regional solidarity within the context of the Caribbean Community (CARICOM); or, alternatively, are national positions born out of the perception by the individual States of their national interest insofar as this is irreconcilable or at least incompatible with that of their partner States.

On the level of common coordinated positions within the context of CARICOM, Commonwealth Caribbean Governments took the initiative at the Sixth Conference of Commonwealth Caribbean Heads of Government held in Kingston, Jamaica, in April 1970 in setting up an Intergovernmental Working Party with terms of reference which include the formulation of recommendations on the possibility of harmonizing policies and legislation in the law of the sea, and also on possible joint action by independent Commonwealth Caribbean countries in relation to the United Nations Conference on the Law of the Sea and the Latin American Meeting on the Law of the Sea.

In its resolution establishing the Working Party, the Sixth Heads of Government Conference took note of the developments which were taking place in the United Nations in relation to the possibility of convening a new Conference on the Law of the Sea, and of the importance of the topics which would form the agenda of the conference for developing countries in general and for small island states in particular, and expressed the desire of achieving maximum harmonization of practice and legislation with regard to the sea among Commonwealth Caribbean countries, paying due regard to special problems which may be faced by individual countries.

The significant advance was made in this Working Party in the direction of harmonizing common policies with respect to questions of the law of the sea. It was agreed, however, to support the convocation of a new conference on the law of the Sea to examine comprehensively all the problems involved.

In the year following this first meeting, various meetings, both at an Official and Ministerial level, have been held among the Commonwealth Caribbean States with the objective of arriving at common positions on certain aspects of the law of the sea in preparation for the United Nations Law of the Sea Conference. In November 1971, a Special Ministerial Committee on the Law of the Sea and related Matters, which met in Barbados, appointed the Standing Committee of Officials on the Law of the Sea and Related Matters which has continued to meet at regular intervals since that date.

At the 1974 Meeting of the Standing Committee held in Kingston, it became clear, however, that positions could be harmonized only on certain of the items which would be negotiated at the Conference. These items included the elaboration of an international regime for the seabed area beyond national jursidiction. On this subject, the meeting recommended that Caribbean States should "seek to establish criteria for the sharing of benefits which will give the most advantageous returns and to this end shall coordinate their efforts." As regards marine scientific research, the meeting also recommended that Caribbean States support the right of coastal states to regulate scientific research.

Other areas which were considered for possible harmonization of Commonwealth Caribbean positions at the Third Law of the Sea Conference were: fisheries, including the basis for negotiating multi-lateral fishing strategy for the area; straits used for international navigation and the high seas and its freedoms. On these questions, however, the Commonwealth Caribbean States either chose to leave all their options open for negotiation at the Conference or declined to adopt final positions on account of the paucity of technical data and expertise on the problems concerned.

With regard to the national positions of the four independent Commonwealth Caribbean territories on the various topics before the Conference, it may be observed from the outset that those States have concentrated their attention only on certain specific issues which they regard as being of vital importance to their national well-being. These items are generally related to the economic benefits which may accrue to States from the establishment of certain new concepts to ocean space in particular, the concept of the exclusive economic zone or patrimonial sea, and the concept of the continental shelf. Most of the controversial discussions within the context of CARICOM have related to these items, while on the other items, generally speaking, the Commonwealth Caribbean continues identifying their positions with those of other developing countries within the Group of 77, and so automatically hold convergent positions among themselves.

As regards the question of the exclusive economic zone, by far the most important single item on the agenda of the conference, the independent Commonwealth Caribbean States had ranged into separate camps. On the one hand, Guyana, Barbados, and Trinidad and Tobago have expressed positions which are more or less similar, but which also differ on certain details. On the other hand, there is Jamaica which has adopted a position on the exclusive economic zone concept which diverges significantly from that held by the other three States, though Jamaica has expressed readiness to accept the concept if certain clearly articulated conditions are satisfied.

The position of Trinidad and Tobago as regards the concept of the exclusive economic zone is that the concept is acceptable to that country as a useful instrument in allocating the resources of the adjacent seas. Trinidad and Tobago's acceptance of the concept has been conditioned, however, upon the recognition of preferential rights of access to the living resources of the economic zones of States of the Latin American region for the geographically disadvantaged States of that region. Closely linked to this position is that country's position with regard to the territorial sea and the continental shelf. For Trinidad and Tobago the territorial sea must be considered as extending up to a maximum distance of 12 nautical miles, and the continental shelf must be defined in accordance with the principle of geomorphological criteria so as to include the entire extent of the natural prolongation of the coastal States' land territory under the sea.

The position of Trinidad and Tobago on these questions reflects both the reality of Trinidad and Tobago's geographical location and its present-day activities in relation to the exploitation of the living and nonliving resources of its adjacent waters. Trinidad and Tobago has exercised sovereignty over a territorial sea of twelve nautical miles since 1969. Its position on this question is only an endorsement of nautical practice.

As regards the continental shelf, Trinidad and Tobago considers that its interests in maintaining the considerable benefits which that country has to date enjoyed from the exploitation of hydrocarbons located on its continental shelf lies in securing firm acceptance of the principle that the continental shelf is the natural prolongation of the continental or insular landmass into and under the sea. It has been estimated that the continental shelf of that country extends in certain areas to approximately 240 miles into the sea, covering an area of approximately 15,000 square miles, so that Trinidad and Tobago, in spite of its firm support for the concept of the "common heritage of mankind" which will be constituted by the International Seabed Area, has seen its interest as lying in the maintenance of the notion that the continental shelf must be considered as extending beyond the 200-mile limit of the exclusive economic zone up to the outer edge of the continental margin.[24]

Trinidad and Tobago's position on the concept of the exclusive economic zone has already been outlined above. From the outset of the discussions leading up to the present Conference, including the meetings held among the Latin American States, Trinidad and Tobago announced its support for the kindred concept of the patrimonial sea propounded by Columbia and Venezuela, among others. This support was always made subject, however, to the preservation of the fisheries rights of the States of the region in the waters of the neighbouring countries which existed by virtue of the freedom of fishing on the high seas. Trinidad and Tobago thus sought to protect its fisheries interests particularly in the waters off the coasts of Brazil and the Guyanas.

In the case of Barbados, support has also been expressed for the concept of the exclusive economic zone, both in the interest of securing acceptance for the concept at the Conference and in accordance with that country's geographical position. Like Trinidad and Tobago, Barbados places considerable emphasis upon the recognition by the Latin American countries of rights of access for Barbadian fishermen for purposes of exploiting the fisheries resources of the exclusive economic zone.

The case of Guyana is slightly more complex. The position of this country has been clearly enunciated both at the Conference and at regional meetings of CARICOM. Guyana supports the concept of the exclusive economic zone but does not support, as a matter of general principle, the concept of preferential rights of access by States within a region. To accept such a principle would be to open the door to the more advanced fishing countries in the region, particularly Cuba—one of the high-ranking fishing nations—to exploit the limited resources of Guyana's exclusive economic zone. Guyana's position did not exclude, however, the participation of States members of CARICOM in the exploitation of Guyana's fisheries on the basis of bilateral or multilateral arrangements.

As regards the concept of natural prolongation of the continental shelf, it seems that Guyana aligns herself with those countries which are seeking to limit the full extent of the economic rights of coastal States to a 200-mile limit. Guyana has stated that there should be a clear cut-off point for all countries in determining the external limit of the continental shelf and that limit ought to be coterminous with the limit of the exclusive economic zone.

Finally, Jamaica's position with respect to the concept of the exclusive economic zone is that this concept ought to be replaced by that of the "matrimonial sea" which ought to be applied to the entire Caribbean Sea. According to this concept, all the resources of the Caribbean Sea would be regarded as the common property of the riparian States which would be entitled to share equally in their exploitation. The matrimonial sea concept seems to have emerged from the idea of considering the Caribbean sea as a *mare clausum* which had been put forward in a Trinidad and Tobago note to the Ministerial Meeting on Territorial Waters, Legal Regime of the Sea-bed, etc., held in Barbados in November 1971. The aim of the Trinidad and Tobago note was to suggest the closing of the Caribbean Sea for exploration and exploitation of its resources to peoples that do not belong to the area. Title to these resources would thereby be vested in all the peoples of the region.

Jamaica (which claims to be a geographically disadvantaged country both in terms of geographical position being hemmed in on the north-west and south by the American continent and in all other directions by the outer fringe of the Caribbean archipelago, as well as being surrounded by waters which are purported to be a low-density fishing area) no doubt found the idea of a Caribbean *mare clausum* to be an attractive one, tailored to suit her own situation. As shown earlier, Guyana has resisted the application of such a notion to the Caribbean sea, while not ruling out entirely the possibility of sharing her *living* resources with her Caricom partners on the basis of consensual arrangements.

At the Third United Nations Conference on the Law of the Sea, the independent Commonwealth Caribbean States form part of the Latin American Group which itself is a subgroup of the wider Group of 77.

The positions of these Caribbean countries with respect to the majority of topics on the agenda of the Conference are accordingly aligned with those of the Group of 77. The most important of these topics relate to the elaboration of a regime governing the management of the International Seabed Area; pollution control; scientific research; archipelagos, etc.

This is not to say, of coure, that there is a coincidence of viewpoints among all the members of the Group of 77 on these various questions, or that all the members of the Commonwealth Caribbean subgroup attach the same degree of importance to these problems. For instance, Trinidad and Tobago has been monitoring closely the development at the Conference on the pollution control question, since she finds herself cast in the role of protector of the marine environment against pollution, especially vessel-resource pollution, and at the same time has vital interests in maintaining unobstructed passage for oil tankers which are potential polluters of the environment.

Nevertheless, it is the topics which deal with the allocation of the resources of the seas which have attracted the greatest interest of the Commonwealth Caribbean States and which have activated the negotiating skill and diplomacy of these countries at the Conference, dictating the strategies which they have either individually or collectively adopted.

On the question of the continental shelf, for instance, Jamaica, Barbados, and Guyana appear to be ranged in a single camp, while Trinidad and Tobago identifies her interests with those States which possess a continental shelf beyond 200 nautical miles. These three countries are members of the group of Landlocked and Geographically Disadvantaged States and, as such, hold the view of the Group that the shelf ought to end at the 200-mile distance in order to reserve a sufficiently significant area both in terms of size and resource endowment to the International Seabed Authority. The solution to this problem could not be found in the context of the Group of 77 and so the question has been entrusted to the "Group of 21" Coastal and Landlocked and Geographically Disadvantaged States for its consideration.

At the same time, all four countries identify with the above-mentioned Group to a greater or lesser extent on the question of rights of equitable participation in the exclusive economic zones of States belonging to the same region or subregion. Unlike her three partners, Trinidad and Tobago is not an official member of the Group of Landlocked and Geographically Disadvantaged States, yet has expressed sympathy with their position on this question. It will indeed be recalled that this participation was originally articulated as the *sine qua non* for the acceptance by Trinidad and Tobago of the concept of the exclusive economic zone.

The prospects at the Conference for the successful negotiation by the Commonwealth Caribbean States of rights of participation of the living resources of regional exclusive economic zones appear to be reasonably good, given the fact that the Latin American Group of States, which forms a substantial majority of the Coastal States Group (adherents to a strong exclusive economic zone concept), depends upon the support of these States for their exclusive economic zone concept. The Latin American States are accordingly disposed to accommodate the demands of the Commonwealth Caribbean States.

The outstanding difficulty relates to whether the formulation of the rights of participation will take the form of what has been proposed by the Jamaican delegation for instance, that is *equal* participation, or whether the preference of the Latin American States themselves for the lesser equitable participation will win the day. In the meantime the member States of CARICOM are continuing their efforts to harmonize their positions on questions where their national interests appear to diverge.

CONCLUSION

The experience of the Commonwealth Caribbean States in the field of the development of international law in general has been limited. The relatively recent accession to independence by these States has naturally accounted for the relative lack of involvement in the creation or development of the law. Nevertheless, the United Nations has provided a forum in which these States have made meaningful contributions to the development of various aspects of the law.

Being absent from the two former conferences on the law of the sea, sponsored by the United Nations, these States were not in a position to influence the direction in which the law was codified in the four Geneva Conventions of 1958. In spite of this, however, these States have adhered to certain of the Conventions and regulate their maritime affairs in accordance with the rules which they enunciated.

On the occasion of the convocation of the current Third United Nations Conference on the Law of the Sea, as we have seen earlier, the Commonwealth Caribbean States have played a vital role from the very outset of the deliberations preceding the Conference. In this way, they have been able, either singly or as a group, to make important inputs into the negotiations in order to safeguard their various positions.

As a pressure group, their overall impact on the conference will not tend to be too considerable on account of their numerical weakness.

Their effectiveness has lain rather in the support which they have been able to bring to the wider Latin American grouping and the Group of 77, particularly on questions which are of importance to the generality of developing countries. In the final analysis, however, the five votes which these States muster will be of *invaluable* crucial importance in the determination of the major issues before the Conference. In particular, the reality of the importance of these votes may even influence the member States of the wider Latin American grouping to yield on the question of participation in the exploitation of the living resources of the exclusive economic zone, which is of such far-reaching importance to the member States of CARICOM.

FOOTNOTES

[1] For instance, the Hague Peace Conferences of 1899 and 1907, see S. S. Goodspeed, *The Nature and Function of International Organization,* 2nd ed. (New York: Oxford University Press, 1967), pp. 23 *et seq.*

[2] It will be recalled in fact that the San Francisco Conference itself was open only to those States invited to participate in the drafting of the Charter of the United Nations, namely fifty chosen States—nevertheless, the intention was to permit participation in the Organization by all peace-loving States.

[3] International instruments adopted under the auspices of the United Nations Organization include the Vienna Convention on Diplomatic Relations, the Convention on The Law of Treaties, and the four Geneva Conventions on the Law of the Sea.

[4] *Official Records of the General Assembly, Twenty-Fifth Session, Supplement No. 21* (A/8021).

[5] *Official Records of the General Assembly, Twenty-Seventh Session, Supplement No. 21,* (A/8721), pp. 5-8.

[6] See "Declaration of Principles Governing the Sea-bed and the Ocean Floor, and the Subsoil Thereof, beyond the Limits of National Jurisdiction," General Assembly Resolution 2749 (XXV) of December 17, 1970, *Official Records of the General Assembly, Twenty-fifth Session, Supplement No. 21* (A/8021). The Resolution declared that "The Sea-bed and ocean floor, and the subsoil thereof, beyond the limits of national jurisdiction . . . as well as the resources of the area, are the common heritage of mankind."

[7] See U.N. Document A/Conf. 62/25 entitled "Economic Implications of Sea-bed Mineral Development in the international area: report of the Secretary General" dated 22 May, 1974, *Third United Nations Conference on the Law of the Sea, Official Records,* vol. III, Documents of the Conference, pp. 4-40.

[8] It must be recalled, however, that although there were no negative votes cast against the "Declaration of Principles," there were 14 abstentions registered including the major technology-endorsed States.

[9] U.N. Document A/CONF. 62/C.1/L.7 dated 16 August, 1974, *Third United Nations Conference on the Law of the Sea, Official Records,* pp. 172-173.

[10] U.N. Document A/CONF. 62/P.8/Rev. 1/Part II: Article 18 entitled "Meaning of Innocent Passage," *Third United Nations Conference on the Law of the Sea, Official Records,* Vol. V, pp. 151-173, at 156.

[11] More than fifty states today lay claim to a territorial sea of twelve nautical miles, twenty-one states claim a territorial sea of more than twelve miles; approximately twenty States claim a distance of less than twelve miles. See F.A.O. Fisheries Circular No. 127, Rev. 2,—FIO/C.127/Rev.2, Rome, 1975 entitled "Limits and Status of the Territorial Sea, Exclusive Fishing Zones, Fisheries Conservation Zones and the Continental Shelf."

[12] Six States have a territorial Sea of 200 miles: Benin, Brazil, Ecuador, Panama, Sierra Leone, and Somalia.

[13] The most important of these strait States are: Spain, Morocco, Indonesia, Yemen, and Malaysia.

[14] See *Third United Nations Conference on the Law of the Sea, Official Records,* U.N. Document A/CONF.62/W.P.8/ Rev. 1/Part II; Article 37, p. 159.

[15] Article 64 of the RSNT.

[16] This approach is in deference to the natural prolongative principle which is inferred in Article 1 of the Continental Shelf convention and was further endorsed by the International Court of Justice in the renowned *Continental Shelf* Cases judgement of 1969.

[17] Included in the small minority of States which are resistant to the profit-sharing idea are Australia and Pakistan.

[18] Article 2 of the High Seas Convention referred to other freedoms "which are recognised by the general principles of international law."

[19] See, in particular, Articles 50, 51, and 58 of the RSNT.

[20] The "geographically disadvantaged" States are those States which on account of their unfavourable geographical location are unable to extend their jurisdiction seawards in a uniform fashion, or are unable to enjoy any substantial advantage from the establishment of exclusive economic zones. These States also include States with short coastlines and those which are shelflocked.

[21] In effect, the main Committees of the Conference are a transposition, pure and simple, of the three Committees of the Seabed Committee which served as the preparatory body of the Conference, and the items allocated to the Committee of the Conference are identical with those allocated to their forerunners.

[22] Grenada's recent accession to independence precluded its direct involvement in the developments in the United Nations which led to the convocation of the current Conference.

[23] The Committee was established by the General Assembly at its twenty-third session of 1968 and consisted initially of 42 members. It was enlarged subsequently to 86 and 91 members before being disbanded in 1973 on the eve of the opening of the Conference.

[24] The Continental Margin is the term used to refer to the unit favored by three constituent elements: the Continental Shelf, the Continental Slope, and the Continental Rise.

Part IV:

Decision Making

Introduction

Anthony T. Bryan

In the abundant literature on decision-making theory (DM) in foreign affairs, it is rare to find research in which a major concern is the process as it occurs in small developing states of the Third World. Even more unusual are studies that seek to relate current DM hypotheses regarding foreign policy to empirical research conducted in, and data gathered from, the Third World environment. The four papers that comprise this section have as their central theme the process of DM in foreign affairs in several states of the Caribbean region.

It should be emphasized that the character of the majority of Caribbean states as open economies and polities, existing as subsystems dominated by the international capitalist system, raises certain implications for analysis. First, notwithstanding constitutional independence (which some of the states under study enjoy), the dependent nature of these units as historical offspring and contemporary components of the international capitalist system limits the capability of local policy-makers to produce autonomous decisions or policies, which are, theoretically, a function of state systems in the international arena. Second, given the open character of these economies and their firm links with metropolitan systems, governmental DM is usually a mixture of both foreign and domestic considerations.[1] Finally, some traditional analyses, which view foreign policy-making as a series of systematic plans and concrete actions in the pursuit of national objectives, may bear little relevance to the Caribbean environment.

In the effort to establish some empirical basis for conducting theoretical explorations of the international behavior of Caribbean states, researchers face a number of problems. Vaughan Lewis (commenting on the Commonwealth Caribbean specifically) has identified several of the tasks of empirical research as follows: the need for relatively precise

237

analyses of the actual nature of "control" or power which exists within political or territorial units; indications of how the "maturation" of dominant forces within the international capitalist system affects the capacity of local political leaders to exercise discretionary power (i.e. range of choice) in foreign policy affairs; knowledge of whether, or to what extent, current constitutional arrangements and practices hinder or facilitate the expansion of discretionary power; estimations of the relevance of territorial political size to the provision of a viable base for the exercise of meaningful discretion in international affairs. More specifically, there is need to: (1) identify those variables that limit the capacity of local political units to pursue normatively defined goals with success; (2) ascertain the strategies that can increase the capacity for autonomous DM and the pursuit of policies which will accrue to the benefit and welfare of the masses; (3) to examine the nature of penetration or linkage between domestic and external political institutions and the consequence of same for the capacity of the domestic political system to exercise real control over its environment.[2] In general, and at times in the specific, the papers under consideration address themselves to these research problems and tasks.

The article by Basil A. Ince focuses on the DM process in the making of foreign policy in Trinidad and Tobago, and on a specific decision, namely that country's decision to become a member of the Organization of American States (OAS) in 1967. Ince provides insights into data collection, evaluations of DM literature (with particular emphasis on the role of leadership, foreign policy, and DM in small states), and background information on the sequence of events that led to the decision. In his analysis of the DM process, he employs an operational framework which examines the Decisional Setting (both domestic and external), the Decision Situation, the Organization of Decision-making, and the motivation and characteristics of the principal decision-maker.

Ince establishes the close relationship between domestic and foreign policy in the period under examination and concludes that the decision to enter the OAS was strongly influenced by the domestic economic development strategy of industrialization-by-invitation. The country's foreign policy was "acquiescent" (a behavioural response to internationally directed demands and changes) and it behaved in the international milieu in the manner necessary to facilitate its chosen domestic economic strategy. The author documents the highly personalized DM role in foreign policy displayed by the Prime Minister, in contrast to the purely supportive roles provided by governmental institutions, Parliament, Cabinet, and the ruling party. Public opinion, interest groups, the media, and the Opposition were "non-salient" in the decision. Ince is of the opinion that in this instance the informational input (data collection and documentation), as a vital component in proper foreign policy DM, was more than adequate. His study provides an empirical basis for discussion of the relative influences of strong leadership, national attributes, and linkage phenomena on the DM process.

Anthony P. Maingot examines several issues in order to establish the extent of "independent decision-making" by Caribbean leaders in respect of "region-related" issues. His theoretical approach is that the Caribbean region (both the states of the archipelago and circum-Caribbean) are *becoming* an "interest area"—one in which "historical consciousness about shared problems and shared interests" exist. Some of the characteristics of this process are revealed through analyses of: (1) decision-making in both Trinidad-Tobago and Venezuela; (2) the former country's relations with Cuba and Venezuela; and (3) the latter's development of a Caribbean policy with emphasis on its fisheries sector.

Maingot uses "dependency" as a perspective to indicate that, while the overall boundaries of action in international affairs are esablished by the dominant nations, national actors still possess options. He suggests that, from the purely *political* aspects of DM, the effectiveness of national elites depends in part upon their skill and creativity in internal politics. Relationships among nations of the periphery then are based on "autonomous definitions of self-interest rather than independent decisions to act and choose after the weighing of alternate paths or options." In his opinion, the competing definitions of the Caribbean, as upheld by Trinidad-Tobago and Venezuela respectively, is a debate between independent actors and a means of advancing the interests of national elites both externally and internally. The particular definitions are "resources" in DM as he perceives them.

From Maingot's analysis, it appears that Venezuelan policy-makers have been more precise, prepared, and capable in the realm of foreign policy DM than their counterparts in Trinidad and Tobago.[3] Venezuela's new Caribbean consciousness relies on the coordination of state and private sector initiatives, literary and media propaganda, geopolitical thinking, inputs from scientific and cultural groups, and, in the matter of marine resources, the powerful pressure group comprised of fishermen. As the author sees it, the Venezuelan circumstance of the linkage between national and economic and political exigencies, and foreign policy formulation, attests to the fundamental independence of DM in the matter of Caribbean policy. In sum, he suggests that, while the nature of the dependency that encompasses the entire Caribbean region cannot be modified by definition, elites in individual countries do have available options in foreign policy DM *within* the region.

The unprecedented international importance that the Caribbean country of Cuba has acquired and sustained is explored by Jacques Lévesque.[4] In spite of Cuba's heavy dependence on the Soviet Union, "never in the history of the Communist world has another socialist state been able to defy the USSR to such an extent with impunity." He examines the specific character and uniqueness of the Soviet-Cuban relationship at the strategic, economic, and political levels, changes in the decisional setting which conditioned both Soviet and Cuban behavior throughout the years, and the motivations and leadership qualities of Fidel Castro.

Some features of the "special type of relationship" which Lévesque explores include the absence of any signed formal defence or mutual assistance treaty between the USSR and Cuba; the reluctance of the Soviets to implement direct reprisals (such as cuts or reductions in supplies) even at the worst moments in the relationship; and the generosity on the part of Moscow (such as indefinite postponement of the repayment of Cuba's foreign debt in 1972) when political relations were good. The author suggests that the concept of dependence in the economic relations between the two countries is a curious one, since it is Cuba which has undoubtedly reaped the most advantages at the least cost in the prevailing situation.

From the author's analysis, one gains the impression that the Cuban Revolution as it progressed forced a reluctant USSR (which did not envision the possibility of a socialist revolution for Latin America) to eventually support the ill-fated, Cuban-inspired, guerilla movements in Latin American during the 1960s. Only when faced with the failure of the guerilla movement on the continent did the Cuban leadership begin to place priority on domestic economic tasks and to display greater flexibility in their foreign policy decisions. Cuban and Soviet foreign policies, then, began the process of *convergence* characteristic of the present era. While Lévesque negates arguments about the total conversion of Cuba into a "satellite" of the USSR, the Caribbean country's continuing role in Africa, and its pro-Soviet view of "nonalignment," should keep alive the debate over Cuban independence in foreign policy DM.

The status of Puerto Rico, as an existing microcosm of North American imperialist expansion in the Caribbean, is in direct contrast to Cuba which was able to sustain a genuine revolutionary movement. Robert W. Anderson's paper is concerned primarily with this acute form of Puerto Rican dependence and the range of choice facing both United States and Puerto Rican decision-makers in the statehood versus independence controversy.

The "commonwealth" status scheme for institutionalizing dependence has long become irrelevant. However, the attitude of Puerto Rico's political elite toward the rest of the Caribbean is ambivalent in the extreme. In Anderson's opinion, independence for Puerto Rico cannot be ruled out; but the resistance of U.S. decision-makers to either statehood or independence would be great.

In the final analysis the various discussions presented on DM help to expand our horizons on the process in several states of the Caribbean. The capabilities of the decision-makers and their decisions to affect the international environment appear to be determined in part by time, place, and circumstance.

FOOTNOTES

[1] As Vaughan Lewis has noted with respect to the Commonwealth Caribbean, "domestic politics is international politics." See "The Commonwealth Caribbean" in Christopher Clapham (ed.). *Foreign Policy Making in Developing States: A Comparative Approach* (Farnborough: Saxon House, 1977), pp. 110-130.

[2] Vaughan Lewis, "Neo-Colonialism and Foreign Policy Constraints in the Caribbean," in Louis Lindsay (ed.), *Methodology and Change: Problems of Applied Social Science Research Techniques in the Commonwealth Caribbean* (Mona: University of the West Indies, 1978), pp. 290-294.

[3] For a comparative perspective on Trinidad and Tobago see Basil A. Ince, "The Administration of Foreign Policy in a Small New State: The Case of Trinidad and Tobago," in Vaughan Lewis (ed.), *Size, Self-Determination and International Relations in the Caribbean* (Mona: ISER/UWI, 1976), pp. 307-339.

[4] The article by Lévesque has appeared in Spanish as "La unión soviética y Cuba: una relación especial," *Foro Internacional,* XVIII, No. 2 (octubre-diciembre, 1977). A more extensive treatment of the topic is available in his book, *The USSR and the Cuban Revolution: Soviet Ideological and Strategical Perspectives,* 1959-1977 (N.Y.: Praeger Publishers, 1978).

The Soviet Union and Cuba: A Special Type of Relationship

*Jacques Lé*vesque

Cuba changed camps in the early sixties under extremely difficult and precarious conditions. This changeover was at the root of a number of different problems and complications, but, on the international relations scene, it enabled that country to hold a position and play a role of unprecedented importance, totally disproportionate to the traditional power attributes which it could possess. It is true that it was not a completely new phenomenon for a small State to develop far greater international importance than its means would imply. This phenomenon, however, usually emerges in a crisis and disappears when the crisis ends. In the case of Cuba, what is interesting is that the importance acquired did not fade. It showed itself in a number of different ways through almost the whole decade of the 1960s. Naturally, it diminished in the early 1970s but has resurfaced over the past two years with the role played by Cuba in Africa.

It is not only the importance culled by Cuba from the terms of its relations with the USSR that makes these special and interesting. It is also the very nature of these relations when examined in the light of the problematics of dependence.

Indeed, when we consider the military support and massive amount of USSR economic aid which Cuba needed in order to survive, we could have expected a situation of very heavy dependence. Yet, for several years, Cuba has taken it upon itself to defy the Soviet Union, to counter the latter's policies within the international communist movement and in Latin America, all the while receiving economic assistance which Moscow felt obliged to continue. Never in the history of the communist world has another socialist state been able to defy the USSR to such an extent with impunity. Similarly, for as long as the USSR has existed, Cuba is undoubtedly the State which has reaped the most advantage for the least price in dependence terms.

As we will see, these facts can be explained by Cuba's geostrategic location as well as by the overall international political situation of the 1960s and, in particular, that prevailing within the communist movement. In order to bring out the specific character and originality of the Soviet-Cuban relationship, we shall examine it at three levels: the strategic, the economic, and the political.

STRATEGIC AND MILITARY RELATIONS

The Soviet reactions to the Cuban revolution in 1959 showed extreme caution. The Soviet press, while making limited mention of the events in Cuba, spoke favourably and sympathetically of them. However, strangely enough, it avoided the usual vague and relatively noncommital phrases which were used whenever nationalist anti-imperialist revolutions anywhere else in the Third World were mentioned, and which generally stated that these revolutions "could rely on the support of the Soviet people."

The Soviet Union displayed a very clear will for noninvolvement, even at a purely symbolic level. This will could be explained for a time by concern about the political direction being taken by the Cuban leaders. This explanation, however, can no longer hold from the latter half of 1959, when the world witnessed the radical turn taken by the Cuban revolution, as evidenced at that time by the most dedicated agrarian reform ever before seen in Latin America. For years the Soviet theorists had maintained that agrarian reform was the most urgently needed revolutionary measure for Latin America. Why then not support those who dared to carry it out?

The fact is that it was Cuba's proximity to the USA and the extreme vulnerability which the Soviet leaders saw in it which, basically, lay behind their hesitancy to become involved. We could even say that the veritable obsession about the insecurity of the Cuban revolution was to determine and structure, in the first instance, all Soviet behaviour during the first four years of the revolution.

The example of the way in which the J. Arbenz regime in Guatemala had been disposed of in 1954 was still fresh in the memories of the Soviet leaders, who had had no choice but to be helpless spectators. Moreover, in April 1959, the Soviet press stated that the USA "was dreaming of a new Guatemala."[1] Soviet authors carefully refrained from placing much emphasis on Cuba in connection with a theme which had been one of their favourite since 1956, and according to which the world power relationship had changed and the USA no longer had the possibilities they had before to export counterrevolution because of the new powers of deterrence of the USSR. This theory, the basis for the theory of peaceful coexistence, therefore, was selective to all appearances and could not apply to as sensitive a zone as the Caribbean.

Soviet observers took note of Fidel Castro's dismembering of Batista's army and police force as a very positive move. Once again the example of Guatemala had obviously reared its head, since the fall of the Arbenz regime had been caused in the end by the defection of his army which demanded his resignation following the U.S. organized attack by the army of exiles, although this event had not been decisive in itself.

In the latter half of 1959, USSR interest in and sympathy for Cuba increased with the advent of agrarian reform, and the increasingly anti-American nationalism displayed by Fidel Castro enhanced his regime's popularity. Its gradual consolidation in 1959 gave rise to a cautious optimism in the USSR with regard to its chances of survival. In spite of this, the Soviet leaders remained passive.

The reserve shown by the USSR need not be attributed only to its fear of stepping on dangerous ground, but also paradoxically, to the very interest it had in the Cuban revolution. Soviet leaders, in fact, seemed to be careful to avoid making any moves which might provoke an American intervention against Cuba. They feared that too rapid and open involvement in Cuba would precipitate an intervention which they would be at pains to counter.

One of the most widespread themes appearing in 1959 in Soviet press articles on Cuba was the denial of any communist threat in Cuba. Moreover, the Cuban leaders answered along the same lines when accusations to that effect were made by a variety of American newspapers. The Soviets were visibly trying to deny the United States any pretext of communist and Soviet expansion for a possible intervention which, in that case, would have been much less easily justified in the eyes of international opinion.

It was a way for the USSR to protect, at little cost, a promising but not priority situation. Finally, in the context of his United States visit and his meeting with Eisenhower at Camp David—one of the high points of detente from which he hoped would emerge a settlement of the Berlin problem, his number one priority—it was not in Khrushchev's interest to rush his adversary by getting involved in what was the latter's most closely guarded reserve.

Interest, however, cannot be indefinitely sustained by passivity. At the end of 1959, the impatience displayed by the Cuban communists with respect to Soviet passivity,[2] coupled with Fidel Castro's evident desire for contact, called for involvement. Castro's moves were slow, gradual, marked by a very clear desire not to provoke strong reaction in Washington. First Moscow kept to economic relations. USSR sugar purchases in 1959 were inferior in value to purchases under Batista in 1957. There could be no better way to divest them of all political meaning. In February 1960, Anastasio Mikoyan arrived in Havana to inaugurate a Soviet trade pact. This visit was the first opportunity for a top level Soviet-Cuban encounter. While in Havana, Mikoyan was especially careful to emphasize the "business" or purely economic nature of his visit. Economic relations between the two countries were carried to a considerably higher level than prevailed before 1959.

It was not until May 1960, three months after Mikoyan's visit, that diplomatic relations were established between Moscow and Havana. While quite innocent, the delay in accomplishing this is very significant. It emphasized the Soviet desire to mark the stages clearly and to put off the open politicization of Soviet-Cuban relations.

This politicization was to come about brutally, in July 1960, after Fidel Castro's decision to nationalize the American oil companies gave rise to the first, formal, open economic reprisals by the United States. At that point Khrushchev made it known that the USSR would buy any amounts of Cuban sugar that the United States might strike off of their import quota. Not content to let it rest at this first challenge to the United States on the subject of Cuba, Khrushchev accompanied it with a threat by recalling that the USA was thenceforth within a range of Soviet missiles which could be used in the event of an intervention in Cuba.[3]

This spectacular Soviet about-face warrants examination since it demonstrates a peculiar logic which would reappear at other moments of the Soviet-Cuban relationship. First and foremost, we must note that the failure of the Paris Summit Conference in May 1960 and the resulting deterioration of Soviet-U.S. relations, as well as the ideological controversy launched in April by China which reproached the USSR, without mentioning any names, for its over-conciliatory spirit with regard to the United States and its failure to adequately support the revolutionary movement—all created a favourable combination of circumstances for intensified Soviet involvement in Cuba. Paradoxically, however, it was Cuba's very vulnerability which called for such a sudden and apparently provoking involvement on the part of the Soviet leaders.

As soon as vague involvement was no longer feasible and it became necessary to challenge the USA, as on the sugar issue, Khrushchev seems to have thought that it had to be an "all-out fight," that he had to move right in and right away, to show his determination in the hope of deterring the adversary. To issue a challenge and not back it up in this way seemed to him more liable to invite intervention than the "double or nothing" gamble.

The strategic theory of massive reprisals had been put forward by the USA for the defence of Western Europe where they were in an inferior position as far as classical military forces were concerned. The theory had lost some of its credibility from 1957-58 when the Soviets had developed missiles which could reach the United States. This credibility was not yet as poor, however, as it is today and Khrushchev sought to keep it alive in order to be able to use it himself. He was able to believe that it was the determination he had shown which *partially* helped to deter the USA from intervening directly to back the Bay of Pigs invasion staged by Cuban exiles in April 1961.

Moscow's massive support to Cuba from July 1960 resulted in a considerable acceleration of the revolutionary process. All American firms were nationalized, and in autumn, it was the turn of local capital. The result was that, to all intents and purposes, capitalism had been eradicated in Cuba. Notwithstanding, Fidel Castro did not as yet call himself a socialist.

It was only in April 1961, at the time of the Bay of Pigs invasion, that he affirmed the socialist nature of the Cuban revolution. That statement was not formally echoed in the USSR. During the summer of 1961, Fidel Castro merged his political forces with those of the Cuban Communist Party, a step toward the creation of a single party and, in December 1961, he announced his personal total commitment to Marxist-Leninism. This did not cause Cuba to be recognized by the USSR as socialist, however. It is vital to grasp the main reason behind this reticence.

Cuba's being a candidate for membership of the socialist camp was Fidel Castro's strategy to obtain more than just verbal guarantees of protection from the USSR, since he was convinced that failure at the Bay of Pigs had not put an end to Washington's interventionist aims. In the presence of Soviet reticence to recognize Cuba as socialist, Fidel Castro wanted to confront Moscow with a *fait accompli* by proclaiming himself Marxist-Leninist.

Now it was precisely these firmer guarantees of protection that the Soviet leaders did not want or thought themselves unable to give to Cuba by refusing to recognize it as a member of the socialist camp. First of all, they believed that Fidel Castro's professions of the socialist, then of the Marxist-Leninist, faith increased Cuba's vulnerability. Certain events even seemed to prove them right. At the end of January 1962, at the Punta del Este Conference, the USA was able to push through a resolution with a unanimous vote by members of the OAS, stipulating that "Marxist-Leninism is incompatible with the Pan-American system," and to have Cuba expelled from that regional organization. Before this, the USA had been unsuccessful in efforts to mobilize the OAS into sanctions against Cuba. Moscow had thought that the absence of an OAS mandate, by withholding international justification, had helped to dissuade the USA from further involvement at the time of the Bay of Pigs. Cuba's adherence to Marxist Leninism had made it easier for the USA to procure for itself a moral stamp of approval.

The more conservative Soviet leaders still believed in Stalin's theory that "the wheel of history cannot turn backwards," and that a country could not be torn away from the socialist camp. Until then, the socialist camp had always developed around the borders of the USSR, which made a flexible defence easier. Not so with Cuba, which would have been the Achilles heel of the socialist camp, a reverse Berlin. If verbal threats of reprisals had failed with the USA and a direct attack had been launched against Cuba, Soviet leaders would have been faced with an unbearable choice: total nuclear war or, for the first time in the history of the Communist world, the loss of a member State of the socialist camp. This explains why they were little disposed to accept this new, too-fragile member.

While the Soviet leaders were hesitant, some of them were 'tempted,' nevertheless. This was so especially for Khrushchev who was more inclined to take a risk. He declared at the XXIInd Congress of the Soviet Union Communist Party in October 1961 that Cuba had inscribed "the socialist aims on its flags." The fact that his words were neither reproduced nor quoted by Pravda articles proves that he was, at that time, part of the minority.[4] The Cuban revolution and its evolution came as proof of several of Khrushchev's theoretical innovations, contested by the Chinese, particularly those on "the third phase of the general crisis of the world capitalist system" which held that it was possible that new socialist States emerge in the context of peaceful coexistence, and those on "national democracy" which foresaw the merging of nationalism and socialism in the Third World. In his view, the USSR should show itself capable of flowing with the mainstream of history by taking up the Cuban challenge and by not neglecting its possible spin-offs in Latin America.

It was in April 1962, when Soviet-Cuban relations were at a low ebb with the growing annoyance of Fidel Castro, that Khrushchev succeeded in carrying through a majority decision and that Pravda at last recognized Cuba as socialist. It was, however, discreetly done, with no hue and cry,[5] which goes to show that the fears of the Soviet leaders were not dispelled. In all likelihood it was soon after this that the decision, which was to lead to the famous October 1962 crisis, was taken to set up Soviet missile installations in Cuba.

Most of the western authors who have studied the missile crisis have stated that it was totally or almost totally unconnected with the defence of Cuba.[6] Looking at the question solely from the angle of relations between the two big Powers, they attributed the missile installations to a desire on the part of the USSR to change the nuclear balance of power in its favour. While this concern was certainly not absent in the Soviet decision, Cuba's defence was a vital consideration. This is what clearly shows the dynamics peculiar to Soviet-Cuban relations.[7]

Coming as it did soon after the recognition that Cuba was socialist, the decision to set up the missiles appeared to be a means of integrating Cuba in a military sense to the socialist camp and of responding to the demands made by Fidel Castro in the matter of defence. Indeed, had the missiles not been discovered by the USA *before they became operational,* Cuba would have become a "Sanctuary." It is difficult to see how the USA in that case could have threatened, as they did, to bomb the sites unless they were dismantled within three days. By becoming a "Sanctuary," it would have been better protected than by a mere defence treaty, the operativeness of which could be doubtful.

When we know the unfortunate outcome of the crisis for the USSR, we can wonder how it could have embarked upon such a risky venture when its foreign policy has always borne the mark of caution. First of all, we must say that the way in which the incident ended was not necessarily the only possible one. Moreover, Cuba's vulnerability, as the USSR saw it, left it not much room to maneuver and it seems that the same dynamics, observed in the summer of 1960, of the "double or nothing" gamble once more ruled the game.

As we all know, the Soviet Union lost face in the autumn 1962 crisis and was forced to withdraw its missiles and be content, in exchange, with a U.S. commitment not to invade Cuba. This return, which had seemed meagre at the time, was nevertheless not a negligible one for the USSR. It derived great, although not total, relief through it from its obsession about Cuba's vulnerability, which had been the focal point of its entire policy toward that country.

Fidel Castro, on the other hand, was in no way reassured or satisfied by the Americans' promise. The unilateral missile withdrawal by the USSR triggered the first serious deterioration in Soviet-Cuban relations and caused Cuba to move somewhat closer to China.

Soviet leaders set themselves to work to reassure him by various means. First of all, they raised considerably Cuba's supply of classical weapons, thus making that country's army one of the most powerful in the western hemsiphere. It enabled Cuba to effectively resist the sporadic harrassments which continued from bases in the USA, or any other larger attempt to intervene, except, of course, a direct intervention by the USA which, nevertheless, would have had to be massive in order to succeed. Apart from this, they tried to appease Castro by forcefully affirming Cuba's membership in the socialist camp as a full-fledged member and by claiming that the "respectability of the USSR was such that the U.S. promise would be kept. As a member of the socialist camp, Cuba was also entitled to considerably greater economic aid. All this seemed, at least in part, to mollify the Cuban leader, if we are to judge by his words following two visits to the USSR in 1963 and 1964.

However, the U.S. bombings of North Vietnam in 1965, prolonged and intensified, caused great concern to the Cuban leader. He was forced to face the painful fact that membership in the socialist camp, which he had sought so avidly for reasons of security, could offer only very poor protection by the USSR. At first he publicly asked that "the socialist camp take the necessary risks to save Vietnam."[8] In 1966, his pleas having had little effect, he bitterly stated: "We do not believe it good that a people should entrust its security to others or even that it count on others to defend it. We are seeing this in Vietnam."[9]

This situation helped to make Fidel Castro even more ardently convinced than before that the security, indeed the survival, of the Cuban revolution could be really ensured only by the spread of the revolution to the Latin American continent. As a matter of fact, his hardest efforts to spread the guerilla movement in Latin America, denouncing the Communist Party's opposition to it, were made in 1966 and 1967. It was the worst period for the Cuba-USSR relationship. This was also the period during which Cuba, with the aim of putting pressure on the USSR, sought, with a degree of success, to organize a coalition of the three socialist States most directly threatened by the USA: North Vietnam, North Korea, and Cuba itself.

When Soviet-Cuban relations took a turn for the better once more, for reasons to which we will return, the question of Cuba's security and the military responsibilities of the USSR with respect to Cuba continued to be of concern to Fidel Castro. Thus in August 1968, he approved of the Soviet invasions of Czechoslavakia as a measure to prevent the removal by the imperialist camp, of a "link in the chain of the socialist community of States." At the same time, however, he addressed a provocative question to the Soviet leaders: "Would they send Warsaw

Pact forces to Cuba if the Yankee imperialists attack our country, or even if they threaten to attack, if we request it of them?"[10]

Two years later, in 1970, commenting on the American demands for the servering of military ties with the USSR as a condition for the end of the economic blockade, the Cuban leader again declared: "We shall never break off our political ties with the Soviet Union, or even what they call military ties. On the contrary! As far as we are concerned, we will always be willing to increase our military ties with the Soviet Union."[11] No doubt the message was meant for Moscow as much as for Washington.

From 1969, with the improvement of Soviet-Cuban relations, a whole series of periodic visits to Cuba began by Soviet navy vessels. The vessels, including the occasional nuclear submarine, spent prolonged periods in Cuban waters.[12] This military activity was no doubt in response to commitments sought by Fidel Castro. Moreover, it fit perfectly into the general strategy of the USSR.

One of the important lessons which the latter learnt from the missile crisis was surely that of the usefulnesss of having an intervening or deterrent force on the spot, which had been sorely lacking before. The general expansion of the Soviet navy, whether in the Mediterranean or the Indian Ocean, was meant to correct this state of affairs. The objectives were made abundantly clear. In 1970, the Soviet Admiral Gorshtiov stated: "The presence of our ships in all these areas ties the hands of the imperialists and deprives them of the possibility of freely interfering in the internal affairs of peoples."[13]

Thus, the visits to and periods spent in Cuba by Soviet military vessels appeared to stem from the will to gradually bring about a change in the local power relationships in the Caribbean. The absence of a technical base, however, checked the logistic flexibility and the possibility of expansion of the Soviet fleet.

This new form of Soviet military presence close to Cuba perhaps helped to reassure Fidel Castro who has stopped showing signs of dissatisfaction in recent years as to the question of security. It might also be that, with time, he has become convinced of the reality of the American commitment of Autumn 1962.

Whatever his certainties or uncertainties may be, it is strange, nevertheless, that no formal defence and mutual assistance treaty has ever been signed between the USSR and Cuba.

ECONOMIC RELATIONS

Economic matters caused constant rifts between the USSR and Cuba but, in spite of this, they never were a source of major conflict. For the

USSR, the more important side of their relations with Cuba was always the political one, and economic matters, however important, always were subject to the political imperatives.

In July 1960, a few days after Khrushchev committed himself for the first time to defend Cuba, a Cuban delegation led by Raoul Castro left for Moscow to discuss, among other things, economic aid. In the communiqué issued at the end of the visit, the USSR pledged to supply Cuba with those products which the USA and other capitalist countries refused to supply, "on the basis of the development of normal trade relations."[14]

This was a way of putting across a very clear message that there was to be this important restriction with regard to the framework and forms of the aid the Russians planned to give to Cuba. However, the extent of the political commitment which Khrushchev had had to make did not allow him to get off so easily in the economic field, and it was easy for the Cuban leaders to force his hand.

In December 1960, another Cuban delegation, this time led by Guevara, went to Moscow and had the Russians sign a communiqué which this time stipulated that "the Soviet Union agreed to take all the measures in its power to supply the products which were vital and essential to the Cuban economy where, it was impossible for them to buy these from other countries."[15] Moscow had already abandoned the idea of being able to supply Cuba "on the basis of normal trade relations." It was obvious, however, that the USSR did not want to become Cuba's quasi-exclusive supplier. The Russians knew that Cuba could not radically and suddenly change trading partners without causing, by this act alone, costly breaks in an economy equipped with western material. They also knew that they would have to bear a large part of the cost of these breaks and the necessary conversions. They were in no hurry to have their economic burden increased and they did not look forward to a total trade break between Cuba and the USA. In their view, the Cuban leaders were a little too happy at that prospect.

The domestic economic policy of the *guerrilleros* soon prompted reservations on the part of the Soviet Union. The nationalization of the U.S. enterprises during the summer of 1960 was hailed by the Soviet press. It was seen as a measure aimed at creating a strong state sector which could become the moving force of the economy. However, when a few months later Fidel Castro launched into the nationalization of private Cuban enterprise, the Russians maintained a disapproving silence. In Moscow it was thought that the Cuban Revolution was moving with dangerous quickness through the stages of the process, even from the point of view of a transition to Socialism which was not at

...de on investment, resource allocation, etc. Their mistakes are all
...rs.

THE POLITICAL RELATIONS:
CONCURRENCE AND OPPOSITION

Soviet interest in the Cuban revolution which justified the 1960
involvement was largely due to its impact on Latin America. As we all
now, the Cuban revolution, especially in the first years, aroused a huge
wave of sympathy among the peoples of the whole Latin American
continent and proved to be an impressive factor for political mobilization.
The Russians, therefore, saw the Cuban revolution as a strong revolutionary lever for Latin America.

Until then, Soviet writings constantly referred to the "national
liberation movement of the peoples of Asia and Africa." The Latin
American movement was rarely mentioned or, if so, took third and last
place to the others. Moreover, until that time, nationalism had risen up
against the colonial empires of France and Great Britain, the decline of
which had been evident to all.

For the Russians, the importance of the Cuban revolution derived
from the fact that it heralded the entry "of all of Latin America into the
arena for the active struggle against imperialism,"[19] and that this time
the most powerful empire was being attacked—the United States of
America—and its most privileged reserves. Thus the effects of the
Cuban revolution were to reconcile the often irreconcilable interests of
the Soviet State and the social revolution.

Before Fidel Castro's rise to power, Soviet theorists had elaborated a
number of theories on the revolutionary process in Latin America. They
generally believed that the countries of Latin America as a whole had to
deal with three great and pressing tasks, common to all: 1) the
introduction of a radical agrarian reform; 2) the limitation of foreign
capital investments; and 3) the development of industry in order to
overcome a too-narrow economic specialization. The class analysis
made by the Russians revolved around the solution to these problems.
Thus, internally, the main enemy on which all contradictions converged
was the agrarian oligarchy or "latifundistas," the most reactionary class.
This was seen as the main break to the development of the productive
forces of those countries and as the main obstructive force to political
democratization. Because of its opposition to economic progress and its
political conservatism, it constituted, along with the greater bourgeoisie
and its links with foreign investments, the pillar of American penetration
and domination. As a result, the struggle against American imperialism

that time, moreover, an officially recognized objective in Cuba itself.
Indeed, after the difficult experience of the first comings into power of the
Bolsheviks, most of the socialist countries in Eastern Europe and China
insisted on keeping, for quite a long inital phase, a relatively large private
sector during the setting up of the State sector and planning, so as to
prevent acute imbalances and ensure an easier transition. The Russians
feared, and not without reason, that the speed of action of the Cuban
leaders might lead to economic chaos of which they would have to bear a
large part of the cost.

In fact, what Moscow feared the most was that economic hardship of
too serious a nature might cause severe upheavals within the Cuban
population, which would then have constituted an additional, and in no
way negligible, incentive for the USA to intervene. We must not
exaggerate too much, therefore, the importance of the hesitations of the
Soviet leaders on the economic front. This is where they made the fastest
adjustment to Cuban demands. In fact, they gave in much more easily
here than on the question of recognizing Cuba as socialist.

In 1960, the Cuban leaders announced an extremely ambitious
economic development strategy, the long-term objective of which was
maximum economic independence and which proposed in the short-term
to develop various branches of heavy industries. The Russians could not
agree to that strategy since they were then seriously beginning to promote
economic specialization between the countries of Eastern Europe and to
oppose Rumania's plans to build a huge steel complex though it did not
have the necessary raw materials, and the economic rationality of which
must have seemed doubtful in the framework of COMECON. The
objections must have been even stronger in the case of Cuba. Because of
its size, its human technical resources, the Cuban projects must have
been deemed unrealistic. The Soviet leaders probably did not exert much
pressure on their Cuban counterparts since their disapproval was only
indirectly shown by the silence of the Soviet press on the issue. It is true
that since Cuba was not a member of COMECON, its economic projects
did not go against the policy of this organization as in the case of
Rumania. Undoubtedly, the Russians must have communicated their
reservations to the Cuban leaders, but these went unheeded. Apparently,
they handled Cuban nationalism very carefully, bearing in mind what
was happening with Cuban-U.S. relations.

Three years later, in the spring of 1963, the Cuban leaders decided to
abandon this development strategy because of the extremely poor results
obtained. Several of the new businesses launched revealed themselves
to be totally inefficient causing a huge amount of wastage. The decision
was taken to make sugar cane the spine of the Cuban economy, and to

develop an industry closely related to agriculture and sugar production. This time the Soviet commentators openly expressed their satisfaction in terms which left no doubts as to their previous opinions. It was noted that the concentration of efforts on agriculture was going to allow for a much quicker rise in the standard of living of the population, and that the elimination of the one-harvest system would mean the maintaining of productivity in that sector.[16] It is a fact that sugar production had decreased since the Revolution. It was also noted with satisfaction that "the Cuban economy has not followed the risky path of autarchy advocated by the Chinese Communist Party."[17]

Though Moscow now agreed with the Cuban development strategy, for several years the Russians did not approve the methods used. Nor did they approve of the accent placed on moral incentive in lieu of material incentives.

It is difficult to make an exact evaluation of the Soviet economic aid granted to Cuba. American scholars of the sixties estimated the net cost for the Soviet Union at $1 million per day. We know, because Fidel Castro made it public, that all the military equipment and material was supplied free of charge. We have no figures on this. For all the rest, the Russians did try to operate on a trade basis, but an "abnormal" one. That is to say that every year Cuba's trade deficit grew, reaching impressive cumulative figures. Moreover, the price quoted for Cuban sugar has generally been higher than the world market price. Finally, when relations between the two countries were very good and if the world market price was favourable, the USSR authorized Cuba to remove parts of the USSR sugar import quota to sell for foreign exchange on western markets and improve its trade position there.

Even at the worst moments in the Soviet-Cuban relationship, there are no indications of any direct reprisals such as cuts or reductions in Soviet supplies. However, there was certainly some economic pressure exerted. It took the form of a refusal to increase the oil supply by more than 2% while Cuba was asking for an 8% increase to meet the growth needs of its economy. As a matter of fact, Fidel Castro reacted very strongly to this refusal.

On the other hand, when political relations were good, Moscow was generous. Thus in 1972, when Cuba agreed to enter COMECON, the USSR agreed to postpone the repayment of Cuba's foreign debt indefinitely. Indeed, did the USSR really have any choice? It is useful to point out here that Cuba's entry into COMECON held more political than economic interest for the USSR. Since Cuban deliveries had been irregular for the most part, they hardly fit in with the objectives of the rigourous and exact coordination desired by COMECON. On the other

hand, Cuba's entry came as a reinforcement of the i that primarily regional body of the socialist camp, economic links were continually being forged betwe and the western world where its image needed it.

The economic management concepts of both countri closer together only in 1970, two years after the Sovi ciliation. It happened because of the failure and the cons "gran zafra," for which Fidel Castro had set a harvest record 10 million tons of sugar cane. It had become the N aim and an all-out effort was made to reach it in a feverish a general mobilization. In the end, the crop was a record one tons. However, the other sectors of the economy had beer because of the concentration of all efforts on the harvest, and, there followed serious drops in production and acute dislocati in turn caused breaks in supply and popular loss of morale. occasion Fidel Castro carried out a public self-criticism and, u there has been no other "voluntarist leap" by Cuba in economic r

Since then, all sorts of indications point to the fact that Soviet is heeded more carefully, for better and for worse. As a result, ma incentives were increased as well as quantification and surveillance levels. Workers received the "work record book," a well-known fea of work in the USSR. In spite of that, however, it would surely exaggerating to state, as some do, that Cuba has become a characterle carbon copy of the Soviet Union. There are numerous differences whicl strike the observer who is familiar with both countries. In this way, Cuba's educational system resembles more closely China's system, with the accent placed on the relationship between practical and theoretical work. Thus there are no full-time students in Cuba's universities, only "student workers" and "worker students" according to which activity predominates. Similarly, many mechanisms and ideas close to those of China can be found in Cuban agricultural communities,[18] not to mention the specifically Cuban features such as the microbrigade in the construction industry.

One can wonder as to the meaning of the concept of dependence in the economic relations between the USSR and Cuba. It is true that the latter depends almost completely on the former for several of its staple supplies. However, it is obvious that there is no question here of economic exploitation. Similarly, when we speak of dependence, and we consider the former situation of Cuba, the notion of control must be introduced. At present, there are no foreign-owned properties on Cuban territory. Even though Soviet advisers might be more carefully heeded than before, the levers of the economy are in Cuban hands and they are the ones who had to be preceded by the struggle against the "latifundistas" for agrarian reform. To this end, Soviet scholars place their bets on the peasants, the workers, and the national bourgeoisie. The latter was considered a less than negligible ally. Since this class was opposed to the greater bourgeoisie which was ruining it, or slowing its growth, it was in its interest not only to protect the domestic market, which would antagonize the "latifundistas," but to broaden it, allying them to agrarian reform which would increase the number of units and domestic economic activities.

Thus we see that the Russians did not have in mind the possibility of a socialist revolution for Latin America. This was expressed, moreover, very clearly in Moscow by an expert who stated "the national liberation movement in the countries of Latin America is not socialist in character but rather democratic. The immediate task it sets itself is the making of an agrarian, anti-imperialist revolution."[20] In fact, it was believed that the attractiveness and mobilizing power of socialism was not as strong as that of agrarian reform, and, above all, that of anti-Americanism. This is why, in the first stages, that is to say, until the autumn of 1960, the Cuban revolution represented in Russian eyes the model par excellence for Latin America and why it seemed to provide dazzling proof of their theories. Nevertheless, it must be emphasized that while the Cuban revolution could serve as a model, this was only the case for its political content and not for its methods in the conquest of power, that is, armed struggle. On this point Moscow remained silent.

This silence had various reasons. First of all, Fidel Castro's calls for continental guerrilla warfare were deemed politically ill-advised, since they could arouse the hostility of the more moderate Latin Amerian governments, which, on the contrary, should be handled carefully in order to avoid a dangerous isolation within the OAS. Moreover, guerrilla warfare on a continental scale was deemed unfeasible because of the difference in conditions from country to country. Finally, armed struggle was the subject of much discussion in various Latin American Communist Parties, and the Russians were in no hurry to make a pronouncement on the matter in order to avoid wounding sensibilities, including that of Fidel Castro himself.

In the USSR, the immediate effects of the Cuban revolution were applauded since they seemed to favour greatly the medium-term objectives mentioned above. Cuba's popularity, according to Russian scholars, was provoking a beneficial polarization of the national bourgeoisie, a radicalization of the petty bourgeoisie, in particular the students and the intelligentsia, and was bringing about a politicization of the masses. It must be noted that at that point in time, Fidel Castro and

Issues in Caribbean International Relations

the Cuban leaders were officially considered by the Soviet press as "belonging to the petty bourgeoisie" or again, to the more "radical faction of the national bourgeoisie" in Cuba.

The Russians also believed that through its example and its effects the Cuban revolution was fulfilling an important unifying function, bringing together all the progressive forces of Latin America. The movement of solidarity with Cuba also brought together communist, socialist, radical bourgeois and petty bourgeois parties. It was thought that the collaboration of Fidel Castro and his movement with the Cuban Communist Party for the needs of struggle against American domination, because of its results and for those same reasons, was bringing about a reduction in the anticommunist feeling among the rest of the Latin American Left. All this favoured the formation of the huge political front needed to perform the immediate tasks facing Latin America.

In the autumn of 1960, when Fidel Castro began his campaign to nationalize local Cuban capital, he, in fact, was forcing the frame of the model assigned to Latin America. No doubt it was in order to preserve the exemplary value of the model that Soviet scholars chose to close their eyes to what was happening in Cuba. Some of them even distorted reality to quite an extent, by stating that the national bourgeoisie continued to play an important role in Cuba and by writing, even in early 1961: "It must definitely be emphasized that nationalization in no way affects small businessmen and traders. On the contrary."[21]

When in 1961, Fidel Castro declared the Cuban revolution to be a socialist one and more so when he affirmed that he was Marxist-Leninist, he, once and for all, "broke" the model as conceived by the USSR. The latter did not abandon this revolution for the rest of Latin America even so. We have already mentioned that the reasons the Soviet leaders had for finding Cuba's change to Marxist-Leninism ill-advised were mainly ones of security. However, it was also because, in their eyes, Cuba was losing, through this, part of its attractiveness in Latin America and its value as an example at close range. During a visit to Moscow in 1973, the Director of the Latin American Institute of the V. Volski Academy told me that by becoming Marxist-Leninist, Cuba had lost the support of the national bourgeoisie of the continent. Since it was thought that the huge movement of solidarity with Cuba was "the strongest mass movement of struggle in Latin America," any loss of forces by this movement could not only be deemed negative. Moreover, the new wave of anti-communism launched at Punta del Este in January 1962 could gain ground over and beyond the national bourgeoisie.

We might say, therefore, that in Moscow's view, the Cuban revolution, because of its haste, had not allowed time for the consolidation of all positive spinoffs of its first stage in Latin America.

However, some Latin American Communist Parties, including Uruguay's for example, were very pleased with Castro's move to Marxist-Leninism and their press recognized Cuba as socialist long before the USSR did. In this way they could claim to be the legitimate representatives of the ultimate turn taken by the Cuban revolution with respect to the guerilla groupings springing up all over Latin America and claiming to be Cuban. Some years later, Fidel Castro was to personally undertake to withdraw from them this legitimacy.

From 1963 onwards, it became more and more difficult for the USSR to maintain an apparently neutral stand on the issue of armed struggle in Latin America. Within the Communist Parties on the continent debates became stormier not only on the subject of the Cuban experience, but also because of the call issued by China to all those who agreed with the line it had taken, one of the basic points of which was precisely the armed struggle, to break away. The leadership of the Communist Party, opposed to armed struggle, had to intervene with Moscow and request that it take a stand on the matter.

Meanwhile, there were clear signs of a division in the Soviet leadership on that particular issue. A reading of the statements by Soviet leaders and of the Soviet press points to the existence of a debate in late 1963 and during 1964 on the advisability of armed struggle in Latin America. Below the surface official line that either armed struggle or peaceful means were valid according to the particular circumstances of each country, there ran two trends of thought. The first one, which dominated till the summer of 1964, was clearly opposed to armed struggle and was spearheaded by Khrushchev himself and the Director of the Latin American Institute of the time, S. S. Mikhailov. There were two reasons for their opposition. First of all they believed that armed struggle did not favour the unity of as broad a political action front as possible, as had always been advocated for Latin America. Finally, since the missile crisis, Khrushchev was seeking a stable detente with the USA. As a result it was not in his interest to have the USSR openly support armed struggle on the American continent. In spite of the personal stand taken by Khrushchev, scholars at first cautiously asserted the relevance of the Cuban example, in reference to armed strggle as well.[22] The fact that scholars were able to express divergent views on such a delicate subject shows that there was division at the top. The divergences intensified in the summer of 1964 when the journal *Kommunist*, theoretical organ of the Central Committee of the Soviet Union Communist Party, published two articles which clearly held opposite views on the issue.[23]

The debate was decided finally by the policy adopted by the new Soviet leadership after the fall of Khrushchev at the end of 1964. The new Soviet leaders sponsored the organization of a conference of Latin

American Communist Parties which was held in Havana in December of that year. Thanks to the role of mediator previously played by the USSR, the conference led to a commitment agreed upon by Fidel Castro and the parties in favour of armed struggle on the one hand, and the majority of the parties which opposed it on the other. In fact, all the participants at the conference pledged to "actively support" armed struggle in five countries: Venezuela, Colombia, Guatemala, Honduras, Paraguay, and Haiti.[24] Inversely, all the participants also pledged to support the other Communist Parties who were using peaceful means.

The Soviet Union officially endorsed the terms of the commitment and began to support the armed struggle in the various countries involved. This was done not only through favourable statements in its newspapers but also materially, mainly by forwarding large sums to the guerrilla forces of the Party in Venezuela, the country where the armed struggle was the most developed.[25]

In 1965 Fidel Castro showed his satisfaction at the commitment. China held it against him at a time when the conflict with the USSR was intensifying. China began to call on all true revolutionaries to denounce Soviet policy in its entirety. This prompted Fidel Castro to say that Cuba had "no lessons in revolutionary behaviour to learn from anyone." In fact, the Cuban leader, who was much more interested in the concrete advancement of the armed struggle than in debates on theory, must have thought that in that field the USSR finally proved more efficient than China which had nothing to offer but a phrase book. Finally, the Soviet leaders did not get involved in giving him "lessons in revolutionary behavior" on this issue. In early 1966 the Chinese leaders made the mistake of cutting by almost half their supplies of rice to Cuba. This earned them a violent outburst from Fidel Castro who accused them of economic blackmail and of having *de facto* joined in the Americn blockade. Sino-Cuban relations went into a decline and in the end never recovered. Naturally, the Soviet leaders gleefully observed this decline which had begun sketchily in early 1965. However, they were soon to be the targets of Fidel Castro's wrath. The compromise of the end of 1964 would have lasted barely more than a year.

The military intervention to overthrow the government in Santo Domingo by the USA in the spring of 1965, based on a very hypothetical fear of another Cuba, caused a certain amount of anxiety in Moscow. It gave birth to the so-called Johnson doctrines according to which the U.S. President claimed that the USA would not tolerate the establishment of another communist State in the Western hemisphere. At the same time, the intensification of the action of the Green Berets and of efforts by the USA to suppress guerrilla movements in Latin America gave rise, in Moscow, to a new theory which one could term the theory of the American "backlash" as a result of the Cuban revolution and its consequences. This, along with the serious setbacks befalling the guerrilla movement in 1965 in all quarters, helped to make the Soviet leaders very sceptical as to its chances of success. However, formally they stuck to the December 1964 commitment.

On the Cuban scene, Santo Domingo, in addition to U.S. bombings in North Vietnam, came to increase feelings of insecurity which, as we have seen, only forced them into extending the guerrilla movement. However, it was the Communist Party's withdrawal from the armed struggle in Venezuela in early 1966 which caused Cuba to break the commitment. Thus the Communist Party in Venezuela withdrew from the armed struggle because of the stinging defeats suffered in 1965. Meanwhile Fidel Castro had placed his greatest hopes in the guerrilla movement in that country. He no doubt hoped that the USSR would intervene to encourage the Venezuelan Communist Party to remain in the armed struggle. Because of its scepticism, the USSR probably had not the least intention of so doing and was able to retire behind the principle of non-intervention in the affairs of other parties.

Fidel Castro therefore began to denounce the Venezuelan Party in violent terms as a party led by traitors to the revolution and to reaffirm that, in all of Latin America, the only way to revolution was the armed struggle. Those who refused to join it, that is to say, the majority of the Communist Parties, were denounced as being pseudorevolutionary. The Soviet Union did not get as large a share of the criticism as the Latin American Parties, but at times severe criticism was levelled at it. Thus Fidel Castro declared in May 1966: "It may well be that a country believes that it is building communism when, in truth, it is building capitalism." He claimed, furthermore, not to believe that a communist society could exist "in a world that is still poverty stricken."[26]

At the beginning of 1967, the Cuban position was drafted in the form of a theoretical synthesis by Regis Debray, following long conversations with Fidel Castro. Debray's work was presented as a charter or revolutionary programme for Latin America. He maintained that the only relevant way to revolution for Latin America was the Cuban brand of armed struggle. As a result, the "foco," or mobile guerrilla centre should not be subject to the political or ideological leadership of any one Party. As happened in Cuba, the guerrilla would ultimately be the nucleus out of which the Party would emerge. He was thus refuting the usefulness of most Communist Parties, deemed hidebound, buried in the sterile tactics which belonged to the stage theory, and were as unreal as the revolutionary potential of the national bourgeoisie. The challenge thus issued to the

communist movement on the theoretical plane, moved to an "organiza-
tional" one in August 1967 with the first Conference of LASO (Latin
American Solidary Organization) in Havana. Most guerrilla groups of
Latin America were invited to send representatives while most of the
Communist Parties were not and were severely criticized. Castro carried
two resolutions through a vote, one which condemned the Communist
Party of Venezuela, and the other condemn "certain socialist countries"
for their economic relations with counterrevolutionary regimes in Latin
America. He stated that Cuban solidarity lay only with those who were
concretely involved in the revolution, even if they did not subscribe to
Marxist-Leninism. He also stated that Cuba belonged to no international
organization   except LASO. Cuba was thus sponsoring a regional
international organization rivalling the communist movement. It was a
weighty challenge coming at a time when Moscow was making great
efforts to reorganize the communist movement.

Therefore it is very likely that Latin American Communist Parties
asked the USSR to take sanctions against Cuba, as Fidel Castro claimed
in his speech to LASO. This is probably why one of the leaders of
Argentina's Communist Party assimilated Castroism to Maoism in an
article written for Pravda.[27] As we saw, the USSR did not get carried
away into direct reprisals. This would have endangered Cuba, constituting, to all intents and purposes, an invitation to the United States to
finish that country off. In view of the USSR's effort thus far to support
Cuba, it could not hand such an important victory to the United States on
a silver platter. Moreover, the USSR thought it ill-advised to add to the
cleavage within the communist movement, already torn apart by the
Sino-Soviet conflict. Therefore it opted for silence and tolerance, still
maintaining, on the surface, a neutral position between Cuba and the
Latin American Parties, although, in fact, its sympathy lay completely
with the latter.

Finally, it was the accumulation of misfortunes suffered by the Latin
American guerrilla movement, the worst of which, symbolically, was
the death of Guevera in Bolivia in October 1967, which caused Cuba to
change its position. Still one year went by after Guevera's death before
the Cuban leaders accepted the harsh facts and began the slow
rapprochement with the USSR at the end of 1968 and in early 1969.

Faced with the failure of the guerrilla movement on the continent, the
Cuban leaders decided to place the priority on the economic consolidation of their country. They displayed greater flexibility in their foreign
policy and learnt to make do with less. Thus they deemed the military

regime of Juan Velasco Alvaredo in Peru a progressive one, even though it had not emerged from a guerrilla movement aimed at an immediate and total break with the USA. By changing from maximalism to minimalism, Cuban foreign policy began to converge with the policy of the USSR. Cuba began to cultivate relations with the States of Latin America which showed the slightest serious desire to oppose American hegemony. Thus, not only did Cuba salute Peru's military regime, but also those of Panama and Ecuador. In spite of Fidel Castro's reservations about the possibility of achieving a changeover to socialism by peaceful means, when the movement of popular unity came to power in Chile, he nevertheless thought it an important step forward for the anti-imperialist movement in Latin America. Through this more flexible foreign policy, Cuba was able to break the economic, political, and diplomatic blockade which the United States had led almost all Latin American States to enforce since 1962. Naturally, the USSR congratulated itself on this. Following the lead of the USSR, Cuba gambled on the policy of a number of states for a change in the power relationship in Latin America. Thus, Allende's Chile, Peru, and for a brief spell, General Torres' Bolivia formed a progessive bloc within a regional organization—the Andean Pact, which was growing stronger and the aim of which was to put a serious check to the economic hegemony of the USA.

These hopes of the gradual reduction of American domination in a limited geographical region was to suffer a serious blow with the coup d'etat in Chile in 1973, and the recent evolution of the situation in Latin America.

In view of these stymied prospects, it is not surprising that Cuba's revolutionary energies and desires for change have shifted to Africa. Therefore there is no need to see in it, as some do, the reflection of a total conversion of Cuba into a USSR "satellite." In the Angolan case, Cuba was, in fact, going back to its initial preference for anti-imperialist guerrilla movements. Naturally, contrary to what was the case in Latin America in the late sixties, the USSR backed this enterprise completely. In its pragmatic approach, the latter believes the chances of success to be higher for the revoutionary movements in Africa today, in the post Vietnam context, than they were for Latin America at the time of LASO.

For Fidel Castro, anxious above all to secure the concrete advancement of the revolution, concertation with the USSR must seem more like a guarantee of efficiency which he did not have in the sixties rather than a submitting to the Soviet will.

FOOTNOTES

[1] *Izvestia,* April 10, 1959.

[2] Edward Gonzales, "The Cuban Revolution and the Soviet Union" Ph. D. diss., University of California, 1966).

[3] *Pravda,* July 10, 1960.

[4] For further details on the divisions within the Soviet leadership on this issue, see Jacques Lévesque *L'URSS et la révolution cubaine* (Paris: Presses de la Fondation Nationale des Sciences politiques et Presses de l'Université de Montréal, 1976), pp. 50-58.

[5] *Pravda,* April 11 and 15, 1962.

[6] Mainly Andres Suarez, *Cuba: Castroism and Communism, 1959-66* (Cambridge, Mass.: MIT Press, 1967); Michel Tatu, *Le pouvoir en URSS* (Paris: Grasset, 1967); A. Horelick, *The Cuban Missile Crisis: An Analyis of Soviet Calculation and Behavior* Santa Monica, Calif.: The Rand Corporation, 1963).

[7] For a detailed development of this theory, see Jacques Lévesque, *op. cit.,* Chapter 1.

[8] *Pravda,* March 18, 1965.

[9] Fidel Castro, *Révolution cubaine II* (Paris: Francois Maspero, 1968), p. 145.

[10] *Granma,* August 25, 1968 (weekly selection in French).

[11] *Granma,* May 3, 1970.

[12] See James D. Theberge, ed., *Soviet Seapower in the Caribbean: Political and Strategic Implications* (New York: Praeger, 1972).

[13] Quoted by D. W. Mitchell, in J. D. Theberge, *op. cit.,* p. 36.

[14] *Pravda,* July 21, 1960.

[15] *Pravda,* December 20, 1960.

[16] B. B. Nikiforov, "Urgent Problems of Latin America," *International Affairs,* no. 8 (August 1964), pp. 93-97.

[17] M. A. Serebrovskaja, "La formation de la méthode socialiste de production," in the collective work, *Osvoboditel noe dvizenie v Latinso Amerike* (Moscou: Nauka, 1964), pp. 57-58.

[18] See "Cuba dans la tourmente," *Le Monde Diplomatique,* February 1977, pp. 7-10.

[19] "Cuba et l'Amérique Latine," *Mirovaja Ekon omika i mezdunarodnye Otnosenija,* no. 7 (July 1961), pp. 26-30.

[20] Maria, V. Danilévić, "Les Forces motrices de la lutte de libération nationale en Amérique Latine," *Morivaja Ekonomika i Meždunarodnye Otnoseniga,* no. 9 (September 1960), pp. 90-98.

[21] A. Negrin, "Cuba oui, Yankee non," *Vsemirnoe profsojuznoe dviženie,* no, 1 (1961), pp. 3-17.

[22] For more details on these differences of view, see Jacques Lévesque, *L'URSS et la révolution cubaine, op. cit.,* pp. 117-124.

[23] See M. Kudackim, and N. Mostovec, "The Liberation Movement in Latin America," *Kommunist,* no. 11 (July 1964, pp. 121-130, and A. Sivolobov, "The peasant movement in Latin America," *Kommunist,* no. 12 (August 1964),pp. 100-107.

[24] See the text of the conference communiqué, *Pravda* January 19, 1965.

[25] Note that the Director of the Institute of Latin America, S. S. Mikhailov, who had taken a hostile stand against armed struggle was replaced in early 1965.

[26] Fidel Castro, *Revolution Cubaine II* pp. 133-138.

[27] *Pravda,* October 25, 1967.

Leadership and Foreign Policy Decision-Making in a Small State: Trinidad and Tobago's Decision to Enter the OAS

Basil A. Ince

In his "Foreign Policy-Making in Small States: Some Theoretic Observations based on a study of the Uganda Ministry of Foreign Affairs,"[1] Maurice East lamented the fact that it was virtually impossible to find any research which has focused "on the *process* of decision-making in foreign affairs in developing states."[2] Almost four years later, although the literature on the Ministries of External Affairs and diplomatic services in developing countries has grown, the position remains virtually the same.[3] About the decision-making (DM) process Kirk-Greene states in his article on Black African diplomatic cadres that "For obvious reasons, we do not really know enough about the decision-making process in an African Ministry of External Affairs."[4] This writer, in an article published a year ago, treated the governmental and nongovernmental environments in which foreign policy was made in Trinidad and Tobago and devoted some space to the DM process.[5] This article, however, focuses on the DM process in the making of foreign policy in Trinidad and Tobago, with special emphasis on the leadership in that sphere of activity, and on a specific foreign policy decision, namely the entry of Trinidad and Tobago into the Organization of American States (OAS).

METHODOLOGY

This paper is essentially on decision-making in foreign policy and a study of this nature forces the author to resort to the conventional

265

informational sources for data collection. The sources in this case are the daily newspapers, official party organs, legislative records (Hansard), books by a major decision-maker, and interviews with decision-makers, not only those involved in the particular decison at hand, but those who had a first-hand knowledge of Cabinet DM policy in general. A distinct limitation with interviews is that some interviewees may suffer from a lapse of memory or may wish to colour the facts after the events.

Few scholars of DM have had the opportunity to observe or participate in policy-making at the highest governmental levels. Not only is the field of DM a difficult one for scholars, but an equally difficult one for the decision-makers themselves. The terrain of foreign policy is less familiar to them, they are dealing with external factors beyond their control, and societies with their own national characteristics and cultures.

DECISION-MAKING THEORY: A PARTIAL GLANCE AT THE LITERATURE[6]

DM analysis stems from as far back as the Greek historian Thucydides in his *The Peloponnesian War.* He was most interested in the factors which led the leaders of the city-states to decide on the issues of war and peace, alliance and empire under the then prevailing conditions. Employing content analysis of speeches, statements, and actions of the officials of both parties, he concluded that the motives of the Peloponnesian War were due to three human impulses: (a) the desire for safety or security (b) the desire for honour, prestige, or glory and (c) the desire for wealth (gain or profit). Thucydides was interested not only in chronicling the history of war *per se,* but in discovering the nature and rationale of the decisions by which the war was being fought. The next known student of DM appeared in the early fifteenth century, and utilizing both diagnostic and prescriptive approaches to explain and predict the political behaviour of decision-makers, Machiavelli stressed power maximization in inter-city state politics as the basic rationale in DM theory.

These classical DM-theorists were replaced by the moderns whose theories and models attempted to identify a larger number of relevant variables and to posit more heuristic mechanisms among these variables. There were two major trends among these moderns, those emphasizing macro-analysis and the other concentrating on micro-analysis. The former were predominant during the period after the Second World War and early fifties. This group emphasized the national interest as the basic unit of analysis and held that it was the major motivating factor explaining the actions and interactions of states on the international political scene. Among these scholars were Charles Beard, Harold Laswell, Hans Morgenthau, Norman Palmer, and Robert Osgood.[7] Of these, Morgenthau contends that behind the action of the State or the statesman, the ulterior motive has been the quest for personal or national interest defined as power. Therefore "to search for the clue to foreign policy exclusively in the motives of statesmen is both futile and deceptive."[8] To Morgenthau, motives were not only illusive but also unmeasureable and, therefore, cannot yield any clue by which to predict the foreign policy of any DM process.[9]

But those scholars were to give way at the beginning of the sixties to a host of scholars expressing the micro-analysis approach to the study of international relations. These scholars were critical of the macro-approach.[10] Verba in his research stressed the importance of the individual decision-maker's total personality, including his attitude based on his innate emotions and temper, past experiences, skills, responsiveness, and responsibilities. Frankel also emphasized the personal values of the decision-maker, but pointed out that the latter based his decision on his perception of reality. Braybrooke and Lindblom questioned the ability of the decision-maker to analyze all the information. The environment of foreign policy is so large in scope that it is virtually impossible for the decision-maker to collect all the information. The authors argue that the decision-makers in foreign policy deal with large-scope areas unlike those in the synoptic model (in domestic politics, economics, and organizations) who deal with small-scope areas. Deutsch demonstrates that DM involves both the human and nonhuman capabilities of the State—the extent of the individual's allegiance to his political system and the capability of his regime to enforce its will and norms within and without its society.[11] Allison has attempted to construct models through which foreign policy decisions might be explained or predicted. Model 1, the Rational Actor model, answers the question: Why did so and so make such a decision, or do what he did? Model II, the Organization Process Model, attempts to answer the question: Under what organizational structure or auspices was the decision made? Model III, the Bureaucratic Politics Model, attempts to answer those questions related to consensus-building in policy formulation.

The work of Snyder, Bruck, and Sapin was immediately recognized on publication as a major addition to the literature of the field. It was the first extended and systematic attempt to conceptualize the role of DM in the formulation of foreign policy and in the process of international politics. These authors list ten fundamental constraints through which the interactions of States can be explained and predicted:

(i) The Nation-State as a prime actor in a given international political system; (ii) actions in terms of its strategies and commitments; (iii) the situation in which the State exists and interacts with other States in a given international political system; (iv) in individual actors as decision-makers; (v) definition of the situation by the decision-makers—their perception, choice, and expectation; (vi) external and internal setting—international and domestic political interpretation; (vii) reactions of domestic non-governmental forces to actions of the government in foreign affairs; (viii) interpretation and reactions of other States to the acts of the State in question; (ix) feedback—awareness and evaluation of the success and failure of the policy in force by the decision-maker; (x) appraisals and counter appraisals—new action by the decision-maker and reactions of other States and domestic organizations in response to such action.[12]

Space does not permit a critique of the models of these DM theorists, but something must be mentioned of the critical issue of rationality in the DM process before moving on. Scholars who have had experience in high government circles warn against the rationality models employed by others in the study of the decision-making process in foreign policy. The rationality model presumes that decision-makers generally follow certain patterns, namely, (a) gather and scrutinize all information possible relevant to the event; (b) consider all possible alternatives in terms of their relative net gains; (c) consider all possible consequences or appraisals of each alternative; and (d) choose and implement only that alternative with potential maximum net gains.

Unfortunately, this is not the reality, according to one U.S. scholar who served in the early sixties as Director of the Bureau of Intelligence and Research in the State Department and Assistant Secretary of State for Far Eastern Affairs. He writes:

Very often "policy" is the sum of a congeries of separate or only vaguely related actions. On other occasions, it is an uneasy, even internally inconsistent compromise among competing goals or an incompatible mixture of alternative means of achieving a single goal. There is no systematic and comprehensive study of all the implications of the grand alternatives—nor can there be. . . . Rather than through grand alternatives, policy changes seem to come through a series of slight modifications of existing policy, with the new policy emerging slowly and haltingly by small and usually tentative steps, a process of trial and error in which policy zigs and zags, reverses itself, and then moves forward in a series of incremental steps.[13]

Most of DM literature deals primarily with the bureaucracies of developed countries which have complex organizations which small developing countries do not possess. It is recognized, therefore, that all aspects of sophisticated DM models are not applicable to a small underdeveloped state like Trinidad and Tobago. In this paper, therefore, the writer will utilize only those DM models that are applicable to the Trinidad and Tobago situation to assist in explaining the actions of the decision-makers in joining the OAS.

SMALL STATES, LEADERSHIP, FOREIGN POLICY, AND DM

We have already referred to the paucity of the DM literature on small states. Since Trindad and Tobago is a small state it may be instructive to briefly review some findings on the literature of small States in order to examine their behaviour in the international system, their uses of foreign policy, and the external and domestic factors which have an impact on their DM processes. In appraising the literature on small states, two scholars concluded that there were four approaches to the foreign policies of small states.[14]

The first is the "Great powers writ small" approach, which has been expounded by scholars like Liska, Rothstein, and Fox.[15] This approach is concerned with the degree to which having 'less power' affects a State's security and the spectrum of responses to this fact of life. The assumption is that all states, large and small, are motivated by the same factor. East himself sums up the impact of size on foreign policy behaviour and presents us with this traditional model which is the outcome of the "Great Powers writ small" approach. In comparison with large states, small states exhibit:

(a) low levels of overall participation in world affairs; (b) high levels of activities in intergovernmental organizations (IGOs); (c) high levels of support for international legal norms; (d) avoidance of the use of force as a technique of statecraft; (e) avoidance of behaviour and politics which tend to alienate the more powerful states in the system; (f) a narrow functional and geographic range of concern in foreign policy activities; (g) frequent utilization of moral and normative positions on international issues.[16]

In that very article East advances an alternative model based on the assumption that foreign policy processes are fundamentally different.[17]

The second, "the capacity to act" approach, concerns itself with the nation's overall capacity to act in foreign affairs, not only in military and security matters, but also in economic and diplomatic affairs. Resources are yet of major concern, but now the impact of modernization on resources and on capacity to act dominates the centre statge. Good, Singer, and O'Leary are among the proponents of this approach.[18] The third approach, "Demands and Needs," shifts somewhat from the idea of resources and focuses on the "demands" or "needs" generated by a nation's size factors and modernization level and the effects these have on foreign policy. The major assumption of this approach, which is well-illustrated by Morse,[19] is that foreign policies of modern and less modern states will differ in fundamental ways due to the special constraints and conditions created by the differences in levels of modernization. The fourth approach, "the uses of foreign policy," is somewhat similar to the "Demands and Needs" approach, but differs in that the focus is on those factors affecting the basic structure and conditions of the domestic political system in which foreign policy is made. Special emphasis is placed on the characteristics of the political arena that are influenced by modernization levels and that in turn influence a state's foreign policy. The size factor is not as important here. Weinstein exemplifies this approach in his study on Indonesia.[20]

One method of understanding and explaining the behaviour of all States is analyzing their actions from a perspective that treats foreign policy as a form of adaptive behaviour. Small states are no exceptions to this type of behaviour. Adaptive behaviour appears when a state takes foreign policy actions which arise because the domestic structures of its society (its economy and polity) are affected to some degree by events external to the state. In addition, if these structures are to perform at levels acceptable to the governmental and nongovernmental elites in the society, action must be taken in the international system toward international institutions and other states to ensure this objective. In the final analysis, therefore, foreign policy is motivated by elite concerns with domestic tensions and the problems generated at least in part by the impact of external demands and changes on the structures of the society. The adaptive approach to the comparative study of foreign policy could yield dividends in viewing decision-makers as adapting to external events in order to secure satisfactory performance of domestic structures. The adaptive approach, therefore, is particularly useful for the study of the decision-makers of small states, especially when there exists two behavioural patterns that are shared by the vast majority of small states of the Third World, namely political and economic dependence.

The foreign policies of small states, then, seem to be greatly influenced by national attributes and linkage phenomena.[21] Two scholars believe that "within a context of powerlessness and dependence, character and ideas alone cannot overcome a passive-subordinate role in international affairs."[22] However, there is another school of thought which believes that personalities and ideologies bear more weight than national attributes and linkage phenomena.[23]

The question of personalities brings to the fore the issue of leadership in Third World states. A Third World scholar has gone so far as to categorize the four major styles of black African leaders.[24] Some comparison with the styles of leadership may be relevant at a later stage for the situation in Trinidad and Tobago. What the literature on leadership in foreign policy does indicate is that the chosen policies are those of the dominant leader and his friends. Rothstein finds what he calls 'personalized foreign policy' commonplace in developing countries. He writes:

> Foreign policy tends to be the unfettered presence of the leader and his friends. The result is a highly personalized foreign policy. When the dominant leader is particularly popular, and his rule is unchallenged the distinction between his personal views and state policies may disappear. As some observers have noted, India may not have had a foreign policy but Jawaharlal Nehru certainly did.[25]

In any case, it is a fact that wherever there is a strong leader he will tend to dominate foreign policy, and this is applicable not only to Third World States but also to developed countries. Thus all dominant leaders cannot but help place their personal stamp on foreign policy. One scholar has observed that "the higher in the hierarchy of the foreign policy organization an individual's role is, the more are his personality characteristics likely to affect foreign policy decision."[26] If this is true, the Prime Minster of Trinidad and Tobago, who was also Minister of Foreign Affairs at the time his nation decided to enter the OAS, must have had a major role in that decision. The style of the Prime Minister is also important in the DM process in foreign policy-making. Does he prefer to centralize the control of policy in his hands? Does he rely on anyone? The fusion of the prime ministerial and external affairs portfolios in his hands is an indicator of the style of the Trinidad and Tobago leader, but the fusion of other portfolios along with that of Prime Minister or Premier is a feature of politics in the Commonwealth Caribbean.

A final word on leadership in foreign affairs. A notable trend in DM in contemporary international relations is the dominance of executive influence over foreign ministries. In his empirical study of the Uganda Ministry of Foreign Affairs, East discovered that the Ministry provided "very little substantive input into the foreign policy-making process." In his view, the ministry "serves primarily as the executor of foreign policy decisions and as a body carrying out a large number of essentially non-policy or non-substantive activities."[27] The role of Obote in the foreign policy DM process was a major one and has increased immensely with Amin. The chief executive officer in the person of the Prime Minister also predominated in foreign policy DM in India during the Nehru years. Illchman informs us that the Informal Consultative Committee for External Affairs was so unwieldy in size that whenever it was called it "served the opportunity for the Prime Minister . . . to lecture to the members on the achievements of Indian Foreign Policy."[28] The author's research findings on the major role of the Prime Minister of Trinidad and Tobago in the nation's foreign policy process yield the same conclusions as Illchman and East found in India and Uganda respectively.[29]

THE DECISION TO ENTER THE OAS: BACKGROUND INFORMATION

In spite of the shortcomings of the rationality approach, this is the approach that will be utilized in this study for it is certain that decision-makers, acting in a collegial fashion, believe in accordance with their perception and with all the available information at their disposal, they are behaving in a rational manner. We believe that the notion of Simon's "satisficing" behaviour is applicable. Decision-makers, instead of weighing all the grand alternatives, examine alternatives sequentially until they come upon one which meets their minimum standards of acceptability.[30]

When scholars read *From Columbus to Castro: The History of the Caribbean, 1492-1969,* written by the principal decision-maker in this study, what they will learn about Trinidad and Tobago's decision to join the OAS is that "in 1967 Trinidad and Tobago followed by Barbados joined the OAS."[31] Williams' autobiography gives a little more information, namely (i) the OAS seemed hostile to Commonwealth independent countries; (ii) the ruling PNM discussed and voted for Trinidad and Tobago's entry into the OAS; (iii) the party's resolution was presented in both Houses of Parliament; and (iv) the application was forwarded to the OAS on February 9, 1967.[32] To students of DM, these bits of information do not shed sufficient light on the DM process in foreign policy. One method of shedding light on this topic and posing the relevant questions regarding Trinidad and Tobago's entry into the OAS is to lay bare some pertinent facts. The list below, providing the bare bones of the information, is as follows:

1. *November 25, 1960,—* Dr. Williams, then Premier, announced that he was West of the Iron curtain not East of it. ". . . I am for the West Indies taking their place in the Western Hemisphere and for membership in the Organization of American States, without any loosening of ties with the Commonwealth."[33]

2. *February 1962,—* After the Punta Del Este Resolution had been passed, Williams stated: ". . . the question of each new Caribbean state's association with the OAS must be worked out separately, for each entity must ask itself the inevitable question—What does Punta del Este mean to us?"[34]

3. *April 1962—* The Nation carries the text of a speech by Teodoro Moscoso, U.S. Coordinator for the Alliance for Progress, made the year before at Punta del Este at an IA-ECOSOC meeting. At that meeting US Secretary of the Treasury, Douglas Dillon, explained: "Latin America, if it takes the necessary internal measures, can reasonably expect its own effects to be matched by an inflow of capital during the next decade amounting to at least $20,000 million."

4. *November 9, 1962—The Nation* carried a report of a press conference by Dr. Williams held in London on the subject of nuclear weapons in Cuba. Dr. Williams stated: "We are opposed to all further attempts to embroil the Caribbean after all these centuries in outside quarrels. No nuclear weapons at all in the Caribbean."

5. *December 6, 1963—* The Prime Minister told Parliament that Jamaica had made a formal application to the OAS but the question of membership of new members had not been resolved. He found this situation 'curious' since the OAS had been trying to bring in Canada for years. He went on to relate that Trinidad and Tobago was "now considering the question of taking a stand on the matter . . . no formal decision has as yet been taken of the Cabinet of Trinidad and Tobago; the matter is being intensively studied now, so that when or if a decision is taken . . . then it would be possible for Cabinet to take action on the decision."[35]

6. *March 1964—* It was mentioned in the Throne Speech in Parliament that the question of association with the OAS was being studied.

7. *April 1965—* Dr. Patrick Solomon, in the course of a debate on the UK's proposed entry into the ECM, referred to the Act

of Washington which had been passed: "there was a special meeting . . . held in Washington in December of last year, for the specific purpose of finding a formula for the admission of new members. Realizing that we belong to the Western Hemisphere . . . we must proceed to give some thought to the advisability or inadvisability of joining the OAS."[36]

8. *October–December 1965*—The Prime Minister was reviewing a series of books and articles on Cuba and the OAS in *The Nation*. Among them were: Theodore Draper, *Castroism: Theory and Practice* (1965). Leo Huberman, "Cuba: A Revolution Revisited" in *The Nation* August 2, 1962; A. J. Thomas and A. V. Thomas, *The Organization of American States,* (1963); Rene Dumont, *Cuba: Socialism and Development,* (1970).

9. *May 1966*—A Strong Case for entry made by Dr. Solomon, Minster of External Affairs, at the Caribbean Regional Conference of the Commonwealth Parliamentary Association.

10. *September, 1966*—The PNM Election Manifesto stated that efforts were being made to achieve a Caribbean Economic Community "whilst taking our rightful place in the affairs of the Western Hemisphere."

11. *September 1966*—The Prime Minister in an Address to Special Convention of the PNM made reference to the question of subversion. "The third danger facing Trinidad and Tobago relates to the subversive activity deliberately conceived at the Tri-Continental Conference in Havana in January of this year." Several Trinidadians had attended that Conference.

12. *November 1966*—Throne Speech in Parliament. "In the field of external affairs my Government will take further steps in respect of regional alignments, with reference to the OAS and the Caribbean Economic Community."

13. *December 1966*—Jose Mora, Secretary-General of the OAS, invites Commonwealth Caribbean States to join the OAS.

14. *January 18, 1967—Trinidad Guardian*—Commonwealth Caribbean countries invited as observers to attend OAS meeting dealing with Charter Reform.

15. *January 27, 1967, The Nation*—Special Meeting of the PNM General Council called to decide if Trinidad and Tobago should join the OAS. The Council had asked a Committee to study the question and the Committee was to present its report at the General Council Meeting. The General Council accepted the Committee's report to join the OAS.

16. *February 3, 1967*—The Prime Minister succesfully moves within the House for Trinidad and Tobago's entry into the OAS.

17. *February 9, 1967*—Senate approves similar motion.

18. *February 17, 1967*—Results of Opinion Poll on OAS entry released.

19. *April 1967*—Jose Mora informs that ECM membership not incompatible with OAS membership.

20. *May 1967*—The Prime Minister at OAS Summit expounded on Trinidad and Tobago's reasons for joining the Organization.

21. *July 1967*—Headline in *The Nation*—"OAS Summit Adopts Education, Health Programmes Similar to Ours."

22. *August 1967*—OWTU four-man delegation attending Solidarity Conference in Cuba.

The skeletal information above would have to be fleshed out and subjected to systematic analysis if we are to carefully observe the DM process in this particular case. In order to do this we propose to utilize the following framework and to examine sequentially the decisional setting, the decision situation, the organization of decision making, and finally the motivation and characteristics of the decision-makers.

THE DECISIONAL SETTING: DOMESTIC POLITICS

The first official statement came from the lips of the Prime Minister, then Premier, in November 1960, and it was not until six years later that Trinidad and Tobago entered the OAS, twenty days after the official decision had been made in Parliament.[37] The date on which the first official statement was made is significant because it preceded Trinidad and Tobago's independence date by nearly two years. In May 1960 Dr. Williams made his "West of the Iron Curtain" speech, and five months later signified his intention of leading his nation into the OAS. These two moves would certainly confirm to the unsuspecting that events immediately before had been in the same vein. Nothing could be further from the truth. In fact, in April 1960 Dr. Williams had led a march to the U.S. Consulate where demands for the return of Chaguaramas were read to U.S. officials. The struggle to have the U.S. return the entire Chaguaramas Naval Base to be used for the capital site had begun in 1957. The struggle for the return of the base from 1957 to 1960 marked the apogée of the nationalist movement in Trinidad and Tobago led by Dr. Williams. This nationalist movement came to an end on February 10, 1961, when Dr. Williams signed an agreement that retreated from his original demands. He, however, saw the results of the Conference as "eminently satisfactory."[38] Not so with Lloyd Best who saw the Prime

Minister's going to the negotiating table with the Americans as a betrayal, and labelled the negotiations a sell-out.[39] With an opportunity to chart its future course in a nationalist fashion, many believed the ruling party had opted for the "colonial dirt track instead of the Independent Highways."[40] On the other hand, the Prime Minister had already explained that he had gone to the final conference at Chaguaramas with "the problem of the economic need of Trinidad and Tobago dominant."[41]

In retrospect, the short nationalist period was an aberration from the norm. The strategy of economic development in the late fifties was that of industrialization by invitation.[42] In 1956 Texaco took over Trinidad Leaseholds with the approval of the British Government. This policy failed to yield the economic development it had promised, and some fifteen years later the population was still contending "with large scale and chronic unemployment, and the government with widespread disenchantment."[43] The Chaguaramas decision, along with others, "alienated the masses and forced the PNM into the hands of right-wing 'parasitic' elements of the coalition."[44]

In pursuit of the strategy of industrialization by invitation, the role of business in the pre-1970 decision-making policy was an important one.[45] Government persistently borrowed from multinational corporations. For example, under the Development Loan (1964) the Government agreed to borrow from the following: Texaco ($8,850,000 US); Tate and Lyle ($3,000,000); Shell (Trinidad) $3,000,000); Barclays ($1,000,000); Royal Bank of Canada ($1,000,000). The high interest rates that were to be paid to these foreign companies moved an opposition member to declare that Government was running the country in partnership with Tate and Lyle and Texaco. "Who elected Tate and Lyle and Texaco to govern the peoples of this country?"[46] he exclaimed. In 1965 the Industrial Stablisation Act (ISA) was passed after there had been an alarmingly high number of strikes. The Prime Minister estimated that there were 230 strikes between 1960 and 1964.[47] The ISA, among other things, was an attempt to gain the industrial stability so necessary for the appropriate climate for foreign investment.

Generally, this was the domestic political scene which was marked by industrial strife which eventually built up to the 'revolution' of 1970. The cause of the revolution, Best claimed, was "dispossession: economic and political." We now turn to the relationship between domestic and foreign policy in the period under study.

THE DECISIONAL SETTING:
DOMESTIC POLITICS AND FOREIGN POLICY

Foreign policy is but an extension of domestic policy. The developmental strategy that the government employed in the pre-1970 period made it imperative for the government to follow a certain type of conduct on foreign policy matters—if it did not wish its domestic equilibrium disturbed. In brief, the Trinidad and Tobago government was adapting its foreign policy to conform with the strategy of development preferred by the influential political groupings within the society. As McGowan and Gottwald have written: "... foreign policy is motivated by elite concerns with domestic tensions and problems generated at least in part by the impact of external demands and changes on the structures of the society."[48] Trinidad and Tobago's foreign policy in the pre-1970 period would fall into the category of adaptive behaviour known as "acquiescent"—a behavioural response to internationally originated demands and changes.

The Government's foreign policy decision to enter the OAS was no doubt influenced by its domestic development strategy. Once this strategy was decided upon, the break with CLR James came, the West of the Iron Curtain speech followed, in addition to the signing of the Chaguaramas agreement which the Prime Minister had described as 'eminently satisfactory.' The die had been cast. All that was necessary now was for the state to await the amendment to the OAS Charter to facilitate its entry into the Organization. In the interim, the Prime Minister began the cleansing process. In that very speech, in which he signified his intention of taking the country into the OAS, he declared Trinidad and Tobago in the Western Camp and took a parting shot at the local Communists. The Nation paraphrased: "if the Communists and fellow travellers were counting on him to pull their chestnuts out of the fire they would be disappointed."[49] As domestic problems arose, the cleansing process was intensified. Red-baiting appeared more regularly.

After a Trinidad and Tobago delegation attended the Tricontinental Conference in Havana in January 1966, the Nation printed headlines attacking the conference and those Trinidadians who had attended. In an address to a Special PNM Convention in September 1966, he stressed that subversive activity 'conceived at the Tri-Continental Conference' was facing the country. Three months earlier The Nation captioned its July 15 issue PAWNS in red capitals and informed: "A Spectre is haunting the trade union movement . . . the spectre is the political ideology of Marxism dressed up in the roles of white purity." But if these cleansing gestures were not sufficient, the then Minister of External Affairs in 1966, Dr. Solomon, confirmed Trinidad and Tobago's acquiescent foreign policy. In a speech at the Caribbean Regional Conference of the Commonwealth Parliamentary Association, the Minister verified a U.S. charge that some states had received less Alliance for Progress funds because they "had failed to undertake the essential pre-requisites in the Charter" e.g. financial stability, land reform, etc. He continued: "We have taken as a matter of course these steps many of which are outlined in the OAS Charter which would make us eligible for the assistance which the Alliance for Progress is designed to give. We did not have this object of qualifying for Alliance for Progress funds at the time when this movement for reform started. We were concerned only with putting our house in order . . . for Independence."[50] His closing remarks on this subject are indicative of the fact that if Trinidad and Tobago had not fulfilled the requirements, the Government in any case would have made an effort to do so. "At least," the Minister explained, "the charge could not be made against us that we have failed to fulfil the requirements."[51]

The Government had not only fulfilled the requirements desired by the North American giant for access to Alliance for Progress funds—though it was *ex post facto*—but it has also feverishly worked on maintaining the proper domestic and external settings required to enter the OAS through which Alliance for Progress Funds would come. In fact the Prime Minister had decided to enter the OAS since his speech of November 1960 when he delcared for "the West Indies taking their place in the Western Hemisphere and for membership in the Organization of American States. . . ." However, the major drawback to admission after independence had been achieved was the inability of the OAS Charter to accept Trinidad and Tobago until it had been amended by the Act of Washington in 1964. The Minister of External Affairs, Dr. Solomon, in the debate on an opposition motion concerning the U.K.'s initiatives to gain entry into the ECM, began to explore for alternate organizations and this is what he said of the OAS:

> . . . prior to December last year, we did not make any move to consider actively the possibility of joining the OAS . . . we do not go knocking on somebody's door when he has locked it in our face or if there is no possibility of opening it. But now the door has been opened . . . we must proceed to give some thought to the advisability or inadvisability of joining the OAS.[52]

In brief, as soon as the Act of Washington appeared in the OAS Charter, the government of Trinidad and Tobago began to knock on the Organization's door immediately. The next move was to enshrine the entry into the OAS in the 1966 elections plank.

PARTIES, INTEREST GROUPS, THE MEDIA— PUBLIC OPINION AND THE DECISION TO ENTER

The decision to enter the OAS seemed to be solely a governmental matter and the Prime Minister's thinking was paramount in this matter.

No interest groups were pushing for Trinidad and Tobago's entry into the Organization and none seemed to be against it. In fact, very few people knew what the Organization was. The position of an independent senator epitomizes this view point very well. When the bill to gain admission to the OAS was being debated in the Senate, a member confessed ". . . I do not believe that I have had in my possession sufficient literature or knowledge of what the OAS is, or what it involves. . . ."[53] The attendance at the session when the bill was being debated was dismal and led a government minister to lament: "I think that it is a sad commentary on the state of public opinion in the country that a matter of this importance coming before the senate, so few people should have thought it worth their while to come and listen to at least some part of what is being said here."[54]

The only party that seemed to be involved to any extent in the issue was the governing party. A committee appointed by the party's General Council conducted a public opinion poll in 1965 among non-members of the party to determine "the public sentiment on any such action by the Government." Three questions were asked:

(i)   Do you know what the OAS is?
(ii) Do you think Trinidad and Tobago should join the OAS?
(iii) Any comments?

The response was poor and only a small majority (53.6%) of the respondents claimed to know what the OAS was.[55] The committee, however, voted to enter the Organization. After Parliament voted to enter the OAS, a special correspondent of the *Trinidad Guardian* supported the government's decision but noted that ". . . while the occasion meets with world wide acclaim and comment, the vast majority of our citizens seem not to understand the meaning of it all."[56] Prior to Trinidad and Tobago's entry a *Guardian* editorial had supported the country entering the Organization in spite of its shortcomings. The editorial read ". . . after all, these criticisms stem from within the body itself. . . .We feel that as a member we can contribute as much as we receive; not in material things perhaps, but certainly from the example of our attitude to politics and the quality of our government."[57] This was certainly a reference to one of the Prime Minister's speeches in which he extolled Trinidad and Tobago's virtues in not having a revolution every other morning, compared to the Latin American states. Besides the editorial and the comment of the special correspondent, there was no analytical coverage in the press. There was straight reporting but there was no feedback from the public in terms of letters to the press, etc.

The Opposition seemed to have no position on the matter. During a major foreign policy speech the Prime Minister had remarked that it was 'curious' as the question of new members' entry into the Organization had not been resolved as yet and continued ". . . there has been a feeling of resentment that our rights were being tampered with . . ."[58] An Opposition member, although not arguing against Trinidad and Tobago's entry, pointed out that the OAS had to be careful because in his view the UN Charter had provided for the entry of all states, including small ones, and the latter had been the cause of "a great deal of difficulty for the original members." He concluded ". . . I cannot see that Trinidad and Tobago or Jamaica have got a right to be there if members of the club do not want them for any reason, and I do not see that it is necessary for them to give any reasons for not wanting them."[59] The Opposition member absented himself when the vote on the bill was taken in Parliament but this could not be construed as opposing the bill. It was more a case of pique at how the government had been treating foreign affairs issues in Parliament. The Opposition had felt that it had been generally ignored and not consulted in foreign affairs matters. When an Opposition member commented on the nonfunctional character of the Foreign Affairs Committee in Parliament, he made specific reference to the case of the OAS. "We have in this House a Rip Van Winkle committee on foreign affairs," he charged. "When the question of seeking admission to the OAS was raised, it pleased the government to seek the opinion of the People's National Movement's (PNM) Central Committee instead of referring this matter of such vital importance to the Committee on Foreign Affairs."[60]

It has been noted in this section that the state of public opinion on the country's entry into the OAS was very low. The Opposition party seemed to have no position and even the poll sponsored by the ruling party pointed out the low interest in foreign affairs in general and, more specifically, in joining the OAS. This is not surprising granted the low interest evinced in foreign policy issues.[61] In addition, the decision to enter the OAS did not seem to present a crisis situation to the public at large. This issue seemed remote to the people, and whenever this situation occurs in foreign policy, foreign policy decision-makers are not locked in by the views of the public and have more leeway in that respect. Since the public knows less about foreign policy matters than domestic matters, it tends to leave decisions on such issues to the government. Research in the United States concluding that "A majority of the public tends to support the general tenets of national policy relating to foreign affairs"[62] is applicable to most countries, especially when no crisis situation obtains. Thus the role of parties, interest groups, the media, and the Opposition were not salient in the decision to join the OAS.

THE DECISIONAL SETTING: EXTERNAL INFLUENCES

States do not make decisions in a vacuum. The conjuncture of the domestic and external settings are vital in the decision-making process. If all the domestic factors were conducive to Trinidad and Tobago's decision to enter the OAS, the external setting was sufficiently appropriate. In analyzing the external setting it may be appropriate to utilize the various subenvironments presented by Rosenau in his *Linkage Politics*.[63] The cold war subenvironment was definitely linked up with the regional subenvironment. The cold war had officially come to an end in 1962 after the Soviet Union and the United States came to an agreement on the removal of missiles from Cuba. But the residue of the cold war remained in the Caribbean simply because Cuba is in the Caribbean. In this case, the values of the decision-makers are important. We have touched on this because of the various statements by the Prime Minister. Both Cuba and ideological values were important in the mind of the decision-makers. The Prime Minister had already gone out of his way to damn and ridicule the Cuban approach to economic development and stressed how the Trinidad and Tobago model was different.[64] This behaviour seemed necessary because the lure of Punta del Este was enticing.[65] In addition, the USA is the validation power in the hemisphere and most states in the hemisphere take their cues from U.S. actions. All the arguments that the Prime Minister advanced for joining the Organization—peace and security of the hemisphere and the access to Alliance for Progress funds—have the USA as the central actor. And the Prime Minister had long asserted which side of the Iron curtain Trinidad and Tobago was located geographically and ideologically.

Another factor to be considered in the decision-makers' minds was the U.K.'s application for entry into the ECM. The fear of what would happen to our Commonwealth preferences was raised and discussed openly by an Opposition member, the Prime Minister, and the committee created by the PNM General Council to decide admission to the OAS. Thus the OAS as an alternative economic source to Commonwealth preferences was desirable in the eyes of the decision-makers. As Vaughan Lewis has written on the decision of Trinidad and Tobago and Jamaica to enter the OAS, "the financial bait of the system: the Alliance for Progress and the Inter-American Development Bank"[66] were important.

The racial subenvironment must have emerged within the OAS itself in addition to the size and cultural questions which some Latin nations raised openly. This delay from independence to the passage of the Act of Washington (1964) was the length of time that the Latin states had to think over the entry of non-white states. The Prime Minister himself had indicated that the OAS was 'hostile' to Commonwealth Independent countries without further elaboration. In other words, the racial factor from the perspective of the decision-makers must have been among the thoughts of some member states of the OAS. It did not prevail sufficiently to debar Trindad and Tobago from entering the OAS.

There is no doubt that the U.S. position in the hemisphere and the lure of Alliance for Progress funds were important factors in helping the government of Trinidad and Tobago arrive at the decision to enter the OAS. But what sort of information did the government of Trinidad and Tobago have in its possession? What had its diplomatic sources abroad reported on the matter? It would appear that the decision-makers had all the information they needed. At least the Prime Minister did. The security and economic arguments had already convinced him that to do so was the right thing. But he wished to know more of the Organization and the situation in the Caribbean. Therefore he proceeded to read as much as possible to be double certain of what he had planned to do.[67] He did not take Trinidad and Tobago into the OAS starry-eyed. He and his officials were aware of the U.S. behaviour in the hemisphere. Dr. Solomon, the Minister of External Affairs in 1966, recognized U.S. domination in the hemisphere, deplored U.S. interventionist behaviour in Guatemala, Costa Rica, and more recently the Dominican Republic, but thought that Trinidad and Tobago should join the Organization and fight from within.[68] The PNM Committee recognized U.S. domination of the OAS but did not believe that ". . . actual steps to secure admission should be held back as a result."[69] Therefore, the informational input for the decision-makers seemed to be more than adequate. In sum, the external setting provided no problem for Trinidad and Tobago's entry after the Act of Washington had been passed in 1964. After the passage of this Act, Trinidad and Tobago's entry was only a matter of time.

THE DECISION SITUATION

How did the decision-makers define the situation in relation to the problem confronting them? How did they see objects, conditions, and other sectors? What were the goals of the government and what were the values that struck them as most important in the particular situation? These are some of the questions that need to be answered if we are to see how the decision-makers perceived the situation.

Evidently they perceived the domestic and external settings as favourable for the country's final acceptance. The domestic scene was being tempered (ISA, charges of subversion, etc.) to make the USA take a positive stance towards Trinidad and Tobago's admission. The policy-makers saw the Organization as satisfying the nation's economic and security purposes, although it had some imperfections.

Without doubt the USA, which would find it more convenient to deal with all the states in this hemisphere in one organization, was not opposed to this country's entry. There was no U.S. public official word but there must have been words of encouragement and assistance in Government files. The United Kingdom could not care less. That country had its hands full essaying to enter the ECM. Canada was watching the situation with some interest. The United States had encouraged Canadian entry into the Organization for many years but the latter had resisted successfully.[70] Canadian interest in the situation extended no further than agreeing to make available to Trinidad and Tobago any studies Canada conducted on the matter. Trinidad and Tobago's position *vis-à-vis* Canada was the same. Canada did not wish to become too enmeshed with U.S. foreign policy—at least via an Organization at the hemispheric level. A respected Canadian scholar wrote "It is hard to see how Canada could... join the OAS until there has been some change in its relations with Cuba."[71] Trinidad and Tobago did not swing around to a positive Cuban position until 1970 when the Prime Minister called for the reintegration of Cuba into the Western Hemisphere.

Some Latin American states had questions on size and culture, and were perplexed about this country's membership in the Commonwealth. After 1964, they intimated in the Act of Washington that the questions they had asked had been answered. Trinidad and Tobago had the support of Jamaica and Barbados, who were both trying to enter the OAS. It would have presumably had the support of Guyana, had the Guyanese nation been eligible for admission. The official organ of the PNC, the *New Nation,* was disappointed with both Trinidad's and Barbados' applications because there had been no Caribbean consultation. On the OAS's view toward West Indian culture, the *New Nation* had this to say: "There is no regard for West Indian identity. We are looked upon as strange types, speaking English and playing cricket."[72] In sum, the path seemed clear for the decision-makers, for none of the countries above had negative intentions towards Trinidad and Tobago's entry. This includes Latin American States after 1964 and Guyana who had commented only after Trinidad and Tobago had applied for admission.

Trinidad and Tobago's decision to seek admission to the OAS was predicated on the fact that economic assistance would come from the Organization to assist the country in its developmental strategy. Therefore, the immediate short-term objective the decision-makers had to pursue to assist in advising their developmental strategy was to gain admission to the OAS. This, the decision-makers believed, was certainly in the country's national interest.

THE ORGANIZATION OF DECISION-MAKING AND THE OAS DECISION

The Role of Parliament

Foreign policy decisions are made in an institutional context, and to analyze seriously any foreign policy decision it is important to identify the decisional unit. Therefore, it is imperative to identify the individuals who made the decision and to locate that group in its proper institutional setting. The formal governmental process in the making of foreign policy is as follows:

> For a foreign affairs bill to become law, the Ministry of External Affairs puts up a note on the matter in question to the Foreign Policy Committee. The issue is discussed in the Foreign Policy Committee which comprises senior civil servants from various ministries and senior Cabinet Ministers. The relevant details are then passed on to Cabinet which makes the final decision. If legislation is necessary, the required readings in the House and Senate take place before the bill is passed into law.

This is the formal aspect of policy-making but we need to focus on the *dramatis personnae* and the machinery to get at the process itself. Parliament has played a minor role in influencing foreign policy decisions throughout the world. The decline of Parliament and the dominance of the executive is well-known. The Trinidad and Tobago scene has fitted into this pattern since independence. There are several reasons for the limitations on the role of Parliament in foreign policy-making. One is the character of external affairs. Whereas legislation is needed for any important change in domestic policy, this is not the case with external affairs. The essence of foreign policy is negotiation which may or may not lead to having legislation placed before Parliament. The average member of Parliament is elected on domestic issues and his knowledge of international issues leaves a lot to be desired. Governments are seldom toppled on foreign policy issues so the average parliamentary representative, burdened by the more pressing socioeconomic needs of the community (water, roads, housing, hospitals, schools, etc.) concentrates on these issues. After all, he is desirous of seeking an extended term of office in parliament.

Another factor limiting the role of parliament is the lack of consultation on foreign affairs matters and the inaccessibility to opposition legislators of information. The fact that a legislator charged the lack of consultation on the OAS matter is worth recalling.[73] The words of an Opposition member voicing his comments on a bill for Trinidad and Tobago to become a member of three international financial organizations are also instructive: ". . . The Prime Minister seems to be making separate arrangements outside of parliamentary requirements because we may have to meet our commitments, but he seems to make his commitments separate and outside of Parliament. Sometimes,I even wonder if he recognises Parliament. . . ."[74] The most telling indictment of the minimal role accorded Parliament in the foreign policy-making process has been the nonfunctioning of a Joint Select Committee for Foreign Affairs created in 1963. Noting that the Committee seldom met, a legislator pleaded: "If the government appoint a Foreign Affairs committee, it should not be for the mere fact of putting on record that there is such a committee: it must function:. . . ."[75] The plaintive cry of the legislator was to go unheeded.

The Role of Cabinet, the Prime Minister, and the Ministry of External Affairs

We have established the minimal role of Parliament in foreign policy-making in Trinidad and Tobago and the role played by the Joint Committee for Foreign Affairs in the OAS decision. Since Parliament is not the locus of power in decision-making in foreign policy and was not the prime mover in the OAS decision, it behoves us to look at other areas of the foreign policy machinery, namely, the Cabinet and its leader, the Prime Minister, and the Ministry of External Affairs and its head, the Minister of External Affairs. The cabinet is the Government as far as external affairs are concerned and the Prime Minister has dominated the Cabinet.[76] Since independence there have been five ministers of External Affairs and the Prime Minister has officially been Minister of External Affairs for a period as long as all the five combined. The preeminence of the Prime Minister in foreign affairs decision-making and the minimal role assigned to Cabinet are described by a former ambassador who is also a former Cabinet member. He wrote:

Our missions are set up when and where and how considered necessary by one and one man only—the Prime Minister, Dr. Williams. Perhaps this is how it has to be: but as far as I know there is no question of consulting anyone on the matter. Cabinet is told that so and so place has become important or even vital to our country's external relationship and a mission is going to be set up in that country. The head of mission is chosen by the same person and Cabinet is informed accordingly. That is the end of the matter for all practical purposes.[73]

There have been many suggestions that Cabinet was a 'one man show' and 'personal monarchy' but it is the first time that a former Cabinet member has publicly declared so. The constant comments on the role of the Prime Minister forced him to defend himself in an interview given to *The Nation* wherein he explained, "I am a member of no committee . . . the members are free to discuss . . . Cabinet is normally prepared to accept the recommendations of the committee. If the committee cannot reach agreement, it then recommends that the matter should be discussed in Cabinet where meetings are relatively short."[78]

The above indicates that the collegial approach to Cabinet decision-making in Trinidad and Tobago is more in the realm of fiction than fact. The evidence suggests that decision-making in foreign policy falls into this category also. The role of the Prime Minister is quite unlike the role of Jomo Kenyatta in foreign policy-making in Kenya, if we are to believe the observations of one scholar who has written: "Foreign affairs policy-making was very much a collegial responsibility in the Cabinet with the President, Jomo Kenyatta, playing a senior stateman's role as an arbiter . . . of policy."[79] The input of the Cabinet in the decision to become a member of the OAS can be gleaned from the above account.

When the decision in Parliament was made to enter the OAS, the Prime Minister also held the portfolio of Minister of External Affairs. One scholar has enumerated the advantages and disadvantages of both these portfolios being held simultaneously by one individual in the British case.[80] East has commented on the low input by the Ministry of External Affairs in decision-making in Uganda and attributes this to the comparative youth of the Ministry (at the time of his study it was ten years old), the style of leadership of the head of State, the emergence of the 'new diplomacy' necessitating specialists rather than generalists, and the move towards 'summitry' in international relations (thus reducing the dependence of the government on the Ministry of External Affairs), the lack of manpower and other organizational problems.[81] Space does not permit discussion of the historical, international, and organizational problems that have existed in the Ministry of External Affairs and make for its low input in foreign policy decision-making in Trinidad and Tobago, but some discussion must be done on the style of the leadership in foreign affairs decision-making in Trinidad and Tobago.[82]

Leadership in Foreign Affairs

All that has been written before suggests that the Prime Minister has not been inconsequential in the foreign policy process in Trinidad and Tobago. His style, personality, intellectual capacity, and his penchant for hard work make him appear to his ministers more of a *deus inter homines* rather than a *primus inter pares*. No other member of the Cabinet, at the time the OAS decision was taken or now, has distinguished himself as a scholar of the history of world affairs as the Prime Minister has. Above them he seems to tower as a Gulliver among Lilliputians. Witness the adulation of an opposition member after the Prime Minister had revealed his position on various issues at a Prime Ministers' Commonwealth Conference in 1965: "I make no apology to anybody for saying that in Trinidad business I would oppose him, but as soon as he talks for Trinidad in the councils of the world he would find that the voice of Simboonath Capildeo is definitely behind him."[83]

The role of the individual has been emphasized in some of the literature on decision-making in foreign policy. Rothstein has stressed that in developing countries the decisions in foreign affairs bear the personal stamp of the leader. The OAS decision, like all foreign policy decisions in Trinidad and Tobago, bears his personal stamp. His strong personality and his style are dominant features of his leadership. This dominant hold in the realm of foreign policy is not the preserve of the Trinidad and Tobago Prime Minister alone. It has been the striking characteristic of strong Third World leaders. Jawaharlal Nehru of India, Sekou Toure of Guinea, and Kwame Nkrumah come readily to mind. Third World leaders are not the only ones who have this strong hold in the realm of foreign affairs. De Gaulle of France, Adenauer of West Germany, and Churchill of England also overwhelmed their Foreign Affairs ministers.

The decision to enter the OAS was made by the Prime Minister, and instrumental in leading him to such a decision were domestic factors and the external environment. The economic development of the country was foremost in his mind, and the policy of industrialization by invitation was not hostile to foreign capital. Any funds that could be obtained from the OAS would be welcome. Externally the USA was the dominant power in the hemisphere, and was influential, via Texaco, in the country's economic health. It did not make any sense to unduly aggravate the USA by opting to stay out. In addition, the lure of the U.S. sugar market was also inviting. In addition, since Commonwealth preferences were disappearing as Britain headed for the ECM, the Prime

Minister thought it made sense to establish closer relationships with Latin nations to fill any market void.

The Prime Minister decided to enter the OAS, intimated his views to Cabinet Ministers, and had the General Council of the PNM create a committee to study the issue. This Committee was fully cognizant of his position on the matter, for he himself had already made it clear. The Committee in its report noted that the "(General) Council heard that all our ambassadors who were consulted in the past three weeks were of the view that membership was desireable and even inevitable." The style of the Prime Minsiter suggests otherwise. He informed the ambassadors of his position on OAS membership and they all agreed. A clue of the dominant figure can be seen lurking in the major speeches made by his ministers who spoke on the issue. The speeches are patently similar in style and content. The speeches referred to are ones made by the Minister of External Affairs, Dr. Solomon, at the Caribbean Regional Conference of the Commonwealth Parliamentary Association in May 1966, that of the Attorney General in the Senate on February 9, 1967, and another by Dr. Solomon in April 1965.

In the last-mentioned speech Dr. Solomon commenced in a tone so similiar to that of the Prime Minister that one legislator remarked: "Here is a second historian. . . ."

The personality of the Prime Minister has been so dominant in foreign affairs that we feel obliged to pose the familiar question. Which is more important in decision-making in a small new state, the strong leader or the national attributes and linkage phenomena of a country? Our final section attempts to provide some guidance in this respect when it examines the motivations and characteristics of the principal decision-maker in leading Trinidad and Tobago into the OAS.

MOTIVATIONS AND CHARACTERISTICS OF THE PRINCIPAL DECISION-MAKER

Richard Snyder has emphasized the importance of motivational analysis as a major determinant of the decision-making process.[84] Scholars often talk of state-behaviour, but the bald truth is that it is men who speak on behalf of states and rationalize their policy actions. It is in this context, therefore, that we attempt to analyze the motivations and characteristics of the principal decision-maker. This paper contends that the Prime Minister, influenced by political and economic consider-ations, made the decision to enter the OAS and elicited the support of his party, Cabinet, and Parliament.

In order to proceed with our analysis we will examine the major speeches of the Prime Minister in and out of Parliament. We will utilize the two types of motivation that Snyder has discussed, namely "in order to" motives and "because of" motives.[85] The former are conscious and verbalizable; the decision-makers are taking a particular line of decision in order to accomplish an objective of the state which they serve. "Because of" motives are unconscious or semiconscious motives, those which arise out of the previous life experience of the decision-makers, and which predispose or impel them toward certain kinds of policy orientations for private psychological reasons.

The Prime Minister's entire speech was published in *The Nation* of February 10, 1967, and the caption was "Westward Ho!" The speech is lengthy but its thrust can be categorized into two "in order to" motives, namely (i) economic advantages and (ii) peace and security. The trend in the world, argued the Prime Minister, was toward regional groupings and he cited several of them around the world. Most of them were getting together for economic benefits, and in this hemisphere there were the Central American Common Market (CACM) and the Latin American Free Trade Asssociation (LAFTA). Since Trinidad and Tobago is located in the Western Hemisphere, he continued, it was expedient that the country join the Organization in this hemisphere because it "will complement and strengthen our position and our influence with the Latin American nations."[86] The "in order to" motivations were inviting. The OAS was to provide access to Alliance for Progress Funds, loans from the IADB, and entry into the huge proposed LAFTA where 75% of the trade among LAFTA members was expected to move freely. Finally, the Prime Minister enumerated the economic benefits that would redound to the country afer Charter amendments took place in Rio at a Foreign Ministers' meeting to be held later in February.

Certainly questions had been raised about Trinidad and Tobago being a member of both the OAS and the Commonwealth, but the Prime Minister assured all that there was nothing in the OAS Charter which prevented membership in both Organizations. In any case, not only was Commonwealth trade declining but Commonwealth preferences were to disappear completely when Britain joined the ECM. The lure of the U. S. sugar market also beckoned and although Trinidad and Tobago enjoyed a very limited quota in the U.S. market, "it was not inconceivable" that Trinidad and Tobago "will have access as of right as all other members of the OAS to the sugar markets of the U. S. A." Membership in the OAS also did not rule out membership in the Caribbean Economic Community, the Prime Minister opined.

These were the full brunt of the "in order to" arguments of the principal decision-maker as far as the economic aspects were concerned. With the help of hindsight it would be unfair to comment on the current situation with respect to LAFTA, the decline of the U.S. quota after the establishment of diplomatic relations with Cuba, and the present straits Trinidad and Tobago and the Caribbean find themselves in with respect to ECM arrangements.

The peace and security agreements are fairly brief when compared with the economic inducements offered by OAS entry. The Prime Minister quoted from the relevant articles of the Rio Act to discuss peace and security arrangements in the hemisphere, As he saw it, Trinidad and Tobago must be concerned with the peace, stability, and security of the hemisphere and the "treaties and charters will continue and will be applied whether or not Trinidad and Tobago joins the OAS. If we are to influence and to guide the deliberations and progress of the OAS we can only do so inside. . . ."[87] The Prime Minister is on firm ground when he assumes that treaties and Charters will continue to be applied with or without Trinidad and Tobago's membership in the OAS, but he possibly overstates his case when he believes that Trinidad and Tobago could fight from within.

Some would say that the Prime Minister's arguments on behalf of economic benefits redounding to Trinidad and Tobago via entry into the Organization would indicate a certain amount of political realism on his part. He was desirous of promoting a particular strategy of economic development and joining the OAS was the way to do it. The decision to join the OAS could be construed as falling within two of the foreign policy behavioural patterns of small states, namely

(1) avoidance of behaviour and policies which tend to alienate the more powerful states in the system, and

(2) a narrow, functional and geographic range of concern in foreign policy activities.

What can we say of the Prime Minister's 'because of' motives? In this author's view it demonstrates the dual character of a type of intellectual—the academic revolutionary and the politician, a realist with sober action. C.L.R. James has another view of Williams' incipient nationalism, namely that he was a property of the colonial past and existing class relations in the West Indies. He was travelling the path well worn by individuals like Manley (Senior) and Adams who began as radicals and were later strangled by the facts of life—the West Indian environment.

Whatever socialization influences may have played a part in his decision—living in a colonial environment and being a young colonial at Oxford—we can say that Dr. Williams' personality and his country's national attributes and linkage phenomena were both instrumental in leading him to his decision. The domestic environment—a pliable political party (PNM), an Opposition without an alternative, interest groups who did not register any concern in the matter, a parliamentary majority great enough to assure easy passage of the bill, and a Cabinet which abdicated its collegial responsibility to the wishes of the Prime Minister—was tailor-made for the domination of the political leader. In addition, the petroleum industry, as he saw it, so vital an ingredient for his strategy of economic development, was in the hands of the United States which should not be antagonized.

This paper has attempted to analyze Trinidad and Tobago's decision to enter the OAS in 1967. Firstly, we examined DM literature, the role of leadership and DM in small states, and provided basic background information on the events leading to the decision. We then proceeded to analyze the decision from four vantage points, namely, The Decisional Setting, both domestic and external, The Decision Situation, The Organization of Decision-making, and the Motivation and characteristics of the principal decision-maker. We found Trinidad and Tobago wished to pursue a particular strategy of economic development (industrialization by invitation) and consequently behaved in the international milieu in such a way as to facilitate its chosen strategy. The governmental machinery, Parliament, Cabinet (with the exception of the Prime Minister), and the Ministry of External Affairs played only supportive roles. The principal role was played by the Prime Minister. His dominant personality and strong leadership lead us to believe that he was the most important factor that led his colleagues to ratify the decision to join the OAS. This, to him, was a way of pursuing his strategy of industrialization by invitation and, at the same time, not causing offence to the validation power in the hemisphere.

FOOTNOTES

[1]This paper was presented for discussions at a meeting of the Inter-University Comparative Foreign Policy Project, sponsored by the University of Southern California, June 18-22, 1973, and was later published in *Policy Sciences* (December 1973), pp. 491-508. References to this article will be cited from the paper presented at the Inter-University Comparative Foreign Policy Project.

[2]East, "Foreign Policy making . . . " *op. cit.* p. 4.

[3]The articles that have come to this writer's attention since 1973 are A. H. M. Kirk-Greene, "Diplomacy and Diplomats: The Formation of Foreign Service Cadres in Black Africa," in *Foreign Relations in African States,* ed. K. Ingham (London: Buttersworth, 1974), pp. 279-319; Peter Boyce, "Foreign Offices and New States," *International Journal* vol. 30, no.1 (Winter 1974-75), p. 151-161; Basil A. Ince, "The Administration of Foreign Affairs in a Very Small Developing Country: The Case of Trinidad and Tobago," in *Size, Self-Determination and International Relations: The Caribbean,* ed. Vaughan Lewis (Kingston, Jamaica: Institute of Social and Economic Research, U.W.I., 1976), pp. 307-339; Benedict V. Mtshali, "The Zambian Foreign Service 1964-1972," *The African Review,* vol. 5, no. 3 (1975), pp. 303-316.

[4]Kirk-Greene, *op. cit.*

[5] Basil Ince, *op. cit.,* 310-322; pp. 329-330.

[6] The author has relied heavily on Auma-Osolo's article for this synopsis of DM literature. See Agola Auma-Osolo, "Rationality and Foreign Policy Process" (London: Steven's & Sons, 1977), in the *Yearbook of World Affairs,* 1977.

[7] Charles Beard, *The Idea of the National Interest, An Analytical Study in American Foreign Policy* (New York: Greenwood Press,1977).

[8] Harold Lasswell, *World Politics and Personal Insecurity* (New York: The Free Press, 1965).

[9] Hans Morgenthau, *In Defence of the National Interest* (New York: Knopf, 1957).

[10] Hans Morgenthau, *Politics Among Nations* (New York: Knopf, 1967).

[11] Karl Deutsch, "On the Concept of Politics and Power," *Journal of International Affairs,* vol. 21 (1967).

[12] Snyder et al, *op. cit.,* pp. 60-74.

[13] Roger Hilsman, "Policy Making in Politics," in Rosenau, *op. cit.,* p. 223. For similar views on rationality in the decision-making process and its limitations see Frankel *op. cit.,* pp. 166-172: Agola Auma-Osolo, *op. cit.,* pp. 260-284 pp. 260-263: pp. 272-283; Sidney Verba in Rosenau, *op. cit.,* pp. 217-231: James E. Dougherty and Robert L. Pfaltzgraff, Jr., *Contending Theories of International Relations* (Philadelphia: J.B. Lippincott Company, 1971), pp. 317-318.

[14] Maurice East and Joe Hagan, "Approaches to Small State Foreign Policy: An Analysis of the Literature and Some Empirical Observations," paper prepared for delivery at the International Studies Association Convention, Toronto, Ontario, Canada, February 25-29, 1976.

[15] George Liska, *Alliances and the Third World* (Baltimore: Johns Hopkins Press, 1968); R. L. Rothstein, *Alliances and Small Powers* (New York: Columbia University Press, 1969); A. B. Fox, *The Power of Small States* (Chicago: University of Chicago Press, 1958).

[16] Maurice East, "Size and Foreign Behaviours: A Test of Two Models," *World Politics,* vol. 25 (July 1973), 557.

[17] *Ibid.,* p. 558.

[18] R. C. Good, "State-Building as a Determinant of Foreign Policy in the New States," in *Neutralism and Non-alignment,* ed. L. W. Martin (New York: Praeger, 1962), pp. 3-12; Marshall Singer, *Weak States in a World of Powers* (New York: The Free Press, 1972), pp. 70-74; Michael O'Leary, "Linkages Between Domestic and International Politics in Underdeveloped Nations," in *Linkage Politics,* ed. James Rosenau (New York: The Free Press, 1969).

[19] E. L. Morse, "The Transformation of Foreign Policies: Modernization, Interdependence, and Externalization," *World Politics,* vol. 22 (April 1970), pp. 371-392.

[20] F. B. Weinstein, "The Uses of Foreign Policy in Indonesia: An Approach to the Analysis of Foreign Policy in the Less Developed Countries," *World Politics,* vol. 3 (April 1972), pp. 356-381.

[21] See James Rosenau, ed., *Linkage Politics* (New York: Free Press, 1969), and his "Pre-Theories and Theories of Foreign Policy" in *Approaches to Comparative and International Politics,* ed. R. Barry Farrell (Evanston, Illinois: Northwesten University Press, 1966).

[22] Patrick J. McGowan and Klaus-Peter Gottwald, "Small State Foreign Policies: A Comparative Study of Participation, Conflict and Political and Economic Dependence in Black Africa," *International Quarterly,* vol. 19, no. 4 (Dec. 1975), p. 471.

[23] See Vernon McKay, ed., *African Diplomacy* (New York: Praeger, 1966); A. A. Mazrui, *On Heroes and Hero-Worship* (London: Longman, 1967).

[24]Mazrui classifies African Leaders into the following four styles: (1) the intimidatory Leader—one who relies primarily on fear and on instruments of coercion to assess his authority; (2) the patriarchal leader—one who commands neo-filial reverence—a real father figure; (3) the leader of reconciliation—relies for his effectiveness on qualities of tactical accommodation and a capacity to discover areas of compromise between otherwise antagonistic viewpoints; (4) the healer of mobilization—tends to be activated by ideological factors than do the other kinds of leader. He also needs personal charismatic qualities more than the other three. See Ali Mazrui "Leadership in Africa: Obote of Uganda," *International Journal,* vol. 30, no. 3 (Summer 1970), pp. 538-539.

[25]Robert Rothstein, "Foreign Policy and Development: From Non-alignment to International Class War," *International Affairs* vol. 52, no. 4, p. 599.

[26]Margaret Hermann, "Leader Personality and Foreign Policy Behaviour," in *Comparing Foreign Policies: Theories, Findings and Methods,* ed. James N. Rosenau (New York: John Wiley and Sons, 1974), p. 201.

[27]East, "Foreign Policy Making . . .," *op. cit.,* p. 7.

[28]Warren Illchman, "Political Development and Foreign Policy: The Case of India," *Journal of Commonwealth Political Studies,* (November 1966), p. 223.

[29]See my "Parliament and Foreign Policy in a Commonwealth Caribbean State: The Case of Trinidad and Tobago," in *Caribbean Yearbook of International Relations, 1976* (Trinidad & Tobago: Institute of International Relations, 1977), pp. 325-346.

[30]Herbert A. Simon, "A Behavioural Model of Rationality Choice,' in *Models of Man: Social and Rational,* ed. H. A. Simon (New York: John Wiley and Sons, 1957), pp. 241-260.

[31]Eric Williams, *From Columbus to Castro: The History of the Caribbean 1492-1962* (London: Deutsch, 1970), p. 475.

[32]Eric Williams, *Inward Hunger: The Autobiography of a Prime Minister* (London: Deutsch, 1969), p. 290, 326.

[33]*Trinidad Guardian,* February 11, 1961.

[34]*The Nation,* (Organ of the PNM), February 16, 1962.

[35]*Hansard,* (House), December 6, 1963, col. 581.

[36]*Hansard,* (House) April 1965, Col. 569.

[37]See p. 273.

[38]Williams, *Inward Hunger, op. cit.,* p. 239.

[39]Lloyd Best, "From Chaguaramas to Slavery," *New World Quarterly* (Dead Season 1965), pp. 43-70.

[40]*Ibid.,* p. 37.

[41]*Trinidad Guardian,* December 17, 1960.

[42]One economist describes it as a policy which "posits that the way to develop a manufacturing sector in a small country is to attract metropolitan business which brings not only capital, but also technology, organization, and market connections. In addition it was hoped that such industry would use some local raw materials. In exchange for creating employment, generating low income and earning foreign exchange, the industrialists were to be offered a period free from income tax, duty rebates on their imports of equipment, machinery, and raw materials, accelerated depreciation allowances, subsidized industrial sites provisioned with water and electricity, and the services of an Industrial Development Corporation." See Edward Carrington, "Industrialization by Invitation in Trinidad and Tobago since 1950," in *Readings in the Political Economy of the Caribbean,* eds. Norman Girvan and Owen Jefferson (Kingston, Jamaica: New World Group, 1974).

[43]*Ibid.,* p. 149.

[44] Selwyn Ryan, "Restructuring the Trinidad Economy," in Girvan and Jefferson, *op. cit.*, p. 197.

[45] For a detailed study of the role of business in this period see the author's "Role of Business and Labour in the Foreign Policy of Trinidad and Tobago," paper delivered at the 34th Annual Conference of the International Studies Association held in Washington D.C., February 19-22, 1975.

[46] *Hansard* (House), 4 December 1964, Col. 453.

[47] Eric Williams, *Inward Hunger, op. cit.*, p. 311.

[48] McGowan and Gottwald, *op. cit.*

[49] *The Nation*, November 1960.

[50] *The Nation*, May 20, 1966.

[51] *Ibid.*

[52] *Hansard* (House) 5, April 9, 1965, Col. 569.

[53] *Hansard* (Senate) 6, February 9, 1967, Col. 423.

[54] *Ibid.*, Col. 374.

[55] For the results of the poll see *The Nation*, February 17, 1967.

[56] *Trinidad Guardian*, February 27, 1967.

[57] *Trinidad Guardian*, January 31, 1967.

[58] *Hansard* (House) 3, December 6, 1963, Col. 580.

[59] *Ibid.*, Col. 627.

[60] *Hansard* (House) 5, April 9, 1965, Cols. 606-610.

[61] See my "Elections and Foreign Policy in Trinidad and Tobago: A Note," in *Contemporary International Relations in the Caribbean*, ed. Basil A. Ince (St. Augustine, Trinidad: Institute of International Relations, 1978).

[62] Martin Abravnel and Barry Hughes, "The Relationship between Public Opinion and Governmental Foreign Policy: A Gross National Survey," in *Sage International Yearbook of Foreign Policy Studies*, vol. 2, ed. Patrick J. McGovan (Beverly Hills: Sage, 1973), pp. 107-134.

[63] James Rosenau, "Toward the study of National-International Linkages," in *Linkage Politics: Essays on the Convergence of National and International System*, ed. James Rosenau (New York: Free Press, 1969), pp. 44-63.

[64] See an excerpt from a speech by Dr. Williams made in 1963 entitled "International Perspective for Trinidad and Tobago," in *Documents on International Relations in the Caribbean*, ed. Roy Prieswek (Rio Peidras, Puerto Rico: Institute of Caribbean Studies, 1970). pp. 65-67.

[65] The Punta del Este Conference was held in 1962 and it was there that the Alliance for Progress was born. It held out hope for the socioeconomic development of Latin American countries.

[66] Vaughan Lewis, "The Commonwealth Caribbean and Self-Determination in the International System," in *Size, Self-Determination and International Relations: The Caribbean*, ed. Vaughan Lewis (Mona, Jamaica: ISER, 1976), p. 228.

[67] See pp. 15-16 above.

[68] *The Nation*, May 20, 1966.

[69] *The Nation*, May 1966.

[70] See articles by J. C. M. Ogelsby "Canada and the Pan American Union: Twenty Years On," *International Journal*, vol. 24, no. 3 (Summer 1969), pp. 571-589 and John W. Holmes, "Canada and Pan America," *Journal of Inter-American Studies*, vol. 10, no. 2 (April 1968), pp. 173-184.

[71]Holmes, *op. cit.,* p. 180.

[72]Quoted in the *Trinidad Guardian,* February 21, 1967.

[73]See p. 26 above.

[74]*Hansard* (House) 2, July 5, 1963, Col. 1007.

[75]*Hansard* (House), 10, March 28, 1969, Col. 1119.

[76]The members of Cabinet when the OAS bill was passed in parliament were as follows: Dr. Eric Williams, Prime Minister and Minister of Planning and Development; Mr. A. N. R. Robinson, Minister of External Affairs; Mr. Robert Montano, Minister of Home Affairs; Dr. Max Awon, Minister of Health, Mr. Kamalludin Mohammed, Minister of West Indian Affairs; Mr. A. G. Richards, Attorney General; Mr. Lionel Robinson Minister of Agriculture, Lands and Fisheries; Mr. Donald Pierre, Minister of Education and Culture; Mr. Errol Mahabir, Minister of Public Utilities; Mr. J. O'Halloran, Minister of Industry and Commerce, and Petroleum; Mr. A. C. Alexis, Minister of Labour, Miss I. Teshea, Minister of Housing; Mr. A. A. Thompson Minster of Local Government and Social Welfare; Mr. V. L. Campbell, Minister of Works; Mr. Robert Wallace, Minister of State in the Ministry of Finance, Planning and Development; Mr. Basil Pitt, Mr. F. C.. Prevatt, Ministers of State in the Ministry of Finance, Planning and Development, and Mr. W. J. Alexander, Minister of State and Special Adviser to the Prime Minister.

[77]The writer of this piece in a local newspaper was Ambassador to Venezuela and High Commissioner to Canada and the United Kingdom. See the *Express,* November 6, 1970.

[78]*The Nation,* January 30 and February 6, 1970.

[79]See an article by Robert F. Stephens, "Foreign Relations Establishments in British East Africa," presented at the Northeastern Political Science Association, Ambest Mass., November 9-11, 1972, p. 11.

[80]Donald Bishop, *The Administration of British Foreign Relations* (New York: Syracuse University Press, 1961), p. 86.

[81]East, "Foreign Policy Making in Small States . . ."*op. cit.,* pp. 10-23.

[82]For a discussion of some of these problems see my "Administration of Foreign Affairs in a Very Small Developing Country: The Case of Trinidad and Tobago," in Vaughan Lewis *op. cit.,* pp. 319-329.

[83]*Hansard* (House) 5, June 11, 1965, Col. 1542.

[84]Snyder, *op.cit.,* pp. 137-171.

[85]*Ibid.,* p. 144.

[86]*The Nation,* February 10, 1967.

[87]*Ibid.*

Puerto Rico Between the United States and the Caribbean

Robert W. Anderson

In 1971, Ambassador Ben S. Stephansky, later to become a low-profile director of the Office of Puerto Rico in Washington under the Hernandez Colon administration, wrote that the "Commonwealth" of Puerto Rico has been since 1952, "America's border state in the Caribbean."[1] After discussing the possible consequences for Caribbean relations of a statehood-oriented government on the island as a result of the election of 1968, he affirms on the last page of the same article that as a state of the U.S. federal union, Puerto Rico "would be a new border state in the Caribbean."[2]

This illustrates one of the realities of Puerto Rico's situation as a member of the Caribbean region. It is not so much a theme as a basic assumption of this paper. U.S. policy in its direct Caribbean colony has from the beginning been conducted in the context of a contest between forms, that is, how best to integrate the island into the U.S. political system. One is reminded of the positions enunciated early on in the period of U.S. colonization of the island. Preparation for immediate statehood for an "alien," non-English speaking, Catholic, and racially mixed population unacquainted with the alleged virtues of Anglo-Saxon democracy and moral values was too much for the new conqueror to contemplate. But after a period of "tutelage" and a thorough indoctrination of the proper langague and the proper values, principally through the educational system, the final destiny of Puerto Rico within the North American Empire would be solved and assured. In the words of William F. Willoughby, writing in 1905:

If success is achieved in these efforts it will then be time to determine whether the territory (of Puerto Rico) shall be erected into a commonwealth enjoying autonomy in some other form.[3]

The colonial distinction between "autonomy" and "assimilation" was inculcated from the very beginning, and that issue has dominated Puerto Rican politics to this day. The choices have been restricted to traditional statehood and some special arrangement for "self-government" within the famework of overall federal domination. This has been a convenient choice from the point of view of the imperial power, since it serves to keep the colonial system functioning properly. That it might no longer be so convenient due to new developments in the arena of international politics, rising statehood sentiment on the island, and new currents in the Caribbean itself, forms one of the themes—or at least questions—of this paper.

Any discussion of the role of Puerto Rico in the Caribbean must rest on the recognition that the subject is inextricably intertwined with the perennial "status question." As the late Kalman Silvert put it in a general overview of the problem:

the weak fabric in the web of Puerto Rican social development is political in the grand sense: a confusion of cultural identities, a lack of ideological conviction, discomfort with the juridical structure of the state in its relation with the United States, a sneaking suspicion that the Puerto Rican experience is not transferable to neighboring islands . . . and a lack of definition of how much responsibility to accept as a part of the United States and how much as Puerto Rico.[4]

In a word, the period of tutelage in the American way of life and politics has not been uniformly successful. A sense of cultural, linguistic, and political identity persists in the face of the enormous impact of American economic and cultural domination; and within the last decade, the classical confrontation within the colony between the statehood and autonomy variants (which up to then had been an abstract and rhetorical confrontation in an electoral system dominated by pragmatic coalitionists and later by declared autonomists) has taken on a direct salience with the emergence into power in 1969 and again in 1977 of a political party openly committed to statehood.

One is under the impression that something new is occurring in Puerto Rico; that political definitions and alignments of the past are disappearing and new ones taking their place; that new roles and new solutions to old problems are in the offing. This paper will look briefly at some of the phenonmena underlying this impression. It will touch on the problem of the changing role of the United States in the world at large and in the Caribbean in particular, the significance of Puerto Rico as an outpost of the U.S. imperial system, and the current internal political situation in Puerto Rico itself.

The times seem to call for a reappraisal of the U.S. role in the international system. Within the United States itself, there is a view that the world is in a state of transition and that the basic assumptions of the postwar period are no longer valid. To some it appears as if the international assumptions of Liberalism no longer hold; that non-ideological economic development under the aegis of the "free world" led by the United States is now seen as the chimera it always was; that a multipolar world within the three so-called world camps is an irreversible fact; and that foreign alignments, perceptions, and policies must be modified somehow to acknowledge this in ways not threatening to U.S. hegemony in areas where it can be maintained without serious challenge.

In the Caribbean and circum-Caribbean area the redefinition of U.S. strategy is necessitated by some crucial issues, which can no longer be hidden from the effective scrutiny of the international community. The success and consolidation of the Cuban revolutionary government, the negotiation with Panama over the canal, the independent line of development announced by Guyana and Jamaica, the inexorable trends towards juridical independence in the Caribbean are situations which, from the point of view of U.S. foreign policy, must be managed with a maximum of diplomatic flexibility.

Puerto Rico dramatizes, in a particularly poignant fashion, both the problems the U.S. has in the Caribbean and the problem of the Caribbean in coping with the U.S. presence. In a sense, the history of Puerto Rico in the twentieth century reflects in microcosm the North American imperialist expansion in the Caribbean. It demonstrated the naked cutting edge of colonialism, U.S. style, and stands in interesting contrast to its sister island, Cuba, whose subjection to indirect imperial control through the Platt Amendment was substituted in the early thirties by a system of political and economic hegemony which proved eventually incapable of sustaining itself in the face of a genuine revolutionary movement.[5] The case of Puerto Rico is a classic example of the inherent contradictions of a colonial society—contradictions made more poignant by the politics of open liberal eclecticism which is the presumed hallmark of North American political society. The result of almost eight years of "tutelage" under direct U.S. aegis has been the development of a gigantic blind alley, which will lead either to a breakthrough into new pathways, a constant travelling about in circles in order not to come to the wall at the end of the road, or a backtracking into the imperial sanctuary.

The cul-de-sac in which Puerto Rico finds itself at present is illustrated by events since 1968 which have led to the present political debate on the island. The Caribbean and Puerto Rico's role in it figures hardly at all in this debate, although the international and regional projections of it are of enormous significance. Since the status plebiscite of 1967 and the formation of a strong political party (PNP) pledged clearly to statehood, the question of Statehood vs Autonomy has monopolized electoral politics in the island. The 1968 electoral victory of the PNP marked the end of twenty-four years of unquestioned domination by the Popular Democratic Party (PDP), under whose local guidance Operation Bootstrap and the Commonwelth arrangement were inaugurated. During the previous PDP administration of Muñoz Marin and Sánchez Vilella, certain movements were made in the direction of the Caribbean region, through the transferral of the Caribbean Organization to headquarters in San Juan, its subsequent dismantling by the Puerto Rican government, and its substitution by CODECA— a model of a pragamtic, low-profile, non-political, functional institution for project-oriented endeavours with other communities, under the aegies of the Puerto Rican government. The Ferré administration (PNP) of 1969-1972 gave the axe to CODECA and created something called the North-South Center, which had not even the pretension of carrying on an autonomous Puerto Rican presence in the Caribbean.

When the PDP returned to power in 1973, the Hernández Colón administration dissolved the North-South Center and proclaimed, in various forms, most notably in an address the Governor delivered at Yale University early in his term, that Puerto Rico "as such" was to play a role in the Caribbean region and that the Commonwealth, as the chosen political status of the island, would permit such a semi-autonomous role. This role was presumably to be confirmed and strengthened by modifications in the terms of the commonwealth arrangement as propounded in the so-called "New Pact," which the Hernández Colón administration attempted to get Congress to pass during the years of Watergate, an unsympathetic and non-elected presidency, and of a deepening economic crisis with particularly drastic consequences for Puerto Rico. The "New Pact" was scuttled definitively, and its demise accentuated the irrelevance and bankruptcy of the idea of commonwealth as a status subject to growth and continuous development in the direction of autonomy.

The victory of the PNP again in 1976 has seemed to seal the fate of commonwealth as an ideological issue in Puerto Rican politics. The present Governor, Carlos Romero Barceló, and the Resident Commissioner in Washington are hard-line statehood advocates, and although as a candidate the Governor was careful to insist that the status was not at issue directly in the elections, the commitment to statehood and a pledge to educate the people in the advantages and desirability of statehood are clearly on this administration's agenda. The Governor has stated publicly that he is not disposed to defend the commonwealth status before the United Nations—where it is under constant attack by many members of the Decolonization committee because of its "colonial vestiges."

Various resolutions and declarations of the U.N. Decolonization Committee, insisting on maintaining the Puerto Rican status question under consideration, keep the issue alive in the international arena. It is clear that some sort of reevaluation of the Puerto Rican situation is being carried out in the pertinent forums within the U.S. government and influential non-official groups. Serious attention is being given to pro-independence as well as pro-statehood views. (See, for example, the articles by Rubén Berrios, head of the Puerto Rican Independence Party (PIP) in the April 1977 issue of *Foreign Affairs,* in which the arguments for independence are set forth lucidly and in a manner designed to appeal to the perceived self-interest of the United States.)

In sum, there is a feeling in Puerto Rico today that a showdown is near, and that whatever form that showdown assumes—between Statehood and Commonwealth or between Statehood and Independence—it will eventually result in the decline of the Commonwealth.

The commonwealth status was a typically "liberal" attempt at solving the colonial status question. It was consistent with the scheme of U.S. imperial hegemony which appeared as a consequence of world realignments after the Second World War. It fitted into the self-congratulatory "non-ideological" North American liberal imperialism. It gave Puerto Rico a slightly longer leash in the form of self-government in exchange for the whole-hearted embracing of capitalist industrialization by invitation. It was attuned to the way the internal political system in Puerto Rico developed, towards claims for enhanced autonomy within the American system. For Washington (and the North American academic establishment), it was a happy scheme for institutionalizing dependence by providing economic development of sufficient durability to ensure its eventual legitimization. Colonialism would gradually develop itself out of existence. Integration into the U.S. economy, an unavoidable consequence of the policy, would bring its own rewards in such a way as to convert Puerto Rico into a "showcase for democracy" and bring evidence that U.S. imperialism is both benign and a motor for a continuing and expanding world economy.

The Commonwealth was based on a set of premises and expectations, all of which would have to hold if the experiment were to be successful. The first was that economic development would be continuous and unabated. The second was that the distribution of the wealth would in the long run take care of itself and would not exacerbate political divisions. It was also assumed—or hoped—that the politics of status in Puerto Rico would disappear gradually as the "middle road to freedom" way of pragmatic commonwealthism would be recognized as the pathway to the better life. And finally, it was assumed that Puerto Rico would continue to be isolated politically from the rest of the world, immune to the anticolonialist bleatings emanating from the emerging Third World, while shining like a beacon signaling America's good intentions to that world.

These were unrealistic assumptions to begin with; and given the complex character of Puerto Rico's problem of political identity, they were a frail reed upon which to lean the vulnerable vessel of commonwealth. At present, the commonwealth—the very structure of the political community itself—is on the precarious defensive against the claims of statehood, claims which its own policies have helped mightily to strengthen. In domestic political terms—expressed in the politics of the electoral system—the living question now is whether statehood sentiment will augment its popular force to such a degree that it can present a sufficiently strong threat to Commonwealth so that Congress will be obliged to deal with it directly.

In terms of the United States, the issue is whether the Commonwealth is to be viable much longer as a vehicle for U.S. interests in the Caribbean and in the anti-colonial Third World in general. This issue is the result of the convergence of four factors, whose interrelations in the coming years will determine which scenario is to be enacted. They are: (1) the fact of the "failure" of the commonwealth/PDP strategy and structure; (2) what I would call the "denial of the Caribbean" by the dominating Puerto Rican political elites; (3) the revisions in the United States of its strategy in the Caribbean within the context of world politics; and (4) the new and unexpected facts of the possibility of mineral extractions and of petroleum deposits in Puerto Rico.

The Commonwealth was designed in such a way that its only success would be in its survival. It has failed to "develop" in the direction of more autonomy because the economic relations on which it was built could lead only to an increased dependence on the United States—or "interdependence" or "integration" to use the more euphemistic term. The "New Pact" scheme was destined to be stillborn because it asked for a kind of development in two inconsistent directions at once: enhanced local autonomy in several areas—such as control of immigration, communications, participation in applicable feudal legislation, and the like—while maintaining or expanding participation in federal programs of economic assistance, welfare and social development. Even if the North American constitutional system were sufficiently flexible to permit such a special status state, the realities of Congressional politics would almost certainly preclude it, as they have indeed in the three attempts since 1952 to culminate, improve, or further develop the Commonwealth. So we are again faced with the crude fact that "commonwealth" must be defined, not in terms of its ideal or what it might develop into, but in terms of "what we've got." As a political ideology it is moribund.

The attitude of Puerto Rico's political elite towards the rest of the Caribbean is ambivalent in the extreme, an ambivalence which not only reflects the colonial indifference to its neighbours and almost exclusive attention to the metropolitan power, but has been compounded by the ambiguities, uncertainties, and lack of political consolidation of the Commonwealth status itself. A recent student of the problem of integration in the Caribbean arrived at the inescapable conclusion that Commonwealth participation in the Caribbean in the early and mid sixties—in the Caribbean Organization and later through CODECA—revolved around the felt need to give lustre and respectability to Commonwealth itself rather than as a result of genuine identification with the region.[6] The idea was that Puerto Rico ought to be able to play a role of principal rather than of U.S. agent in the Caribbean, to show that bootstrap democracy was self-supporting, as it were. This was a naive illusion to begin with, but the political assaults of the Statehood-oriented opposition were a lethal torpedo in any case. The Statehood people, as the Ferré administration quite clearly expressed, are uninterested in any autonomous role in the Caribbean—a role inconsistent with their status ideology. The Romero Barceló adminstration seems to be not at all different.

Perhaps the most crucial factor in the reevaluation of Puerto Rico's status situation at the present time is the new international strategy of the United States, beginning with the Nixon-Ford administrations and which is apparently being refined, or at least articulated more precisely, by the Carter administration.

As far as Puerto Rico and the Caribbean are concerned, the first signals of such a shift were contained in a brief "case study" paper on

Puerto Rico prepared in 1975 for the Senior Seminar on Foreign Policy of the Department of State by an official of that Department, C. Arthur Borg.[7] It was critical of the proposals contained in the "New Pact" draft and gave evidence for the first time on the record that the Commonwealth status was not necessarily the preferred baby of the State Department. The long-run vulnerability of the present status was outlined in the study, and the suggestion is made that perhaps the United States ought to begin to consider directly preparing the way for either statehood or independence, if it is deemed—as is hinted very strongly in the study— that commonwealth is no longer a convenient arrangement. After suggesting the creation of a presidential assistant for Puerto Rico's affairs to help "steer" the Puerto Rican political status question rather than let the matter drift into "real trouble on the island," Borg closes his paper as follows:

> One possible initiative which comes to mind is a Presidential statement or Congressional resolution setting forth an updated public position on Puerto Rico's status; there is no doubt this would help greatly to clear the political air. But even if it were not possible to go that far, it should at least be possible to decide internally how far the thrust for greater Puerto Rican autonomy could be permitted to proceed before it placed too great a burden— constitutionally or politically—on the U.S.-Puerto Rican relationship. A *prior* conception of that limit would help us to decide whether we are really prepared to support commonwealth status in perpetuity, or whether we must prepare now for an eventual move to either statehood or independence.

The Borg paper was made public sometime after it was produced at the Seminar, and some months later, on New Year's Day of this year, outgoing President Ford made his generally unexpected announcement in favour of Statehood for Puerto Rico. A task force was hurriedly put together in the Domestic Council to draft legislation detailing the possible steps to be traversed before enabling Puerto Rico to be admitted as a state. This lame duck operation was disavowed by incoming President Carter, but Carter was careful not to oppose Statehood or to support Commonwealth. He limited himself to expressing the need to respect the wishes of the Puerto Rican people, *whatever they might be.*

(It should be noted that a group of Puerto Rican Statehooders, many associated with the PNP, were the only Puerto Ricans from the island who actively supported Jimmy Carter during his campaign for the nomination.)

The Ford declaration was greeted with universal disdain from the North American liberal press. But Carter's sense of redirection in foreign policy might very well carry important repercussions on the way Puerto Rico may develop in the next decade. The division of imperial capitalist labour as expressed by the influential Trilateral Commission might presage a degree of retrenchment in the spheres of direct American involvement. Shifting accommodations in relation with Cuba and others might mean a more relaxed international atmosphere, as the capitalist world apportions its influences and hegemonies in a more pluralistic arrangement. It is possible that within this "multipolar" capitalist world, faced with an equally multipolar and politically sensitive Third World, the old North American tradition of territorial expansion followed by political consolidation and incorporation might be resuscitated in the case of Puerto Rico. (Carter's vocabulary about the new integrative pluralism of American society, the preservation all the same of ethnic integrity, his and Rosalyn's elaborately publicized Spanish lessons—all might be seen as subtle indications that a way is being paved towards making the idea of Statehood for Puerto Rico somewhat more acceptable from the North American point of view.) Besides, it is clear that the need to guarantee Puerto Rico's permanence within the American hegemonic system, in the face of increasing resistance on the part of some of the other lands in the region, militates in the same direction.

Just a few days before President Ford made his surprise New Year's announcement, he had received a report from the Department of Interior confirming the possibility of significant hydrocarbon resources on and just off the northern coast of Puerto Rico. No one can be sure yet whether such petroleum resources are there or not, but there are few people in Puerto Rico who can believe that the reasonable geological possibility of such a discovery is not playing a role in these processes of apparent revision of the stance regarding the relations between the USA and Puerto Rico.

Let me conclude with a possible scenario of events over the next decade, based on the assumptions and factors dealt with above.

First, on the international level, it is to be expected that the U.N. Decolonization Committee, and possibly later the General Assembly, will declare Puerto Rico formally a colony. (The United States might be able to keep this from occurring for a few years yet, but it will not be able to forestall it indefinitely.) Puerto Rico, with or without the formal declaration, will continue to be a symbol of remaining colonialism in the Third and Socialist Worlds, at least.

In Puerto Rico itself, the lines will be increasingly drawn between the

Statehood and Anti-Statehood forces. The latter will probably not be able to agree on the kind or degree of autonomy as the final solution and will have to be a very loose coalition, limited only to the sentiment of anti-assimilation. The PNP will be working towards the holding of another plebiscite sometime after the elections of 1980, assuming that the party acquires a significant electoral victory that year and can be assured of a substantial Statehood victory of, let us say, some 70% of the vote. (If the PNP is unable to hold on to its electoral strength over the next three and a half years—and it is faced with staggering economic problems, budget deficits, and undeclining unemployment rates—all bets will be off and the status question will remain on the shelf.) The PDP, presently in opposition, is in deep organizational, as well as ideological, trouble and its survival as an "anti-statehood" party is questionable. With the demise of commonwealth as an ideology, and the defensive connotations of being merely a rearguard action against statehood, the PDP runs the risk of dissolving into irrelevance, of being simply a "loyal opposition" to the reigning party. If that is ever the case, then it would be able to offer no effective resistance to statehood, and might even be converted into another statehood party itself.

At the same time the organized independence sentiment is rising slowly, though it is still a small minority, as far as electoral force is concerned. The thrust toward Statehood by the present government party tends to focus attention on the contrast between Statehood and Independence as the two "classic" or "legitimate" permanent solutions. Independence feelings and nationalist slogans are cultivated, not only by traditional independentist groups, but now even by Statehood advocates as well.

Romero Barceló has asserted that the Spanish language and Puerto Rico's cultural identity are "un-negotiable" in the petition for statehood. He has stated that he will deign to ask for statehood "only once"; and if it is refused, he will opt for independence. And he endorsed poet Francisco Matos Paoli, a long-time nationalist follower of the late Pedro Albizu Campos, for the Nobel Prize in literature!

This can have two possible consequences. When the plebiscite comes, if it does, the defeat of independence will be made to seem all that more devastating; or, if Statehood is stalled or refused humiliatingly in Congress, a resurgence of independence as a real popular alternative would result. Since these contingencies are in the realm of possibility, independence can certainly not be ruled out.

From the side of the United States, we can expect lengthy or indefinite delays in Congress if ever the Statehood, even the Statehood favouring plebiscite, is held in Puerto Rico. Some inferences are being made at present in Puerto Rico as to the sinister designs of the USA to impose Statehood on the island in order to ensure continued military control and control over the newly-discovered and potential mineral resources on the island. Such a design would be consistent with a national appraisal of U.S. imperial interests at the present juncture in world politics. However, there is probably no such clear-cut scenario being worked out in Washington. Congressional resistance to Puerto Rican Statehood would be enormous, not to mention the profound adjustments that would have to be made in Puerto Rican political and cultural life before Statehood could even be imminently contemplated.

Whatever happens, the problem as sketched here will persist for a good time into the future. As far as the Caribbean area is concerned, it goes without saying that as long as it does there will be no autonomous role played by Puerto Rico in the region. Its role in the Caribbean is, obviously, inseparable from the status question. Any kind of an autonomous, genuinely regional orientation will be impossible as long as this particularly dramatic colonial dilemma persists.

FOOTNOTES

[1] Ben Stephansky, "Puerto Rico," in *The United States and the Caribbean,* ed. Tad Szulc (Englewood Cliffs, N.J.: Prentice-Hall, 1971), p. 71.

[2] *Ibid.,* p. 96.

[3] William F. Willoughly, *Territories and Dependencies of the United States: Their Government and Administration* (New York: The Century Co., 1905), p. 420.

[4] K. Silvert, "The Caribbean and North America," in Szulc, *op. cit.,* p. 200.

[5] For a discussion of the differences between the concepts of "imperialist" and "hegemonic" modes of domination, as alluded to here, see Jorge I. Dominguez, "The Impact of Cuban Internal Politics and Economics, 1902-1958: from Imperialism to Hegemony," paper prepared for the American Political Science Association meeting, September 25, 1976.

[6] Herbert Cokran, Jr., *Patterns of International Cooperation in the Caribbean, 1947-1967* (Dallas: Southern Methodist University Press, 1970), pp. 172-73.

[7] The report is called "The Problem of Puerto Rico's Political Status" and was prepared for the Seventeenth Seminar in Foreign Policy, 1974-75.

National Pursuits and Regional Definitions: The Caribbean as an Interest Area

Anthony P. Maingot

"What is the Caribbean?" is no longer an academic question. How a particular government answers might determine initiatives of all kinds; to mention a few of an institutional nature: participation in development banks, shipping arrangements, scholarships and aluminum smelter arrangements. Then there is that equally important dimension of international relations: the attitudes of the peoples of the region towards each other—friendships and understanding or ignorance and mistrust.

Recently, and for the first time, the people (or at least the leaders) of this geographic region have had an opportunity to lead the discussion on this vital question, a discussion which has taken on the appearance of a debate. Yet, it is clear that if measured, for instance, in terms of press coverage,[1] the two principal protagonists are Prime Minister Eric Williams of Trinidad and Tobago on the one side, and the collective leadership of Venezuela on the other.

The Venezuelan "definition" is not so much a definition as it is a geopolitical claim; that Venezuela is a Caribbean country through the "simple" fact that it has 1,100 miles of coast on the Caribbean and 72 islands therein. By that accounting, Colombia, Central America and Mexico are Caribbean countries and are so considered by Venezuela. Together with the islands (the archipelago) they form what Venezuela calls the "Caribbean Basin."

Challenging this whole concept is Eric Williams' definition of the Caribbean archipelago as a "culture area,"[2] a definition which has geohistory as its center of gravity. The Caribbean area, he notes, has a "fundamental unity and distinctive identity":

. . . The product of a *common historical experience,* a common social movement, and the similarity of our economic problems and political aspiration—the long and oppressive domination of sugar in the colonial period, *the ethnic diversity* encouraged by it, the subordination of our colonial interest to the exclusive requirements of the metropolitan economies, our political struggles for freedom and independence.[3]

Williams' definition of the Caribbean with its emphasis on geohistory explicitly leaves out Venezuela, Colombia, Central America and Mexico, an "archipelago" approach widely shared by students of the region.[4] It is the common historical experience in colonialism, says Philip Mason, that made the Caribbean "the most colonial of all colonial societies."[5] Similarly, David Lowenthal feels that because of this common past, ". . . in the Caribbean, European culture and institutions, artifacts, and ideas, are the only generally recognized heritage."[6] Sidney Mintz, who like the others limits his definition to the islands, Belize and the Guyanas, talks about "the special distinctiveness of the Caribbean area,"

One of the ways to clarify the contemporary importance of the Caribbean islands is to limn their social and cultural characteristics against the backdrop *of regional history;* much of their commonality, their meaning as a bloc of societies, is the result of *demonstrably parallel historical experiences during more than four centuries of power* (though intermittent and whimsical) *European influence.*[7]

It is not at all certain that these scholars explicitly intend to define the Caribbean in terms of a "culture area"; many seem to shy from such an outright claim and for obvious methodological reasons.[8] Be that as it may, it is clear that the similarities of attitudes and outlook they attribute to a "common historical past" amounts to at least something of a culture area. Even if one could agree on what "culture" comprises exactly, there are other problems with such an approach to the Caribbean. The varieties of colonial past have led to such disparate cultures as that of Cuba and that of Barbados for instance. Similarly, Jamaica and Trinidad show strong dissimilarities, a reflection of their quite different colonial experiences. Again, does the colonial past have to be European as these scholars would suggest or merely colonial? The position of Gordon Lewis reflects something of the confusion. Speaking of the Caribbean as having "a common historical experience and a common imprint upon its people,"

Lewis concludes that "In that sense Puerto Rico, even though it may be the most Americanized society in the Caribbean Sea, belongs by historical fiat to the West Indies."[9] His subsequent study of the West Indies, however, uses language and common colonial past as its criteria of selection (and presumably exclusion). Puerto Rico is not included.[10]

It is clear that a definition of the "Caribbean" will vary with the perceived interests of the parties and that these will in turn determine just what is defined as a "Caribbean" problem. Williams has been emphatic that Caribbean "problems have to be carefully selected in terms of their "Caribbean" relevance—Caribbean, meaning the archipelago. "I was particularly careful to warn," he recently told his Party, "that we were importing into the Caribbean the tensions of Latin America."[11] It is obvious that such a "culture area" approach which additionally dichotomizes the region into "problem" areas makes no sense to those who see the region in geopolitical terms. Is Guatemala's claim on Belize a Caribbean problem, or France's plans to colonize French Guyana with Frenchmen, the Cuban-USA conflict, the Panama Canal issue, the Bahamas' "lobster conflict" with the U.S., the potentially serious Venezuelan-Brazilian border tension, perhaps even Cuba's involvement in Angola, especially since it involved air stopovers in Barbados and potentially Trinidad and Guyana? How to deal with Fidel Castro's claim that Cuba is not only a Latin American nation but a "Latin-African" one as well?[12] How to deal with the joint Cuban-Panamanian Communique which highlights the Sistema Economico Latinoamericano (SELA) as the appropriate institutional context for regional development (with specific mention of the integration of the "English speaking" Caribbean therein), calls for a special regime of the Law of the Sea for the Caribbean (including the Circum-Caribbean), and generally addresses itself to the common economic problems of raw material exporting countries.[13]

It would appear, thus, that even though the Eric Williams interpretation of the Caribbean area as an archipelago culture area has the support of much of contemporary English-speaking scholarship, it is being challenged and a debate is in the offing. In 1966, Richard M. Morse fired what has to be considered one of the early shots of the debate when he told a group of Caribbean scholars that

> ... a primary task for historians at this stage of a Caribbean *prise de conscience* is to identify the enduring substrate of Caribbean regionalism which will outlast the imperialism and strident nationalisms of the moment, or of the century.[14]

The fast moving events and trends in the region make this a task of utmost importance.

There is yet to be demonstrated that even the archipelago Caribbean, in all its linguistic, racial and religious variety, shares enough values, customs and mores to warrant being called a "culture area." On the other hand, it is widely accepted that the archipelago and the Circum-Caribbean nations do experience certain major problems and share certain major interests in common. While different nations might have been introduced to these problems at different historical moments and thus developed interests later than others, they all share today a degree of historical consciousness regarding these problems. Where such historical consciousness about shared problems and shared interests exists one can avoid the potential pitfalls of the "culture area" approach by defining the region as an "interest area."

The Venezuelan approach best approximates such an "interest area" focus. Fundamentally concerned with geopolitics and economics, it points to common problems and challenges: the struggle for economic independence, the need for transportation, the risks and opportunities of tourism.[15] Such a focus was evident in the approach of President Carlos Andres Perez of Venezuela. It is difficult, he noted, for "Barbados, Cuba, Peru, or Venezuela" to fulfill their true destiny unless efforts are joined towards a common effort of these "Latin American" nations. Their common "great Latin American nationality," Perez continued, stems from the recent awakening of all these nations to a common reality.[16]

The theme of this paper is that the Caribbean region is becoming an "interest area" that includes not just the archipelago but also the Circum-Caribbean nations. The emphasis on "becoming" indicates that it is a process, not just a static "reality" of some European colonial past. At the center of that process are geopolitical and economic interests and considerations.

Some of the characteristics of this process are revealed through an analysis of two critical areas of decision-making in Trinidad and Tobago and Venezuela: the former country's relations with Cuba and Venezuela and the latter's development of a Caribbean policy and emphasis on its fisheries sector. Official Venezuelan policies and pronouncements in both these areas have stimulated Trinidadian measures and counter-measures as the governing elites of both nations pursue their defined interests. The use of power in the midst of dependency are the central themes in that process.

POWER AND DEPENDENCY

Whether adhering to a "culture area" or a "geopolitical basin" concept of the area, both parties tend to use a point of departure for historical analysis a variation of dependency theory. President Carlos Andres Perez' own explanation of his country's belated awareness of its Caribbean heritage is in that vein:

> Venezuela has lived with its back turned to its responsibilities in the Caribbean. . . . And the essential and effective cause of this reality is that we have not been masters of our own destinies. Our decisions have not been our own, they have been made from other centers of power.[17]

This position has a parallel in Eric Williams assertion (cited above) of the "subordination of our colonial interest to the exclusive requirements of the metropolitan economies." This emphasis on dependency has a solid basis in the literature. That literature will not be reviewed here, but it should be emphasized that this paper uses dependency not as "theory", but as a frame of reference, a perspective.[18]

This perspective encompasses several dimensions.[19] Fundamental among these is the notion that while the overall boundaries of action are set by the dominant nations, this does not eliminate or nullify the possible options of national actors. Separating analytically the political from the economic aspects of decision-making, it is clear that the effectiveness of national elites depends in part upon their skill and creativity in internal politics.[20] Logically related to this is the assumption that the analysis of historical trends is necessary because each country shows a different development, the realities of power vary in each instance. Both dimensions, then, require that we focus on the internal response to external dependency. And as Fernando Enrique Cardoso states, at all times one should keep in mind "that there are historical options, alternative political possibilities inside a nation."[21]

Such a flexible perspective on dependency requires a relational rather than absolute approach to the concept, *power*. The use of absolute rather than relational definitions of power comes rather easy in the study of international relations in the Caribbean given the history of the European and North American presence in the region. Additionally, since the Caribbean nations are assumed to be dependent on the same dominant nation, there is also a danger of viewing regional conflicts as a form of sibling rivalry. When all power is located at the center, relationships on the periphery are, at best, based on semi-autonomous definitions of self-interest rather than independent decisions to act and choose after the weighing of alternate paths or options.

The evidence indicates that the debate on the nature of the Caribbean is being carried on by independent Caribbean actors pursuing their self interests in the area and, as such, neither the notion of a "culture area" with its accompanying "historical backdrop" nor the across-the-board transferral of a blanket theory of dependency to the field of intra-Caribbean foreign relations advances our understanding of the new dynamics of the area. What is unfolding within the broad parameters of Third World dependency is a process of clashing and coinciding national interests with competing conceptions and definitions of the Caribbean as a means of advancing the interests of national elites, externally and internally. Power, then, is measured in terms of the range of options open to each elite studied in terms of particular situations, specific instances of competition for shared values. The particular definitions given the Caribbean, insofar as it is a resource in decision-making, becomes a value. Control of that definition advances the interests of whichever party controls it.

TRINIDAD'S RELATIONS WITH CUBA AND VENEZUELA

In a real sense Eric Williams' legitimacy as a politician was from the beginning based on his reputation of personal independence, even rebelliousness—first from the Caribbean Commission for which he worked, then as Premier of autonomous Trinidad. A few years after coming to power in Trinidad Williams would fight a battle for "unit-participation" in foreign policy during the short-lived West Indies Federation.[22]

Accompanying this unwillngness to relinquish any sovereignty in the area of foreign policy has been a fairly consistent approach to West Indian integration. "Our stand on this," he wrote in 1968, "has always been crystal clear from as far back as January, 1962. . . . It was to work towards the formation of a Caribbean Economic Community, beginning with, but not limited to, the Caribbean Commonwealth countries."[23] Such an alignment, he argued, was warranted by a common history, geographical proximity, similarity of economic structure and limited national markets.

Over the years, Williams has been consistent in his insistence on the need for an economic community in the area. He has been less consistent, however, on just exactly how that Caribbean community would fit into the Latin American context. Note his stance in 1968:

I turn next to the question of possible alignments with our Latin American neighbors. Trinidad and Tobago has also made its position clear on this. We have recognized our geographical position on this Hemisphere by deciding to become a member of the Inter-American Community. As such we are now participating in the Alliance for Progress mainly through membership in the Inter-American Development Bank and we have great interest in all the various possible forms of economic cooperation with our Latin American neighbors. Indeed, we have established a Mixed Commisson with the Government of Venezuela for the purpose of formulating and executing all practicable forms of economic cooperation.

And then, the crucial formulation on options:

We do not see any conflict beeween alignment with the Caribbean and participation in the economic instrumentalities of the inter-American Community. In short, we do not regard the Caribbean and Latin American as alternatives. [24]

Not that the relations between Trinidad and Venezuela had been smooth sailing throughout. In 1963 Williams warned a high level Venezuelan delegation that unless the 30% surtax on goods from Trinidad was removed, he intended to initiate dicussions in the United Nations on remaining colonialism in the Caribbean, "and he wished to indicate that that included the 30% Antillean surtax the importance of which should not be minimized." [25] Generally, however, Williams was interested in keeping good relations with Venezuela for a fundamental reason: ideology and national security. On both scores, Williams had placed Trinidad on the side of Venezuela and anti-Communism, in an anti-Castro stance.*

The evolution of Eric Williams' policy and attitude toward Cuba reflects both his attempts to promote his own conception of "archipelago" Caribbean politics as well as his independence of action. One of the earliest pronouncements was made in 1963 (on the first anniversay of Trinidad and Tobago's Independence) in *Monde Diplomatique* of Paris:

*The appearance in Trinidad of a newspaper ("The Circle") which carried news of Venezuela's guerrilla movement (including a verbatim reprint of a F.A.L.N. Statement (cf. vol. I, No. 11 (Nov. 1963)) tends to indicate some degree of transnational contact and cooperation between radical circles.

This then is the significance of Trinidad and Tobago as an independent country in the modern world, that it represents a confrontation
in the Caribbean of the two dominant points of view that face the
world today:

(a) Active partnership between government and investors in
    Trinidad and Tobago as against the state direction of the
    economy in Cuba;

(b) a direct democracy superimposed upon a parliamentary tradi-
    tion in Trinidad and Tobago as against Cuba's one party state
    dominated by its caudillo;

(c) the vision in Trinidad and Tobago of a Caribbean Economic
    Community with some sort of independent existence as against
    the submerging of the Cuban personality in the international
    behind the Iron Curtain.[26]

Again in 1967, on the occasion of Trinidad and Tobago's presentation
on September 27, 1967 to the Twenty-Second General Assembly of the
United Nations, the Trinidad and Tobago position on Cuba was made
clear by its then Minister of External Affairs, A.N.R. Robinson:

I cannot end this brief review of areas of tension over which my
delegation is particularly concerned without reference to those states
which indiscriminately seek by force to impose a pattern of
government and of society on people outside of their borders. I refer
particularly to the activities of the government of Cuba in the
Western Hemisphere. I say to the representative of the government
of Cuba: "Unwarranted intervention in the affairs of other states
cannot but justify intervention in your own. Exporting revolution,
be it remembered, is a two-edged sword.[27]

Previous to that (on September 24, 1967), the Trinidad and Tobago
position *vis-à-vis* Cuba was put even more emphatically to the Final
Plenary Session of the Twelfth Meeting of Consultation of Foreign
Ministers of the OAS:

We have extended assurances to the government of Venezuela
that we will not permit the soil of Trinidad and Tobago to be used for
purposes of subversion against the democratic regime of the
Republic of Venezuela. . . . We propose to take all necessary action
within our community to avoid the danger of communist infiltra-
tion; . . . finally, in the dispute between the Government of
Venezuela and the totalitarian state of Cuba, and in all the
circumstances demonstrated at this Meeting of Foreign Ministers,

we wish to state emphatically and unequivocably for public opinion in the Hemisphere and elsewhere in the world. We stand by Venezuela.[28]

By 1967 the value of Trinidad's trade with selected countries and with Venezuela and Cuba specifically reflected very nicely the absolute and relative relationship with the two:

TABLE I

Country	TT$ Imports (cif)	TT$ Exports (fob)
U.K.	104,078,600	96,923,200
Canada	37,417,900	33,666,400
Guyana	9,932,100	19,389,400
Jamaica	2,110,300	2,919,800
Netherlands	8,156,500	28,901,200
U.S.A	108,679,500	298,137,900
China	1,714,200	500
Venezuela	283,675,700*	1,486,800
Cuba	100	—

Source: Overseas Trade Report
*Reflects the importation of Venezuela crude for refining and re-export.

By 1969, however, the Trinidad government recommended that "The door should be left open for the inclusion of Cuba" into CARIFTA.[29] No explanation of whether this meant with, or, perhaps, after Castro; the position on Cuba was not at all clear. In his *From Columbus to Castro* book published in 1969 Williams did note that "Castro's programme is pure nationalist, comprehensible and acceptable by any other Caribbean nationalist."[30] And in the field of race relations he saw Cuba as "the only bright spot" in the area.[31] But Williams' old reservations were still there:

. . . Cuba has illustrated the basic weakness of West Indian countries—the tendency to look for external props. But the real tragedy of Cuba is that she has resorted to a totalitarian framework within which to profoundly transform her economy and society. This is the real point about the essentials of the political system in Cuba today.[32]

The "Cuban Model," as he called it was not recommended for the Caribbean. Yet, by 1970, Williams used the occasion of his Chairmanship of the Economic and Social Council of the OAS meeting in Caracas to call for "reabsorption" of Cuba into the OAS. Whether this was to counterbalance his call for the admission of Guyana (then locked in a border dispute with Venezuela), or an outright statement of conviction, is difficult to tell. By 1972 Trinidad joined its CARIFTA partners in extending diplomatic recognition to Cuba.

It was not until June 1975, however, that Williams would make Cuba a central part of his foreign policy through a state visit to that island. "In this mighty effort to achieve greater Caribbean solidarity," he told the students of the University of Havana, "Cuba has a great role to play."[33] The search, Williams stressed, was for the Caribbean's "fundamental unity and distinctive identity." To Fidel Castro, Williams wrote that "Cuba's progress is something that has to be seen to be believed."[34]

What explains this dramatic shift in Eric Williams' foreign policy? Part of the explanation lies in an understanding of the dynamics of an evolving Venezuelan consciousness about the Caribbean, its roots in national politics and its manifestations in foreign policy.

THE VENEZUELAN FACTOR

That there are important geopolitical trends underway in the Caribbean is evident.

Since in politics the one thing which cannot exist is a vacuum, it stands to reason that the gradual withdrawal of the English and Dutch from the Caribbean would be replaced by other forces. Certainly the U.S.A and Cuba have taken a new and active interest in the changing situation. But so has Venezuela, and never more assertively than during the period of the early 1970s.

The most important area of interest in Venezuelan-Trinidad relations, then and now, however, has been modern Venezuelan geographical thinking on its maritime position. This thinking is heavily laden with historical interpretations of the country's past weakness, always a powerful source of aggressive defensiveness. Note, for example, the words of Pascual Vanegas Filardo, a prominent Venezuelan geographer: "The threats to our coast and sea are historical in character and the aggressive greed of the treaties, which were not fully successful in hiding such greed, led to the dismembering of the Netherlands Antilles and Trinidad. . . ."[35]

One final point will illustrate the question. The writings of a major Venezuelan geographer, Ruben Carpio Castillo, have developed a keen consciousness of what is called Venezuela's "interior sea" (Mar Interior).[36] This is the body of water lying between the coast and the chain of 72 Venezuelan islands which stretch from Los Monjes in the west to Islas Aves in the north to Los Testigos in the east, and constitute a total of 14,650 square miles of land—seven times that of Trinidad and

Tobago. No other Latin American country has such a coastal configuration and certainly none have foreign-controlled islands as close to their coast as does Venezuela.

No one demonstrated the depth of this new consciousness more clearly than President Carlos Andres Perez in his inaugural address to the III United Nations Conference on the Law of the Sea in Caracas, 1974. Perez was especially emphatic when explaining why it had taken Venezuela so long to develop such a consciousness of its maritime potential and wealth ". . .Venezuela cannot forget that in its past as a weak nation it had been the victim of the maneuvres of great international interests."[37] He was quick to reassure his audience that such memories would not be used to feed infertile feelings of vengeance or rancour but rather to make them "permanent and constructive lessons for the future."

In common language, Venezuela would no longer be "pushed around."[38] It is the kind of language often applauded and encouraged in "Third World" leaders. The fact that in the Venezuelan case it generates fear among her neighbors, only demonstrates the complexity of international relations in the Caribbean, an area of developing consciousness of vital national interests and definitions to suit those interests.

In Venezuela, the new consciousness of its position as a maritime nation, in the Caribbean and the Atlantic, transcended particular parties; it had become a national posture. The official visit of Jamaica's Prime Minister, Michael Manley, to Venezuela in March-April 1973 provides some telling insights into Venezuela's Caribbean policy during this period. The level of protocol attending that visit was of the highest order; the red carpet and the champagne toast were everywhere in evidence. In short, Manley was given much more than entertainment and decorations (he was honored with the "Gran Cordon de la Orden del Libertador"); he was given the status and recognition usually reserved for leaders of much larger countries. With the warm glow of such high level diplomatic courting permeating the atmosphere, it is understandable that Manley should have been moved to toast then Venezuelan Foreign Minister, Aristides Calvani, as "the architect of the spirit of regionalism in the Caribbean." It would be easy to dismiss Manley's statement as mere diplomatic expansiveness or to fault it on factual grounds. Be that as it may, the fact is that the whole Manley-Calvani cordiality reflected the success of what Calvani himself called the "new deal" in their Caribbean foreign policy. During the four years of the Social Christian COPEI Government of Rafael Caldera (1969-1974) the Caribbean was given unprecedented emphasis and attention, and 1973 was officially termed "the year of our Caribbean policy."[39] A new office of Caribbean Affairs was established in the Foreign Ministry, and Calvani (born in Trinidad and known as the "Kissinger" of Latin America) courted Caribbean statesmen up and down the island chain. In many ways the launching of this Caribbean "new deal" was signalled by the "Informal Meeting of Consultation of the Ministers of Foreign Affairs of Countries of the Caribbean Sea" held in Caracas in November 1971.[40] The agenda included the following topics: Marine Resources, Multinational Corporations, Marine and Air Transport, Tourism, External Commerce, Scientific and Technological Development. The final communique of that conference gives a preliminary insight into the dimensions of the new foreign policy's grand design. The diplomatic thrust would be a three-pronged one: political, economic and cultural. Cultural diplomacy comes easily to the Venezuelans because of their considerable resources in folklore and the arts; their talents span the spectrum from "classical" to Afro-Venezuelan and thus fits the Caribbean context admirably. New emphasis was placed on the functions of their various "Andres Bello" institutes which already were quite successful in language training. From a practical plane, the establishment of a ferry service between Aruba, Curacao, and Coro, Venezuela insured greater tourist exchanges and general travel within that zone. From a political, regional plane it was seen as fulfilling the "imperative" of integration in the region.[41]

The most important area of negotiation, however, remained that of national boundaries including the question of the Continental Shelf.* Not surprisingly Venezuela seems to be gearing for an immediate future of hard international negotiations. In 1974 two new foreign policy bodies were created. The Assessory Commission on External Relations (the importance attached to this new Commission is attested to by its composition: ex-Presidents—only those democratically elected—ex-Ministers of External Affairs—of democratic governments, the Chief of Staff of the Armed Forces, the Presidents of the Chamber of Deputies and of the Senate, each chamber to have two representatives who sit for five years. The Commission's terms of reference are broad but include a specific role in territorial and frontier questions, of land and sea.[42] The other was the National Council on Frontiers which seemed to have the function of suggesting social and economic development *on both sides* of

---

*Venezuela shares land and sea and/or continental shelf boundaries with Colombia, Trinidad, the Netherlands Antilles, The French Antilles, Dominica and Guyana. The mix of national laws and the continued presence of metropolitan powers (France, Britain and Holland) all present Venezuela with an extraordinarily complex international panorama.

Venezuela's borders; it would be based on the Chancellor's Office and be composed of different state agencies which are concerned with all aspects of frontier development.[43] Both these bodies were designed to pull governmental, university and private sector talent together in a national effort in foreign affairs. Similarly the investments of oceanographic and other scientific research indicates that the decision-makers intended to come prepared for these negotiations. This preparation was also evident in the upgrading of the diplomatic corps.

The coordination of State and private sector initiatives in foreign policy was a major feature of the "new deal" and was as evident in the cultural as it was in the economic sphere. The main instrument of the economic thrust was the joint venture. An example of this is the cardboard box factory built in St Lucia, West Indies with 50 percent Venezuelan capital and which was inaugurated by Calvani himself. At one level, "mixed commissions" of every type sprang up in the region; at another level Venezuela was joining the Caribbean Development Bank, sponsoring Trinidad for membership in OPEC and encouraging the newly-independent states to take an active role in the multiple functions of the OAS. The political thrust was characterized by continuous State visits—Eric Williams, Michael Manley, R. J. Isa (Netherlands Antilles)—the putting on ice of the Guyana border dispute and the general alignment with "Third World" aspirations on the international scene.

But since in politics, as in physics, every action has a reaction, there was bound to be a reaction to all this. The reaction to Venzuela's "new deal" was two-headed. On the one hand there can be no doubt but that some Caribbean governments and many business communities publicly welcomed and encouraged further Venezuelan initiatives.[44] The other response was not as friendly; voices began to be heard calling for caution if not outright distrust of the Venezuelan motives. Among the many voices was that of a "senior official" from an English-speaking island who told a foreign journalist: "With Venezuela, it is more than idealism. . . . Its policy is disturbing because it could become some new sort of over-lordship, a new economic paramountcy."[45]

If these news stories from the British islands had a ring of "small-island" paranoia to it, it was mild compared to what was going on in the press of the Netherlands Antilles. A report presented by Curazaleño international relations expert Dr. Boeli Van Leeuwen to the Parliamentary Committee on the Status of the Dutch islands created a sensation. Van Leeuwen claimed that there was a secret agreement between Holland, Venezuela and Royal Dutch Shell Oil Co. on the future status of these islands. The report led the respectable *Beur en Nieuwsberichten*[46] to headline the question: "Antilles: Sold and Betrayed?" Van Leeuwen's evidence appears circumstantial if not outright unfounded, but the context of his report did provide grounds for serious speculation. So that when in June 1974 the Dutch government announced that it was withdrawing its military protection from the oil refinery in Aruba while at the same time suggesting that they be substituted by Venezuelan troops, Arubanos must have recalled the Van Leeuwen report and rejected the suggestion outright.

Was it something of the fabled camel getting his head into the tent? Or was it merely a suggestion for Arubanos to accept or reject as was their sovereign right.

Contributing to the atmosphere of suspicion was the Venezuelan release in 1973 (the "year" of the Caribbean) of a batch of State documents detailing a 1942 "understanding" between President Roosevelt and President Isaias Medina of Venezuela. The gist of their discussions was that the U.S. understood that Venezuela would be "responsible" for the off-shore islands after the war. The documents created something of a sensation in Venezuela itself; one national newspaper even ran the unfortunate headline, "Curacao, Aruba and Bonaire Complement Venezuelan Territory."[47] That same year—1973—saw the then U.S. Secretary of State William Rogers in Caracas saying things which appeared to be official U.S. encouragement of Venezuela's Caribbean orientation.

The appearance in Venezuela of books such as Ruben Carpio Castillo's *Mexico, Cuba, Venezuela: Triangulo Geopolitico del Caribe* (Caracas, Imprenta Nacional, 1961) alarmed those who would not bother to read more than the title or read too assiduously between the lines. Little things (such as the title given to the Spanish version of Dr. Jesse Noel's book published in Caracas: *Trinidad, Province of Venezuela* [Noel's doctoral thesis carried another English title]) began to be added to a growing theory of some Venezuelan *Realpolitik* conspiracy. The outlines of that "theory" were that the Venezuelan "new deal" fit into a broader design engineered in Washington which would have new "great power" roles for Mexico, Brazil and Venezuela in Central America, South America and the Caribbean respectively. But it would be Dr. Eric Williams, Prime Minster of Trinidad and Tobago, who would provide the most elaborate interpretation of Venezuelan intentions. This was done in two speeches given in 1975, just before the dramatic shift in his policy towards Cuba.

In the first speech (in May 1975), Williams attacked the notion that Venezuela was a Caribbean country, ("I expect next to hear that Tierra del Fuego is.") and pointed to "Venezuela's relations, territorial ambitions in respect to our area." The second speech, was delivered at his party's convention June 15,[48] just two days before his trip to Cuba (and to the USSR, Rumania and the USA where he met with Henry Kissinger). In what amounts to one of the most scathing attacks by one country on another in the Caribbean area during peace time, Williams warned of Venezuela's "penetration" of the Caribbean, berated that country's "belated recognition of its Caribbean identity" and chastized his CARICOM partners for falling for the new Venezuelan definition of the Caribbean (the "Caribbean Basin") and leading a "Caribbean Pilgrimage to Caracas."

The sources of friction with Venezuela were many: multilateral vs. bilateral trade and arrangements between CARICOM members and Venzuela, especially as regards bauxite and oil, differences regarding law of the sea, objections to certain Venezuelan claims to islets in the Caribbean, Venezuelan loans, tourism initiative, and cultural "penetration" through scholarships. Fundamentally, however, Williams' fear was that the Caribbean and Latin American primary products were "jumping from the European and American frying pan into the South American fire," and that the net result would be the recognition of Venezuela as "a new 'financial centre' of the world."

Yet Williams' most detailed analysis was reserved for an inventory of his attempts to get a fishing accord with Venezuela, a reflection of the long-standing controversy on the matter and the simmering tensions built up on both sides. By 1975 Williams concluded that "one man can only take so much, and I have had enough."[49] Before turning to an analysis of this controversy, however, it is worth reiterating the central hypothesis of this study: even in the midst of overall dependency, nations will pursue foreign policy options which respond both to internal political pressures as well as to autonomously defined targets of interest to the elites.

In the pursuit of their own individual national interests, both Trinidad and Venezuela advanced definitions of the Caribbean appropriate to those interests. Both would make fundamental shifts in foreign policy: Trinidad moving to consolidate its definition of the "archipelago" Caribbean culture area, shifting its policy towards Cuba and attempting to exclude Venezuela; Venezuela, pushing its definition of the "Caribbean Basin," changing its policy towards the Caribbean dramatically. An analysis of this Venezuelan initiative and especially its new emphasis on fisheries illustrate the interlocking relationships between national economic and political exigencies and foreign policy formulation. It also attests to the basically autonomous nature of decision-making in at least this one area of policy formulation.

THE FISHERIES ISSUE

Clearly Venezuela's main concern is with oil, whether it be inland, just off-shore or in the Continental Shelf. But Venezuela is also deeply concerned with its marine riches. "Fisheries," President Carlos Andres Perez noted, "lies at the very center of our concern for the development of our resources. . . ."[50]

This relatively new Venezuelan concern with its marine resources[51] and the resulting clash with ongoing and developing Trinidadian initiatives provides an important case with which to test our initial proposition on developing interests in the Caribbean and independence of decision-making.

The immediate interests involved are clear. Trinidadian small-bait shrimpers and "fillette" net drifters fish in Venezuelan waters; Venezuelan "a-la-vive" fishers find many of their best catches in Trinidad's north coast waters. It would be easy to say that the simple and most obvious solution would be to regard the situation as a fair-exchange-no-losers situation and "call it George." Even the monetary differential (shrimping is much more lucrative an enterprise) could be solved arithmetically by a system of prorating or some other purely mechanical formula. But such an approach would probably not succeed because it disregards that fundamental dimension already mentioned: attitudes toward national interests, the new consciousness. Trinidadians have no particular prejudice against Venezuelan surface fishing—except, of course, when there is competition for the same "school" or fishing "ground." Venezuelans, on the other hand, have a deep-rooted fear and prejudice against trawling for shrimp, and in the past ten years this attitude has taken on the proportions of near-obsession, encouraged no doubt by the idea that trawling is done mainly by big-time foreign concerns.

When the Commander General of the Venezuelan Navy announced in July 1974 that six new patrol boats and six anti-submarine planes were being acquired in order to, among other things, "preserve our riches and care for our natural and ichthyological resources,"[52] he was in fact indicating an expansion of the traditional role of the navy. Most naval men even today would have to run to their dictionary to find out what they were defending should an order be received to "defend our ichthyological resources at all costs!" What such an order means is that all activities which threaten the marine flora and fauna of the nation be stopped. Such an activity, for example, would be trawling ("pesca de arrastre") in certain areas or with nets of certain mesh. Intentionally or unintentionally, the Navy Commander was contributing fuel to an ongoing struggle between interest groups in Venezuela over the best protection and use of that nation's ichthyological resources. Venezuelan law now prohibits trading within eight miles of the coast,* nearly the distance between Cedros in Trinidad and Pedernales in Venezuela. One governor in Venezuela (of the State of Anzaoategui) went so far as to order the Coast Guard to shoot at any shrimper—Venezuelan or foreign—found fishing within that 8-mile zone. Confiscation of shrimp caught within that zone was a weekly occurrence all along the Venezuelan coast during 1974. How to explain this prejudice? One clue is language. Language engenders attitudes above and beyond the specific interests involved, thus lending poignancy to any discussion of those interests.

In English the word "trawling" is benign sounding, even romantic in the imagery it engenders. In Spanish, however, the word is "pesca de arrastre," literally "fishing by dragging." Immediately the imagery clashes with ecology conscious visions of the flora and fauna of marine life being scraped away by the shrimpers' gates and nets. But there is more: the very verb "arrastrar" is a hard and fearsome one. In much of Latin America the saying "andar arrastrado" means to live in the utmost misery and distress. To do something against one's will is usually expressed as a popular localism, "lo estoy haciendo arrastrando." Once a political consciousness is aroused, language can lend an additional edge or dimension to that consciousness. So it is with the new consciousness over Venezuelan interests in its "inner sea." In English the area within the 200 miles from the coastal baseline is called an "economic" zone, or with some differences, a "contiguous" zone. The language points unequivocally to the specific interests and purposes behind the demand for 200 miles of sea. In Spanish, on the other hand, the term is "mar patrimonial," a term derived from "patria" or fatherland. Few terms in the lexicon of Latin American nationalism have the motive power of that word, or concept. "Patria" is derived from the Latin word for father, and the proper translation for "patri-monial," thus, is "claimed by right of birth." Language adds an "emotional" or psychic interest and investment to the legal and economic one.

Sociolinguistics, however, only scratches the surface of the dynamics of Venezuelan decision-making in fisheries. The true core of those dynamics are found within the political bargaining process, the conflicts over power within the system itself. In both Venezuela and Trinidad, fishing interests had entered the political process and the consequences were both national and international. In fact, this awakening of political

*See Appendix "A"

consciousness among the fishermen goes a long way in explaining the fisheries conflicts between the two countries.

THE FISHERMAN AS POLITICAL ACTOR

It has long been nearly axiomatic in political science that rural poeple are less active politically than urban dwellers. The land-tiller and fisherman, so goes the theory, are too busy surviving against the natural elements to worry about what those "city politicians" are up to. The farmer and fisherman, one concludes logically, are less of a pressure group and thus have less influence on political decisions. This theory is beginning to weaken in the face of recent developments. Farmers and fishermen are awakening to their political interests and rights and are organizing and behaving like any other pressure or interest group. To cite but one example, in the Northeastern coastal region of the United States organized fishermen backed by ecology-minded citizens have had oil refineries declared off-limits in Delaware, stopped Aristotle Onassis from building a refinery in New Hampshire, and in St. Mary's County in Maryland, 1,200 tenacious crab and oyster fishermen forced a major petroleum company into a public referendum on its proposed refinery. After a David vs. Goliath-type political battle, the fishermen won 2 to 1; plans for the refinery were shelved, illustrating that political awareness, once awakened, tends to broaden the sphere of action. These same fishermen from the Northeast U.S. succeeded in getting Congress and then President Nixon to declare the New England lobster a creature of the U.S. Continental Shelf and it was pressure from this same area that compelled both Houses of Congress and President Ford to sign the 200 mile economic zone law. Thus the United States has declared its rights over this creature as going way beyond the 12-mile territorial limit: reaching, in fact, to the point where the shelf achieves a 200 meters depth.

Stimulated in part by the growing nationalism and activity of the Americans, the Bahamians were awakened to their fish resources. The Bahamian Minister of External Affairs who is also Attorney General, Paul Adderley, stated openly in 1974 that new legislation on lobstering follows the nationalistic American initiatitves.[54] With 700 islands and 100,000 square miles of territorial waters, the Bahamas began pushing fisheries in an area heatedly contested by Cuban and Cuban-exiled Miami-based fishermen. The Bahamaian Fisheries Act imposes fines of U.S. $10,000 plus one year in jail plus confiscation of craft for illegal (unlicensed) fishing. New legislation declaring the spiny lobster a creature of the Bahamian Continental Shelf is now on the books and, as Adderley noted, is not negotiable in any way.[55] As early as 1972 Prime

Minister Pindling noted the aggressive and illegal behaviour of Maimi-based fishermen and warned that "something very, very serious could happen at any time."[56] Confrontations between Bahamian Coast Guard and Cuban-exiled lobster fishermen have been on the rise and the need for high level talks to forestall the increasing possibility of violence was evident.* It is in this type of political context that one must view at least part of the problem of the fishing dispute with Venezuela. The Venzuelan fishermen have succeeded in having their voices heard—the first step towards having their interests and needs attended to. The southern Trinidad fishermen are affected by this emergence of the Venezuelan fishermen as an interest group. A good beginning to the specific problem of the Gulf of Paria fishing dispute, therefore, would be to analyze the Venezuelan fishing industry as a political group and see what their new consciousness has produced in terms of their government's decision-making.

An important preface to the discussion is that fisheries was a very minor part of the total economic panorama of Venezuela in 1974: 1.33 percent of the labor force and Bs. 113 million of a total GNP of Bs. 45 billion.** Given what they represent statistically, their recent political achievements appear all the more remarkable. The fishing industry and population of Venezuela is divided into "artisanal" fisheries and "industrial" fisheries. The latter group fish tuna, redfish, codfish, and, crucially, shrimp. This "industrial" sector occupies a total of some 450 trawlers, 4,500 men each earning between Bs. 11,000 and Bs. 27,000 a year.[57] Organized and active as a pressure group (Asociacion Venezuelana de Industriales de la Pesca de Arrastre) members of the powerful Venezuelan Chambers of Commerce (FEDECAMARAS), this sector had important influence during the past government of Rafael Caldera. As an example of their gains, one can cite the development of

---

*The most serious clash, however, occurred with the Cuban armed forces in May 1980. Cuban MIG fighter planes sank a Bahamian gunboat which had taken a Cuban fishing trawler into custody off Ragged Island.

**The average world consumption of fish is 30 to 35 pounds a year; in Trinidad and Tobago it is only 17.5 pounds of which 8.5 pounds is imported processed fish—the lowest consumption rate in the Caribbean. In Venezuela the consumption rate is 20 pounds a year, higher than Trinidad's but still considerably below world standards. Fish is a much cheaper source of protein than beef, yet in Venezuela it represents only one-quarter of the total meat consumption. Both availability and taste are involved. Nevertheless, it is significant that while the Venezuelan agrarian working force has been declining, its fishing sector has been increasing. There is clearly a future seen in fishing. Cf. Ministry of Planning and Developing, *Fisheries Feasibility Study* (Halifax, Canada: Canadian Plant and Process Engineering Ltd., 1973 pp. 141-55 *passim;* Lygia Sanchez de Isturiz y Ulpiano F. Nascimiento, *Consumo de pescado y productos pescueros en Venezuela.* Caracas: MAC-PNUD-FAO, no. 17, 1970, p. 5.

several major fishing ports, especially at Punto Fijo, the Puerto La Cruz-Barcelona Complex, and, more recently, the port of Guiria in the Gulf of Paria.

Buoyed by the apparently insatiable world market for fish (especially shrimp) this sector invested heavily in new equipment. The expansion of the trawling fleet from its start in 1950 with immigrant Italian fishermen has been substantial, and although returns from shrimping have been declining, this has not stopped investment in the industry.[58] This growth is illustrated by the fact that while the growth rate of investment between 1959 and 1966 was 1.5 percent per year, it has been a phenomenal 85.2 percent since 1967. Sixty-five percent of the trawling fleet was added between 1969 and 1971.[59] Other factors, however, are beginning to put a damper on this industrial expansion. First of all, the most unfortunate for the industrial sector, the "artisanal" sector, long an organized group within AD, achieved significant representation with the election of Carlos Andres Perez in 1972. Divided between coastal fishermen (about 25,000) and river fishermen (some 15,000), the artisanal fisherman's income varies between an incredible low Bs. 500 and Bs. 2,400 annually.[60] Compare this to the $175 per month median income for Trinidad inshore fishermen. A clearly underprivileged and depressed sector, they see their interests as conflicting with the industrial fishermen. Trawling, they maintain, is clearly prejudicial to all other types of fishing and should be banned or strictly regulated. The conflict with the Trinidad trawlers is a direct spin-off from the "artisanal-industrial" fishing battle now being waged in Venezuela, and the recent victories of the artisanal sector. Clearly they have emerged as one of the most effective pressure groups within the rural Venezuelan sector. Their interests are represented through the Asociacion Venezolana de Pesca which has 50,000 members and a President who speaks the fishermen's language, yet is as articulate as any city politician. Much recent legislation stands as testimony to the new-found strength of the artisanal fishermen. In short, they have become an effective pressure group.[61]

The main thrust of their pressure has been to have the clearly outdated Ley de Pesca de 1944 updated. In the Oficina Nacional de Pesca, which is in the Ministry of Agriculture, the artisanal fishermen have found a co-lobbyist and 1974 was a bumper year for fishing legislation. Resolutions No. 335 through 349 set the minimum legal size for capture of a number of fish (trawling, in which all sizes are indiscriminately hauled in, is logically affected), regulate sizes of net-mesh, prohibit a long list of fishing accoutrements; specifically ban the capture of certain species (mejillon, anchovets) and in general make detailed and precise what the law of 1944 left vague. Resolution No.

342 is contained in Article 2: "The zone of four miles from the coast is reserved for artisanal fishing." Even beyond four miles, trawling is limited to four "campaigns" of five days per month including the going to and from the shrimping grounds. Article 4 declared a moratorium on any new trawling permits for that area.[62]

Again the goals of both conservation and improvement of the living standards of the artisanal fishermen is evident in Resolution No. 345. A total prohibition is set on lobster fishing in any part of the national territory until November 30, 1976, except in the Archipelago Los Roques and there only by "the fishermen permanently resident in the Archipelago." A survey by the Oficina Nacional de Pesca would determine who legitimately qualifies and stiff fines ranging up to Bs. 10,00 were set for violations. That all this affects the South Trinidad fishermen, who admittedly trawl within a stone's throw of the Venezuelan coast,* and generally with net-mesh banned by Venezuela, is clear. And in this regard one should mention that artisanal fishermen's political pull was also felt through the appointment of a Congressional committee to study the question of fishing permits for Trinidadians. With a number of prominent Venezuelans as members, the Committee's report was bound to carry weight, and the report did indeed conclude that the 1973 permits granted by Venezuela were illegal. The permit-giving provisions of the 1944 Fishing Law (Article 13), they concluded, are applicable only to Venezuela citizens.[63] Any future plans for permits will have to contend with the findings of this Congressional Committee. As in the United States, the Bahamas, Iceland and so many other countries, Venezuelan politicians are listening to the newly articulate fishermen. The prohibition affects Venezuelan trawlers no less than Trinidadian. Appendices "A' and "B" show the three trawling zones in the Gulf of Paria and the new prohibited areas which vary from 2 to 5 miles off the coast. Within the Gulf, then, there are three clearly identifiable shrimp-rich zones. Chances are that should permits be given, they will apply only to zones B and C as shown on Appendix "B." With port and other projects under way in zone A it would be politically unfeasible to have Trindadian trawlers within constant view of the Venezuelans. But even if permits are given for Zones B and C, all indications are that these will be relatively short-term solutions. Three reasons can be cited. First of all, Venezuelan trawlers have been moving further and further to the northeast, that is towards Trinidad as shrimping returns have diminished in the west. In the technical language of fisheries, shrimping and sardine fishing in the west of Venezuela have "stabilized"; in the eastern part they are in a

*See Appendix "B"

"development" stage.[64] With the estuaries of the Orinoco and its tributaries being rich shrimping grounds, it is only a matter of time before Venezuelans begin doing what now is done exclusively by Trinidadians—small local trawling in the Gulf of Paria.

This move has been accelerated by the mobilization of artisanal interests. Venezuelans are now fishing as far east as Surinam.[65] Navigational passage as well as fishing makes the Serpent's Mouth strategically crucial to these trawlers. Secondly, plans for the creation of a state-run national fishing industry (Corporacion Nacional Autonoma de Pesca) have been actively pushed by politicians and scientists alike. The idea is a state-sponsored plan to incorporate all fishermen into a nation-wide fisheries industry which would eliminate the industrial vs. artisanal conflict and harmonize ecological with socio-economic goals. In 1974 this plan took on great urgency when one of the Directors of Venezuela's major marine research institute—Instituto La Salle—was made "Director de Pesca" with overall authority in the economics and ecology of fisheries.

The third reason is that, should this area prove to be as rich in oil as it is believed, it will be off-limits when explorations and exploitation begin.

It appears at least plausible that Venezuela is quite within its legal rights in exercising maximum independent action in all three areas. But beyond the question of legality lies the issue of autonomy of decision-making. In this case, as in the case of most other legislation, fishing legislation (or the lack thereof) is often a direct result of a bargaining process in which interest groups have a say (or lack one).

The Venezuela case is interesting because of the distinctive interests of industrial and artisanal sectors and its interplay with legitimate ecological and conservation needs. In the case of Trinidad and Tobago there was no such felicitous meeting of interests.

Traditionally in Trinidad and Tobago the fishermen were not politically active. At no time did they present a united group or front. In part this stems from their geographical isolation: fishing villages are located on 53 beaches in Trindad and 32 in Tobago, all areas quite remote from any major center of political activity. In part also because the traditionally Indian-Black divisions were also evident among the fishermen.

In 1970, however, fishermen were also affected by the general malaise which swept the society and led to the "Black Power" uprising of that year. That year Trinidad fishermen began to understand that a two-pronged approach to the fishing question with Venezuela was needed: (a) an awareness of the growing concern over conservation and scientific exploitation of their fish resources; (b) an understanding of how the politics of interest group bargaining takes place. By 1973 it was the Trinidad fishermen's turn to organize, unionize and bargain as any other interest group, putting pressure on the regime of Eric Williams to reach a settlement with Venezuela, to improve marketing conditions in the city and make credit available. In fact, the fishermen (especially in the outlying villages such as Icacos and Cedros) were eager to see a change in the urban and bureaucratic bias against agriculture in general and fisheries specifically.

Fishing like most other agricultural work was still considered demeaning as the major study on the industry reports:

> . . . the (educational) system remains largely British Oriented in curriculum and emphasis. . . . This means that participants in the system would be adverse to performing manual occupations such as offered in the fishing industry. . . . The increasing urbanization of the society is another factor which prevents the unemployed entering the fishing industry. . . .[66]

From the government side, the Trinidad fisherman received little attention and his sense of alienation was expressed by his continual agitation against the government, including a week-long encampment in the Savannah in front of the Prime Minister's Office. Often the fishermen would express their support for the Venezuelan side as a means of prodding an apparently disinterested government. By 1975 the pressure had had its impact; Prime Minister Eric Williams' move was to make this internal conflict a foreign policy issue, with Venezuela as the villain of the piece. He expressed his frustrations to his Party's Congress:

> As far as I am concerned, I have had my fill of this fishy business, and as Prime Minister I wash my hands of it. . . . If we can't agree on fish, how can we agree on oil.[67]

It is evident that Williams had utilized a particular definition of the Caribbean to achieve two purposes: (1) to make the fisheries issue with its intractable internal aspects part of a broader Caribbean vs. Venezuela (or more broadly, "Latin American") conflict, and (2) to portray the behavior of the newly aroused fishermen as part of a wider "Latin Americanization" of the Island's politics.

To do this he had to redefine the Caribbean as a means of distinguishing Trinidadian from Venezuelan interests and problems. In fact it was precisely in terms of interests and problems that Trinidad and Venezuela were Caribbean countries, parts of the same interest area.

CONCLUSION

The Caribbean is a part of the Third World. As such it shares many common features of this Third World. That dependency in some form is part of that world is too well established to need repeating here. It is the extent and characteristics of that dependency which requires defining; blanket politically or ideologically-derived definitions are not adequate to the task.

The analyses of Trinidad-Venezuela-Cuban relations, of Venezuela's expanding interest in the Caribbean area and of the Trinidad-Venezuela fishing dispute were intended to show that these issues all involved independent decision-making by the area's leaders to internal pressures and towards *region-related* issues. The debate over the definition of "the Caribbean" was similarly a debate between independent actors. The particular definition will, to a certain extent, affect the process of regional integration now taking place as well as the outcome of some of the processes of conflict and cooperation discussed in this paper. Should the Eric Williams "archipelago" culture area definition be adhered to, for instance, integration in the region will start from a base which is largely a legacy of the European colonial history and thus perpetuate existing (and often inherited) conflicts. Those advocating a geopolitical "Caribbean basin" argument such as the one advanced by Venezuela, run the risk of overlooking important cultural-historical differences in the region which, if ignored, might well become stumbling blocks to future cooperation.

The concept of an "interest area" is suggested as a means of focussing on the broad common issues to which national elites in the whole area have to respond, regardless of their degree of general dependency. Some indication of their actual or potential capacity to deal with the broader issue of regional dependency can be derived from an understanding of their responses to issues within the interest area. This study attempted to show that a significant capacity is there. The will to do so is a different story.

FOOTNOTES

[1] See for instance the major coverage given by the *Miami Herald* to the Williams vs. Venezuela controversy: June 25, 1973, p. 4B, April 16, 1975, p. 3B, July 6, 1975, p. 6A, August 14, 1975, p. 22B.

[2]Cf. Melville J. Herskovits:
". . . When cultures are viewed objectively, they are seen to form clusters, so to speak, sufficiently homogeneous that the regions in which they occur can be delimited on a map. The area in which similar cultures are formed is called a culture area." *Men and His Works,* New York: Knopf, 1948, p. 183.

[3]*Trinidad Guardian,* June 21, 1975, p. 1, emphasis added.

[4]Of 27 major scholars of the Caribbean surveyed by UNITAR, only "a few" included Venezuela, Colombia and Central America. The majority defined as "comprising all the islands, plus the mainland territories of the Guyanas and Belize." (cf. Joan T. Seymour, Hans J. Geiser and Christian McDougall, "Reach and Training in the Caribbean: A Unitar Inquiry," mimeo January, 1976, pp. 1-3)

[5]"Introduction" in David Lowenthal, *West Indian Societies* (London: Oxford University Press, 1972), p. ix.

[6]*West Indian Societies,* p. 5.

[7]Sidney Mintz, "The Caribbean as a Socio-Cultural Area," in Michael M. Horowitz (ed.), *Peoples and Cultures of the Caribbean* (New York: The Natural History Press, 1971), p. 18.

[8]Cf. Raoul Naroll: "The primary weakness of the *culture area* concept is that no clear agreement can be found on principles of classification which will permit the drawing of comparable area boundaries." Julius Gould and William L. Kolk (eds.), *A Dictionary of the Social Sciences,* UNESCO, 1964, p. 168.

[9]Gordon K. Lewis, *Puerto Rico, Freedom and Power in Caribbean* (New York: Monthly Review Press, 1963), p. 27.

[10]Gordon K. Lewis, *The Growth of the Modern West Indies* (New York: Monthly Review Press, 1968). Lewis says he has limited his study to the "English-speaking Antilles." p. 9.

[11]Speech to the San Fernando PNM Group, May 4, 1975, *Trinidad Guardian,* June 13, 1975, p. 8.

[12]Fidel Castro's speech, April 19, 1976. For an interesting analysis of the implications of this statement see Herbert L. Mathews, "Forward with Fidel Anywhere," *New York Times,* 3/4/76. A Cuban elaboration of this position is contained in Armando Hart, "Africa is Waking Up . . ." speech, May 28, 1976.

[13]"Communicado conjunto Cuba-Panama," *Matutino* (Panama) January 16, 1976, p. 6.

[14]Richard M. Morse, "The Caribbean: Geopolitics and Geohistory," in Sybil Lewis and Thomas G. Mathews (eds.), *Caribbean Integration* (Rio Piedras: Institute of Caribbean Studies, 1967), p. 155.

[15]Hurtado Hector Navarro, (Minister of France), "Primer Reunion Extraordinaria del Consejo Latinoamericano," *Venezuela Ahora,* enero 26, 1976, p. 14.

[16]Carlos Andres Perez, "Turismo: Via hacia la integracion," Conferencia de Turismo del Caribe, Caracas, enero 9, 1975 (pamphlet), p. 7.

[17]*Turismo: Via hacia la integracion, op. cit.,* p. 2.

[18]The focus of dependency addresses a situation in which "the economy of certain countries is conditioned by the development and expansion of another economy to which the former is subjected." (Theotonio Dos Santos, *La crisis de la teoria del desarrollo y las relaciones de dependencia en America Latina,* IX Congreso de Sociologia, Mexico, 1969), p. 6. There is a real danger of expanding this position into a general theory which is all encompassing-covering all areas of decision making. "This new approach" proclaims

one student, "emphasizes the role of this dependence in shaping the internal economic, *social and political structures and external relations* of underdeveloped countries that impede any real development." Charles K. Wilbur in his edited work,*The Political Economy of Development and Underdevelopment* (New York: Random House, 1973), p. 107.

[19]This more flexible approach to "dependency" is central to the work of Fernando Enrique Cardoso. cf. Cardoso and E. Faletto, *Dependencia y desarrollo en America Latina* (3rd ed., Mexico: Siglo XXI, 1971); Cardoso, *Ideologias de la burguesia industrial en sociedades dependientes* (2nd ed., Mexico: Siglo XXI, 1972).

[20]For an example of the fruitful use of such a flexible approach to external politics, see Jorge I. Dominguez, "The U.S. Impact on Cuba in Internal Politics and Economics, 1902-1958: from imperialism to Hegemony," paper American Political Science Association, Sept 5. 1976.

[21]Interview with Cardoso in Joseph A. Kahl, *Modernization Exploitation, and Dependency in Latin America* (New Jersey: Transactions Books, 1976), p. 177.

[22]Eric Williams, *Inward Hunger*, p. 194. Interestingly, he would justify this acting by citing his experience in dealing with Venezuela as contrasted to the lack thereof in the federation's leadership.

[23]Eric Williams, "Feature Address and Official Opening," *Seminar on the Foreign Policies of Caribbean States*. Institute of International Relations, Trinidad, 1968, p. 9.

[24]*Ibid.*

[25]Report on Conference Between Representatives of the Governments of the Republic of Venezuela and Trinidad and Tobago. Whitehall, January 16-18, 1963 (mimeo).

[26]Cited in *Inward Hunger*, p. 302.

[27]This speech is reprinted in A.N.R. Robinson, *Areas of Conflict: A Review of the External Scene* (P.O.S.: Government Printery, 1967). Later, an independent A.N.R. Robinson would maintain that "The fact is that Cuba does offer an alternative and however unpalatable it may be to others, that alternative will undoubtedly be probed if other avenues prove impassible." (*The Mechanics of Independence,* Cambridge: MIT Press, 1971), p. 167.

[28]Robinson, *Areas of Conflict, op. cit.*

[29]Kamaluddin Mohammed, (*Minister of West Indian Affairs*). *Caribbean Integration* (Port of Spain, 5 April, 1969), p. 19.

[30]Eric Williams, *From Columbus to Castro* (London: Andre Deutsch, 1969), p. 486.

[31]*Ibid.,* p. 503.

[32]*Ibid.,* p. 510.

[33]*Trinidad Guardian,* June 21, 1975, p. 1.

[34]*Trinidad Guardian,* June 24, 1975, p. 1.

[35]"Fronteras maritimas de Venezuela," *El Universal,* June 24, 1974, p. 4. For an even stronger stand and call to redress "a painful past" see, General (r,) Adolfo Ramirez Torres, "Politica exterior con Colombia," *El Universal,* July 1, 1974, p. 5.

[36]Cf. Ruben Carpio Castillo, *Fronteras maritimas de Venezuela,* Caracas, 1974.

[37]*El Universal,* June 21, 1974, p. 1.

[38]Much of Venezuela's claim to Guyana territory is based on the interpretation of British coercion of a weak Venezuela; this interpretation forms part of a wider theory of a "dependent" past.

[39]"La politica del Caribe," *El Universal,* December 12, 1972.

[40]Reunion Consultativa Informal de Cancilleres de Paises del mar Caribe. Caracas, Venezuela, Comunicado, November 26, 1971 (mimeo).

[41]*El Nacional,* March 28, 1973, Section D.

[42]*El Universal,* May 29, 1974, pp. 2-6.

[43]*El Universal,* June 12, 1974, pp. 1-4.

[44]For the established newspaper response, see editorial "Bilateral Good News," *Trinidad Guardian,* November 15, 1975.

[45]Witness the bold headlines in the Miami Herald last year (June 23, 1973), p. 4B: "Venezuela Sparks New Imperialism Cries."

[46]For a review of some complaints see "Caricom Problems Over Venezuela?" *West Indies Chronicle News,* (May, June, 1975).

[47]*El Nacional,* January 4, 1973, p. 1—see p. 13 for a transcript of the "For-Medina" talks. The response in Curacao was immediate and with full headlines (cf. *Buers en Nieuwsberichten* January 8, 1973, p. 1).

[48]*Trinidad Guardian,* June 18, 19, 20, 1975.

[49]*Trinidad Guardian,* June 16, 1975, p. 1.

[50]Speech to III Conference of the Sea, *El Universal,* June 21, 1974, p. 10.

[51]Cf. R. C. Griffiths and J. G. Simpson, "The Present Status of the Exploitations and Evaluation of the Fishery Resources of Venezuela," Gulf and Caribbean Fisheries Institute, *Proceedings of the 25th Annual Session,* Miami, Fl., November 1972, pp. 129-155; Juan Pischedda, *et al., Analisis de la estructura institucional de la pesca en Venezuela.* Caracas: MAC-PNUD-FAO, no. 59, 1973.

[52]*El Nacional,* July 25, 1974, p. D-19.

[53]*El Nacional,* May 29, 1974, p. D-15.

[54]*Miami Herald,* September 15, 1974, p. 2.

[55]*Miami Herald,* January 11, 1976, p. 32.

[56]*Miami Herald,* December 3, 1972, p. 25A.

[57]Cf. H. Lundberg, *et al., La flota de arrastreros de Venezuela en 1968,* Caracas: MAC-PNUD-FAO, Informe Tecnico, No. 10, 1970.

[58]AROPESCA, "Porque nos vamos a Guyana," *El Nacional,* June 12, 1974, p. B-14.

[59]Cf. Ulpaiano Nascimiento y B. Rojas C., *Aspectos economicos de la flota pesquera de Venezuela.* Caracas, MAC-PNUD-FAO, no. 36, 1971.

[60]Ulpiano F. Nascimiento y Octavio Hernandez M., *Poblacion y mano de obra pesquera en Venezuela.* Caracas, MAC-PNUD-FAO, no. 15, 1970, pp. 10 ff.

[61]Personal, on the spot observation, Caracas, July 15-25, 1974.

[62]For the legislation cited, see the *Gaceta Oficial,* no. 30.440, 30,441 (1974).

[63]*Ibid.*

[64]Cf. D. Novoa, *et al., La Pesca de arrastre en la zona nor-oriental de Venezuela.* Caracas: MAC-PNUD-FAO no. 55, 1972; J. J. Ewald *et. al., La pesca de arratre en el Golfo de Paria.* Caracas, MAC-PNUD-FAO, no. 29, 1971.

[65]AROPESA, *op. cit.*

[66]*Fisheries Development Plan, op. cit.,* p. 224.

[67]*Trinidad Guardian,* June 16, 1975, p. 1.

Appendix "A"
Areas Banned to Shrimp Trawling

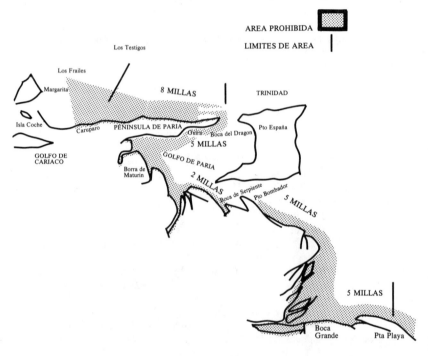

AREA PROHIBIDA

LIMITES DE AREA

Los Testigos

Los Frailes

Margarita

8 MILLAS

TRINIDAD

Isla Coche

Caruparo

PENINSULA DE PARIA

Guiria

Boca del Dragon

Pto España

5 MILLAS

GOLFO DE
CARIACO

GOLFO DE PARIA

Borra de
Maturin

2 MILLAS

Boca de Serpiente

Pto Bombador

5 MILLAS

5 MILLAS

Boca
Grande

Pta Playa

Appendix "B"
Principal Zones of Trawling for Shrimp
in Gulf of Paria

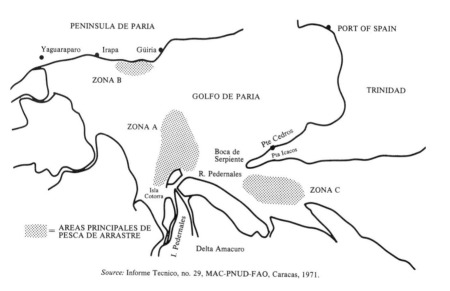

Source: Informe Tecnico, no. 29, MAC-PNUD-FAO, Caracas, 1971.

Subject Index*

A

Act of Washington 274, 278, 281, 282
Africa 5, 7, 243, 263
Agrarian reform 256, 257
Albania 9, 19
Alliance for Progress 273, 277–278, 281, 282, 289, 315
Andean Pact 116, 263
Antigua 140
Argentina 57, 59, 68
Aruba 322
Asia 5
Autonomy 7–11. See also small states.

B

Bahamas 326–327
Bahrain 19, 25
Barbados 88, 98, 100, 102, 272, 310
and Law of the Sea 225, 227, 228, 230
Belize 98, 102, 136
Bolivia 262, 263
Brazil 57, 59, 68
Britain 5, 15, 43, 281, 283, 287
British Empire 112
Burma 9

C

Cambodia 10
Canada 112, 121, 273, 283
Capital accumulation 35–37, 40, 42, 48, 62, 63, 65, 67. See also small states.

Capitalist systems 56, 62, 98, 120, 237
Cartels 55–56, 66
Caribbean 5, 19, 68, 112, 309–335.
See also Caribbean Community, CARICOM and Commonwealth Caribbean.
Capitalist class of 98, 100, 101
colonial experience of 310
common external tariff 100, 101
decision-making in 239, 332
definitions of, debate on 309–314, 332
definitions of 323
geopolitical definition 123
Venezuelan 311, 312
Williams' 309–310, 311
Caribbean Basin 309, 332
as culture area 332, 309–311, 312
as interest area 312, 332
external patrons of 98
fiscal incentives 100, 101
free trade process 100
independence in 237
and international capitalist system 237
international relations of 319
mineral deposits in 139
Caribbean Community 85, 86
power in 85
economic system of 85
integration of 89–110
decision-making as process in 86–110
issue areas 86–89, 91, 92–97, 103

*Prepared by Margaret Blenman Harris

337

Name Index*

A

Adams, Grantley 290
Adderley, Paul 326
Adenauer, Konrad 287
Allende, Gossens Salvador 263
Allison, Graham T. 267
Alvaredo, Juan Velasco 263
Amin, Idi 53, 272
Amstrup, Niels 30, 34, 46
Anderson, Robert W. 240
Arbenz, J. 244, 245
Aron, Raymond 122, 123

B

Barceló, Carlos Romero 301, 303, 306
Batista, Juan 245, 246
Beard, Charles 267
Berrios, Rubén 301
Best, Lloyd 275, 276
Borg, C. Arthur 304
Braybrooke, David 267
Brewster, Havelock 75, 130

C

Caldera, Rafael 319, 327
Calvani, Aristides 319, 320, 321
Campos, Pedro Albiz 306
Capildeo, Simboonath 287
Cardoso, Fernando Enrique 313
Carter, Jimmy 56, 57, 58, 59, 60, 66, 67, 303, 304, 305
Carter, Roselyn 305
Castillo, Rubén Carpio 318, 322
Castro, Fidel 240–263, 311, 318

Castro, Raoul 252
Churchill, Winston 287
Colón, Hernández 297, 300

D

Dadone, Aldo 130
Debray, Regis 261
De Gaulle, Charles 287
Demas, William 136
Deutsch, Karl 267
Dillon, Douglas 273
Di Marco, Eugenio 130
Draper, Theodore 274
Dubchek, Alexander 23
Dumont, René 274

E

East, Maurice 265, 269, 271, 272, 286
Eisenhower, Dwight D. 245
Extavour, Winston 161, 166

F

Farrell, Trevor 161, 163, 169
Ferré, Luis 300, 303
Filardo, Pascual Vanegas 318
Ford, Gerald 303, 304, 305, 326
Fox, A.B. 269, 271
Frankel, Joseph 267

G

Good, R.C. 270
Goodwin, George 75, 76
Gorshtiov, Admiral 251

*Prepared by Margaret Blenman Harris

347